3rd International Conference on Inventions (ICI 2017)

MATEC Web of Conferences Volume 201 (2018)

Sun Moon Lake, Taiwan
29 September - 2 October 2017

Editors:

Cheng-Chi Wang

ISBN: 978-1-5108-7117-5

Printed from e-media with permission by:

Curran Associates, Inc.
57 Morehouse Lane
Red Hook, NY 12571

proceedings.com

Some format issues inherent in the e-media version may also appear in this print version.

Printed by Curran Associates, Inc. (2018)

For additional information, please contact EDP Sciences – Web of Conferences at the address below.

EDP Sciences – Web of Conferences
17, Avenue du Hoggar
Parc d'Activité de Courtabœuf
BP 112
F-91944 Les Ulis Cedex A
France

Phone: +33 (0) 1 69 18 75 75
Fax: +33 (0) 1 69 28 84 91

contact-edps@webofconferences.org

Additional copies of this publication are available from:

Curran Associates, Inc.
57 Morehouse Lane
Red Hook, NY 12571 USA
Phone: 845-758-0400
Fax: 845-758-2633
Email: curran@proceedings.com
Web: www.proceedings.com

TABLE OF CONTENTS

edp sciences

MATEC Web of Conferences

Statement of Peer review

In submitting conference proceedings to MATEC Web of Conferences, I certify to the Publisher that I adhere to the **Policy on Publishing Integrity** of the journal in order to safeguard good scientific practice in publishing.

1. All articles have been subjected to peer review administered by the proceedings editors.
2. Reviews have been conducted by expert referees, who have been requested to provide unbiased and constructive comments aimed, whenever possible, at improving the work.
3. Proceedings editors have taken all reasonable steps to ensure the quality of the materials they publish and their decision to accept or reject a paper for publication has been based only on the merits of the work and the relevance to the journal.

Title, date and place of the conference 2017 International conference on Inventions, 2017/09/29-10/2 Taiwan.

Proceedings editor(s): Cheng-Chi Wang

Date and editor's signature 2018/8/29

https://doi.org/10.1051/matecconf/201820101001

Study on the Cutting Efficiency of High-Speed Band Saw Blade by Taylor Tool Life and Fractal Equations

Sung-Hua Wu[1,*], *Ming-Shyan* Huang[1], *Cheng-En* Jhou[1], *and Chin-Chung* Wei[2]

[1]Department of Mechanical and Automation Engineering, National Kaohsiung First University of Science and Technology, No.1 Chuangxin Road,811 Kaohsiung, Taiwan
[2]Department of Power Mechanical Engineering, National Formosa University, No.64 Wenhua Road,632 Yunlin, Taiwan

Abstract. The study proposed the chip formation steady-state model and cutting efficiency model for multi-cutters by Taylor tool life and fractal equation according to uniform chip thickness in high-speed band sawing process. Furthermore, a kind of new hook-tooth can be successfully applied on continuously uniformed chip formation in order to raise the production precision. The study developed MDOF cutting dynamics, which can be applied on multi-cutting process by Taylor tool life and fractal equations. Factors of affecting band-sawing included the cutting force, the cutting geometry, the cutting heat, the local stress-strain and the chip thickness formation uniformity. These factors had an important influence on tool wear, surface roughness, production precision and cutting efficiency in high-speed sawing process. The simulated results shown that, the wear resistance property is better at coating TiN 0.6 μm. In high-speed cutting process, the cutting improvement rate can be increased at least 13%. While the hook-tooth cutting speed achieved 120 m/min, comparing with non-coating cutting tooth, coating 0.6 μm coating-layer can make the temperature decreased, obviously.

1 Introduction

Factors of affecting band-sawing include cutting force, cutting geometry, cutting heat, local stress-strain and chip thickness formation uniformity. These factors have an important influence on tool wear, surface roughness, production precision and cutting efficiency in high-speed sawing process. It is effective to improve machining quality, raise cutting efficiency and reduce the cost by controlling these factors. The study proposed cutting factors of tool geometry in band-sawing process, simulated and improved the machining characteristics and investigated the effects of vary kinds of cutters geometry in sawing process. By using the optimal process parameters, including coating factors, cutting velocity, tool geometry, tool material and workpiece material to improve cutting temperature, cutting resistance and the production qualities will achieve a better standard.

1.1 Paper Review

Band-saw types can be distinguished from the straight-cutters, wave-cutters, sinusoidal-cutters, circle-cutters and wire-saw depended on saw-blade geometry, and machining mechanism applied on multi-points cutting. According to the band-saw with different kinds of saw-blade, it can be processing on metal, wood, plastic material and even in semi-conductive chip. Earlier studies, there were a lot of papers investigated about band-sawing process. According to the studies, the cutter design has greater effects on cutting process, and then, it will cause tool wear fast and bad surface roughness, especially for the tool life decreasing. Ko and Kim **[1]** analyzed saw-blade geometry and mechanistic cutting force prediction agreed well with experimental trends. Andersson **[2-4]** used the FEM demonstrated that, the maximum stress had decreasing with cutter radius increasing. The kind of tool geometry variation caused cutting force variation along feed direction and linear increasing with undeformed chip thickness. Marusich **[5]** et. al simulated the cutting process under residual stress with considering heat performance, tool geometry and machining parameters on workpiece. They found the relations of stress, cutting velocity and chip load. Xu and Yu **[6]** investigated sawing performance of diamond with alloy coatings, and the coating can raise the TRS performance. Okai **[7]** et. al used saw-blade analyzed to investigate the effects of cutting velocity and cutting force, however, the cutting tool caused wear because of cutting heat and local stress concentrated. Buyuksehir **[8]** investigated specific wear ratio and obtained specific energy under up-cutting modes, and determined the optimal performance between process parameters, cutting depth and workpiece moved velocity. Besides, wire-saw is another important machining application for natural stones and architecture. Wu **[9]** et. al studied multi-points by chip fractal geometry and hack-sawing mechanism, and predicted cutting force, boundary conditions, undeform cutting areas and specific energy trends, successfully. Thaler **[10]** et. al studied the stability diagrams and chatter avoidance in horizontal band sawing, and the experimental results the analysis of chatter avoidance is better than unstable cutting force signals. To raise the cutting efficiency and cutting velocity, the cutting stratray is to reduce chatter occurred. Patten **[12]** et. al used AdvanEdge to establish cutting

* Corresponding author: jackywoo0923@gmail.com

model, such as feed, edge radius, cutting depth 10 micrometer and cutting velocity 1~300 m/min. They found the toughness shearing occurred in high-speed sawing process. Usui **[13]** et. al proposed a kind of finite element model to calculate chip geometry, cutting force and surface hardening by applying Lagrangian method to predict AISI 4130 chip breaking. Grzesik **[14]** et. al used FEM the orthogonal cutting process by coating tool and uncoating tool with adding TiC and Al_2O_3 deposited on P20 carbo-material. Fang **[15]** et. al proposed the heat-elastic-plastic coupling model to simulate 3 dimensional FEM, and the results demonstrated the stress concentration on tool-edge section and the higher stress focus on the main deformation zone. Usui **[16]** studied 3D FEM, including adaptive meshing, heat-mechanical coupling, strain rate and high temperature deformation for tool. Stephenson **[17]** et. al proposed 3-D FEM for drilling model, including adaptive meshing, heat-mechanical coupling effect, strain rate and high temperature deformation for tool. Mohammadpour **[18]** et. al observed the residual stress influence of cutting velocity and feed rate in orthogonal cutting process, and the results the chip formation and stress distribution can be successfully predicted by MSC. Superform. Huang and Yang **[19]** indicted the energy reduced from the cutting heat in high-speed cutting process, resulted in the non-uniform heat distribution on workpiece. Fractal is a kind of mathematical tool to solve the transient problems by Mandelbrot **[20]**, who proposed W-M fractal function in order to simplified Weieratrass equation to simulate roughness profile by topothesy and random phase.

2. Theoretical Modelling

The study developed MDOF cutting dynamics, which can be applied on multi-cutting process by Taylor tool life and fractal equations. The maximum material removal rate (MMR) and chip thickness uniformity were the objective functions, which simulated on S45C in order to find out the optimal geometric and process parameters in multi-points sawing process.

2.1 MDOF Cutting Dynamics

From **Fig. 1 (a)-(e)**, the MDOF cutting dynamics can be established by steady-state chip formation without self-excited vibration. In brief, the governing equation for MDOF can be written as Eq. (1)

$$[\mathrm{M}][\ddot{x}]+[c][\dot{x}]+[k][x]=[0] \quad (1)$$

Hence, Eq.(2) to Eq.(4) can be obtained as generalized matrix by conservation of energy.

$$[\mathrm{M}]=\begin{bmatrix} m_1 & 0 & 0 & \cdots & 0 \\ 0 & m_2 & 0 & \cdots & 0 \\ 0 & 0 & m_3 & \cdots & 0 \\ \vdots & \vdots & \vdots & \cdots & \vdots \\ 0 & 0 & 0 & \cdots & m_n \end{bmatrix} \quad (2)$$

$$[c]=\begin{bmatrix} c_1 & c_1+c_2 & 0 & \cdots & 0 \\ c_1+c_2 & c_2 & c_2+c_3 & \cdots & 0 \\ 0 & c_2+c_3 & c_3 & \cdots & 0 \\ \vdots & \vdots & \vdots & \cdots & c_{n-1}+c_n \\ 0 & 0 & 0 & c_{n-1}+c_n & c_n \end{bmatrix} \quad (3)$$

$$[k]=\begin{bmatrix} k_1 & k_1+k_2 & 0 & \cdots & 0 \\ k_1+k_2 & k_2 & k_2+k_3 & \cdots & 0 \\ 0 & k_2+k_3 & k_3 & \cdots & 0 \\ \vdots & \vdots & \vdots & \cdots & k_{n-1}+k_n \\ 0 & 0 & 0 & k_{n-1}+k_n & k_n \end{bmatrix} \quad (4)$$

For furthermore, take Laplace Transform, and assumed $\{x\}=\{\bar{x}\}e^{st}$ subinto Eq.(1)

$$s^2[\mathrm{M}][\bar{x}]+s[c][\bar{x}]+[k][\bar{x}]=\{0\} \quad (5)$$

Through reduced order, assumed $\{\hat{x}\}=s\{\bar{x}\}$ subinto Eq.(5), Eq.(6) can be obtained.

$$\begin{Bmatrix}\bar{x}\\ \dot{\bar{x}}\end{Bmatrix}s\begin{Bmatrix}\bar{x}\\ \dot{\bar{x}}\end{Bmatrix}=\begin{bmatrix}0 & \mathrm{I}\\ -[\mathrm{M}]^{-1}[k] & -[\mathrm{M}]^{-1}[c]\end{bmatrix}\begin{Bmatrix}\bar{x}\\ \dot{\bar{x}}\end{Bmatrix} \quad (6)$$

To solve the eigenvalues and egigenvectors from 2n set, $\{S_k\}_{n*1}$ and $\{S_n^*\}_{n*1}$, where $S_k=-\delta_k+j\omega k$, $s_k=-\delta_k-j\omega k$

The generalized displacement of cutter edge can be written as Eq.(7)

$$\begin{aligned}\{\mathrm{X}_k(t)\}&=c_{1k}e^{S_k t}\{\mathrm{X}_k\}+cc_{2k}e^{S_k^* t}\{\mathrm{X}_k^*\}\\ &=e^{-\delta_k t}\left(e^{j\omega kt}cc_{1k}\{\mathrm{X}_k\}+e^{-j\omega kt}\{\mathrm{X}_k^*\}\right)\\ &=\{\mathrm{XX}\}_k e^{-\delta kt}\cos(\omega kt-\theta_k)\end{aligned} \quad (7)$$

Where $\{\mathrm{XX}\}_k=\sqrt{(cc_{1k}\mathrm{X}_k+cc_{2k}\mathrm{X}_k^*)^2-(cc_{1k}\mathrm{X}_k-cc_{2k}\mathrm{X}_k^*)^2}$;

$$\theta_k=a\tan\left(\frac{j(cc_{1k}\mathrm{X}_k-cc_{2k}\mathrm{X}_k^*)}{cc_{1k}\mathrm{X}_k+cc_{2k}\mathrm{X}_k^*}\right) \quad (8)$$

Hence, Eq.(7) can be rewritten as Eq.(9)

$$\{\mathrm{X}(t)\}=\sum_{k=1}^{n}\{\mathrm{XX}\}_k e^{-\delta t}\cos(\omega kt-\theta_k) \quad (9)$$

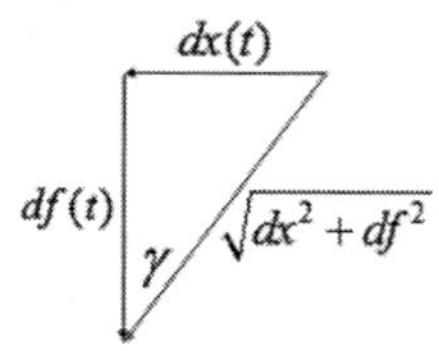

For a tiny displacement dx at differential-cutter, the tiny feed df will be occurred at the same time *t*, hence, Eq.(10) can be derived.

$$\gamma=\tan^{-1}\left(\frac{dx}{df}\right) \quad (10)$$

If the chip formation is steady-state, the γ is uaually constant, called differential-cutter angle. For two dimensional orthogonal cutting, Eq.(11) can be expressed MDOF cutting from every single unit cutter.

$$\int_0^l\{X(t)\}dx=\int_0^h\tan(\gamma)df \quad (11)$$

Where l means the cutting length from the workpiece, and h means the average cutting depth. For furthermore, the transient chip load for every single cutters can be derived from feed $df(t)$, cutting width b and cutting overlap ratio α from chip fractal geometry. Average specific energy K_t can be obtained through unit cutting areas of multi-cutters as Eq.(12)-Eq.(15)

$$K_t = \frac{W}{\Delta V} \tag{12}$$

For single cutters,

$$W = K_t V_s = K_t L A_s \tag{13}$$

For multi-cutters,

$$W = K_t V = K_t \sum_{i=1}^{n} A_i l_i \tag{14}$$

The study denotes average sprcific energy Kt and average cutting force for multi-cutters,

$$\bar{F} = \bar{K}_t\left(\sum_{i=1}^{n} a_i\right) \tag{15}$$

2.2 Fractal Differential Equation

In order to obtain chip fractal self-similarity, the cutting tool can be expressed as sinusoidal-wave through one-dimensional projection and become 84 cutter topologies. According to sinusoidal multi-cutters, the cutters interference ratio of cutter arrangement can be written as Eq. (16).

$$\alpha_{n+1} = 1 - \frac{\lambda}{n \cdot b}\left(\tan\theta_{n+1} - \tan\theta_n\right) \tag{16}$$

Where α_{n+1} means $(n+1)^{th}$ cutter; λ denotes the length of unit wave; n means cutter number of period; b means cutter width; θ_{n+1} means the banding angle of unit cutter. The equivalent depth under cutter interference in cutting process can be demonstrated as Eq.(2) and Fig.1, called fractal- algebraic operators.

$$d_{i,\max} = d_1^*\left(\frac{\alpha_i}{1-\alpha_i}\right)^{n-1} + (1-\alpha_i)(d_{i-1} - d_{i-2}) + d_1^* \tag{17}$$

Where d_1^* means the initial cutting depth according to experimental results; d_i means the transient cutting depth for i^{th} cutter of total working cutters. To consider the chip load of the equivalent depth and cutting width in two-dimension, the chip load can be presented as Eq. (17) without energy dissipated.

$$\begin{aligned} P_i &= A_i \\ &= b_i \times d_i \\ &= b_i\left[d_1^*\left(\frac{\alpha_i}{1-\alpha_i}\right)^{n-1} + (1-\alpha_i)(d_{i-1} - d_{i-2}) + d_1^*\right] \\ &= (1-\alpha_i)b^*\left[d_1^*\left(\frac{\alpha_i}{1-\alpha_i}\right)^{n-1} + (1-\alpha_i)(d_{i-1} - d_{i-2}) + d_1^*\right] \end{aligned} \tag{18}$$

A_i means the chip load under geometry interference, and the shape has strictly fractal self-similarity It is key point to determine the boundary orders in order to obtain exact convolution function. Due to geometric characteristics, Eq. (18) can be shown as chip-load geometric factors of cutting process, called chip load function of sinusoidal multi-cutters. Eq. (18) can be also rewritten as a functional expression as Eq. (19)

$$\begin{aligned} &P(d_i,\alpha_i,b,n,\theta_i) \\ &= (1-\alpha_i)b^*\left[d_1^*\left(\frac{\alpha_i}{1-\alpha_i}\right)^{n-1} + (1-\alpha_i)(d_{i-1} - d_{i-2}) + d_1^*\right] \end{aligned} \tag{19}$$

From Eq. (19), $\tan\theta = R\sin\left(i \times \frac{2\pi}{n}\right)/t_p$; R means amplitude of sinusoidal-set cutters; t_p means cutter pitch

2.3 Taylor's Tool Life and Cutting Efficiency Model

The traditional Taylor's tool life can be demonstrated as Eq. (20)

$$VT^n = C \tag{20}$$

Where $n = \frac{\log\left(\frac{C}{V}\right)}{\log T}$, V means cutting velocity and T denotes the tool life, n means exponent.

Extend Eq. (20), the generalized form can be rewritten as Eq. (21) for more process parameters

$$[F_c]^f [P]^m [N]^d [f]^q V[T]^n = C_1 \tag{21}$$

Where f means the cutting force exponent; m means the exponent for the cutting numbers of workpieces; d means the exponent of coating layer thickness; q means the exponent for feed.

Simultaneously, the raising cutting efficiency model for multi-cutters can be derived from Taylor's Tool life equation as Eq. (22)

$$E = \eta(\%) \cdot e^{-\eta \cdot 10} \tag{22}$$

Where E means the cutting efficiency for multi-cutters, and η means the percentage of single-cutter cutting efficiency. From the simulation of single-cutter, it can be extended to the multi-cutters cutting efficiency obtained by Eq. (22)

In order to obtain the temperature variation of cutter edge and chip surface, where the Johnson-Cook equation used as Eq. (23), it assumed the temperature conduction between tool and workpiece. The study doesn't be considered cutting temperature conducting into the air.

$$\sigma_{eq} = (A + B\varepsilon_n)\left(1 + C\ln\left(\frac{\dot{\varepsilon}}{\dot{\varepsilon}_0}\right)\right)\left(1 - \left(\frac{T - T_{room}}{T_m - T_{room}}\right)^m\right) \tag{23}$$

Where T_m means the melting point temperature; T_{room} means the environmental temperature; T means the workpiece temperature; A means the yielding stress; B means the strain factor; n means the strain coefficient; m means the temperature coefficient; ε means the plastic strain ratio; ε_0 means the stain ratio

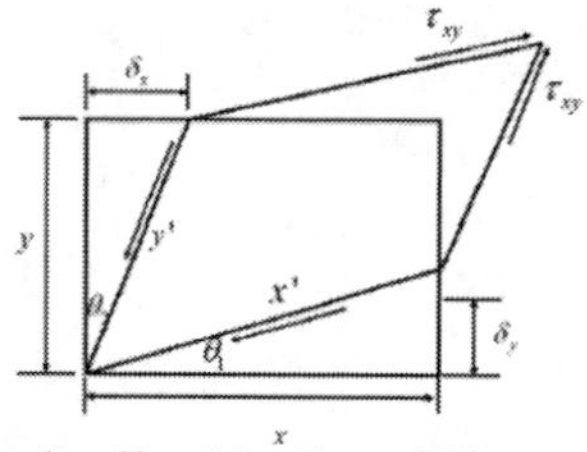

Cutting tool suffered loading will be occurred stress and strain, result in the body deformation. The strain can be distinguished from normal strain and shear strain. The physical meanings are length deformation and the variation of angle. If the model considers shear strain without normal strain, the Eq. (24) and Eq. (25) can be expressed.

$$\varepsilon_{xx} = \frac{x' - x}{x} = \frac{\sqrt{x^2 + \delta_y^{\,2}} - x}{x} \cong \frac{x - x}{x} = 0 \tag{24}$$

$$\gamma_{xy} = \theta_1 + \theta_2 \cong \tan\theta_1 + \tan\theta_2 = \frac{\delta_x}{x} + \frac{\delta_y}{y} \tag{25}$$

The simulation processes the band-saw orthogonal cutting by Lagrangian finite element method and numerical analysis.

3. Results and Discussion

The study proposed the chip formation steady-state model and cutting efficiency model for multi-cutters by Taylor tool life and fractal equation according to uniform chip thickness in high-speed band sawing process as **Fig. (a)-(d).** The uniformity of the study has two, one is the chip thickness uniformity, and the other is cutting temperature uniformity. Furthermore, a kind of new hook-tooth can be successfully applied on continuously uniformed chip formation in order to raise the production precision. **Fig.1 (b)** demonstrates a kind of hook-tooth design with coating TiN 0.2 ~0.6 μm and uncoating simulation. Initial chip formation and mesh has good uniformity from **Fig. 1 (d).** H-adaptive model can cause the fine mesh to the cutting precision raising.

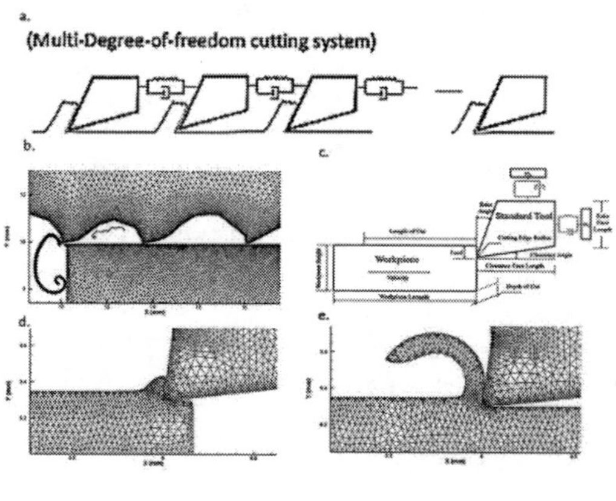

Fig.1. (a) Multi-degree-of-freedom cutting modelling; (b) chip formation for multi-cutters; (c) mathematical model for single cutter; (d) initial chip formation and mesh; (e) steady-state chip formation without considering self-excited vibration

3.1 Hook-Tooth Design and Simulated Parameters

Hook-tooth design can cause the higher shear strain rate to remove the chip, and furthermore, the tool obtained the smaller cutting temperature in order to extend the tool life. **Fig. 2** and **Table 1** demonstrated that, the cutting temperature for the relations of variations of cutting velocity from 40 m/min to 80 m/min and feed rate from 45 cm^2/min to 65 cm^2/min (at the middle section 1.51~3.00 mm of cutting length).

Table 1. Simulated Parameters

Workpiece Parameters					
Material	S45C				
Hight (mm)	0.35				
Width (mm)	4.5				
Process Parameters					
Chip Load (mm)	0.05				
Band Saw Thickness (mm)	1				
Cutting Length (mm)	5				
Cutting Velocity (m/min)	40	50	60	80	120
Feed Rate (mm/s)	0.58		0.71		0.83
Coating Parameters					
Layer	1				
Coating Material	TiN				
Coating Layer Thickness (μm)	uncoating		0.2		0.6

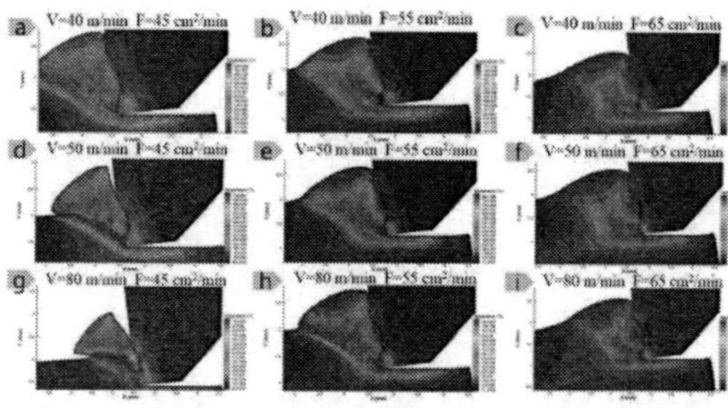

Fig.2. The cutting temperature for the relations of variations of cutting velocity from 40 m/min to 80 m/min and feed rate from 45 cm^2/min to 65 cm^2/min (at the middle section 1.51~3.00 mm of cutting length)

The study investigated the effect of cutting velocity from lower velocity 40 m/min to high-speed 120 m/min. In ultra-speed sawing process, the WC tool-edge will achieve transient higher temperature 400 deg. C. In order to solve the problem under high temperature, the edge coating for adaptive coating-layer range is very important. TiN coating is an anti-wear layer to reduce the cutting temperature raising. Besides, cutting efficiency model from **Eq.(22)** can predict the steady-state chip formation or unsteady-state chip formation form single-cutter to multi-cutters. Obviously, **(a)-(c)** mean the single cutter (V=60m/min), the temperature on coating-layer 0.2~0.6 is lower than single cutter of uncoating-layer; **(d)-(f)** mean the single cutter (V=120m/min); the temperature on coating-layer 0.2~0.6

is lower than single cutter of uncoating-layer from **Fig. 3-Fig. 5.**

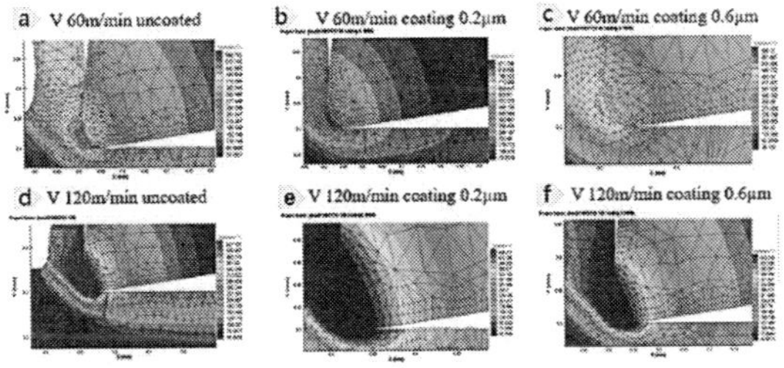

Fig.3. Temperature at section (Local 1/3 length 0.00 mm~1.50 mm); (a)-(c): single cutter (*V*=60m/min), the temperature on coating-layer 0.2~0.6 μm is lower than single cutter of uncoating-layer; (d)-(f): single cutter (*V*=120m/min); the temperature on coating-layer 0.2~0.6 μm is lower than single cutter of uncoating-layer

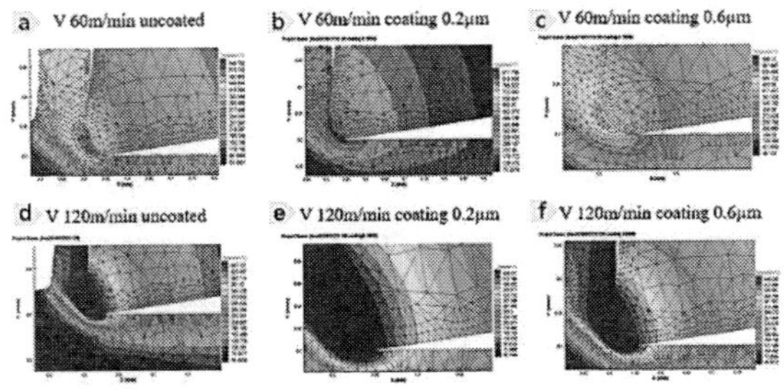

Fig.4. Temperature at section (Local 2/3 length 1.51mm~3.00mm); (a)-(c): single cutter (V=60m/min) , the temperature with cutting length increasing on coating-layer 0.2~0.6 μm is lower than single cutter of uncoating-layer; (d)-(f): single cutter (*V*=120m/min); the temperature with cutting length increasing on coating-layer 0.2~0.6 μm is obviously lower than single cutter of uncoating-layer

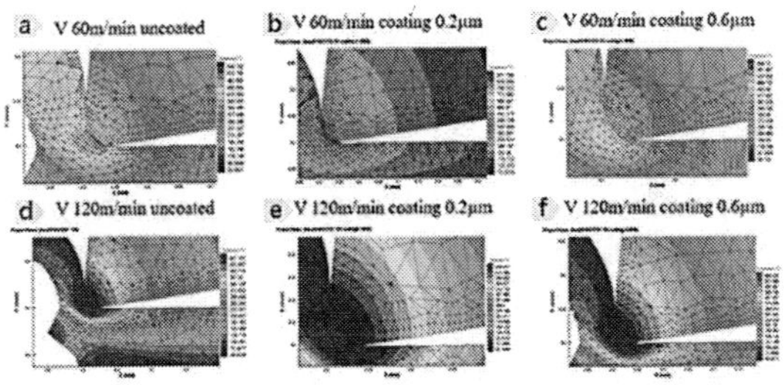

Fig.5. Temperature at section (Local 3/3 length 3.01mm~4.50mm); (a)-(c): single cutter (*V*=60m/min) , the temperature with cutting length increasing on coating-layer 0.2~0.6 μm is lower than single cutter of uncoating-layer; (d)-(f): single cutter (*V*=120m/min); the temperature with cutting length increasing on coating-layer 0.2~0.6 μm is obviously lower than single cutter of uncoating-layer; temperature on cutter edge has decreasing with coating-layer increasing, and benefits for tool life.

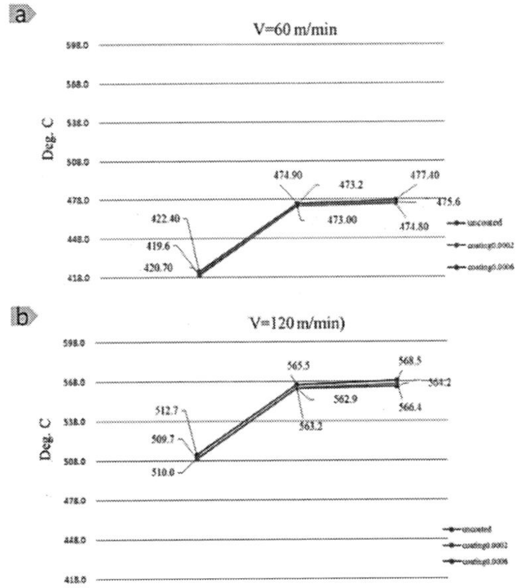

Fig.6 (a) *V*=60m/min for single cutter; (b) *V*=120m/min for single cutter is lower down than uncoating cutter (0.6 μm)

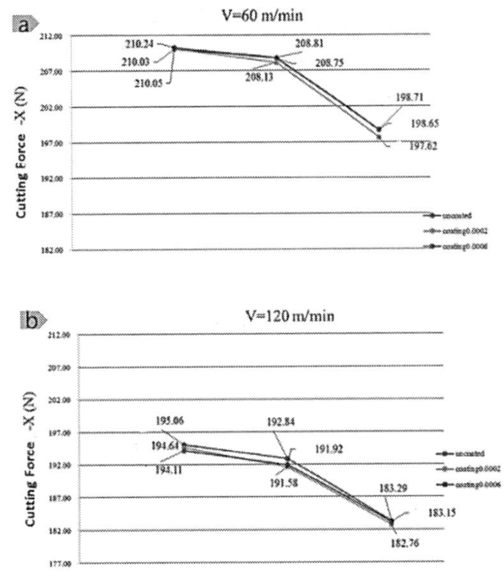

 https://doi.org/10.1051/matecconf/201820101001

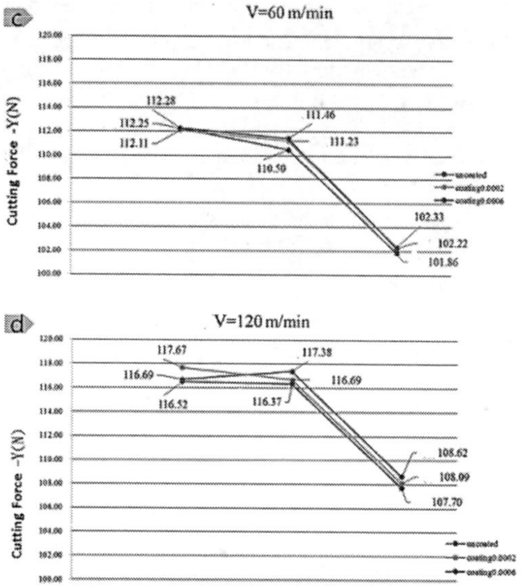

Fig.7. (a)-(b) for single cutter on *V*=60m/min (coating0.2~0.6 μm is better than uncoating); (c)-(d) single cutter on *V*=120m/min (coating0.6 μm), no variation for average force

In high-speed sawing process, the cutting temperatures at different locations are different due to the contact time of tool on workpiece. The relations of cutting velocity and cutting temperature from V=60 m/min to v=80 m/min have the same trends, summarized as **Fig. 6**. **Fig. 6 (a)** expressed the variation of the average cutting temperature at three sections of cutting length (420 Deg. C to 470 Deg. C); **(b)** means the variation of the average cutting temperature at three sections of cutting length (510 Deg. C to 560 Deg. C). Through cutting efficiency model, the cutting efficiency can be improved at least 13% by coating TiN layer 0.6 μm. The average cutting force for cutting velocity 60 m/min to 120 m/min has the same trends for three sections of cutting length, and the cutter with coating TiN has lower cutting force than one without coating TiN as **Fig. 7 (a)-(d)**.

To observe the simulation of stress-strain for multi-hook tooth design, **Fig.8** expressed the first cutter of new hook-tooth design obtain the uniform cutting stress. First cutter design can simultaneously add chip thickness uniformity and lower cutter edge stress, but flank wear still existed. Shear stress from von Mises will be increasing, and it can help chip break. The maximum shear stress 933 MPa distributed on tool-edge, reasonably. The stress X-X and stress Y-Y were under controlled as **Fig. 8**. **Fig.9** shown the second cutter of new hook-tooth design in order to obtain uniform cutting stress as (a) maximum principle stress; (b) von Mises stress; (c) stress Z-Z; (d) uniform chip formation. The analysis of von Mises can find the maximum stress on tool flank, which means the flank wear will be occurred in high-speed dynamics. Due to **Fig. 9 (d)**, the hook-tooth design indeed produced the better uniform chip formation, continuously.

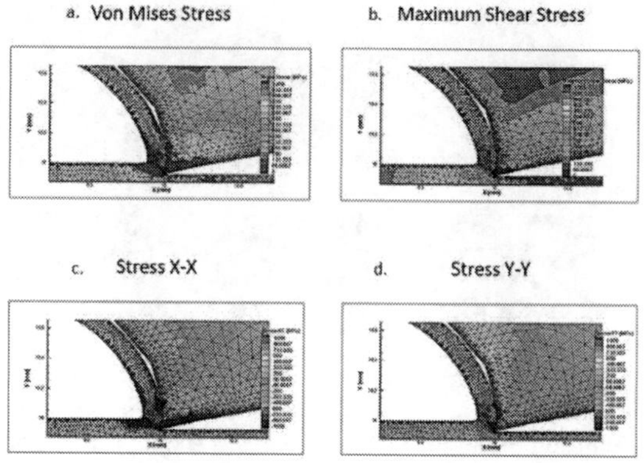

Fig. 8. First cutter of new hook-tooth design in order to obtain uniform cutting stress; (a) von Mises stress; (b) maximum shear stress; (c) stress X-X; (d) stress Y-Y

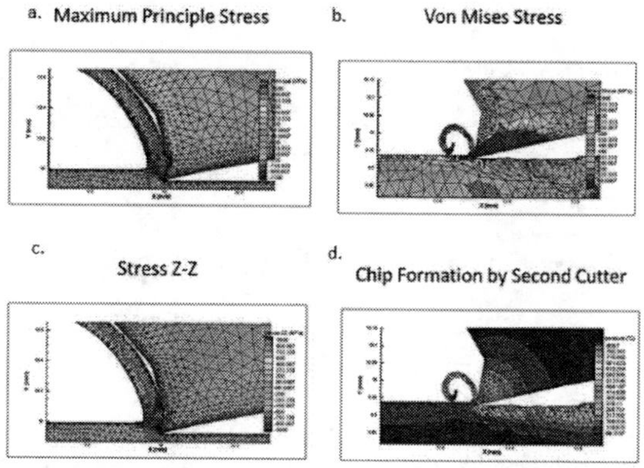

Fig.9. Second cutter of new hook-tooth design in order to obtain uniform cutting stress; (a) maximum principle stress; (b) von Mises stress; (c) stress Z-Z; (d) uniform chip formation

3.2 Vibration and Frequency Response in High-Speed Sawing Process

The mainly measured locations were on S45C first, middle and last sections, and the values were expressed as vibration energy RMS. The RMS increased with cutting velocity increasing. The acceleration gages No.3 and No.4 had larger vibration RMS, because the locations were on cut-out, where the stiffness was not enough strong. The middle section on S45C has larger vibration because of the longest cutting length. The experimental vibration trends agreed well with the simulated cutting force profile as **Fig. 10 (a)**, and the average cutting force distributed on 400 N ~500 N. Through a new tooth design, the smooth frequency response can be achieved as **Fig. 10 (b)**.

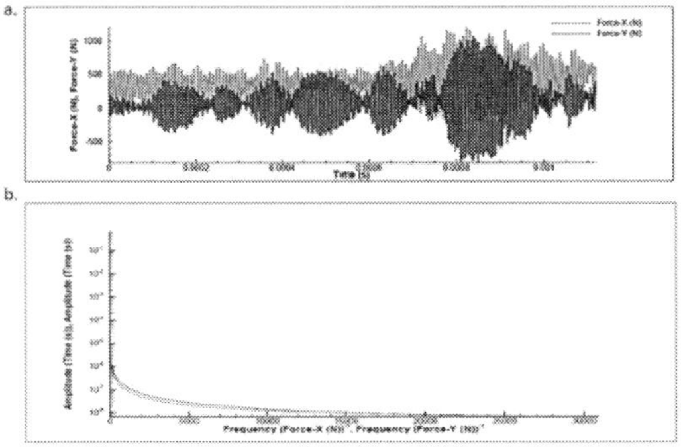

Fig.10. (a) Two-dimensional cutting force for new hook-tooth has better uniformity; (b) smooth frequency response

The validation used the 4 acceleration gages to measure the vibration (**Fig. 12 –Fig. 13**) compared with the simulated vibration and frequency reponse (**Fig. 10-Fig. 11**) has nicely trends from the three sections on S45C. Experimental preparation as **Fig. 12** (a) the location for No.1 to No.4 acceleration gage and S45C for first, middle and last section ; (b) COSEN company C-320GNC ; (c) PCB352C22 acceleration gage (d) NI-9234 vibration sampling device.

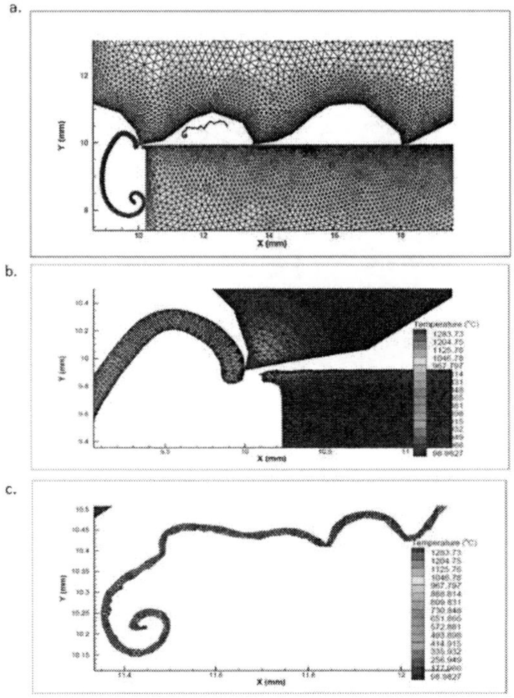

Fig.11. (a) Simulation of new hook-tooth design in order to obtain uniform cutting stress; (b) Burr for cutting out and uniform temperature distribution on chip surface (c) second chip temperature uniformity and continuous chip formation;

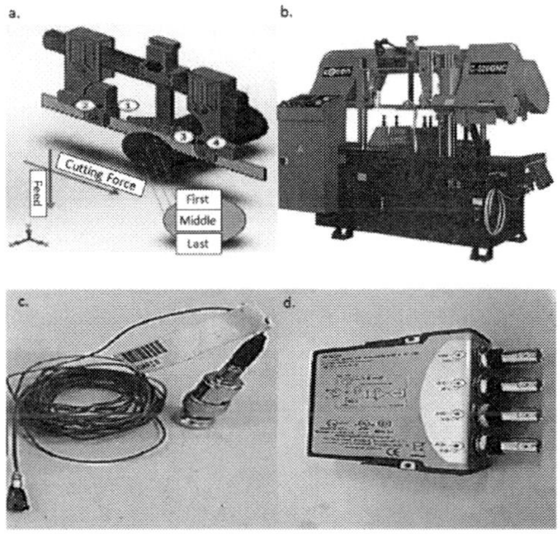

Fig.12. Experimental measurement device; (a) the location for No.1 to No.4 acceleration gage and S45C for first, middle and last section ; (b) COSEN company C-320GNC band-saw machine ; (c) PCB352C22 acceleration gage (d) NI-9234 vibration sampling device;

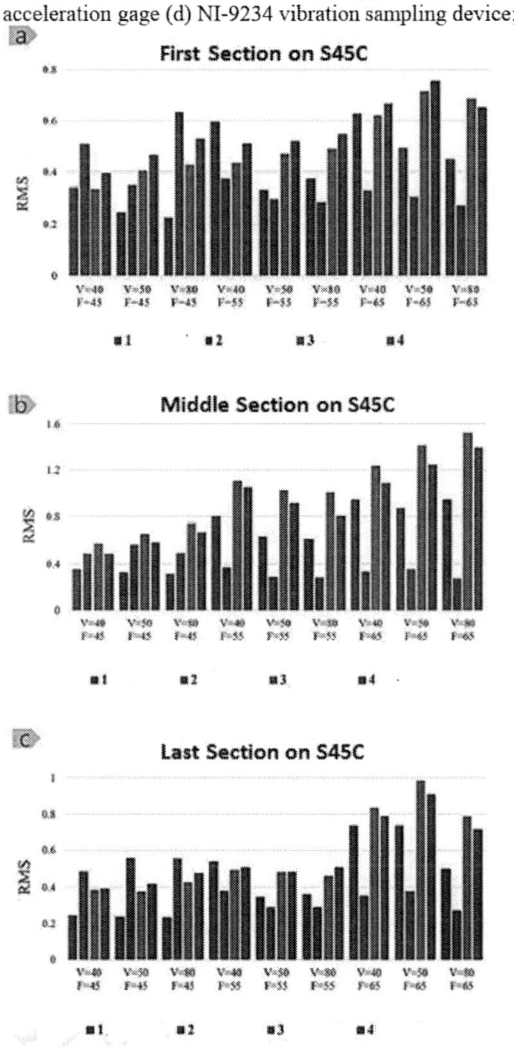

Fig.13. Vibration RMS on S45C first, middle and last section; the experimental results compared with the cutting force profile (Fig, 10 (a)) has the same trends from first, middle and last section on S45C

3.3 Chip Thickness Uniformity and Chip Temperature Uniformity

Simulation of new hook-tooth design can achieve chip thickness uniformity and chip temperature uniformity, simultaneously. To observe from Fig. 11, chip shape is an important feature. The chip formation from first cutter was nicely uniform and continuou. While the tool cutting out, the burr will be occurred on S45C. The chip surface temperature was about 500 deg.C, and the advantages of hook-tooth included that,

1. Good Surface Roughness
2. Good Cutting Force Distribution
3. Nice Chip Formation in High-Speed Sawing Process

Fig.14 The author Prof. Sung-Hua Wu stood around the COSEN Band-Saw Machine for MOST plan

The study can simulated the residual temperature about 256 deg.C on S45C. From the second cutter, it can occur the second chip temperature uniformity and continuous chip formation. The tooth design and coating under process parameters in high-speed sawing can be achieved the COSEN plan propurse (**Fig. 14**). By cutting mechanism adjusting, the MMR will be raising and tooth-bite improvement for future work.

4. Conclusions

The finding results in the study has been summarized as follows,

1. The study proposed the chip formation steady-state model and cutting efficiency model for multi-cutters by Taylor tool life and fractal equation according to uniform chip thickness in high-speed band sawing process.
2. The simulation successfully processed the band-saw orthogonal cutting by Lagrangian finite element method and numerial analysis.
3. Through cutting efficiency model, the cutting efficiency can be improved at least 13% by coating TiN layer 0.6 . The average cutting force for cutting velocity 60 m/min to 120 m/min has the same trends for three sections of cutting length, and the cutter with coating TiN has lower cutting force than one without coating TiN.
4. The study can simulated the residual temperature about 256 deg.C on S45C. From the second cutter, it can occur the second chip temperature uniformity and continuous chip formation.
5. The tooth design and coating under process parameters in high-speed sawing can be achieved the COSEN plan propurse.
6. First cutter design can simultaneously add chip thickness uniformity and lower cutter edge stress, but flank wear still existed. The maximum shear stress 933 MPa distributed on tool-edge, reasonably. The stress X-X and stress Y-Y were under controlled
7. If the chip formation is steady-state, the differential-cutter angle is uaually constant.
8. For two dimensional orthogonal cutting,the MDOF cutting dynamics has been established on the study. In additions, the tool life equation can effectively predict the cutting performance of the band saw in order to improve the process efficiency and served as the reference of actual machining process.
9. While the hook- tooth cutting speed achieved 60 m/min, comparing with non-coating cutting tooth, coating 0.2~0.6 μm was the highest temperature decreased obviously and the cutting force of hook-tooth also decreased.
10. The research put forward the cutting factors of the geometric structure of the band saw cutter, simulated and improved the processing characteristics during the cutting process, the impact of different cutting types by taking advantages of different process parameters, such as coating parameters, cutting speed and cutting feed.

This work was supported in part by Taiwan NSC under Grant No. MOST 105-2221-E-327 -015, and the industril plan –Development of Ultra Speed Intelligent CNC Band Saw Machine from No.105RB07. Appreciation is expressed to the COSEN Company for the provision of the band-saw and for its subsequent contribution to the success of this study. Additional thanks to Prof. Sheng-Jye Hwang, Prof. Ta-Hui Lin and Prof. Rong-Shean Lee at NCKU for the supporting in studied process. Besides, external thinks to Prof. Yunn-Lin Hwang and Prof. Jeng-Haur Horng for the research cooperation at National Formosa University.

References

[1] T.J. Ko, H.S. Kim, Mechanistic cutting force model in band sawing, Int. J. Mach. Tool. & Manu., **39**, 8,118–119 (1999)

[2] C. Andersson, M.T Andersson, J.-E Ståhl, Bandsawing. Part I: cutting force model including effects

of positional errors, tool dynamics and wear, Int. J. Mach. Tool. & Manu., **41**, 227–236 (2001)

[3] C. Andersson, J.-E S.H. Hellbergh, Bandsawing. Part II: detecting positional errors, tool dynamics and wear by cutting force measurement, Int. J. Mach. Tool. & Manu., **41**, 237–253 (2001)

[4] C. Andersson, Bandsawing. Part III: stress analysis of saw tooth microgeometry, Int. J. Mach. Tool. & Manu., **41**, 255-263 (2001)

[5] T.D. Marusich, E. Askari, Modeling Residual Stress and Workpiece Quality in Machined Surfaces, *Proceedings of the 4th CIRP International Workshop on Modelling of Machining Operations, Delft*, The Netherlands, 105–109 (2001)

[6] X. Xu, Y. Yu, Sawing performance of diamond with alloy coatings, Surf. & Coat. Tech., **198**, 459- 463 (2005)

[7] R. Okai, S.J. Mitchual, K. Frimpong-Mensah, Optimization techniques for minimizing saw teeth deflection and lumber thickness variation, Prec. Eng., **30**, 1, 39–46 (2006)

[8] I.S. Buyuksagis, Effect of Cutting Mode on the Sawability of Granites Using Segmented Circular Diamond Sawblade, Int. J. Mach. Tool. & Manu., **183**, 399-406 (2007)

[9] Sung-Hua Wu, J.-J. Junz Wang, R. S. Lee, Chip fractal geometry and loading characteristics of sinusoidal multi-cutters in hack-sawing process, Int. J. Mach. Tool. & Manu., **111**, 68. Corrigendum (2016)

[10] T. Thaler, P. Potocnik, I. Bric, E. Govekar, Chatter detection in band sawing based on discriminant analysis of sound features, Appl. Acou., **77**,114–121 (2014)

[11] T. Thaler, B. Krese, E. Govekar, Stability diagrams and chatter avoidance in horizontal band sawing, CIRP Anna.-Manu. Tech. , **64**, 81–84 (2015)

[12] T.G. Kumbera, J.A. Patten, H.P. Cherukuri, C.J. Brand, T.D. Marusich, Numerical simulations of ductile machining of silicon nitride with a cutting tool of defined geometry, Int. J. Mach. Tool. & Manu., **5**, 341–352 (2001)

[13] T.D. Marusich, J.D. Thiele, C.J. Brand, Simulation and analysis of chip breakage in turning processes, *Technical Paper Presented in Caterpillar Inc*, 1–10 (2001)

[14] W. Grzesik, M. Bartoszuk, P. Nieslony, Finite element modelling of temperature distribution in the cutting zone in turning processes with differently coated tools, J. Mate. Proc. Tech., 1204–1211 (2005)

[15] G. Fang, P. Zeng, Three-dimensional thermo–elastic–plastic coupled FEM simulations for metal oblique cutting processes, J. Mate. Proc. Tech., **168**, 1, 42–48 (2005)

[16] T.D. Marusich, S. Usui, S. Lankalapalli, N. Saini, L. Zamorano, A. Grevstad, Residual Stress Prediction for Part Distortion Modeling, *Copyright SAE International* (2006)

[17] T.D. Marusich, S. Usui, J. Ma, D.A. Stephenson, A. Shih, *Finite Element Modeling of Drilling Processes with Solid and Indexable Tooling in Metals and Stack-ups* (2007)

[18] M. Mohammadpour, M.R. Razfar R. Jalili Saffar, Numerical investigating the effect of machining parameters on residual stresses in orthogonal cutting, Simu. Mode. Prac. & Theo., **18**, 3,378–389 (2010)

[19] K. Huang, W. Yang, Analytical model of temperature field in workpiece machined surface layer in orthogonal cutting, J. Mate. Proc. Tech., **229**, 375–389 (2016)

[20] B.B. Mandelbort, *The fractal geometry of nature*, W.H. Freeman, New York (1982)

MATEC Web of Conferences **201**, 01002 (2018)
ICI 2017
https://doi.org/10.1051/matecconf/201820101002

Sensitivity Study of Polysilicon Nanowire Based on Scattering and Quantum Mechanics Models

Aanand[1], *Gene* Sheu[1], *Syed Sarwar* Imam[1], *Shao Wei* Lu[2], *Shao-Ming* Yang[1,3*], *Ming Jen* Fan[1]

[1]Department of Computer Science and Information Engineering, Asia University, 500, Lioufeng Rd., Taichung 41354, Taiwan.
[2]School of Software and Microelectronics, Peking University, Beijing, China.
[3]Department of Medical Research, China Medical University Hospital, China Medical University, Taichung, Taiwan.

Abstract. In this paper, we report nanowire drain saturation current sensitivity property to measure femtomol level change in drain current due to different proteins i.e. DNA with numerical simulation and fabricated polysilicon nanowire based on the theoretical predictions. In addition, the drain current will also be affected by the back-gate voltage and will increase as the back-gate voltage increases. A 3-dimensional Synopsis tool is used to investigate the drain current behavior for a polysilicon nanowire. The scattering compact model reported result of detailed numerical calculation shows in good agreement, indicating the usefulness of scattering compact model. Whereas 3D synopsis unable to explain the whole region of the drain current characteristics in linear region which uses quantum mechanics model approach.

1 Introduction

Nanowire (NW) have attracted wide attention, and analyses that focus on various aspects of the device operation have accumulated. We have offered an experimental and analytical method to observe the poly silicon NW MOSFET threshold voltage based on a simple ballistic MOSFET modeling from the private communication with Natori. [1] In previous paper we proposed scattering effects into the ballistic modeling and to provide a compact model of the quasi-ballistic Si NW MOSFET. Now our current study compares the tow different approach of physics to study the electrical characteristic of device. Based upon Sentaurus device simulation which uses quantum mechanics approach and theoretical study of semi classical physics. Silicon NW MOSFETs attract wide attention as a promising Nano device for future high-density LSI application. For development of the device including the circuit application, a handy tool that affords accurate prediction of device characteristics is indispensable.

Semiconducting silicon nanowire field effect transistors (SiNW FETs) have been shown to function as a transducers for label-free, high-sensitivity and direct electrical detection of biomolecules.[1][4] The ultrahigh sensitive detection can be attributed to their small size and large surface-to-volume ratio, enabling local charge transfers to result in a current change due to a field effect, such as when the analytical molecules bind to specific recognition molecules at the surface of the nanowire. This effect is sufficiently strong that single charge at the surface of the nanowire can be sensed because the depletion or accumulation of charge carriers affects the entire cross-sectional conduction pathway of these nanostructures. [5]

2 Device fabrication approach

2.1 Botton up Fabrication approche

A simple and low-cost method to fabricate poly-crystalline silicon (poly-Si) NW FET for bio sensing application has been demonstrated [6][7]. The poly-SiNW channel can be fabricated by employing the poly-Si 'bottom up' process, in an approach which is compatible with current commercial semiconductor processes. Throughout the fabrication, no expensive lithography tools are needed for definition of the nano-scale patterns. The fabricated devices exhibited good performance and showed great potential to be developed to an ultrasensitive biosensor because of their excellent electrical characteristics in aqueous solution. [8]

2.2 Fabrication steps

The device samples were manufactured on standard 6-in. p-type wafers. A proposed hybrid sensor/memory/CMOS poly-Si nanowire structure is illustrated in Figure 1. The bottom-gate poly-Si

* Corresponding author: rickyyang121@asia.edu.tw

 https://doi.org/10.1051/matecconf/201820101002

nanowire formation can be inserted specifically after metallization of the back-end process (BEOL).

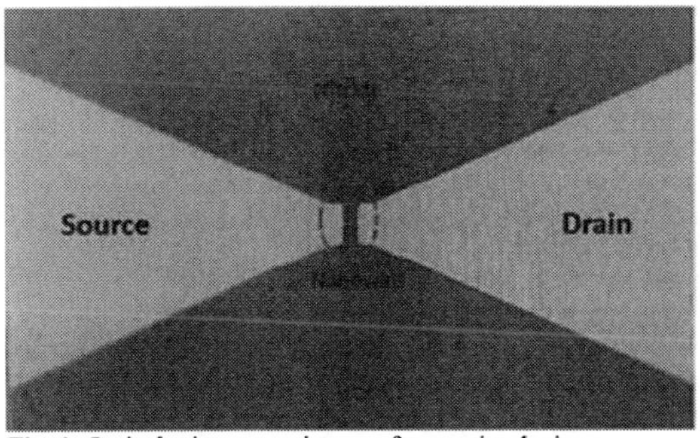

Fig. 1. Optical microscope image of nanowire device.

At the beginning, buried oxide was deposited on a substrate surface as the gate dielectric of nanowire FETs. A 50-nm polysilicon layer was then deposited using the CVD process. Subsequently, the poly-Si wire was patterned by the standard I-line stepper of the CMOS semiconducting process. By using reactive plasma etching for photoresist trimming followed by silicon etching, the NW dimension was scaled to a level of approximately 100 nm. Figure 2. Showed the zoomed view of Nanowire.

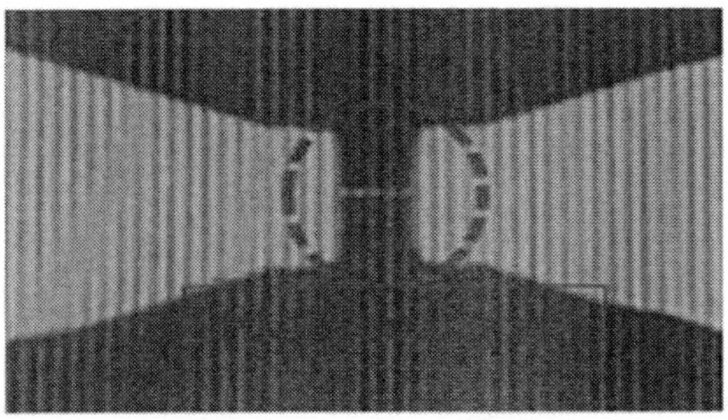

Fig. 2. Zoom optical microscope image of nanowire device.

A NW shrinkage technique using poly re-oxidation and oxide stripping was employed to scale down the NW width to less than 50 nm. A channel protection photoresist pattern was then formed by I-line lithography.

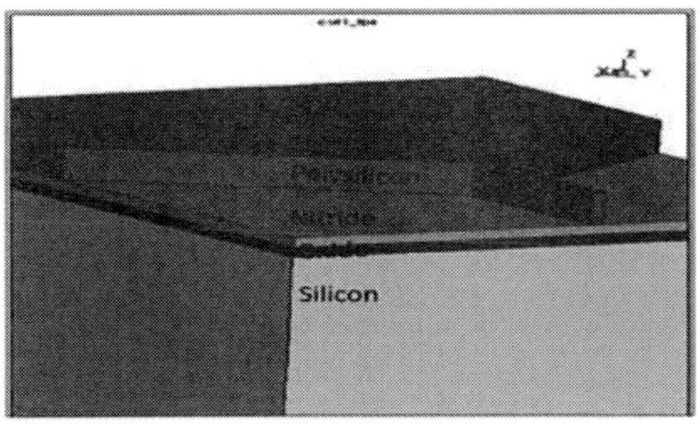

Fig. 3. 3D Cross-section of the simulated device.

Figure 3. Show the 3D cross section of the simulated device. The objective of the channel protection patterning was to keep the channel intrinsically from n+ source/drain (S/D) implantation, to increase NW FETs sensitivity. Subsequently, the n+ S/D implant was performed with a 5e14 cm^{-2} arsenic ion beam at 10 KeV to reduce the parasitic resistance of the NW. Thereafter, the channel protection photoresist was removed. Finally, the S/D dopant was activated by annealing treatment at 600 °C for 30 min in a N_2 ambience.

3 Simulation methodology

Simulation is one of the stages that are important before manufacturing device. In simulation, the device can be analysis the optimal functionality and the performance. By using simulation tool, it allows the user produce the prototype even the device become more complex and become more difficult to do experimentally. Simulation program will reduce the time and enable the researcher from the based on the concept of the chip potential and their characteristic performance.

In this paper, the result of polysilicon nanowire is observed for the conductance of the device. The simulations of the model design characterized are using the boundary conditions as described in our previous study. In our simulation, various simulation models have been used to match the silicon result.

In this study, a simulation methodology is presented based on a 3D drift diffusion (DD) simulator including quantum confinement effects to accurately describe the electrostatics related characteristic. But the simulation tool fails to explain the Id-Vg curve in all regions i.e. also the simulation results fits only in the saturation region, but fails to explain the linear region of the curves.

The drain current is readily evaluated by following a simple procedure if device parameters and bias conditions are specified. A comparison with a reported result of detailed numerical simulation [4] showed good agreement, indicating the usefulness of the compact model. The compact model includes the energy integration as well as the sub-band summation, and numerical procedures are inevitable for the detailed evaluation. But here, we introduce some reasonable approximations in the NW structure and the carrier statistics in the compact model, and intend to derive analytic expressions of the device current.

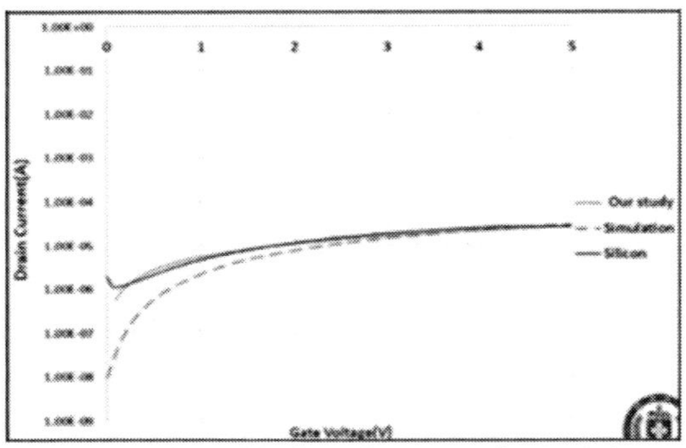

Fig. 4. Comparison of the three Id-Vg curves for simulation result, compact model curve with the fabricated silicon chip at drain biased at 3V.

Also, our compact analytical equation for the drain saturation current derive the injection velocity equation for the fully degenerate condition. And can we have calculated with the handy calculation. This drain current formula is obtained from Kenji Natori with the private communication of Prof. Gene Sheu, equation 1. [5]

$$I_D = C_G(V_G - V_t)V_{inj}\frac{(1-R)\left\{1-exp\left(-\frac{qV_D}{k_BT}\right)\right\}}{(1+R)+(1-R)exp\left(-\frac{qV_D}{kT_B}\right)} \quad (1)$$

$$V_{inj} = \frac{I_d}{C_{eff}(V_g - V_t)} x \frac{(1+r)+(1-r)\,exp^{-\frac{qV_d}{kBt}}}{(1-r)\left\{1-exp^{-\frac{qV_d}{kBt}}\right\}} \quad (2)$$

The above equation we propose for the injection velocity calculation for the fully degenerate condition, in non-degeneracy condition the injection velocity supposed to be constant as shown in equation 3. [9]

$$v_{inj} = \sqrt{\frac{2k_BT}{\pi m_x}} \quad (3)$$

Also, we take the Vinj curve as a reference from the Purdue University, they have quantum mechanics approach to solve for the Vinj equation but also our equation derived from the compact model [9] as shown in equation 1 can also be able to calculate the injection velocity.

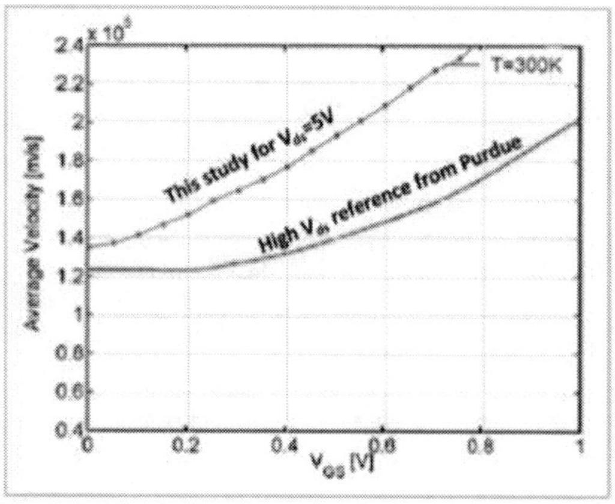

Fig. 5. Red line is the reference line from Purdue University and blue line is our work proposed equation for Vinj for higher drain biased voltage at 5V

4 Conclusion

Nanowire drain saturation current sensitivity property to measure femtomol level change in drain current due to different proteins i.e. DNA with numerical simulation and fabricated polysilicon nanowire based on the theoretical predictions. In addition, the drain current will also be affected by the back-gate voltage and will increase as the back-gate voltage increases. A 3-dimensional Synopsis tool is used to investigate the drain current behavior for a polysilicon nanowire. The scattering compact model reported result of detailed numerical calculation shows in good agreement, indicating the usefulness of scattering compact model. Whereas 3D synopsis unable to explain the whole region of the drain current characteristics in linear region which uses quantum mechanics model approach.

Acknowledgment: The authors would also like to thank National Center for High-performance computing, National Nano Device Laboratories, and the National Chip Implementation Center for supporting us.

References

1. Y. Cui, Q. Wei, H. Park and C. M. Lieber, *"Nanowire Nanosensors for Highly Sensitive and Selective Detection of Biological and Chemical Species"*, Science **293**, 1289-92 (2001)
2. Z. Li, Y. Chen, X. Li, T. I. Kamins, K. Nauka and R. S. Williams, *"Sequence-Specific Label-Free DNA Sensors Based on Silicon Nanowires"*, Nano Letters **4**, 245-247 (2004)
3. E. Stern, J. F. Klemic, D. A. Routenberg, P. N. Wyrembak, D. B. Turner-Evans, A. D. Hamilton, D. A. LaVan, T. M. Fahmy and M. A. Reed, *"Label-free immunodetection with CMOS-compatible semiconducting nanowires"*, Nature **445**, 519-522 (2007)
4. N. Elfstro¨m, R. Juhasz, I. Sychugov, T. Engfeldt, A. Eriksson Karlstro¨m and J. Linnros, *"Surface Charge Sensitivity of Silicon Nanowires: Size Dependence"*, Nano Letters 7, 2608-2612 (2007)
5. M. Lundstrom, *"Elementary scattering theory of the Si MOSFET"*, IEEE Elec. Dev. Lett. **18**, 361-363 (1997).
6. H. C. Lin, M. H. Lee, C. J. Su, T. Y. Huang, C. C. Lee and Y. S. Yang, *"A Simple and Low-Cost Method to Fabricate TFTs With Poly-Si Nanowire Channel"*, IEEE Electron Device Lett. **26**, 643-645 (2005)
7. C. J. Su, H. C. Lin and T. Y. Huang, *"High-Performance TFTs With Si Nanowire Channels Enhanced by Metal-Induced Lateral Crystallization"*, IEEE Electron Device Lett. **27**, 582-584 (2006)
8. H. C. Lin, C. J. Su, C. Y. Hsiao, Y. S. Yang and T. Y. Huang, *"Water passivation effect on polycrystalline silicon nanowires"*, Appl. Phys. Lett. **91**, 202113 (2007)
9. K. Natori, *"Compact Modeling of Quasi-Ballistic Silicon Nanowire MOSFETs"*, IEEE Trans. Elec. Dev. **59**, 79-86 (2012)

Damage Assessment of a Structure by Using Frequency Responses Function Curvature Method and Cubic Spline Interpolation

Wei-Chih Su [1,]*and Chiung-Shiann Huang [2]

[1]National Center for High-performance Computing, National Applied Research Laboratories, Hsinchu 30076, Taiwan
[2]Department of Civil Engineering, National Chiao Tung University, Hsinchu 30076, Taiwan

Abstract. This study explores the possibility of using frequency responses function curvature method and cubic spline interpolation to locate the storeys of a building that is damaged in an earthquake, and corresponding frequency responses function curvature of storey often change in the earthquake. The frequency responses function of a building in each floor is established from the full structural dynamic responses. Next, the frequency responses function of storeys that be obtained by cubic spline interpolation would be used to detect the damage location of a building. The effectiveness of the proposed procedure is verified using numerically simulated earthquake responses of the finite element model of an eight-storey frame.

1 Introduction

The severe loading, such as a strong earthquake, and structural material is degraded would cause damage in a structure. The serviceability and safety of structures depend on the detection and location of structural damage. It is well-known that vibration-based damaged detection methods are simple and widely adopted [1-8]. Vibration-based damage detection methods are using the measured vibration responses of a structure to detect its damage location. Theoretically, if the stiffness and mass of a structure are changes, its dynamic properties, such as natural frequency, damping ratio, mode shapes or frequency responses function etc., are also changes. Pandey et al. employed curvature mode shapes to detect the damage in a beam, and Sampaio et al.[9] proposed frequency responses function curvature method for reducing the time-consuming on modal identification process. However, only the measured degree of freedoms could be obtained its curvature in this method.

This study using the frequency response functions curvature method and cubic spline interpolation for directly pointing out the damage location. The measured raw data will direct use for damage detection. The measured responses are in terms of acceleration or velocity. The acceleration responses are used herein. The proposed procedure is validated using the numerically simulated earthquake acceleration responses of an eight-storey finite element model.

2 Methodology

The dynamic responses of a linear structure satisfy the equation of motion

$$\mathbf{M}\ddot{\mathbf{x}} + \mathbf{C}\dot{\mathbf{x}} + \mathbf{K}\mathbf{x} = \mathbf{f} \qquad (1)$$

where **M**, **C** and **K** are mass, damping and stiffness matrices, respectively; $\ddot{\mathbf{x}}$, $\dot{\mathbf{x}}$ and $\mathbf{x}$ are the acceleration, velocity, and displacement responses vectors of the system, and f is the input force vectors. Applying Fourier transform into Eq.(1) and denoting $\mathscr{F}\{\mathbf{x}\} = \overline{\mathbf{X}}(\omega)$

$$\overline{\mathbf{X}}(\omega) = \mathbf{H}(\omega)\overline{\mathbf{F}}(\omega) \qquad (2)$$

where, $\mathbf{H}(\omega) = \left(-\mathbf{M}\omega^2 + i\mathbf{C}\omega + \mathbf{K}\right)^{-1}$ is well-known frequency response function. The frequency response function can be calculated by applying the weighted least-square approach on Eq. (2).

The frequency responses function curvature method is an extension of the curvature mode shapes method to all frequencies in the measurement range and not just considers the modal frequencies. In fact, the operation of this method is similar to the curvature mode shapes method. The curvature for each frequency is given by

$$h''(\omega)_{i,j} = \left[h(\omega)_{i+1,j} - 2h(\omega)_{i,j} + h(\omega)_{i-1,j}\right]/l^2 \qquad (3)$$

where $h_{i,j}$ is the receptacle FRF measured at the ith degree of freedom for a force input at location j.

* Corresponding author: wichcv86@gmail.com

 https://doi.org/10.1051/matecconf/201820101003

The absolute difference between the FRF curvatures of the damaged and undamaged structure at the ith degree of freedom, along the chosen frequency range, is calculated, for an applied force at point j, by the following equation

$$\Delta h''_{i,j} = \sum_{\omega} \left| h''_d(\omega)_{i,j} - h''_u(\omega)_{i,j} \right| \tag{4}$$

where, $h''_d(\omega)_{i,j}$ and $h''_u(\omega)_{i,j}$ are denoting as the curvature of damaged and undamaged structures, respectively. Finally, the each force location will be summed up and yielded

$$S(i) = \sum_j \Delta h''_{i,j} \tag{5}$$

However, the curvature of the FRF calculated by Eq. (3) is difficult to apply on boundary degree of freedoms. Besides, this procedure that used to detect the stiffness change between the i-1th and i^{th} degree of freedoms is indirectly. To address these issues, the spline interpolation will be used to the curvature between the i-1th and i^{th} degree of freedoms.

A cubic spline is a spine constructed of piecewise third-order polynomials which pass through a set of m given points. The frequency responses function between the i-1th h and i^{th} degree of freedoms for a force input at location j, denoted by $h(\omega)_{i-1/2,j}$, can be easy obtained by the cubic spline interpolation. Then, the FRF curvature between the i-1th and i^{th} degree of freedoms for a force input at location j is given by

$$h''(\omega)_{i-1/2,j} = 4\left[h(\omega)_{i,j} - 2h(\omega)_{i-1/2,j} + h(\omega)_{i-1,j} \right] / l^2$$

$$D.I.(i) = S(i-1/2)/S(i_{max}-1/2) \quad i = 1,2,\text{L}\ ,I \tag{6}$$

$\Delta h''_{i-1/2,j}$ and $S(i-1/2)$ can be calculated by the same procedure. Finally, the damage index can be defined as

$$D.I.(i) = S(i-1/2)/S(i_{max}-1/2) \quad i = 1,2,\text{L}\ ,I \tag{7}$$

Here i_{max} is the maximum order location, and I is the measured degree of freedoms.

3 Numerical Verification

To demonstrate the feasibility of the proposed procedure, the finite element model of eight-storey frame was built and this frame was subjected to a simulated 1999 Chi-chi earthquake at its base in X direction (see Fig. 1). The eight-storey frame under consideration was 1.5m long, 1.1m wide and 1.06m high. The simulation was conducted at 5% of the modal damping ratio. Plates were fixed on each floor, such that the total mass of frame at each floor was approximately 6.732 kg. The columns have rectangular sections of 2.5x15, with units in cm. This original frame was defined as "frame A". And "frame B" was created by replacing each column on the first storey with columns of rectangular sections of 2.5x13.5. Each frame was subjected to base excitations of the 1999 Chi-Chi earthquake. The acceleration responses of the base and all floors at t=5~45 seconds were used in evaluating frequency responses function for the frames. Fig. 1 displays the time history of base excitation and acceleration responses in X direction of "frame A" subject the Chi-chi earthquake. Fig.1 also shows the FRFs of the "frame A" and "frame B", plotted for a frequency range of 0-20 Hz, measured on each floor for an input force on the base.

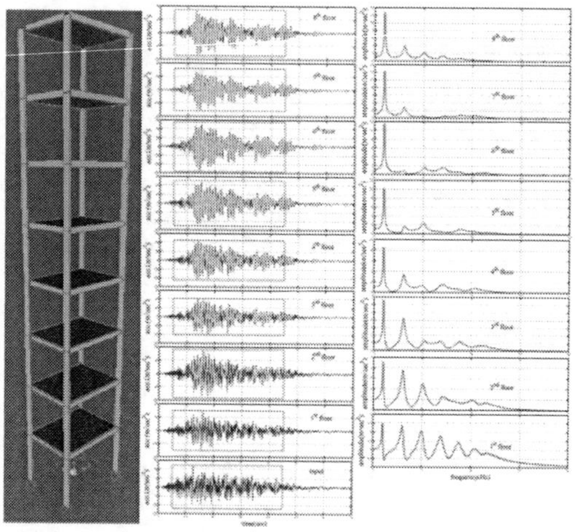

Fig. 1. Schematic diagram of an eight-storey frame and its simulation responses

This paragraph further applied this procedure to the calculated frequency responses function. Fig. 2 compares the results obtained using the presented method and the traditional frequency response function curvature method. The results in Fig. 2 are normalized the variation of the curvature of the FRFs between the "frame A" and "frame B". In theoretically, the normalized indexes induced by the "FRFCM only" in the observation points nearby the damaged elements are close to one. Fig. 2 clearly demonstrates the ability of the both method in identifying the storey in the reference structure. However, it is directly to locate the storey with stiffness reduce in the proposed procedure.

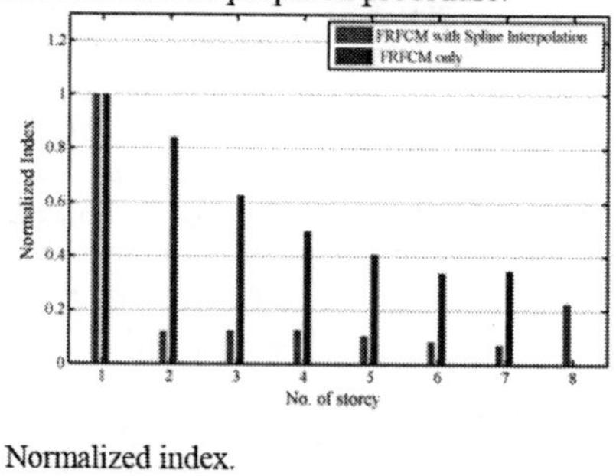

Fig. 2. Normalized index.

The success of the proposed procedure, as revealed in capturing the difference in properties of numerical models, demonstrates the practical applicability of this procedure to a shear building model.

4 Conclusions

This study developed a simple and efficient approach for locating damaged storeys in a structure, based on the fact that damage to a storey changes the frequency responses function curvature of the structure. The frequency response functions are directly estimated from the measured acceleration responses. Next, the FRFs curvature between the observed locations will be obtained by applying the cubic spline interpolation on the FRFs. Comparing the FRFs curvature in the current state with those in the undamaged state enables damaged storeys to be accurately located.

The proposed approach was demonstrated on an eight-storey finite element model under earthquake excitation. A finite element model with single-site damage was considered. The proposed approach was validated by successfully identifying damaged storeys by processing numerically simulated responses. The proposed procedure did provide more directly locating the damaged storeys than the process without the cubic spline interpolation.

Acknowledgement

The authors would like to thank the Ministry of Science and Technology of the Republic of China, Taiwan, for financially supporting this research under Contract No. MOST 106-2622-M-492-001-CC2.

References

1. H.G., Natke, Probab Eng Mech. **3**(1), 28-35 (1988).
2. M. Imregun, W.J. Visser, Shock Vib Dig. **23**, 9-20 (1999).
3. J.E. Mottershead, M.I. Friswell, J Sound Vib. **167**(2), 347-75 (1993).
4. O.S. Salawu, Eng Struct. **19**(9), 718-2 (1997).
5. S.W. Doebling, C.R. Farrar, Shock Vib Dig. **30**(2), 91-105 (1998).
6. C.r., Farrar, S.W. Doebling, D.A. Nix, Philosophical Transactions of the Royal Society. Math Phys Eng Sci. **359**(1778), 131-50 (2001).
7. P.C. Chang, A. Flatau, S.C. Liu, Struc Health Monit, Int J. **2**(3), 257-67 (2003).
8. J.M.W. Brownjohn, Philosophical Transactions of the Royal Society. Math Phys Eng Sci. **365**(1851), 589-622 (2007).
9. R.P.C. Sampaio, N.M.M. Maia, J.M.M. Silva, J Sound Vib. **226**(5), 1029-42 (1999).

Structural Damage Assessment by Using Stiffness-based Method and Cubic Spline Interpolation

Wei-Chih Su[1,*], *Chiung-Shiann* Huang[2], and *Jyh-Horng* Wu[1]

[1]National Center for High-performance Computing, National Applied Research Laboratories, No. 7 R&D 6th Rd Hsinchu, Taiwan
[2]Department of Civil Engineering, National Chiao Tung University, 1001 University Rd Hsinchu, Taiwan

Abstract. This study explores the possibility of using stiffness-based method and cubic spline interpolation to locate the damaged storey of a building during a strong earthquake, and corresponding stiffness matrix of structure often change in the earthquake process. The time series model of a building is established from the full structural dynamic responses. Next, the coefficient matrix of the time series model could be solved by recursive least squares (RLS) algorithms. Then, the model parameters of a building are calculated by the coefficient matrix of time series model. Finally, the identified natural frequencies and mode shapes of structure that corrected by cubic spline interpolation would be used to construct the stiffness matrix of a building. Then, the damage location of a building could be detected by the identified stiffness matrix of a building. The effectiveness of the proposed procedure is verified using numerically simulated earthquake responses of the finite element model of a six-storey frame.

1 Introduction

It is essential that detect the damaged location by using the identified modal parameters of an existing structure or bridge from the measured dynamical responses in the field of structural health monitoring. System identification is a process to create mathematical models of structures using measurements of the dynamic responses and base excitation of structure. Based on the properties of coefficient estimation approaches, the process of system identification are divided into two broad categories, online and offline estimation.

- Online estimation algorithms estimate the coefficient matrix of time series model when the new responses are measureable during the dynamic process. These algorithms including: recursive least square approaches [1-3]; recursive gradient approaches [4, 5] and recursive maximum likelihood approaches [6, 7].
- Offline estimation algorithms estimate the coefficient matrix of time series model after collecting all the input and output data. These algorithms including: least square approaches [8]; maximum likelihood approaches [9]; artificial neural network [10]; genetic algorithm [11].

The vibration-based damage detection method would use to locate the damaged sotreys based on examining change in measured dynamic responses. Stiffness matrix based process requires as follows: 1. identifying the modal parameters of structures; 2. constructing the stiffness matrix of structures by identified modal parameters; 3. computing the variation of the identified stiffness matrix between the damaged and undamaged structure.

This study utilizes a simple and efficient modal identification method and stiffness-based damage locating approach to determine which floors of a structure exhibit a change in stiffness. First, the time series model of a structure is established and the recursive least square approach is used to estimate the coefficient matrix of time series model. Next, the modal parameters of structure would be calculated by the estimated coefficient matrix of time series model. Then, the stiffness matrix of structure could be obtained from the identified modal parameters. However, it is difficult to observe the dynamic responses of all degree of freedoms. In here, the cubic spline interpolation would be used to obtain the mode shapes of the unobserved degree of freedom from the identified modal parameters.

The proposed procedure is validated using the simulated earthquake acceleration responses of a six-story finite element model. The incomplete measurement situation would be assumed and the cubic spline interpolation would be used to calculate the mode shapes of the unobserved degree of freedom.

2 Methodology

A building structure could be considered with viscous damping. The dynamic responses of building must

* Corresponding author: wichcv86@gmail.com

satisfy the equation of motion, and could be described as follows

$$\mathbf{M}\ddot{\mathbf{x}} + \mathbf{C}\dot{\mathbf{x}} + \mathbf{K}\mathbf{x} = \mathbf{f} \tag{1}$$

where **M**, **C** and **K** are mass, damping and stiffness matrices, respectively; $\ddot{\mathbf{x}}$, $\dot{\mathbf{x}}$ and $\mathbf{x}$, respectively, are the acceleration, velocity and displacement responses vectors of the building, and **f** is the input force vectors. According to the central difference approach, equation of motion could be rewrite by time series model

$$\mathbf{y}_t = \sum_{i=1}^{I} \mathbf{\Phi}_i \mathbf{y}_{t-i\Delta t} + \sum_{j=0}^{J} \mathbf{\Theta}_j \mathbf{f}_{t-j\Delta t} \tag{2}$$

where, $\mathbf{y}_{t-i\Delta t}$ and $\mathbf{f}_{t-i\Delta t}$ are the vectors of measured responses and input forces at time $t\text{-}i\,\Delta t$, respectively; $1/\Delta t$ is the sampling rate of the measurement, $\mathbf{\Phi}_i$ and $\mathbf{\Theta}_j$ are matrices of coefficient functions to be determined in the model. Rearranging Eq.(2) yields

$$\mathbf{y}_t = \bar{\boldsymbol{\varphi}}_t^{\mathbf{T}} \boldsymbol{\theta}_t, \tag{3}$$

where

$$\begin{cases} \bar{\boldsymbol{\varphi}}_t = [\mathbf{y}_{t-\Delta t} & \cdots & \mathbf{y}_{t-I\Delta t} & \mathbf{f}_t & \cdots & \mathbf{f}_{t-J\Delta t}]^{\mathbf{T}} \\ \boldsymbol{\theta}_t = [\mathbf{\Phi}_{t,1} & \cdots & \mathbf{\Phi}_{t,I} & \mathbf{\Theta}_{t,0} & \cdots & \mathbf{\Theta}_{t,J}] \end{cases} \tag{4}$$

A recursive least square algorithm can be used to estimate and track the time-variant coefficient matrix of time series model as follows

$$\begin{cases} \hat{\boldsymbol{\theta}}_{t+1} = \hat{\boldsymbol{\theta}}_t + \boldsymbol{L}_t \varepsilon_t \\ \varepsilon_t = \mathbf{y}_t - \bar{\boldsymbol{\varphi}}_t^{\mathbf{T}} \hat{\boldsymbol{\theta}}_t \\ \boldsymbol{L}_t = \boldsymbol{P}_t \bar{\boldsymbol{\varphi}}_t = \frac{\boldsymbol{P}_{t-1}\bar{\boldsymbol{\varphi}}_t}{\lambda + \bar{\boldsymbol{\varphi}}_t^{\mathbf{T}} \boldsymbol{P}_{t-1} \bar{\boldsymbol{\varphi}}_t} \\ \boldsymbol{P}_t = \frac{1}{\lambda}[\boldsymbol{P}_{t-1} - \boldsymbol{L}_t \bar{\boldsymbol{\varphi}}_t^{\mathbf{T}} \boldsymbol{P}_{t-1}] \end{cases} \tag{5}$$

where, $\boldsymbol{L}_t$ is the filtering gain; $\boldsymbol{\varepsilon}_t$ is the a priori prediction error; $\boldsymbol{P}_t$ is the estimation covariance matrix and $\boldsymbol{\lambda}$ is the forgetting factor.

Eq. (2) reveals that the modal parameters of a structure are determined from $\mathbf{\Phi}_i$ with i=1,2,…,I. A matrix G is constructed from $\mathbf{\Phi}_i$ as

$$\mathbf{G} = \begin{bmatrix} \mathbf{0} & \mathbf{I} & \mathbf{0} & \mathbf{0} & \cdots & \mathbf{0} \\ \mathbf{0} & \mathbf{0} & \mathbf{I} & \mathbf{0} & \cdots & \mathbf{0} \\ \vdots & \vdots & \vdots & \vdots & \cdots & \vdots \\ \mathbf{\Phi}_I & \mathbf{\Phi}_{I-1} & \mathbf{\Phi}_{I-2} & \mathbf{\Phi}_{I-3} & \cdots & \mathbf{\Phi}_1 \end{bmatrix}_{\bar{N}\times\bar{N}} \tag{6}$$

Consider the response of a structure described by equation of motions such as Eq. (1). Assuming properties damping, the orthogonality property of the mode shapes with respect to the mass and stiffness matrix leads to [13]

$$\mathbf{M}_D = \boldsymbol{\varphi}^{\mathrm{T}}\mathbf{M}\boldsymbol{\varphi};\quad \mathbf{K}_D = \boldsymbol{\varphi}^{\mathrm{T}}\mathbf{K}\boldsymbol{\varphi} \tag{7}$$

in which $\mathbf{M}_D$ and $\mathbf{K}_D$ are the diagonal modal mass matrix and diagonal modal stiffness matrix, respectively. The equation used to express the square of modal frequencies as a matrix is

$$\mathbf{\Lambda} = \mathbf{M}_D^{-\mathrm{T}/2}\mathbf{K}_D\mathbf{M}_D^{-1/2} = \mathbf{M}_D^{-\mathrm{T}/2}\boldsymbol{\varphi}^{\mathrm{T}}\mathbf{K}\boldsymbol{\varphi}\mathbf{M}_D^{-1/2} \tag{8}$$

Assuming the mass matrix was given, then, the stiffness matrix could be obtained

$$\mathbf{K} = \boldsymbol{\varphi}^{-\mathrm{T}}\mathbf{M}_D^{\mathrm{T}/2}\mathbf{\Lambda}\mathbf{M}_D^{1/2}\boldsymbol{\varphi}^{-1} \tag{9}$$

3 Numerical Verification

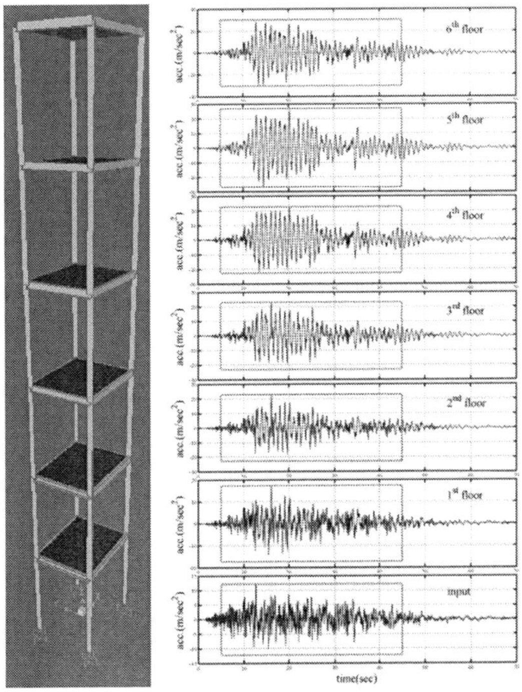

Fig. 1. Schematic diagram of a six-storey finite element model and its simulation responses

The finite element model of six-storey frame was built to demonstrate the feasibility of the proposed procedure, and this frame was subjected to a simulated 1999 Chi-chi earthquake at its base in X direction (see Fig. 1). The geometric parameter of this six-storey frame were 25cm long, 20cm wide and 180cm high. The 5% of the modal damping ratio would be assumed during the simulation process. Plates were fixed on each floor, such that the total mass of frame at each floor was approximately 6.732kg. The columns have rectangular section of 2X18, with units is mm. Table 1 shows the theoretical modal parameters. This frame was subjected to base excitations of the 1999 Chi-chi earthquake. The acceleration responses of the base and all floors at t=5-45 seconds were used in evaluating modal parameters for the frame. Fig. 1 displays the time history of base excitation and acceleration responses in X direction of this numerical model subject the Chi-chi earthquake.

Table 1. Theoretical modal parameters of numerical model

modal	1st	2nd	3rd	4th	5th	6th
f_n (Hz)	0.966	2.842	4.555	6.000	7.095	7.778
ξ(%)	5.000	5.000	5.000	5.000	5.000	5.000
φ	1.000	-0.947	-0.843	-0.685	-0.484	-0.252
	0.942	-0.478	0.225	0.818	1.000	0.675
	0.830	0.233	1.000	0.481	-0.658	-0.945
	0.668	0.825	0.477	-0.939	-0.249	1.000
	0.468	1.000	-0.665	-0.247	0.942	-0.828
	0.241	0.668	-0.944	1.000	-0.827	0.468

3.1 Incomplete measurement

It is difficult to observe the total degree of freedom in the site experiment. To somewhat simulated this situation, the dynamic responses of the second story wouldn't be used to the identification process of modal parameters. To check for agreement between the identified mode shapes and theoretical ones, the modal assurance criterion (MAC) proposed by Allemang and Brown [14] was used, which was defined as

$$\mathrm{MAC}\left(\varphi_{k,i},\varphi_{k,a}\right)=\frac{\left|\varphi_{k,i}^{\mathrm{T}}\varphi_{k,a}\right|^{2}}{\varphi_{k,i}^{\mathrm{T}}\varphi_{k,i}\varphi_{k,a}^{\mathrm{T}}\varphi_{k,a}} \tag{10}$$

where $\varphi_{k,i}$ is the identified i^{th} mode shape and $\varphi_{k,a}$ is the corresponding analytical mode shape. The value of MAC is between 0 and 1. When the two mode shapes are more similar, the resultant value of MAC is closer to one. In other words, when two mode shapes are orthogonal with each other, the resultant MAC value is zero.

The acceleration responses of the base and all degree of freedom at t=5-45sec would be used to identify modal parameters. Figure 2(a) plots the results obtained from processing the simulated input and acceleration responses of all stories by using recursive least square approach. In this study, the forgetting factor would be given as 0.995. In the modal identification process, the accurately and stable modal parameters were obtained.

3.2 Constructing stiffness matrix

In the stiffness matrix construction process, the identified mode shapes of all degree of freedom is necessary. In here, the cubic spline interpolation would be used to calculate the mode shapes of the unobserved degree of freedom. Under the assumption of given mass matrix, combined with the identified natural frequencies and mode shapes, the stiffness matrix of structure can be determined by Eq. (9). Table 2 shows the theoretical stiffness matrix of the six-storey frame extracted from finite element model. Due to the values of off-tridiagonal elements less than 1% of the tridiagonal elements, in the follow numerical study, the relative errors of the tridiagonal element would be discussed.

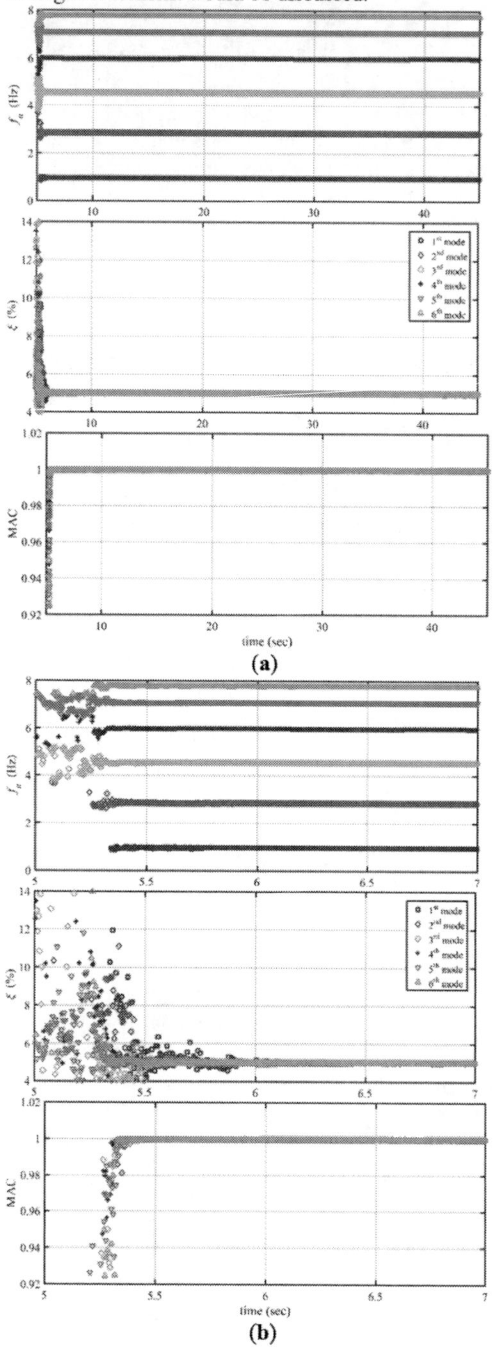

Fig. 2. The identified instantaneous modal parameters (a) t=5-45sec; (b) t=5-7sec

Table 3 shows the relative errors of the calculated stiffness matrix using Eq. (9). The modal parameters that were identified from the simulation dynamic responses of certain observed degree of freedom would be used in Eq. (9). For the identified results from the full measurement, the maximum relative error is 4.221%. It is evidently that the variant of the local stiffness less than 5% is difficult to detect from the identified modal parameters.

Table 2. The theoretical stiffness matrix of the six-storey frame

K matrix (N/cm)					
42.480	-42.585	0.067	0.011	0.011	0.011
-42.585	85.180	-42.652	0.057	0.000	0.000
0.067	-42.652	85.181	-42.652	0.057	0.000
0.011	0.057	-42.652	85.181	-42.652	0.057
0.011	0.000	0.057	-42.652	85.181	-42.652
0.011	0.000	0.000	0.057	-42.652	85.237

Next, for the identified results from the incomplete measurement, the cubic spline could be used to calculate the deformations of the unobserved degree of freedom in each modal. The maximum relative error is 4.725%. It is evidently that the variant of the local stiffness more than 5% is easy to detect from the identified modal parameters.

Table 3. The relative stiffness matrix errors on tridiagonal (unit:%)

	without mode shapes correction					
Full measurement	4.221	3.718	\	\	\	\
	3.718	2.650	0.950	\	\	\
	\	0.950	3.145	2.074	\	\
	\	\	2.074	2.360	2.065	\
	\	\	\	2.065	1.509	0.292
	\	\	\	\	0.292	0.765
Incomplete measurement	4.725	3.494	\	\	\	\
	3.494	2.169	3.447	\	\	\
	\	3.447	2.944	1.716	\	\
	\	\	1.716	3.289	2.266	\
	\	\	\	2.266	3.851	0.629
	\	\	\	\	0.629	1.962

4 Conclusions

This study extended cubic spline interpolation for creating the stiffness matrix of building from structural dynamic responses. The procedure of stiffness matrix creation from the measured vibration would be divided three stages, 1. The modal parameters of s structure would be identified from measured seismic responses; 2. Assuming the mass properties was given and calculating the deformations of the unobserved degree of freedom in each modal via cubic spline interpolation; 3. Constructing the stiffness from the identified natural frequencies and corrected mode shapes.

In modal identification stage, the time series model was constructed in time domain. The time-varying coefficients in time series model were determined by a recursive least square approach. Then, the modal parameters of the structure were calculated from these coefficients. For incomplete measurement case, it is difficult to construct the stiffness matrix from the identified modal parameters. Therefore, the cubic spline interpolation would be used to calculate the deformation of the unobserved degreed of freedom in each modal. Finally, the stiffness matrix of the structure would be constructed via the identified natural frequencies and corrected mode shapes.

The numerically simulated responses of a six-storey finite element model subjected earthquake input were used to validate the proposed procedure. The effects of forget factor on the ability to identify the modal parameters were also investigated. The recursive least square approach apply on full measurement data did provide more accurately stiffness than the process incomplete measurement data.

The authors would like to thank the Ministry of Science and Technology of the Republic of China, Taiwan, for financially supporting this research under Contract No. MOST 106-2622-M-492-001-CC2.

References

1. S. Ljung, L. Ljung, Automatica, **21** (1985)
2. A. Vahidi, A. Stefanopoulou, H. Peng, Veh Mec Mobil, Int J. **43**, 31-55 (2005)
3. F. Ding; Y. Wang, J. Ding, Dig Signal Proc, **37**, 100-108 (2015)
4. S.I. Adachi; A. Sano, Elec Com. Japan, **69**, 1-9 (1986)
5. H. Oku, H. Kimura, Automatica, **38**, 1035-1043 (2002).
6. M. Drton, M. Eichler, T.S. Richardson, J. Mach Learn Res, **10**, 2329-2348 (2009)
7. T. Fujiwara, H. Yamamoto, T. Kasami, Shu Lin, IEEE Trans Inf Theo, **44**, 714-729 (1998)
8. W.C. Su, C.S. Huang, C.H. Chen, C.Y. Liu, H.C. Huang, Q.T. Le, Comp Aid Civ Infras Eng, **29**, 738-757 (2014)
9. J.H Li, F. Ding, G.W Yang, Math Comp Model, **55**, 442-450 (2012)
10. C.S. Huang, S.L. Hung, C.M. Wen, T.T. Tu, Earth Eng Struct Dyn, **32**, 187-206 (2002)
11. T. Kumon, T. Suzuki, M. Iwasaki, M. Matsuzaki, N. Matsui, S. Okuma, Elec Eng. Japan, **142**, 45-55 (2003)
12. C.S. Huang, J. Sound Vib, **241**, 337-359 (2001)
13. J.W. Tedesco, W.G. McDougal, C.A. Ross (Menlo Park, Calif, 1999).
14. R.J. Allemang, D.L. Brown. Mod Analy, Proc Int Conf. 110-116 (1982)

 https://doi.org/10.1051/matecconf/201820101005

Evaluation of the Power Output Performance Improvement of a 2 MW Wind Turbine

Jui-Hung Liu[1*], *and Jien-Chen Chen* [2], *Wen-Jhen Lai*[3], *Wei-Niam Su*[3]

[1]Mechanical Engineering Dept., Southern Taiwan University of Science and Technology, Taiwan
[2]Green Energy and Environment Lab., Industrial Technology Research Institute, Taiwan
[3]Mechanical and System Engineering Program, Institute of Nuclear Energy Research, Taiwan

Abstract. This paper shows the possibility of the output improvement to a large wind turbine, so the operator can earn more and thus reduce the overall cost of energy. For a modern wind turbine certificated by IEC or DNV-GL guidelines, a 20 years design lifetime is a base line. However, the efficiency of the turbine will degrade after 8 or 9 years' operating. Some components, especially the turning blade, the efficiency may vary due to the surface condition change. Meanwhile, the controller technology may also have been improved after years. So, the turbine can regain its original output or even have a better output performance through some adjustments. In this paper, a 2 MW wind turbine with different design and operating parameters like blade efficiency, wind direction alignment, high/low wind control strategy has been evaluated, then with the software DNV-GL BLADED simulation, to calculate the output differences and availability of the turbine. The result shown that a 3~5% yield annually can be obtained for each improved parameter in a 9 m/s mean wind speed situation.

1 Introduction

Wind energy has rapid growth recent years. According to GWEC's report [1], a world's total cumulative wind capacity is 486.8 GW in 2016. And with annual installations in excess of 50 GW which means over ten thousand of turbines have been installed all over the world each year. The forecast statistics also indicates a cumulative capacity growth more than 10% in the coming 5 years [1].

The market growth also shown the highly technology maturity compares to other renewable energies. With so many turbines installed all around the world in the recent 3 decades, the design standards for wind turbines have also been proved and updated for years. These design standards provide a basic and important guideline for the turbine developers, and manufacturers to choose, evaluate or design their turbines.

For a modern wind turbine certificated by IEC or DNV-GL guidelines, the design lifetime shall be at least 20 years [2, 3]. The guideline provides basic requirements for the turbine to operate safely and smoothly in its lifetime. And of course, after the installation of a wind turbine, the manufacturer will go through a fine tuning procedure to optimize the turbine's operation performance based on the design requirement and in-situ measurement. However, the efficiency of the turbine will degrade after 8 or 9 years' operation. Some components, especially the turning blade, the efficiency may vary due to the surface condition change. Meanwhile, new controller methods may also been found during this period. So, the turbine may need an overall examine, retune, and controller re-design to improve the turbine's availability. As shown in Figure 1, two wind turbines' power curves have been plotted. These 2 turbines come from a same wind farm with 2 MW output capacities for each wind turbine. In the plot, the blue dotted line is the real output while the orange dotted line represents the design power curve. It can be clearly seen that the real curve of the turbine A has an obvious difference in the power output. The turbine B also showed a larger output offset in the below-rated wind speed region. This output difference results in a loss of the income from the electricity generation from the turbine.

This paper evaluates a 2 MW wind turbine from a real operating wind farm with different design and operating parameters input like blade efficiency, wind direction alignment, high/low wind control strategy, then with the software DNV-GL BLADED's simulation, to calculate the output differences of the turbine to see how much annual output can be improved through these adjustments.

2 System Description: Wind Turbine Model

In this article, a generic 2 MW turbine model was adopted as a reference to have a general evaluation on this topic. The basic specification of this turbine is listed

* Corresponding author: dofliu@stust.edu.tw

in Table 1 with a nominal rotor speed 22.5 rpm, an optimum tip speed ratio 8, and an optimal mode gain 98815 Nm/(rad/s)^2 as its base line operation parameters. And the resulting design power curve is plotted in Figure 2. The turbine starts to generate the electricity at a cut-in wind speed of 3 m/s, power output to its rated at 12m/s, then when the average wind speed is over 25 m/s, the turbine will stop automatically to prevent the dangerous operation under extreme wind condition.

From the power curve in Figure 2, the annual yield of the turbine can be calculated with the wind speed distribution probability (Figure 3) given the Weibull distribution shape factor 2 and a 98 % availability. Table 2 is the calculation output for different annual average wind speed. For a 9 m/s wind speed, it means more than 7 million kWh electricity can be generated annually. This number is an ideal calculation since the wind conditions, system control response, turbine faults, and maintenance all have influence to the final power output.

Table 1. Specification of the generic 2 MW turbine.

General	
Rotor Diameter	70.65 m
Rotor Speed	Variable, nominal 22.5 rpm
Nominal Power	2.0 MW
Rated Wind Speed	12 m/s
Cut-in / Cut-out Wind Speed	3~25 m/s
Optimum Tip Sppd Ratio	8 (with Optimum C_p 0.478)
Optimum Mode Gain	98815 Nm/(rad/s)^2
Generator Torque	~866 kNm

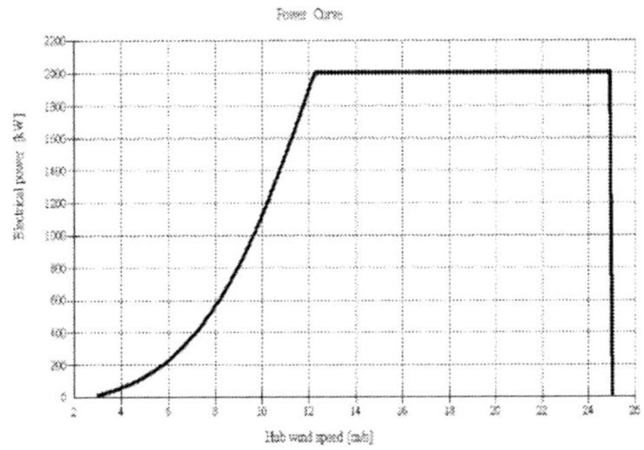

Fig. 2. Power of the generic 2 MW turbine.

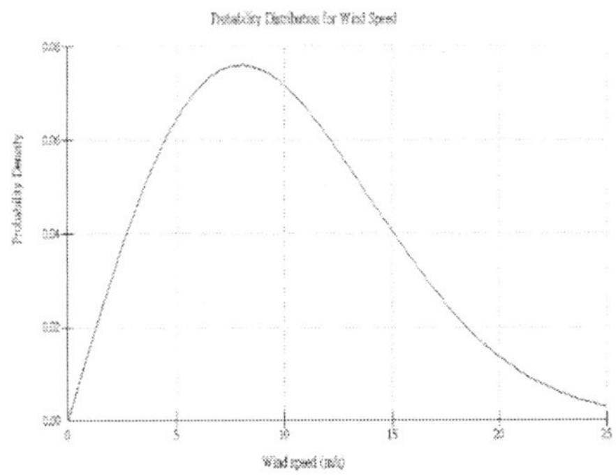

Fig. 3. Wind Distribution Probability.

Table 2. Annual Yield Calculation.

Annual Mean Hub Wind Speed (m/s)	Annual Energy Yield (kWh)
7	5.015e+06
8	6.461e+06
9	**7.754e+06**

3 Output Degradation Analyses

As mentioned in Section 1, the power output may differ from the original design after years' operation. We can quantify the effects through the following analyses and calculations.

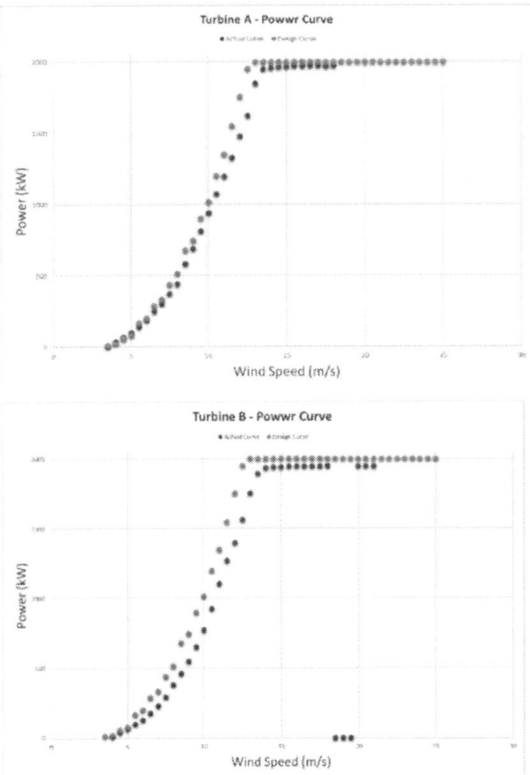

Fig. 1. Two turbines' actual power curve compare to the design one.

10	8.834e+06

3.1. Blade C_p (Power Coefficient)

The turbine blades are rotating parts and have direct contact to the outside environment. So, its surface profile (aerofoil shape) may be changed by the dust's friction and salty water particle's erosion effects. Since the surface profile of the blade decides the energy conversion efficiency, that is the C_p of the blade, the power output and control performance will be influenced, too. However, it's hard to measure exactly the change of the C_p. It can only be calculated and estimated from the actual power curve. Here, C_p can be viewed as a parameter in the simulation, so the difference of the yield can be analysed. From Table 1, the original design optimum C_p is 0.478. Then three different C_p values range from 0.365 to 0.478 were chosen to evaluate the performance differences as shown in Figure 4.

For the wind turbine control in the low wind speed region, C_p and λ (tip speed ratio) are two very important parameters to reach the MPPT (Maximum Power Point Tracking) strategy since the following formulas (1)~(3) shown these two parameters should be kept to their optimum to have a MPPT curve.

$$\text{Power} = \frac{1}{2}\rho A V^3 C_p(\theta,\lambda) \quad (1)$$

$$\lambda = \frac{\omega R}{V} \quad (2)$$

where ρ is the air density, A is the rotor swept area, V is the wind speed, θ is the blade pitch angle, and λ is the tip speed ratio define by formula (2). Since the wind speed measure is not reliable from the anemometer behind the rotor, the formula (1) can be rewrite by replacing wind speed V with the relation of formula (2). Then the power output can be independent from the wind speed as shown in formula (3). In this mode, the blade angle θ and λ should be both stay at its optimum, so the $\mathbf{C_{p,\,opt}}$ and $\boldsymbol{\lambda}_{\text{opt}}$ is denoted in formula (3). Then, the formula can be simplified into a linear proportional relation in formula (4), where K_{opt} is the product of all known parameters except rotational speed W.

$$\text{Power} = \frac{1}{2}\rho\pi R^5 W^3 \frac{C_{p,opt}}{\lambda_{opt}^3} \quad (3)$$

$$\text{Power} = K_{opt}W^3, \text{Torque} = K_{opt}W^2 \quad (4)$$

The internal control algorithm will follow the formula (4) by measuring the rotor speed and then multiply with K_{opt} to give the power or torque command to the system. With this optimum relation, the wind speed can be evaluated to match the power curve. When the real blade C_p decreases, the power or torque command form formula (4) to reach the MPPT will no longer works. This means, for a same rotor speed, it represents a higher wind speed than the ideal one. The power output from formula (4) will thus be degraded. It needs a higher wind speed to reach the same power. This results in the power curve offset as shown in figure 5(a). And figure 5(b) is a zoom in at wind speed from 6~11m/s to see more clear the differences. For the worst case, the black curve with C_p 0.365, the rated wind speed will be moved to 13 m/s. And the annual yields were calculated in table 3 according to different average wind speed. It's about **4% electricity loss** due to a slightly C_p change. An obvious loss over 10% can be seen in the last and the worst case, C_p = 0.365. However, this is an extreme case just to show the influence of C_p and is unlikely to happen with a normal operation.

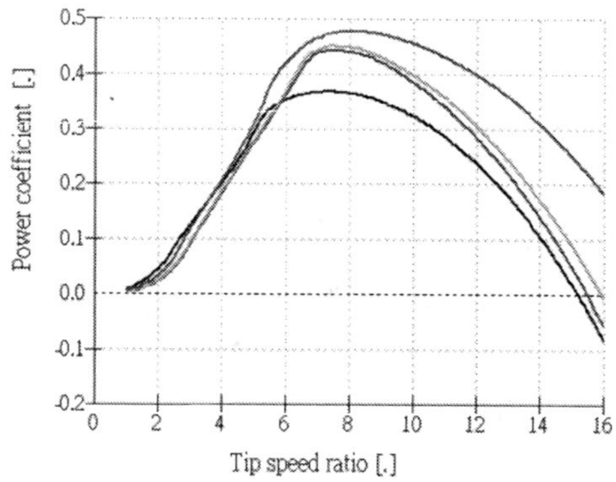

Fig. 4. Different C_p curves with optimum from 0.478 to 0.36

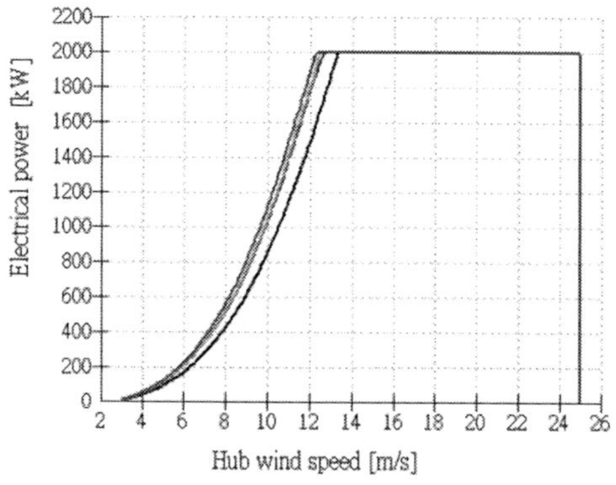

Fig. 5. (a)Power curves generated from different C_p

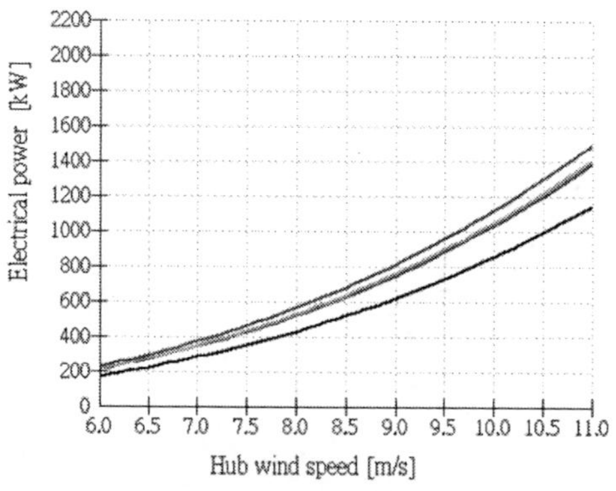

Fig. 5. (b)Zoom in at wind speed from 6~11m/s

3.2. Yaw Alignment Error

The second parameter that may influence the power output performance is the yaw alignment error and the flow inclination. The ideal power curve assumes the wind comes from the upwind direction and directly exerts on the rotor swept surface without any yaw error and inclination. Although the turbine controller will turn the nacelle to align with the wind direction, it is not possible for such a big mass body (>100 tons) to do the alignment exactly and immediately since the wind direction is changing all the time. So the nacelle will not yawing continuously if the alignment error lies in the range about +/- 15 degrees for this turbine. As a whole, this effect will be averaged for a loner time periods. Besides, this yaw alignment error can also come from the measurement of the cup anemometer. Since the yaw error is the difference between the nacelle position and the wind direction. This value can vary with time and need to be adjusted periodically. If not, this error can result in a large power curve offset as shown in figure 6. Its impact is even more than the C_p variation. With a 10 degrees alignment error, the annual yield reveals a **<u>5% more loss</u>** from the yaw error as listed in table 4.

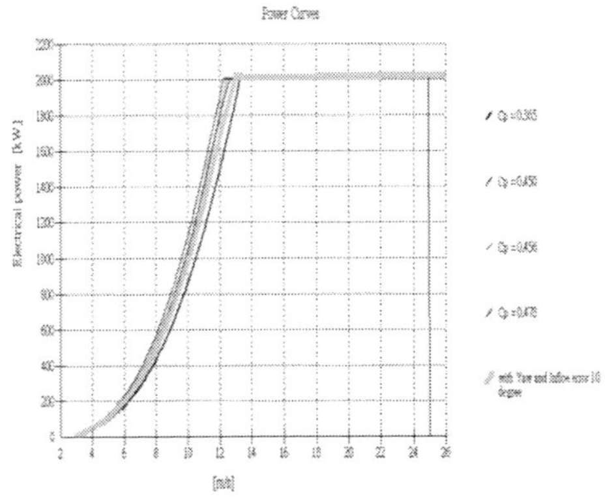

Fig. 6. Power curves comparison with Yaw misalignment and inflow inclination

4. Retrofit Strategy in Controller

From the analysis of two parameters that relates to the annual yield, it's possible for wind farm owner to check the operating power curve to see if the tuning is needed to bring back the power output. Besides these, what we can do to gain extra power is to increase rated power and extend the cutout wind speed [4]. If these strategies can be done carefully, the turbine's lifetime can also be extended as there also exist international standard especially for the lifetime extension of the wind turbines. [5~7].

4.1. Rated Power Upgrade

Assume that the generator's capacity can be overloaded within some small range, the power output will thus be increased if the operating parameters like rotor/stator temperatures can still lies within the safe values. The simulation bellows increased the generator output for 5% more, that is, 2100 kW. Obviously, the power curve in Figure 7 has an offset after the rated wind speed. And the annual yield improvement is calculated and listed in Table 5. The difference is relative small especially when the mean wind speed is small than 8 m/s, only 2% increase in annual yield. For a 9 and 10 m/s mean wind speed, 3% and 4% increase separately, these result is more effective and economical.

Table 3. Annual Yield Calculation of different C_p.

Annual Mean Wind Speed (m/s)	Annual Yield (kWh) C_p=0.478	Annual Yield (kWh) C_p=0.456	Annual Yield (kWh) C_p=0.450	Annual Yield (kWh) C_p=0.365
7	5.02E+06	4.85E+06	4.80E+06	4.14E+06
8	6.46E+06	6.29E+06	6.23E+06	5.50E+06
9	7.75E+06	7.58E+06	7.53E+06	6.77E+06
10	8.83E+06	8.67E+06	8.61E+06	7.87E+06

Table 4. Annual Yield Calculation of different C_p and yaw error.

Annual Mean Wind Speed (m/s)	Annual Yield (kWh) Cp=0.478	Annual Yield (kWh) Cp=0.456	Annual Yield (kWh) Cp=0.450	Annual Yield (kWh) with Yaw Error
7	5.02E+06	4.85E+06	4.80E+06	**4.57E+06**
8	6.46E+06	6.29E+06	6.23E+06	**5.99E+06**
9	7.75E+06	7.58E+06	7.53E+06	**7.28E+06**
10	8.83E+06	8.67E+06	8.61E+06	**8.36E+06**

4.2. Cut-out wind speed Extended

If we extend the normal cut-out wind speed from 25m/s to 28m/s. The difference will not be so obvious since the probability of these wind speed range is relative small as we mentioned in Figure 3. In column 4 of Table 5, the extra energy obtain by this parameter is **only 0.4%** (about 34000 kWh per year). This parameter need a site with higher Weibull shape factor to show its effectiveness.

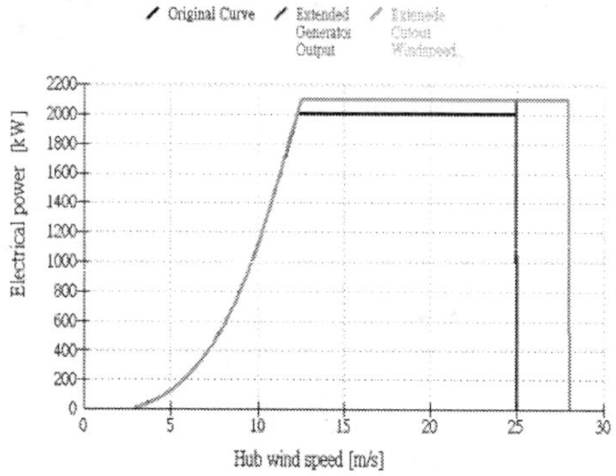

Fig. 7. Power curves comparison with Extended Generator Output and Cut-out Wind Speed

5. Discussion

In this article, investigations on various parameters that may influence the wind turbine output performance have been given. The blade's C_p, yawing misalignment, generator rated output upgrade, and cut-out wind speed extension are all possible and effective ways to bring back or increase the annual electricity yield, that is, much more income for the wind farm owners. From the simulation outcome, in general, a 3~5% yield annually can be obtained for each improved parameter in a 9 m/s mean wind speed situation. For the worst case that the turbine was downgraded due to long time operation and then upgraded by control strategy modification, a 12% increase may be achieved. This paper only addresses the steady state calculation. Much more dynamic simulations will be carried out in the future.

Acknowledgments: The financial support provided by Bureau of Energy and Institute of Nuclear Energy Research (Taiwan) are gratefully acknowledged.

Table 5. Annual Yield Calculation.

Annual Mean Wind Speed (m/s)	Annual Yield (kWh) Cp=0.478	Annual Yield (kWh) Rated Power Upgrade	Annual Yield (kWh) Higher Cut-out Wind Speed	Percentage increased (%)
7	5.02E+06	5.09E+06	**5.09E+06**	**1.4%**
8	6.46E+06	6.59E+06	**6.60E+06**	**2.2%**
9	7.76E+06	7.95E+06	**7.98E+06**	**3.0%**
10	8.83E+06	9.09E+06	**9.188+06**	**4.0%**

References

1. GWEC, Global Wind Report – Annual Market Update 2016, GWEC, 2016.
2. DNV GL, Guideline for the Certification of Wind Turbines 2010 edition, DNV GL, 2010.
3. IEC, IEC 61400-1 wind turbines – part 1: Design Requirements (third edition), IEC, 2005.
4. Upgrading Vestas V47-660kW, Available online: http://www.mita-teknik.com/knowhow/turbine-retrofit/retrofit-v47/ (accessed on 23rd July 2017).
5. New DNV GL standard and service specification for lifetime extension of wind turbines, Available online: https://www.dnvgl.com/news/new-dnv-gl-standard-and-service-specification-for-lifetime-extension-of-wind-turbines-61059
6. DNV-GL, Certification of lifetime extension of wind turbines(DNVGL-SE-0263), DNV-GL(, March 2016.
7. DNV-GL, Lifetime extension of wind turbines(DNVGL-ST-0262), DNV-GL, March 2016.

* Corresponding author: dofliu@stust.edu.tw

Upgrade of a Yaw System and its Operation Strategy to a 2 MW Wind Turbine

Jui-Hung Liu[1*], *Jien-Chen Chen*[2]

[1]Southern Taiwan University of Science and Technology, Taiwan
[2]Industrial Technology Research Institute, Taiwan

Abstract. The yawing system in a wind turbine keeps the nacelle facing the incoming wind direction to obtain a better efficiency while it also induces the vibration and fatigue load to the structure. In this paper, the yawing system was discussed and an upgrade plan been provided to a real 2 MW wind turbine. The result has shown the significant improvement on the load output after the update.

1 Introduction

Yawing system is an important sub-system in a wind turbine. It provides the rotational torque for the turbine head (nacelle + rotor) to rotate into the wind direction to obtain a better energy conversion efficiency. Also, to provide a sufficient brake torque for the nacelle to fixed stably and transfer the dynamic energy to the drive train. Since the wind speed and direction may change continuously every second, the yawing system should turn the nacelle in the same way. However, this is not so realistic for the actuator and may induced extra fatigue load to the structure. Normally, a threshold like +/- 8 degrees [1-2] misalignment could reduce the yawing action while keeping the efficiency within an acceptable range. Taiwan's wind resource is very good, but it also come with a high turbulent wind condition. From the viewpoint of yaw system, this means the yawing action in such wind farm will be much more than the normal one. Combing the high turbulent wind and high wind speed, the brake torque may not enough to stop the turbine head, the yawing torque not efficiently (need more action and time) or results in an overload trip. The unstable yawing also need another hydraulic brake system to provide larger pressure. This induces other maintenance problems in the hydraulic system to lower the availability of the turbine operation [3-4]. In this paper, a yawing system replacement plan has been implemented to show the performance improvement before and after the update.

2 System Description: Wind Turbine Model

In this article, a 2 MW turbine located in central Taiwan was chosen. The basic specification of this turbine is listed in Table 1. The turbine starts to generate the electricity at a wind speed of 3 m/s, rated at 12m/s, then when the average wind speed is over 25 m/s, the turbine will stop automatically to prevent the dangerous operation under extreme wind condition. Table 1 also shows the yawing strategy of this turbine. When the misalignment between nacelle and the wind direction more than +/- 15 degrees and the 60s wind speed average more than 3.0 m/s, the main controller system will initiate the yawing action. And the yawing will stop when the misalignment is less than +/- 2 degrees in 5s average.

Table 1. Specs. of the Z72 2 MW turbine.

General	
Rotor Diameter	70.65 m
Rotor Speed	Variable, nominal 22.5 rpm
Nominal Power	2.0 MW
Rated Wind Speed	12 m/s
Cut-in / Cut-out Wind Speed	3~25 m/s
Auto Yawing Start	+/- 15 degrees misalignment (wind speed 60s avg. >= 3.0 m/s)
Auto Yawing Stop	+/- 2 degrees misalignment (5 second average)

3 Upgrade Plans

To upgrade the capability of the yawing mechanism, an appropriate improvement plan is given in this section to select the motor, driver, brake and the necessary components. From the original system documents, a safe range from 1.5 kW to 3.0 kW is accepted. A 2.2 kW capacity is selected from the exisiting products and vendors. This product can satisfy the performance and

* Corresponding author: dofliu@stust.edu.tw

 https://doi.org/10.1051/matecconf/201820101006

safety requirement at the same time. Table 2 is the specification of the new and original yawing system. The rated current, rated torque, rated power, and the brake torque all have a large increase, which are 30.2%, 50.6%, 47%, and 233% separately.

Table 2. Specs. of the new/original yawing system

	Original	New
Rated Current	4.3 A	5.6 A
Rated Torque	15 Nm	22.6 Nm
Rated Power	1.5 kW	2.2 kW
Brake Torque	15 Nm	55 Nm

To ensure new system can satisfy the operating requirement, simulations have been done by using software DNV-GL Bladed, Adams, and Matlab with new specification parameters like motor electrical parameters and rated values. Combining the high wind speed condition, the system response can be obtained. In Figure 1, a 60 second yawing response is revealed with a 14 m/s average wind speed. The yawing command is set to be 0, 10, -10, and 0 degree. The motor torque is the torque after a gearbox which its maximum is 20 Nm. This result shows that the new yawing system can be operated within the rated torque under a high wind speed condition. It can meet the system requirement and can be installed to the new turbine.

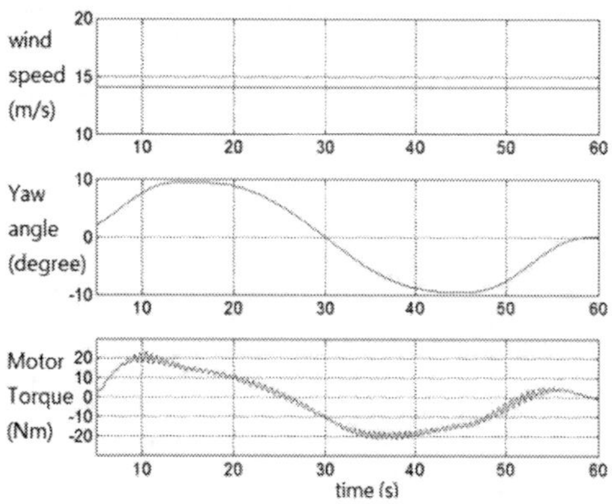

Fig. 1. Simulation Response of the new Yawing System

Besides the motor, other relative necessary components like coupler, control panel, driver, and flange, were also selected to match the requirements. The new motor with integrated into the original mechanism is shown in Figure. 2.

Fig. 2. New Yaw Motor and the original mechanism

Figure 3 is the main control circuit of the new yawing system. MC1 and MC2 are in charge of the forward and reverse turning. When over current raised, a message will be sent to the turbine controller. Unlike the simple start/stop (on/off) control of the yaw motor, new system has a speed up and slow down strategy to control the motor speed fixed and stable. This is an important improvement in this upgrade to decrease the vibration to the structure. Other functionalities of the new yawing system are listed below:

1. Speed up/ Slow down strategy: Stable Yawing Speed
2. Brake Capability: Only works when electricity in on. Free mode when black out.
3. Sliping Coupler mode: protect the mechanism in a excessive torque

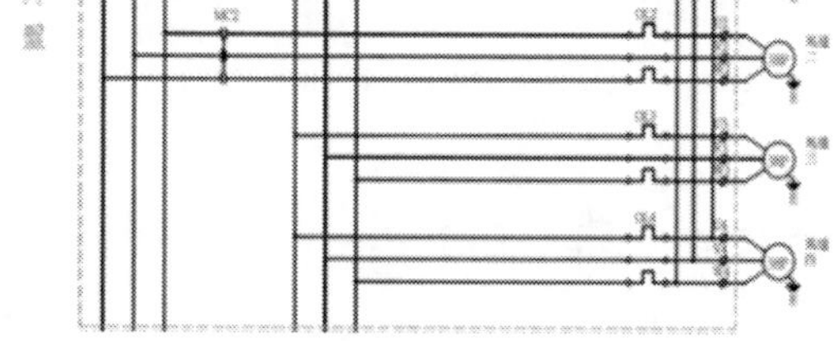

Fig. 3. Main circuit diagram of the new yawing system.

4. Verification

4.1 Case1: 8 days normal operation analysis

For a 8 days operation period as shown in Figure 4, under a normal wind speed condition, the yaw motor current is within 10 A. A load increase will occurred in an anti-wind resistance as shown in the middle and bottom of the Figure 4, the current will exceed 20 A. If a forward wind force is faced, motor's speed will too fast to cause the overload. As a whole, in 8 days monitoring, the maximum motor current is about 25 A, this is still below the new system's limit, 32A. So the new system has enough capability to go through the normal wind condition.

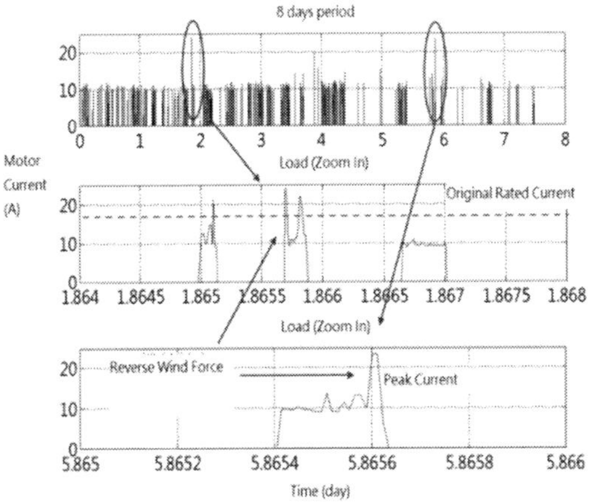

Fig. 4. Long time operation output

4.2 Case2: Extreme Wind Condition Operation Analysis

This operation period is only 4.6 hours (15000 seconds) with a wind speed from 20 m/s to 35 m/s (under Typhoon) but is a very extreme condition with a quite high wind speed and high direction variance. In Figure 5, it can be seen there are many current peaks exceed the rated current 32 A. Because this system also allows 48 A in 60 seconds and 64 A in 3 seconds, the yawing system still can survive through this Typhoon wind condition. And when the driver detects an over current, it will reduce the motor frequency to lower the rotational speed to keep the motor operate within the rated value.

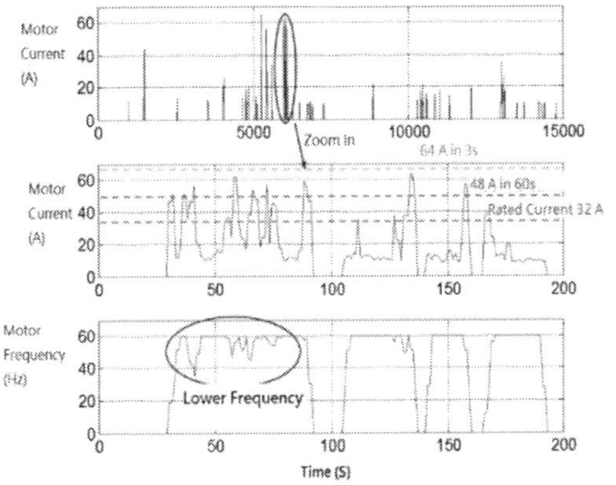

Fig. 5. Yawing System under 20~35m/s wind condition

4.3 Case 3: One Year Operation Analysis

This analysis is a long term observation after the new system has been installed and operated for one year long. We pick up a 13 days data after one year as shown in Figure 6. It can be shown the motor current can be kept in 20 A (rated current) in most time period. Only two peak values exceed 40 A. This shows the motor still work well after one year. The maximum motor current occurs in Day 7, the zoom-in can be seen in Figure 6(b). At the 3rd second, yawing action started, the motor current increased and the motor frequency also increased to 60 Hz to keep a constant speed. At the 15th second, due to a high wind input resistance, yawing system needs an instantaneous power output to remain its original action, so the current increase quickly to 50 A. To protect the system, the driver lowers the frequency to lower the speed of the yaw motor.

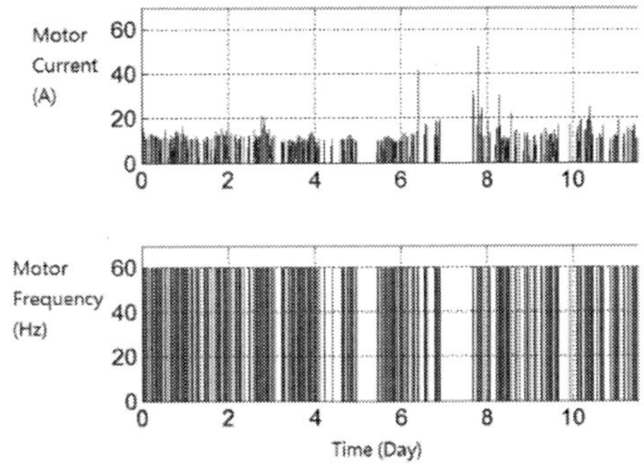

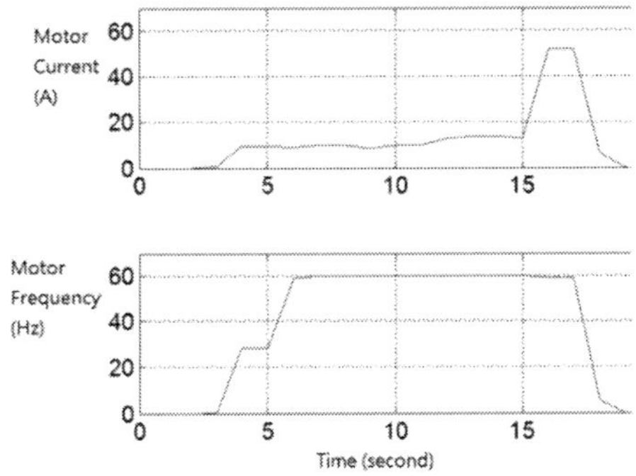

 https://doi.org/10.1051/matecconf/201820101006

Fig. 6. Operation Data after one year: (a) 13 days data, (b) zoom-in for a specified period

5. Conclusions

In this article, we have successfully upgraded a yawing system in a 2 MW wind turbine to increases its moving ability and the peak load resistance. By upgrading yaw motor's rated power, rated current, rated torque, and the brake torque, the final operation data analysis and verification shown that the new system can yawing the nacelle well even under a Typhoon wind condition and a one year long period operation.

Acknowledgments: The financial support provided by Bureau of Energy (Taiwan) is gratefully acknowledged.

References

1. DNV GL, Guideline for the Certification of Wind Turbines 2010 edition, DNV GL, 2010.
2. IEC, IEC 61400-1 wind turbines – part 1: Design Requirements (third edition), IEC, 2005.
3. C. Moerman, "Harakosan Technical Documentation, User's Guide (HE-0378-R03)", Harakosan, 2009
4. C. J. A. Versteegh, "Design of the Zephyros Z72 wind turbine with emphasis on the direct drive PM generator", NORPIE 2004, NTNU Trondheim Norway 14 – 16 June, 2004.

Simulation study on the effects of humidity reduction regulation and detection on indoor temperature comfort

Wen.-An. Wang[1,*], *and Ssu.-Wei. Tung*[2]

[1] Department of Architecture, Tamkang University, 25137 New Taipei City, Taiwan
[2] Department of Architecture, Tamkang University, 25137 New Taipei City, Taiwan

Abstract.. This study would discuss about the installation of indoor smart monitoring and control system and propose a feasible structure to establish a smart system for sensing and controlling the temperature and humidity inside the building. The sensor offers the capability of learning and automatically controlling the indoor temperature and humidity to automatically adjust the indoor heat environment.

1 RESEARCH METHODS AND SIMULATION SETTING

This study was focused on investigating and improving residential thermal environment. Temperature and humidity were manually adjusted, and computer simulation approach was employed to analyze the feasibilities of improving indoor thermal environment and comfort.

1.1 Study Subject

The study subject of this study was a low-rise residential building located in Tainan City of Taiwan. The space of the investigation was on the first floor with a dimension of 702 cm (L) × 620 cm (W) × 330 cm (H). Five indoor monitoring points were established.

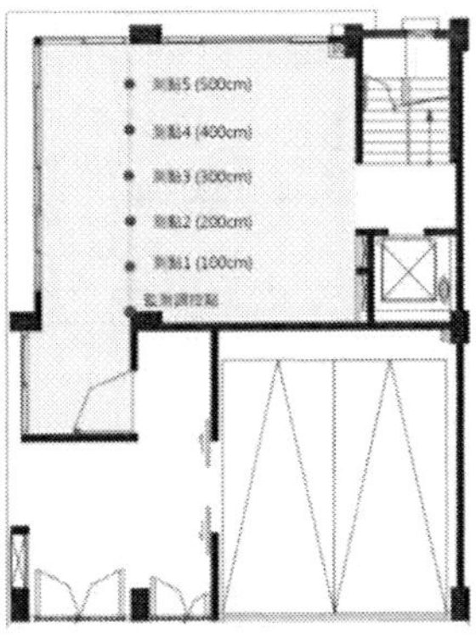

Fig. 1. Floor plan of the study subject.

1.2 Establishment of Local Meteorological Data

Using the same indoor comfort environment, it was assumed that the meteorological parameters measured indoors at 12:00 noon were the basis for defining the indoor parameter boundary condition, and that the indoor air-conditioner was operating at steady state. Table 1 shows the conditions based on the meteorological data.

Table 1. Boundary Conditions of Meteorological Parameters.

Attributes	parameter
WIND	V=2.0 (m/s)
Humidity	69%
Scope of Calculation	Summer T0=32°C

1.3 Establishment of Local Meteorological Data

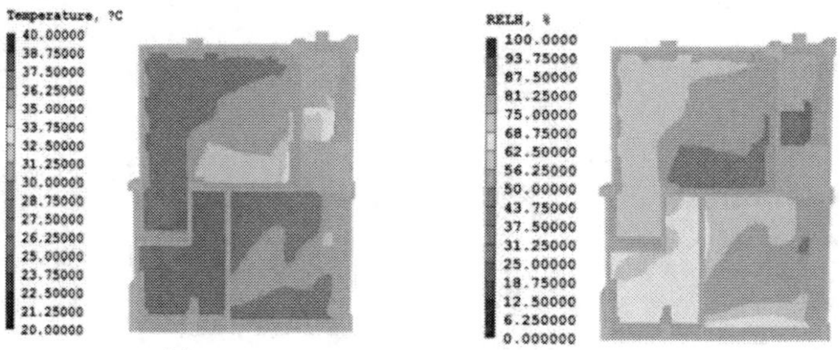

(a) (b)

Fig. 2. (a) Temperature Field Simulation of the current situation ; (b) Humidity Field Simulation of the current situation.

The above analysis results indicate that the monitoring point measured maximum temperature of 32.92°C and minimum temperature of 29.81°C (at Monitoring Point 5). The overall indoor humidity level ranged between 50% and 70%. Therefore, the overall indoor temperature was overly high, indicating an uncomfortable living environment.

Table 2. Simulation design.

Module	Simulation Content
Case1	Adjust temperature to 32°C: Humidity 64%
Case2	Adjust temperature to 32°C: Humidity 59%
Case3	Adjust temperature to 32°C: Humidity 39%

2 NUMERICAL SIMULATION AND ANALYSIS

2.1 CASE 1 Adjust Temperature to 32°C: Humidity 64%

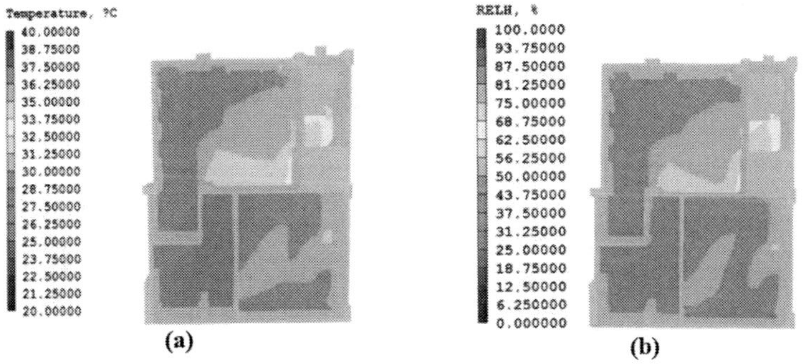

Fig. 3. Simulation of Case 1, Adjust temperature to 32°C: Humidity 64%: (a) Current Temperature Field of the current situation ; (b) Improved Temperature Field Simulation of the current situation.

The above analysis results indicated that when humidity was reduced by 5%, the cooling effect observed in Monitoring Points 1, 2, and 3 was weaker than that of the current situation. The overall average temperature measured at Monitoring Points 4 and 5 was reduced by 0.15–0.37°C compared with the current situation. Therefore, reducing humidity by 5% did not significantly improve the overall thermal environment.

2.2 CASE 2 Adjust Temperature to 32°C: Humidity 59%

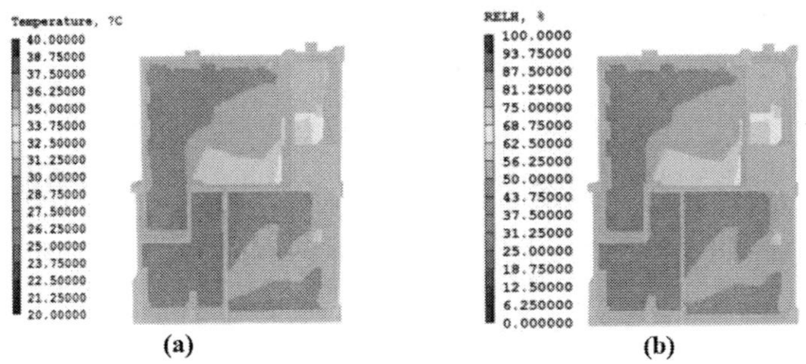

Fig. 4. Simulation of Case2, Adjust temperature to 32°C: Humidity 59%: (a) Current Temperature Field of the current situation ; (b) Improved Temperature Field Simulation of the current situation.

The analysis results showed that when humidity was reduced by 10%, the cooling effect observed in Monitoring Point 3 showed approximately 0.13°C lower in temperature than that of the current situation, and the overall average temperature of Monitoring Point 4 was reduced by 0.47°C, compared with the temperature of the current situation. Therefore, reducing humidity by 10% achieved optimal improvement of 0.13–0.47°C in overall thermal environment compared with the current situation.

2.3 CASE 3 Adjust Temperature to 32°C: Humidity 39%

https://doi.org/10.1051/matecconf/201820101007

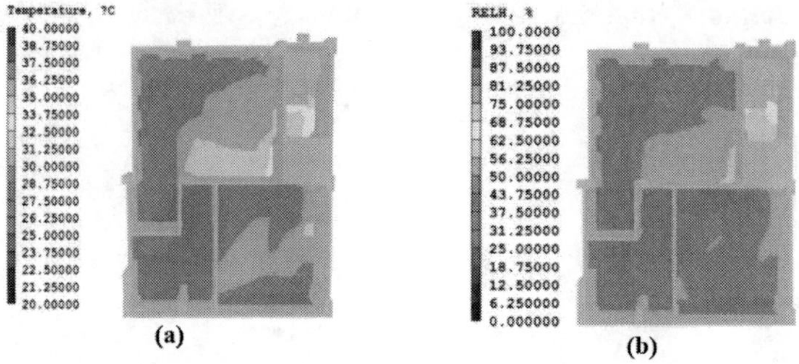

Fig. 5. Simulation of Case 3, Adjust temperature to 32°C: Humidity 39%: (a) Current Temperature Field of the current situation ; (b) Improved Temperature Field Simulation of the current situation.

The analysis results indicated that when humidity was reduced by 30%, the cooling effect observed in Monitoring Points 1, 2, and 3 reflected 1°C cooler in temperature than that of the current situation. The overall average temperature measured at Monitoring Points 4 and 5 was reduced by 1.22–1.38°C compared with the current situation. Therefore, reducing humidity by 30% significantly improved the overall thermal environment in comparison to the scenario in Cases 1 and 2.

3 CONCLUSION

The simulation results showed that when humidity and temperature were not adjusted, the optimal thermal module was indoor temperature of 32°C, humidity of 39%, and wind speed of 2.0 m/s. At this condition, significant cooling effect was observed. The overall average temperature decreased by 1°C when humidity was reduced by 30%. When cooling effect was achieved by adjusting temperature, the overall temperature cooled by roughly 4–5°C; however, according to research, for every decrease in 1°C temperature, it increases 7–10% in electricity load, suggesting that from energy conservation point of view, although directly reducing temperature produced the best effect, but it also consumes the most amount of energy. because the locations of the monitoring points differed, the overall indoor environment can generate erroneous readings, causing some areas to reflect low comfort level. Subsequent studies could analyze the influence of distance and height of different indoor monitoring locations to calculate the mean values of the area, which provides input data for a smart control system to achieve temperature reduction and energy conservation.

References

1. Chou, P.C.; Chiang, C.M.; Li, Y.Y.; Lee, C.Y. & Chang, K.F., Natural Ventilation Efficiency in Bedroomwith Central-Pivoting Window, Indoor + Built Environment , 2008, 17(2).
2. Huang, C.C. A Field Study on Thermal Comfort in University Classrooms. Thesis (PhM). Feng Chia University,2005.
3. Guang Dexin , Zhu Tingyao , Han Shijie. Theoretical model of drag coefficient of isolated tree, Sciental Silvae Sinicae, 2001: Vol.37, No.6.
4. O. HÄLSA. Comfort Climate Evaluation with Thermal Manikin Methods and Computer Simulation Models, Ph.D. Thesis, University of Gävle, Sweden, 2004.

Bifurcation and Chaos Analysis of Gear Pair System Based on Crack Rotor-Bearing System with Rub-Impact Effect

Cai-Wan Chang-Jian [1,*], Cheng-Chi Wang [2] and Li-Ming Chu [3]

[1] I-Shou University; cwchangjian@isu.edu.tw
[2] National Chin-Yi University of Technology; wcc@ncut.edu.tw
[3] National Taitung University; lmchu@nttu.edu.tw
* Correspondence: cwchangjian@isu.edu.tw; Tel.: +886-7-6577711 ext.3231

Academic Editor: name
Received: date; Accepted: date; Published: date

Abstract: This study performs a systematic analysis of the dynamic behavior of a crack rotor-bearing system with rub-impact effect. The dynamic orbits of the system are observed using bifurcation diagrams plotted using the dimensionless damping coefficient, the dimensionless unbalance parameter and the dimensionless rotational speed ratio as control parameters. The analysis methods employed in this study include the dynamic trajectories of the crack rotor-bearing system, power spectra, Poincaré maps and bifurcation diagrams. Lyapunov exponent and fractal dimensional analysis are also used to identify the onset of chaotic motion. The numerical results reveal that the system exhibits a diverse range of periodic, sub-harmonic, quasi-periodic and chaotic behaviors. The results presented in this study provide an understanding of the operating conditions under which undesirable dynamic motion takes place in a crack rotor-bearing system and therefore serve as a useful source of reference for engineers in designing and controlling such systems.

Keywords: rotor-bearing system; cracked rotor; rub-impact

PACS: J0101

1. Introduction

Cracked rotor and rub-impact between rotor/stator are both common faults found in turbo-machineries. Those faults will induce some possible fatigue. The diagnosis the cracked rotor or rub-impact effect can help researchers or engineers understand how to escape the undesired vibration and fatigues. Most literatures also emphasize the importance of cracked rotor or rub-impact effect. Sabnavis et al. [1] presented a very comprehensive study on vibration of cracked shaft and found some interesting vibration phenomena induced by rotor crack. Jun et al. [2] found that cracked rotor would cause periodic steady state lateral vibrations at twice and thrice the rotation speed due to breathing of the crack under gravity loading and thus proved that the relations between dynamic behaviors of system and cracked rotor. Zhou et al. [3] took some experiments to prove cracked rotor would produce some problems of dynamical systems and thus evidenced numerical results of formal literatures. Darpe et al. [4-5] investigated the dynamic behaviors of two cracked rotors and also discussed the effect of bow. They found the dynamics of the system would become more seriously with effects of cracked rotor and bow coexisting.

2. Mathematical Modeling

Figure 1 shows a flexible crack rotor supported by two oil film journal bearings on a parallel with nonlinear springs suspension under rub-impact between rotor and stator. O_m is the center of rotor gravity, O_1 is the geometric center of the bearing, O_2 is the geometric center of the rotor, O_3 is the geometric center of the journal. From the equilibrium of force, the forces applied to the journal center O_3 are

$$F_x = f_e \cos\varphi + f_\varphi \sin\varphi = K_s(1-\frac{\delta_1\delta_2}{2})(X_2 - X_3)/2 \tag{1}$$

$$F_y = f_e \sin\varphi - f_\varphi \cos\varphi = K_s(1-\frac{\delta_1\delta_2}{2})(Y_2 - Y_3)/2 \tag{2}$$

where $\delta_1 = \frac{1}{2}L_R \frac{\bar{\lambda}_\xi - \bar{\lambda}_\eta}{(L_R+\bar{\lambda}_\xi)(L_R+\bar{\lambda}_\eta)}$, $\delta_2 = \frac{1}{\delta_1} - \frac{\bar{\lambda}_\xi + \bar{\lambda}_\eta}{\bar{\lambda}_\xi - \bar{\lambda}_\eta} - \frac{2L_R}{\bar{\lambda}_\xi - \bar{\lambda}_\eta}$, $L_R = \frac{L_1}{3R(1-\nu^2)}$,

$\bar{\lambda}_\xi = \frac{\pi R^3 E}{(1-\nu^2)} c_\xi \int_{-\frac{b}{R}}^{\frac{b}{R}} \int_0^{\frac{\eta}{R}} 32[1-(\frac{\xi}{R})^2](\frac{\bar{\eta}}{R}) F_2^2(\frac{\bar{\eta}}{R}) d(\frac{\bar{\eta}}{R}) d(\frac{\xi}{R})$, $\bar{\lambda}_\eta = \frac{\pi R^3 E}{(1-\nu^2)} c_\eta \int_0^{\frac{b}{R}} \int_0^{\frac{\eta}{R}} 32(\frac{\xi}{R})^2 (\frac{\bar{\eta}}{R}) F_1^2(\frac{\bar{\eta}}{R}) d(\frac{\bar{\eta}}{R}) d(\frac{\xi}{R})$,

$h = 2\sqrt{R^2-\xi^2}$, $\eta(\xi) = a - R + \sqrt{R^2-\xi^2}$ is the local depth of crack, L_1 is the length of shaft between both supported ends, R is the radius of journal, E is the Young's Modulus, a is the depth of crack and ν is the poisson ratio. The following parameters $F_1(\frac{\eta}{h})$ and $F_2(\frac{\eta}{h})$ will be defined, then.

$$F_1(\frac{\eta}{h}) = \sqrt{\frac{2h}{\pi\eta \tan(\frac{\pi\eta}{2h})}} \{0.923 + 0.199[1-\sin(\pi\eta)]^4\} / \cos(\frac{\pi\eta}{2h})$$

$$F_2(\frac{\eta}{h}) = \sqrt{\frac{2h}{\pi\eta \tan(\frac{\pi\eta}{2h})}} \{0.752 + 2.02(\frac{\eta}{h}) + 0.37[1-\sin(\pi\eta)]^3\} / \cos(\frac{\pi\eta}{2h})$$

From assumptions (a) to (c), it means that the whirling is considered, while the wobbling is neglected. The equations of motion of O2 in the Cartesian coordinates and the equations of motion of the bearing center could be written as

$$m\ddot{X}_2 + C_2\dot{X}_2 + K_s(1-\frac{\delta_1\delta_2}{2})(X_2 - X_3) + \frac{\delta_1 f}{2} K_s[(X_2-X_3)\cos(2\omega t) + (Y_2-Y_3)\sin(2\omega t)] = m\rho\omega^2\cos\phi + R_x$$

(3)

$$m\ddot{Y}_2 + C_2\dot{Y}_2 + K_s(1-\frac{\delta_1\delta_2}{2})(Y_2 - Y_3) + \frac{\delta_1 f}{2} K_s[(X_2-X_3)\sin(2\omega t) - (Y_2-Y_3)\cos(2\omega t) = m\rho\omega^2\sin\phi - mg + R_y$$

(4)

$$m_0\ddot{X}_1 + C_1\dot{X}_1 + K_1X_1 + K_2X_1^3 = F_x \tag{5}$$

$$m_0\ddot{Y}_1 + C_1\dot{Y}_1 + K_1Y_1 + K_2Y_1^3 = -m_0 g + F_y \tag{6}$$

where g is the acceleration of gravity, F_x and F_y are the components of the oil film force. R_x and R_y are the rub-impact forces in the horizontal and vertical directions.

Equations (3)-(6) describe a nonlinear dynamic system. The approximate solution of these coupled nonlinear differential equations can be obtained by numerical methods.

3. Results

The nonlinear dynamic equations presented in equations (3) to (6) for the crack rotor-bearing system were solved using the fourth order Runge-Kutta method. The time step in the iterative solution procedure was assigned a value of π/300 and the termination criterion was specified as an error tolerance of less than 0.0001. The time series data corresponding to the first 800 revolutions of the rotor-bearing system were deliberately excluded from the dynamic analysis to ensure that the analyzed data related to steady-state conditions. The sampled data were used to generate the dynamic trajectories, Poincaré maps and bifurcation diagrams of the rotor-bearing system in order to obtain a basic understanding of its dynamic behavior. The maximum Lyapunov exponent and the fractal dimension measure were then used to identify the onset of chaotic motion.

Figure 2 presents the bifurcation diagram for the dimensionless displacement of the rotor center and bearing center in the horizontal direction using the dimensionless rotating speed ratio *s* as a bifurcation parameter. Note that the rotor-bearing system is assumed to be without rub-impact effect in this case. It can be observed that both the rotor center and bearing center exhibit periodic or nT-periodic motions at low values of the dimensionless rotating speed ratio, i.e. $s \leq 2.80$. Besides, we also find that the so-called "Jump phenomena" is also happening at *s* =1.20 for rotor center. However, as *s* is increased from 2.80 to 3.40, the nT-periodic motion is replaced by non-periodic motion both for rotor and bearing dynamic trajectories. As the dimensionless rotating speed ratio is further increased from *s* =3.40 to *s* =5.20, the non-periodic motion transits to periodic motion and then the dynamic trajectory becomes sub-harmonic motion of *8T*-period as *s* >5.20. For 7.80<s<8.90, the trajectory performs non-periodic motion and it becomes synchronous *1T*-periodic motion as s>8.90, finally. Figure 3 are the history of Poincaré maps of rotor dynamic behaviors with rub-impact effect at s= *0.10, 0.20, 0.50, 1.00, 2.00, 2.30, 2.40, 2.60, 2.80, 3.00, 3.20, 3.60, 4.00, 6.00* and *8.00*. We can find that the dynamic trajectory history performs 1T => nT => quasi-peirodic motions. Figure 4 is the bifurcation diagram of rotor dynamic behaviors in the horizontal direction with rub-impact at *s=0.50* using dimensionless damping coefficient, ξ_1 as bifurcation parameter. The dynamic trajectories of the rotor center perform non-periodic at low values of the dimensionless damping coefficient, i.e. ξ_1<0.03 and then 3T-period and period motion would be found at $0.03 \leq \xi_1 \leq 0.032$ and $0.032 \leq \xi_1 \leq 0.034$ respectively. As the dimensionless damping coefficient is further increased from ξ_1 =*0.034* to ξ_1 =*0.05*, the non-periodic motion happen and non-periodic motions transits to sub-harmonic motion of 2T-periodic motions as ξ_1 >*0.05*, but non-periodic dynamic response would occur again at $0.056 \leq \xi_1 \leq 0.064$. Finally, the periodic motion perform at higher values of dimensionless damping coefficient ξ_1 >*0.064*. Figure 5 are the Poincaré maps with rub-impact effect at ξ_1 = *0.0001, 0.001, 0.01, 0.02, 0.028, 0.03, 0.032* and *0.04*. The simulation results show that quasi-periodic motions are found at ξ_1 = *0.0001* and *0.001*, chaotic motions are found at ξ_1 = *0.01, 0.02, 0.028* and *0.04*, *3T*-periodic motion is found at ξ_1 = *0.03* and periodic motion is found at ξ_1 = *0.032*.

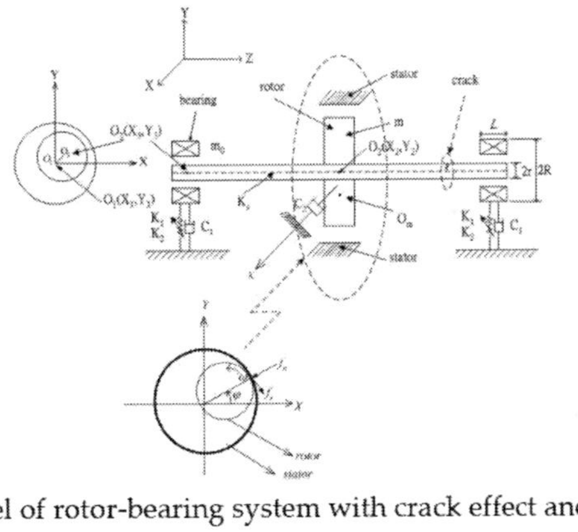

Fig.1 Dynamic model of rotor-bearing system with crack effect and rub-impact effect.

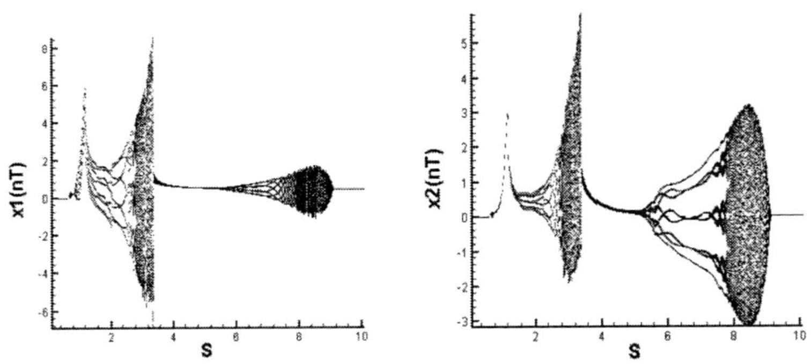

 https://doi.org/10.1051/matecconf/201820101008

Fig.2 Bifurcation diagram of rotor and bearing dynamic behaviors **with** rub-impact effect using dimensionless rotating speed ratio, *s*, as bifurcation parameter.

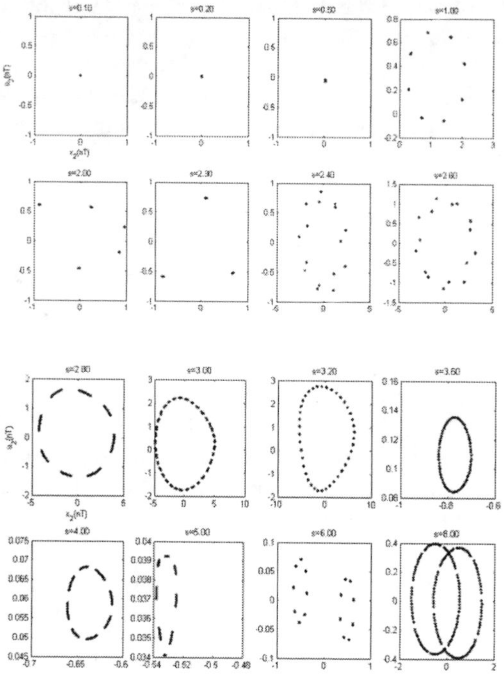

Fig.3 The history of Poincaré maps of rotor dynamic behaviors **with** rub-impact effect at *s= 0.10, 0.20, 0.50, 1.00, 2.00, 2.30, 2.40, 2.60, 2.80, 3.00, 3.20, 3.60, 4.00, 6.00* and *8.00*.

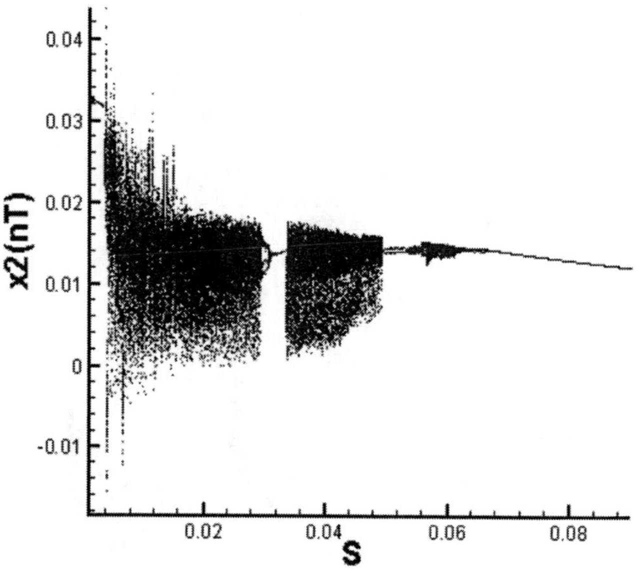

Fig.4 Bifurcation diagram of rotor dynamic behaviors in horizontal direction with rub-impact at *s=0.5* effect using dimensionless damping coefficient, ξ_1, as bifurcation parameter.

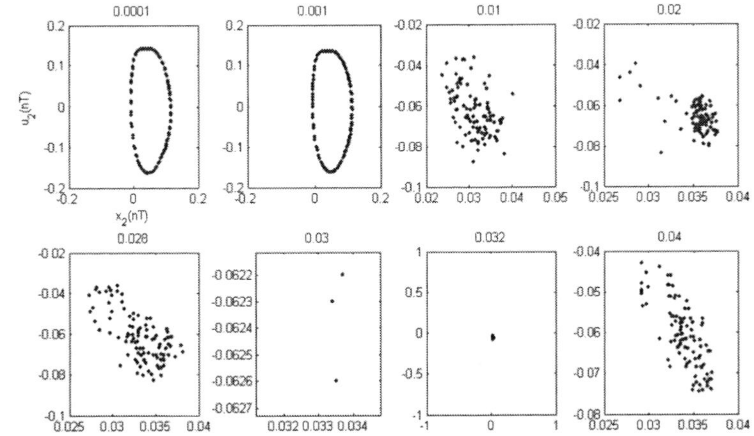

Fig.5 The history of Poincaré maps of rotor dynamic behaviors **with** rub-impact effect at $\xi_1 = 0.0001$, *0.001, 0.01, 0.02, 0.028, 0.03, 0.032* and *0.04*.

Acknowledgments: Financial support for this work was provided by the Ministry of Science and Technology Taiwan, under the contract MOST 106-2221-E-214-023.

References

1. Sabnavis G.; Kirk R.G.; Kasarada M.; Quinn D. Cracked shaft detection and diagnostics: a literature review. Shock Vibr Digest 2004; Volume 36, pp. 287-296.
2. Jun O.S.; Earnme H.Y.; Lee C.W. Modelling and vibration analysis of a simple rotor with breathing crack. J Sound Vibr 1992; Volume 155, pp. 273-90.
3. Zhou T.; Xu Z.; Han W. Experimental analysis of a cracked rotor. J. Dyna Sys Meas Control 2005; Volume 127, pp. 313-20.
4. Darpe A.K.; Gupta K.; Chawla A. Dynamics of a two-cracked rotor. J Sound Vibr 2003; Volume 259, pp. 649-75.
5. Darpe A.K.; Gupta K.; Chawla A. Dynamics of a bowed rotor with a transverse surface crack. J Sound Vibr 2006; Volume 296, pp. 888-907.

Ergonomic Evaluation of Smart Navigation System for Riding on Motorcycle

Po-Hsiang Liu*, *Yong-Cheng* Li, and *Yu-Jung* Tsai

Department of Industrial Engineering and Management, St. John's University, Taiwan

Abstract. A smart navigation device could be provided to keep riders' eyes safely on the road while riding on motorcycle. Present study surveyed the riding behaviors and examined the fifteen design factors about navigation device and determined the priority of each factor. Further, navigation device have been evaluated on road. A total of 550 questionnaires were dispatched, with a response rate of 89 % (n = 491). Results of factor analysis showed the six dimensions of prediction information, real-time information, brand and appearance, cost, functionality, efficacy and utility. Further, the highest priority design factors of smart navigation device are reminder for speeding camera, intersection name of next turn, distance of next turn, lane guide and map guide line. After navigation device have been evaluated on road, the smart device that effortlessly guides rider through the safest and most enjoyable riding routes with intuitive light patterns. Results of this study could provide the information for the design of the smart navigation device for riding on motorcycle.

1 Introduction

According to the statistics data on numbers of motorcycle from the Ministry of Transportations and Communications in September 2017, there are about 13,768,921 registered motorcycles. There are 1,056 traffic accidents occurred in category A1 (1,126 deaths and 570 injuries). Mainly 94.41% (n = 997) of traffic accidents caused by drivers' fault, because drivers did not pay attention to front vehicle states (n = 289), not complying with the regulations to yield the vehicles (n = 149), and in violation of traffic sign control or command (n = 64). Among the accidental deaths caused by all types of vehicles, motorcycling has the highest proportion (44.98%) on statistics data from January to September 2017. Motorcyclists are about 26-times more likely per vehicle mile traveled to die and 5-times more likely to be injured in a crash, compared to passenger car occupants [1]. Wu and Wu [2] investigated the adolescents in school and uses statistical method to analyze the relative factors. The results showed that the riding behaviors on adolescents are affected by personality traits, parental education, incorrect riding styles among peers, and the positive news reports. In addition, results of previous study showed that the proportional hazards model showed that after controlling for age, gender, and riding distance, older riders who had sustained hearing impairment (hazard ratio, HR) =2.58; rode a motorcycle at speeds of ≥41 km/h (HR= 2.31) and had experienced a motorcycle crash in the past year (HR =1.81) were more likely to be involved in a crash, compared to their counterparts.

Traffic accidents mainly due to unsafe conditions and unsafe behaviors. However, distractions have been present since driving began. Given the continuous, widespread and increasing use of mobile phone, however, people have become very concerned about drivers distraction resulting from mobile phone. Results of a literature review showed that concurrent mobile phone use increases the overall level of cognitive and physical demand, inevitably reducing allocation of attention to the driving task, with consequent impact on driving performance [3]. Thus, unsafe behaviors might occur while riding motorcycle with use of mobile phone. Navigation systems play an important role in many vital disciplines. Determining the location of a user relative to its physical environment is an important part. Now, smartphones as navigation is a better way because the mapping is so easy and intuitive. Smart phones could quickly download detailed maps of any country in the world which are easy to zoom in and out of, move around, and create points of interest on. However, riding motorcycle should keep the eyes on the road. How the use of smart phones as a navigation system distracted cycling or riding motorcycle? Present study surveyed the riding behaviors and examined the fifteen design factors about navigation device and determined the priority of each factor. Further, navigation device have been evaluated on road.

2 Materials and Methods

The present study consisted of two stages. In the first stage, a questionnaire was used to survey the design factors of navigation system with respect to riding behaviors. In the second stage, navigation device have been evaluated on road.

2.1 Questionnaire survey

The questionnaire was designed to determine the design factors of navigation system while riding motorcycle. Questionnaire involved five parts about background of participant, riding motorcycle behaviors, purchase navigation system, provided information of navigation system, design factors of navigation system. What information is expected from the navigation assistance system? There are fifteen factors to design of navigation system and determine the priority of each factor. The design factors involved durability, power consumption, operational convenience, brightness, size, modelling, auxiliary equipment, brand, repair prices, failure rate, price, endurance, functionality, quality, and waterproof. Rating of the design attributes was accomplished via a 5-point Likert-type scale: (1) strongly disagree, (2) disagree, (3) neither agree nor disagree, (4) agree, and (5) strongly agree. After rating, principal component analysis with varimax rotation was used for classification of the descriptors into factors.

2.2 Ergonomic evaluation

A navigation tool have been evaluated on road (Hammerhead H1, USA). This smart device that effortlessly guides riders through the safest and most enjoyable routes with intuitive light patterns. Get the information that rider need through the corner of eye and keep rider's eyes safely on the road. Further, the Hammerhead App software and usability have been evaluated as follow [4, 5]:

(1) Learnability: A system should allow users to reach acceptable performance levels within a specified time.
(2) Effectiveness: Acceptable performance should be achieved by a defined proportion of the user population, over a specified range of tasks and in a specified range of environments.
(3) Attitude: Acceptable performance should be achieved within acceptable human costs, in terms of fatigue, stress, frustration, discomfort and satisfaction.
(4) Flexibility: The product should be able to deal with a range of tasks beyond those first specified.
(5) Task match: In addition to the LEAF (Learnability, Effectiveness, Attitude and Flexibility) precepts set out above, a usable product should exhibit an acceptable match between the functions provided by the system and the needs and requirements of the user.

Furthermore, this navigation tool have been evaluated on road from St. John's University to Tamsui MRT station (10 Km). The experiment was conducted in an electric scooter (Gogoro Plus, Gogoro Limited, Taiwan). Dimension of the electric scooter is 1,730 mm x 690 mm x 1,215 mm (Length x Width x Height) and seat height is 745 mm. Gross weight with two batteries is 112 kg. Maximum power output is 6,400W at 3,250 rpm (Figure 1).

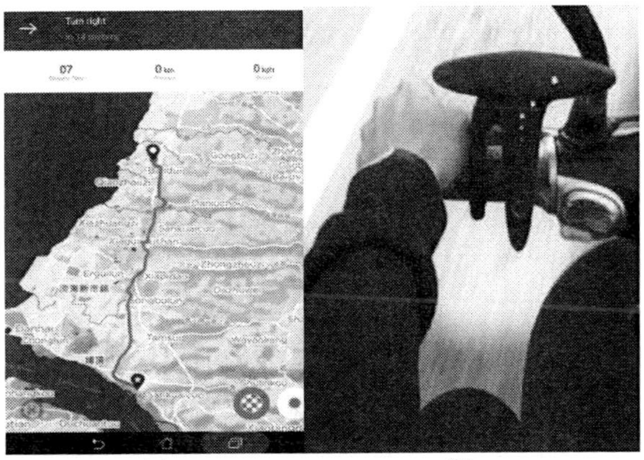

(a) (b)

Fig. 1. Navigation tool have been evaluated on road: (a) Navigation map from St. John's University to Tamsui MRT station (10 Km); (b) On road testing by riding the electric scooter.

3 Results

3.1 Questionnaire survey

A total of 550 questionnaires were dispatched, with a response rate of 89% (n = 491).Female respondents are 42.4% (n=208) and male respondents are 57.6% (n =283). The age distribution is 11.4% (< 20 years old), 66.8% (21-30 years old), 12.4% (31-40 years old), 5.1% (41-50 years old), and 4.3% (more than 51 years old). There are 32.0% (n = 157) respondents riding 2-3 days a week, 23% (n = 113) for 4-5 days a week, 15.3% (n = 75) for 6-7 days a week. The 80.0% (n = 393) respondents using a smartphone navigation to find destinations while riding a motorcycle. Navigation system using Apple map accounted for 22.8% (n = 112), Google map for 82.5% (n = 405), Papago for 5.5% (n =27), Garmin for 4.5% (n = 22), others for 33 6.7% (n =33).

3.2. Design of information and factors

Table 1 showed that riders need to consider information while using navigation system and sorting from high to low. The information of reminder for speeding camera, next turn-intersection name, next turn-reminder for distance, next turn-intersection figure or icon, lane guide should be provided in high priority. Table 2 showed that riders need to consider design factors while using navigation system and sorting from high to low. The design factors of durability, failure rate, quality, operational convenience, power consumption, functionality, waterproof, endurance should be designed in high priority.

Table1. Riders need to consider information while using navigation system.

Information	%
Reminder for speeding camera	89.0
Next turn - intersection name	88.8
Next turn - reminder for distance	85.7
Next turn - intersection figure or icon	85.5
Lane guide	84.9
Map guide line	83.5
Destination name	82.9
The remaining distance	75.4
Traffic signs	73.1
The remaining time	66.2

Table 2. Riders need to consider design factors while using navigation system.

Factors	%
Durability	94.3
Failure rate	94.3
Quality	93.5
Operational convenience	93.3
Power consumption	92.3
Functionality	91.9
Waterproof	91.4
Endurance	91.0

3.3. Factors analysis

For the factor analysis, the Kaiser-Meyer-Olkin (KMO) measure of sampling adequacy was 0.841 and Bartlett's test of sphericity showed that the factor model was appropriate ($p < 0.001$ and KMO > 0.5). For the principle components analysis with varimax rotation, the attributes were classified into six major factors with eigenvalues greater than 1. The six dimensions explained 65.3% of the internal variance. Table 3 showed the factor loading of the attributes. The first dimension contains factors including Reminder for speeding camera, Next turn-intersection name, Next turn-reminder for distance, Next turn-intersection for figure or icon, Lane guide. These factors are labeled 'Prediction information'. The second dimension is labeled 'Real-time information' which includes Map guide line, Destination name, The remaining distance, Traffic signs, Remaining time, Compass. The third factor is about 'Brand and appearance' includes factors of Brand, Size, Modeling. The fourth factor is 'Cost' including the factors of Price, Repair prices, auxiliary equipment. The fifth factor is 'Functionality' including the factors of Operational convenience, Functionality, Waterproof, Durability. The last factor is Efficacy and utility involved the factors of Failure rate, Quality, Power consumption, Brightness, Endurance.

3.4. Ergonomic evaluated

For learnability evaluation of navigation APP software, pair device (Bluetooth) is easy in first time as follow the on-screen instructions. After connect the device, the software provided the demo of light patterns. For example, light patterns involved about keep going forward, next turn on your right, turn right now, next turn on your left, turn left now, slight left now, slight right now, U-turn on the right, U-turn on the left, end ride, arrived the destination, re-routing, error etc. it is good design (Figure 2).

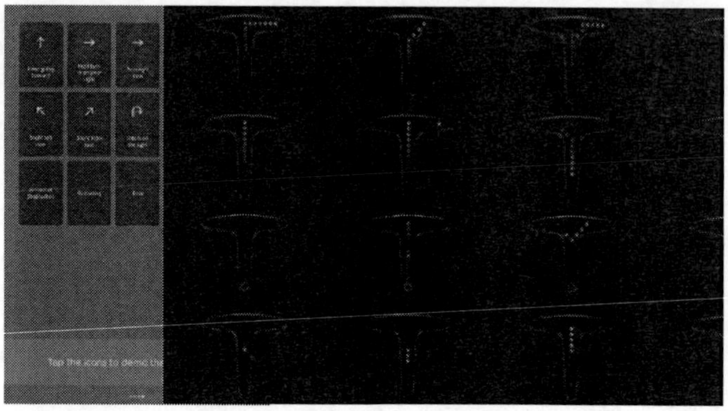

(a) (b)

Fig. 2. The demo of light patterns: (a) tap the icons to demo the light patterns; (b) the light patterns of device.

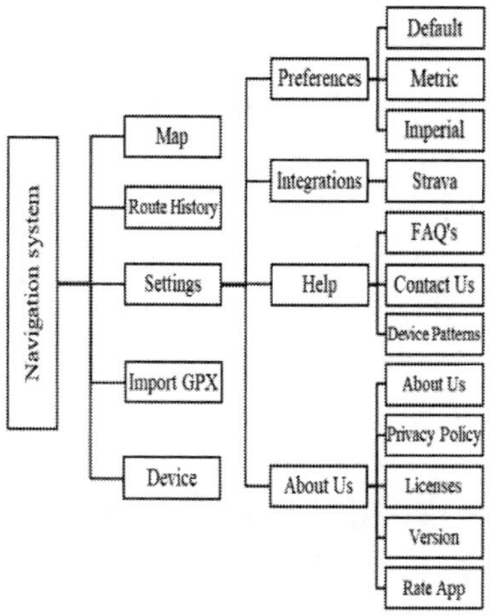

Fig. 3. The system structure of navigation APP software.

For software analysis, the navigation system has only three hierarchies [5]. Open the navigation program showed the map first. Selecting the menu icon in left bottom, screen showed the other selection in fist hierarchy (route history, settings, import GPX and device). Route history showed the previous riding route and could edit and sort by date, distance, elevation, time and name. Four functions on settings involved preferences (unit selection), integration (connect with Strava's global community of athletes), help (Frequently asked question, contact us, device patterns) and about us (about us, privacy policy, licenses, version, rate app). Next function is the "import GPX". GPX, or GPS Exchange Format, is an XML schema designed as a common GPS data format for software applications. It can be used to describe waypoints, tracks, and routes.

Last function is "Device" that involved connection status, device battery level, serial number and firmware version. For usability analysis, some comments could be provided as follow: (1) considering the task match, the function of "Import GPX" is highly related to the map or route history. In addition, "Strava" could also move to route history; (2) function of "Help" could be move to the first hierarchy. The function of "About us" should be under the function of "Help"; (3) the function of "Device patterns" should be moved to "Device" in first hierarchy Figure 3).

A navigation tool have been evaluated on road by riding electric scooter. First, the current location is St. John's University. After searching the destination of Tamsui MRT station and selecting the correct item, the riding route is showed on screen (Figure 1a). However, navigation system did not provide the alternative route for flexibility choice of rider. The route planning could depend on the shortest path, optimal time, or elevation variation. In addition, direction indicator of light pattern are difficult to identify clearly between next turn on your left (right) and turn left (right) now. In addition to light identification, the light color also need to use. The amber (yellow) light could be described the attention and warning to be prepared to turn. The green light could be presented the turning now. Furthermore, navigation device might provide the sound patterns for redundant design of indication.

4 Discussion

Navigation systems are very useful tools because they display a rider's location and guide them to a destination using graphics, text and voice information. Safety concerns have prompted designers of route guidance and information systems to make more use of an 'audible interface' to convey guidance instructions. The study of Jackson [6] examined that participants watched video footage of journeys through an unfamiliar area, while hearing guidance that linked direction instructions to landmarks visible at the decision point. Results showed that heard these amended instructions performed significantly better than other groups at a wide range of tasks designed to measure the spatial knowledge that they had acquired. This group performed better than groups who heard nothing, and groups who heard full guidance. Lee and Cheng [7] explore whether the efficiency to destination and driver behavior were distinguishable when using a portable navigation system compared to a paper map. The results revealed that the drivers performed better when using a portable navigation system compared to those using a paper map, in terms of efficiency to destination and driving performance. In addition, drivers could save time and gasoline using a portable navigation system when in an unfamiliar region, and driving performance may be safer, despite the fact that the display screen of the phone is small. Liu and Wu [8] explore the effect factors on driver's route choice behavior by factor analysis and compared the driver's route planning with electronic map and the shortest path algorithm. The results of factor analysis revealed that traffic environment, interference, change direction, traffic hazard, convenient, the number of lanes and distance/time were important components of route choice behavior. The driver's route planning did not depend only on distance or time factor. Present study indicated that results of factor analysis showed the six dimensions of prediction information, real-time information, brand and appearance, cost, functionality, efficacy and utility. In addition, the highest priority design factors of smart navigation device are reminder for speeding camera, intersection name of next turn, distance of next turn, lane guide and map guide line. Those factors could consider in design of navigation system.

5 Discussion

Providing the smart device that effortlessly guides rider through the safest and most enjoyable routes is an important issue. Riders get the navigation information and need to keep eyes safely on the road. Navigation device simplifies the map complex information to provide the direction guidance only. Six dimensions of prediction information, real-time information, brand and appearance, cost, functionality, efficacy and utility should be considered in design of navigation system. Further, the highest priority design factors of smart navigation device are reminder for speeding camera, intersection name of next turn, distance of next turn, lane guide and map guide line. Applied the light patterns with sound alarm is a better design for navigation device. Results of this study could provide the information for the design of the smart navigation device for riding motorcycle.

Acknowledgments: This study was supported by a grant from the Ministry of Science and Technology in Taiwan, and Project No. MOST 105-2815-C-129-007-E. Researchers are very grateful for all of participants in this study.

References

1. National Center for Statistics and Analysis (NCSA), 2015. Motorcycles: 2013 Data (Traffic Safety Facts. Report No. DOT HS 812 148). National Highway Traffic Safety Administration, Washington, DC.
2. S.U. Wu, C.H. Wu, A study on the risk perception of adolescent motorcyclists in school. Urban Traffic Biannually, **27-28**, 38-53 (2013).
3. B.S. Liu, Y.H. Lee, Effects of car-phone use and aggressive disposition during critical driving maneuvers. Transportation Research Part F, **8**, 369-382 (2005)
4. N. Stanton, *Human factors in consumer products*. (Taylor & Francis: London, UK, 1998)
5. Hammerhead One Navigation System User Manual, 2014; Hammerhead, New York, USA.
6. P.G. Jackson, In search of better route guidance instructions, Ergonomics, **41**, 1000-1013 (1998)

https://doi.org/10.1051/matecconf/201820101009

7. W.C. Lee, B.W. Cheng, Effects of using a portable navigation system and paper map in real driving, Accident Analysis & Prevention, **40**, 303-308 (2008)
8. B.H. Liu, J.H. Wu, The comparison of E-map navigation and subjective route choice. Journal of Ergonomic Study, **6**, 21-28 (2004)

Table 3. Results of factors analysis.

Factors	**Prediction information**	**Real-time information**	**Brand & appearance**	**Cost**	**Functionality**	**Efficacy and utility**
Reminder for speeding camera	.828					
Next turn - intersection name	.799					
Next turn - reminder for distance	.797					
Next turn - intersection for figure or icon	.725					
Lane guide	.637					
Map guide line		.722				
Destination name		.714				
The remaining distance		.714				
Traffic signs		.711				
Remaining time		.684				
Compass		.543				
Brand			.757			
Size			.724			
Modeling			.541			
Price				.667		
Repair prices				.614		
auxiliary equipment				.463		
Operational convenience					.809	
Functionality					.774	
Waterproof					.746	
Durability					.587	
Failure rate						.741
Quality						.624
Power consumption						.599
Brightness						.595
Endurance						.531

Study on Machine Learning Based Intelligent Defect Detection System

Chung-Chi Huang [1,*] **and Xin-Pu Lin** [2]

[1] Dept. of Automaation of Control Enginerring, Far East University ; phdcchuang@gmail.com
[2] The Institue of Manufacturing Information and Systems, National Cheng Kung University; r2hlin@gmail.com
* Correspondence: phdcchuang@gmail.com; Tel.: +886-6-912727958

Academic Editor:
Received: date; Accepted: date; Published: date

Abstract: In the paper, it is proposed to develop a machine learning based intelligent defect detection system for metal products. The common machine vision system has the surface (stain, shallow pit, shallow tumor, scratches, Edge defects, pattern defects) detection, or for the processing of the size, diameter, diameter, eccentricity, height, thickness and other parts of the non-contact numerical parameters of detection. Considering the quality of the work piece and the defects of the standard, so for the quality of customized testing requirements, the study is the development of machine vision and machine learning metal products defect detection system, mainly composed of three procedures: Image preprocessing, training procedures and testing procedures. The system architecture consists of three parts: (1) Image preprocessing: we first use the machine vision. OPENCV to carry out the image pre-processing part of the product before the detection. (2) Training procedures: The algorithm of the machine learning includes the convolution neural network (CNN), chunk-max pooling is used to train the program, and the generative adversarial network (GAN) based architecture is used to solve the problem of small datasets for surface defects. (3) Testing procedures：The Python language is used to write the program and implement the testing procedures with the GPU-Based embedded hardware In industries, collecting training dataset is usually costly and related methods are highly dataset-dependent. So most companies cannot provide Big-data to be analyzed or applied. By the experimental results, the recognition accuracy can be obviously improved as increasing data augmentation by GAN-Based samples maker. Manual inspection is labor intensive, costly and less in efficiency. Therefore, this study will contribute to technological innovation, industry, national development and other applications. (1) The use of intelligent machine learning technology will make the industry 4.0 technology more sophisticated. (2) It will make the development of equipment industry be better by the machine learning applications. (3) It will increase the economics and productivity of countries for the aging of the population by machine learning.

Keywords: convolution neural network; generative adversarial network; machine learning; intelligent detection system; metal products; computer vision system

PACS: J0101

---

1. Introduction

Manual inspection is labor intensive, costly and less in efficiency. Further, the accuracy of the defect detection is lower due to harsh industrial environment and human errors. Therefore, big data, computer vision and machine learning play important roles in the automated defect detection system. In industries, collecting training dataset is usually costly and related methods are highly dataset-dependent. In 2016, Y. Shimizu et al. [1] presented a concept of a micro thermal sensor to be used for defect inspection of a smoothly-finished surface such as a bare wafer or a hard disk. Existences of the defects on a measurement surface will be auto-detected by scanning the surface with the micro thermal sensor, which is utilized to detect the variation of the thermal flow in-between the sensor surface and the measurement surface. The proposed micro thermal sensor has a possibility of auto-detecting various types of surface defects. In 2017, R. Ren et al. [2] proposed a generic approach that requires small training data for automated surface inspection. The approach builds classifier on the features of image patches, where the features are transferred from a pre-trained deep learning network. And then pixel-wise prediction is obtained by convolving the trained classifier over input image. The experiment involves two tasks: (1) image classification and (2) defect segmentation. The results of the experiments showed the proposed method improves accuracy by 0.66%-25.50% in the classification tasks, improves accuracy by 0.66%-25.50% in the classification tasks, and improves accuracies by 2.29%-9.86% in all seven defect types. In 2017, Y. C. Samarawickrama et al. [3] proposed an automated inspection system for ceramic tile industry based on image processing techniques. This system can detect color variations and defects such as corner damages, edge damages and middle cracks on the surface of the tile with high accuracy and efficiency. The results of the experiments were outstanding with of 96.36% detection accuracy rate. And the processing time for one tile was approximately 2 seconds. So this outstanding achievement of results reflects that this automated system can effectively replace manual ceramic tile detection system with better accuracy and efficiency. In 2016, S. Faghih-Roohi et al. [4] proposed a deep convolutional neural network solution to the analysis of image data for the detection of rail surface defects. This huge amount of data obtained from many hours of automated video recordings makes it impossible to manually inspect the images and detect rail surface defects. Therefore, automated detection of rail defects can help to save time and costs, and to ensure rail transportation safety. The advantage of the deep convolutional neural network solution is to skip elaborate procedures of feature extractions required in classical learning approaches. The results of different network architectures characterized by different sizes and activation functions were compared. By the experimental results, the rail defect classes can be successfully classified with almost 92% accuracy. Wood defect detection has an important influence on the automation of wood industry. In 2016, Z. N. Ke et al. [5] proposed the hybrid algorithm of genetic algorithm (GA) and particle swarm optimization (PSO) algorithm in view of the complexity of wood defect segmentation. Firstly, the contrast of the image is enhanced by the linear transformation function. Secondly, applying GA and PSO-GA hybrid algorithm respectively for the image segmentation, and finally morphological processing is performed. The experimental result shows that the PSO-GA hybrid algorithm has a better and more stable effect on detecting wood defects compared with the GA. Image technologies nowadays are used not only for keeping personal events safe, but also are widely applied in conjunction with automated electronic systems. Computer vision is widely used for inspection of the production quality in industries. Food industry is not an exception. Containers for food industry are made in very large quantities. In 2016, A. Laucka et al. [6,7] proposed an automated computer vision algorithms for the control of PET preparation quality. The algorithms and methods were used for the detection of defective products mainly based on the image segmentation, digital production, erosion, smoothing. The most effective filters for the defect detection of the workpieces have been determined. It was carried out that efficiency of algorithms are close to 100 %. And reached throughput is 10,000 workpieces per hour. In 2015, M. Win et al. [8] proposed two new thresholding methods, namely contrast-adjusted Otsu's method and contrast-adjusted median-based Otsu's method, for automated defect detection system for titanium-coated aluminum surfaces. The results of the experiments showed that the proposed contrast-adjusting methods have performance similar to minimum error thresholding (MET) and are generally better than Otsu's method. In 2015, M. W. Ashour et al. [9] proposed the approach of the Support Vector Machine (SVM) classifier with various kernels for the categorization of machined surfaces into the six machining processes of Turning, Grinding, Horizontal Milling, Vertical Milling, Lapping, and Shaping. And the effectiveness of the gray-level histogram as the discriminating feature is explored. The results of the experiments suggest that the SVM with the linear kernel provides superior performance for a dataset consisting of 72 workpiece images. And its training time is less than the training time of ANN. In 2015, C. Huang et al. [10] proposed a method of workpiece recognition and location by Hu moment invariants based on Open Source Computer Vision (OPENCV). Firstly, the methods of image preprocessing including image graying, mean filter, image binaryzation by adaptive threshold segmentation are used. And then, the contours from the binary image are extracted. Finally, the object workpiece can be identified by matching the extracted contours with the object contour from the template image by Hu moment invariants. At the same time, the method of confirming the workpiece position and direction is put forward. It showed that the proposed method can recognize the target workpiece and locate the position effectively by the experimental results. So the used algorithms are simple and fast in operation.

To Sum up, being able to identify machining processes that produce specific machined surfaces is crucial in modern manufacturing production. Image processing and computer vision technologies have become indispensable tools for automated identification with benefits such as reduction in inspection time and avoidance of human errors due to inconsistency and fatigue. And collecting training dataset is usually costly in industries. Therefore, it is very important to develop a machine learning based intelligent defect detection system with small training data.

2. Materials and Methods

The common machine vision system has the surface (stain, shallow pit, shallow tumor, scratches, Edge defects, pattern defects) detection, or for the processing of the size, diameter, diameter, eccentricity, height, thickness and other parts of the non-contact numerical parameters of detection. Considering the quality of the work piece and the defects of the standard, so for the quality of customized testing requirements, the study is the development of machine vision and machine learning metal products defect detection system, mainly composed of three procedures: Image preprocessing, training procedures and testing procedures.

The system architecture consists of three parts: (1) Image preprocessing: we first use the machine vision. OPENCV to carry out the image pre-processing part of the product before the detection. (2) Training procedures: The algorithm of the machine learning includes the convolution neural network (CNN), chunk-max pooling is used to train the program, and the generative adversarial network (GAN) based architecture is used to solve the problem of small datasets for surface defects and (3) Testing procedures: The Python language is used to write the program and implement the testing procedures with the GPU-Based embedded hardware.

2.1. Image preprocessing

In order to improve the efficiency of the operation, a series of integrated image processing will be conducted in advance to facilitate the learning of the machine learning model. It consists of three layers of processing, the first layer is Median filter, the second layer is Canny edge detector, and the third layer is Thresholding. The flowchart of image preprocessing is showed as Figure 1.

• Layer 1: Median filter for grayscale images

The median filter is a nonlinear digital filtering technique and very widely used in digital image processing. It is often used to remove salt and pepper noise from an image or signal and preserves edges while removing noise. The median filter replaces a pixel by the median, instead of the average, of all pixels in a neighborhood.

• Layer 2: Canny edge detector

The Canny edge detector is an edge detection operator that uses a multi-stage algorithm to detect a wide range of edges in images. The Canny Edge detector algorithm aims to satisfy three main criteria: (1) low error rate: a good detection of only existent edges. (2) good localization: the distance between edge pixels detected and real edge pixels have to be minimized. (3) minimal response: only one detector response per edge. The steps of the Canny edge detector are (1) Filter out any noise by using the Gaussian filter. (2) Follow a procedure analogous to Sobel for finding the intensity gradient of the image. (3) Non-maximum suppression is applied. (4) Hysteresis: Canny does use two thresholds (upper and lower).

• Layer 3: Thresholding

Thresholding is a non-linear operation that converts a gray-scale image into a binary image where the two levels are assigned to pixels that are below or above the specified threshold value.

Thresholding creates binary images from grey-level ones by turning all pixels below some threshold to zero and all pixels about that threshold to one.

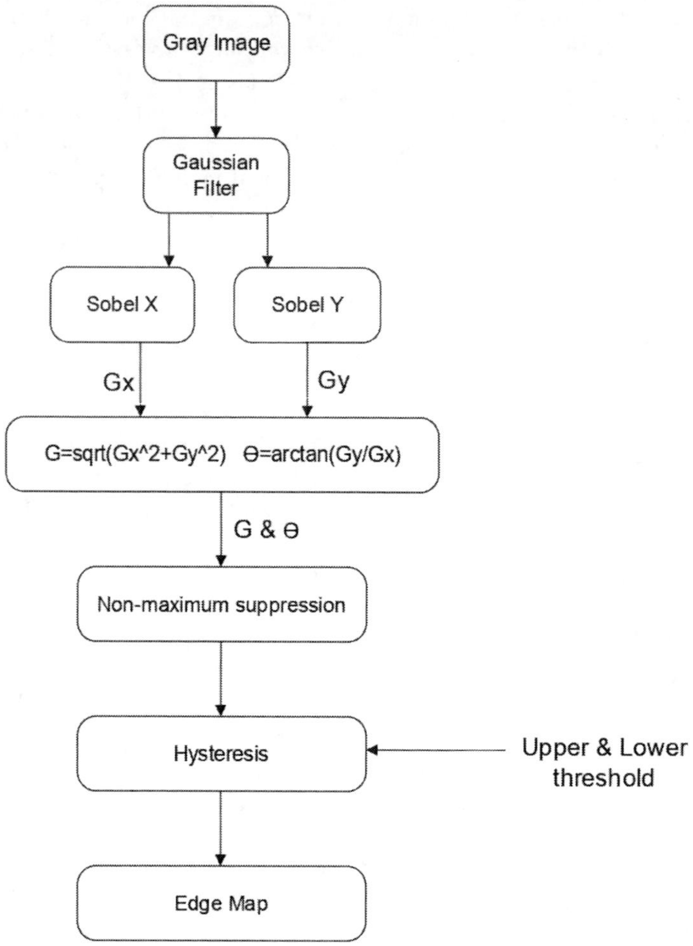

Figure 1. The flowchart of image preprocessing for intelligent defect detection system

2.2. *Training procedures*

Training procedures : The algorithm of the machine learning includes the convolution neural networks, chunk-max pooling is used to train the program, and the architecture of GAN-based samples maker is used to solve the problem of small datasets for surface defects and

(1) Convolution neural network

In the study, the architecture of convolutional neural network (CNN, or ConvNet) showed as Figure 2 is a class of deep, feed-forward artificial neural networks that has successfully been applied to analyzing visual imagery. It consist of convolutional layer, pooling layer and fully connected layer. Convolutional layers apply a convolution operation to the input image, passing the feature result to the next layer. Pooling layers combine the outputs of neuron clusters at one layer into a single neuron in the next layer. Max pooling uses the maximum value from each of a cluster of neurons at the prior layer. Finally, fully connected layers connect every neuron in one layer to every neuron in another layer. It is like the traditional multi-layer perceptron neural network (MLP).

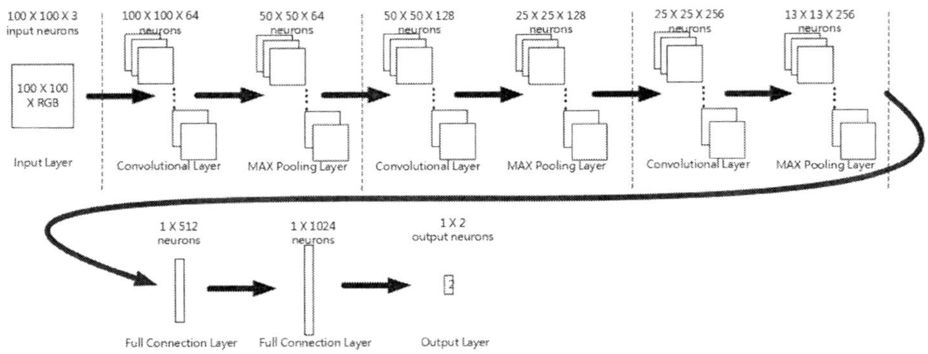

Figure 2. The architecture of convolutional neural network for intelligent defect detection system

(2) GAN-based samples maker

In order to solve the problem of small dataset for surface detects, GAN-based samples maker is built up and auto generates massive, diverse and labeled samples. Generative adversarial network (GAN) is a class of artificial intelligence algorithms used in unsupervised machine learning, implemented by a system of two neural networks contesting with each other in a zero-sum game framework. The standard architecture of the generative adversarial network consists of a discriminator network and a generator network. The generator network generates candidates and the discriminator network evaluates them. Therefore, the generative network learns to map from a latent space to a particular data distribution of interest, while the discriminative network discriminates between instances from the true data distribution and candidates produced by the generator. It is showed as Figure 3. GAN-based architecture plays a role as a samples maker to finish the data augmentation in the defect detection system.

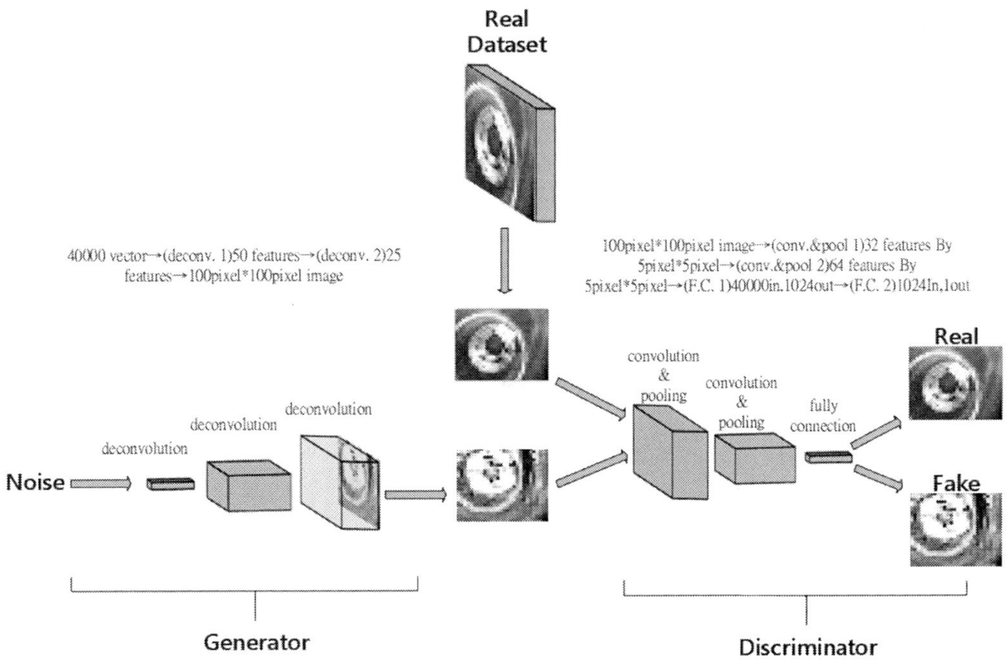

Figure 3. The architecture of GAN-Based samples maker for intelligent defect detection system

The overall architecture of GAN-Based Defect Detector system is showed as Figure 4. The generative adversarial network based architecture is used to solve the problem of small datasets for surface defects.

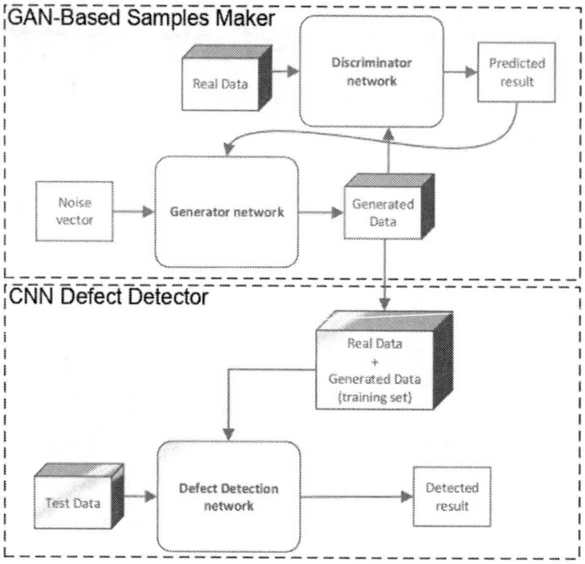

Figure 4. The overall architecture of GAN-Based defect detection system

2.3. *Testing procedures*

Testing procedures : The Python language is used to write the program and implement the testing procedures with the GPU-Based embedded hardware. In order to effectively identify the workpiece surface defects, the architecture of convolutional neural network is chosen in testing procedures. The flowchart of testing procedures for defect detection system is showed as Figure 5.

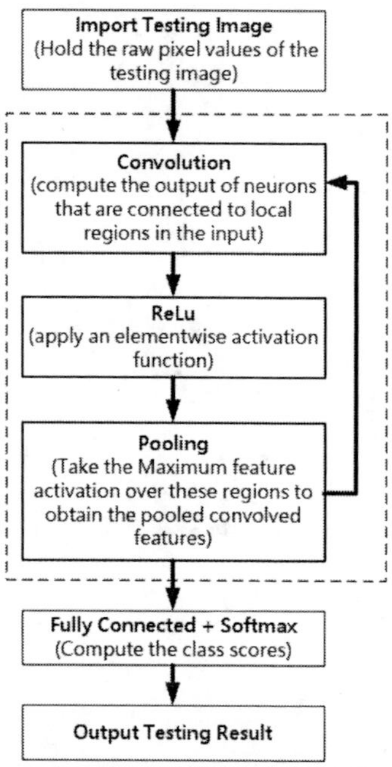

Figure 5. The flowchart of testing procedures for defect detection system

3. Results

The samples of 151 normal surface images and 151 surface defects images are the training datasets for CNN. Moreover, the testing samples of 10 normal surface images and 10 surface defects images are the valid datasets.

In order to make CNN work well, we need to train and adjust the configuration of network several times to obtain a relatively accurate network architecture. The accuracy comparisons of the defect detection can be used to analyze the results of many different hyper parameters for convolutional neural network.

As shown in Table 1, there are eight configuration (type A ~ H) for convolutional neural network. The differences between the eight configurations are the number of layers of convolutional layer and the pooling layer, CNN training epochs and learning rate. The parameter layer_position represents the order of the layers is located in the CNN. The parameter "conv_nb_filter" represents the number of convolutional filters. The parameter "conv_filter_size" represents the Size of convolutional filters. The parameter "pl_kernel_size" represents the Pooling kernel size. The parameter "fc_n_units" represents the number of units for fully connected layer. In addition, the recognition effect of CNN with the Canny edge detector pre-processing was tested. The result of pre-processing image is showed as Figure 6. The eight results of accuracy with or without image pre-processing are showed in Table 2.

Table 1. The configurations for convolutional neural network

Nets Type	*Conv.* (layer_position, conv_nb_filter, conv_filter_size)	*Pooling* (layer_position, pl_kernel_size)	*F.C.* (layer_position, fc_n_units)	*Epoch*	*Learning rate*
A	(1, 64, 5) (3, 128, 5)	(2, 2) (4, 2)	(5, 512) (6, 1024) (7, 2)	999	0.00001
B	(1, 64, 5) (3, 128, 5) (5, 256, 5) (7, 512, 5)	(2, 2) (4, 2) (6, 2) (8, 2)	(9, 512) (10, 1024) (11, 2)	999	0.00001
C	(1, 64, 5) (3, 128, 5)	(2, 2) (4, 2)	(5, 512) (6, 1024) (7, 2)	1999	0.00001
D	(1, 64, 5) (3, 128, 5) (5, 256, 5) (7, 512, 5)	(2, 2) (4, 2) (6, 2) (8, 2)	(9, 512) (10, 1024) (11, 2)	1999	0.00001
E	(1, 64, 5) (3, 128, 5)	(2, 2) (4, 2)	(5, 512) (6, 1024) (7, 2)	999	0.0000001
F	(1, 64, 5) (3, 128, 5) (5, 256, 5) (7, 512, 5)	(2, 2) (4, 2) (6, 2) (8, 2)	(9, 512) (10, 1024) (11, 2)	999	0.0000001
G	(1, 64, 5) (3, 128, 5)	(2, 2) (4, 2)	(5, 512) (6, 1024) (7, 2)	1999	0.0000001
H	(1, 64, 5) (3, 128, 5) (5, 256, 5) (7, 512, 5)	(2, 2) (4, 2) (6, 2) (8, 2)	(9, 512) (10, 1024) (11, 2)	1999	0.0000001

https://doi.org/10.1051/matecconf/201820101010

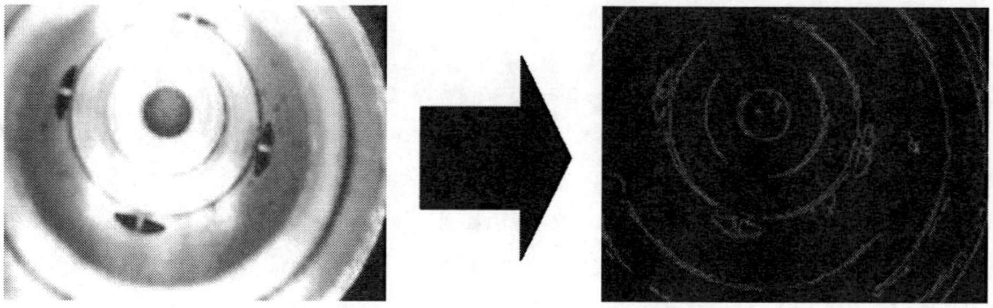

Figure 6. The result of pre-processing image

Table 2. The eight results of accuracy with or without image pre-processing

Nets Type	Accuracy (%)	Accuracy with Image Pre-Processing (%)
A	75	73
B	74	74
C	83	74
D	85	71
E	82	N/A
F	83	N/A
G	90	N/A
H	90	N/A

The best configuration from type A ~ H will be chosen for GAN-Based samples maker for defect detection system. The process of GAN-Based samples maker is shown as Figure 7. Each subgraph shows the sample generated by the initial random vector every 10000 iterations of the generative network. In this study, 30 new samples are generated by using GAN. Therefore, the samples of 15 normal surface images and 15 surface defects images are the new training datasets for CNN.

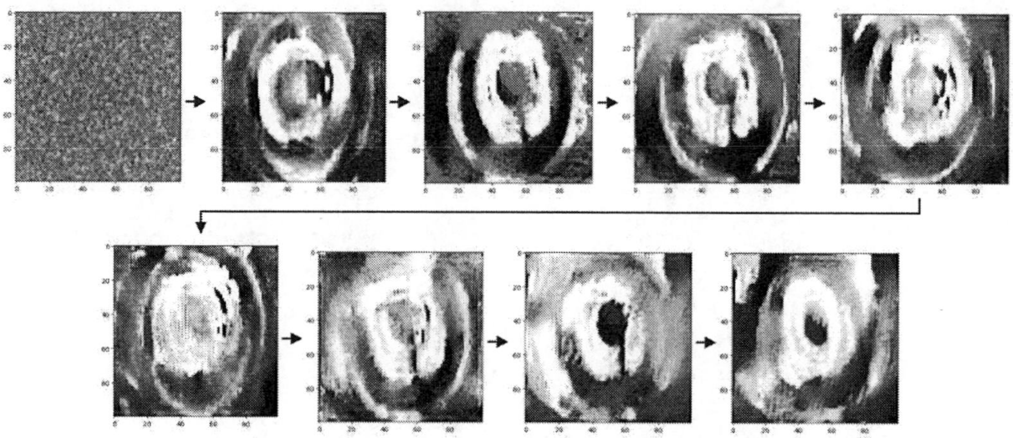

Figure 7. The process of GAN-Based samples maker

In this study, several experiments are conducted to verify the feasibility of data augmentation by using the generative adversarial networks. Firstly, existing samples are used to train and adjust the CNN. The best configuration from Type A ~ H will be chosen for GAN-Based samples maker for defect detection system. The experimental results with data augmentation by GAN-Based samples maker for defect detection system shown in Table 3.

Table 3. The results of accuracy with or without data augmentation by GAN-Based samples maker

Data augmentation (%)	Before (Non-GAN) (%)	After (GAN-Based) (%)
3%	90%	91%
7%	90%	93%
10%	90%	94%

4. Discussion

By the experimental results in Table 2 and Table 3, we can find the following：

(1) The maximum accuracy of the defect detection is only 74%, no matter with the preprocessing of Canny edge detection images or not. It means that the recognition accuracy cannot be obviously improved with or without the preprocessing of Canny edge detection images.

(2) As the number of convolution layers and pooling layers increase, the recognition accuracy of defect detection only increases by up to 2% for type C and type D. As the number of convolution layers and pooling layers increases, the recognition accuracy of defect detection drops from 75% to 74% for type A and type B. It means that the recognition accuracy cannot be obviously improved with or without increasing the number of convolution layers and pooling layers.

(3) As the Epoch increases from 999 to 1999 and the learning rate decreases from 0.00001 to 0.0000001, the recognition accuracy of defect detection is improved 5%~16%. It means that the recognition accuracy can be obviously improved by increasing the Epoch and decreasing the learning rate.

(4) The experimental results of data augmentation by GAN-Based samples maker are shown in Table 3. The recognition accuracy of defect detection increases from 90% to 94% for 10% data augmentation by GAN-Based samples maker. So We can find that the recognition accuracy can be obviously improved as increasing data augmentation by GAN-Based samples maker.

5. Conclusions

In industries, collecting training dataset is usually costly and related methods are highly dataset-dependent. So most companies cannot provide Big-data to be analyzed or applied. By the experimental results, the recognition accuracy can be obviously improved as increasing data augmentation by GAN-Based samples maker. It means it will be a good solution to solve the problem of small dataset in the future. To sum up, the development of a machine learning based intelligent defect detection system will contribute to technological innovation, industry, national development and other applications. (1) The use of intelligent machine learning technology will make the industry 4.0 technology more sophisticated. (2) It will make the development of equipment industry be better by the machine learning applications. (3) It will increase the economics and productivity of countries for the aging of the population by machine learning.

Acknowledgments: We would like to thank the Ministry of Science and Technology of the Republic of China (Taiwan) for the financial support of this research under contract numbers MOST 106-2622-E-269-009-CC3.

References

1. Y. Shimizu, Y. Matsuno, Y. Ohba and W. Gao, "Micro thermal sensor for nanometric surface defect inspection," 2016 IEEE 16th International Conference on Nanotechnology (IEEE-NANO), Sendai, 2016, pp. 978-979. DOI: 10.1109/NANO.2016.7751308
2. R. Ren; T. Hung; K. C. Tan, "A Generic Deep-Learning-Based Approach for Automated Surface Inspection," in IEEE Transactions on Cybernetics , vol.PP, no.99, pp.1-12. DOI: 10.1109/TCYB.2017.2668395
3. Y. C. Samarawickrama and C. D. Wickramasinghe, "Matlab based automated surface defect detection system for ceremic tiles using image processing," 2017 6th National Conference on Technology and Management (NCTM), Malabe, 2017, pp. 34-39. DOI: 10.1109/NCTM.2017.7872824
4. S. Faghih-Roohi, S. Hajizadeh, A. Núñez, R. Babuska and B. De Schutter, "Deep convolutional neural networks for detection of rail surface defects," 2016 International Joint Conference on Neural Networks (IJCNN), Vancouver, BC, 2016, pp. 2584-2589. DOI: 10.1109/IJCNN.2016.7727522
5. Z. N. Ke, Q. J. Zhao, C. H. Huang, P. Ai and J. G. Yi, "Detection of wood surface defects based on particle swarm-genetic hybrid algorithm," 2016 International Conference on Audio, Language and Image Processing (ICALIP), Shanghai, 2016, pp. 375-379. DOI: 10.1109/ICALIP.2016.7846635
6. A. Laucka, D. Andriukaitis, V. Markevicius and M. Zilys, "Research of the Defects in PET preform," 2016 21st International Conference on Methods and Models in Automation and Robotics (MMAR), Miedzyzdroje, 2016, pp. 1273-1279. DOI: 10.1109/MMAR.2016.7575322
7. A. Laucka, D. Andriukaitis, A. Valinevicius and D. Navikas, "Computer vision system for defects detection in PET preform," 2016 21st International Conference on Methods and Models in Automation and Robotics (MMAR), Miedzyzdroje, 2016, pp. 1280-1285. DOI: 10.1109/MMAR.2016.7575323
8. M. Win, A. R. Bushroa, M. A. Hassan, N. M. Hilman and A. Ide-Ektessabi, "A Contrast Adjustment Thresholding Method for Surface Defect Detection Based on Mesoscopy," in IEEE Transactions on Industrial Informatics, vol. 11, no. 3, pp. 642-649, June 2015. DOI: 10.1109/TII.2015.2417676
9. M. W. Ashour, F. Khalid, A. A. Halin and L. N. Abdullah, "Machining process classification using PCA reduced histogram features and the Support Vector Machine," 2015 IEEE International Conference on Signal and Image Processing Applications (ICSIPA), Kuala Lumpur, 2015, pp. 414-418. DOI : 10.1109/ICSIPA.2015.7412226
10. C. Huang, D. Chen and X. Tang, "Implementation of Workpiece Recognition and Location Based on Opencv," 2015 8th International Symposium on Computational Intelligence and Design (ISCID), Hangzhou, 2015, pp. 228-232. DOI: 10.1109/ISCID.2015.143

Study of HCI Reliability for PLDMOS

Ravi Deivasigamani[1], *Gene* Sheu[1], *Aanand*[1], *Shao* Wei Lu[2], *Syed* Sarwar Imam[1], *Chiu-Chung* Lai[2], *Shao-Ming* Yang[1,3*]

[1]Department of Computer Science and Information Engineering, Asia University, 500, Lioufeng Rd., Taichung 41354, Taiwan.
[2]School of Software and Microelectronics, Peking University, Beijing, China.
[3]Department of Medical Research, China Medical University Hospital, China Medical University, Taichung, Taiwan.

Abstract. In this paper, we demonstrate electrical degradation due to hot carrier injection (HCI) stress for PLDMOS device. The lower gate current and the IDsat degradation at low gate voltage (VGS) and high drain voltage (VDS) is investigated. Hot Electrons, generated by impact ionization during stress, are injected into the gate oxide, creating negative fixed oxide charges and interface-states above the accumulation region and the channel. Increase of the drain-source current is induced by the negative fixed oxide charges. The physical model of the degradation has been proven combining experimental data and TCAD simulations.

1 Introduction

Most of the studies about hot-carrier effects concentrated on n-MOSFETs rather than p-MOSFETs simply because the hot-carrier induced problems are more serious in n-MOSFETs due to longer mean free path, hence higher energy of electrons. For example, peak substrate current in n-MOSFETs is about 3 to 4 orders larger than in P-MOSFETs. In near-micrometre CMOS integrated circuits, N-MOSFETs are known to fail earlier than P-MOSFETs. However, the empirical relationship between P-MOSFET DC lifetime and lifetime monitor is usually obtained over narrow V, ranges, for example V, near the peak of ISuB or IG, and may not be suitable for lifetime modeling for arbitrary stressing waveforms. A general expression which can well describe device degradation over a wide range of bias is thus required. In the following, hot-carrier-induced degradation and gate current model in SC p-MOSFETs are presented. The lifetime of a SC p-MOSFET is found to correlate with I, over a wide range of V. Using this correlation and a gate current model based on the lucky electron approach, the lifetime of a SC p-MOSFET under pulse stress can be estimated [4].

However, the use of power semiconductor devices is exponentially growing, because increased efficiency is required in energy conversion process and better circuit solution is continuously proposed. One of the strongest motivations for research in this field is the largest market segment of automotive body control power. In some cases, P-channel power devices can be a better option than the n-channel devices, when the lower performance of the PLDMOS (i.e. Lower switching speed and higher RON) can be less important than the possibility of significant circuit simplification. The new rising market of LED driver for automotive interior and exterior lights, LED daytime running lights and LED front lights is a typical example. One of the key devices in this product is the PLDMOS, which is, for example used in the low-dropout (LDO) regulator of the converter. A low-dropout or LDO regulator is a DC linear voltage regulator, which can operate with a very small input–output differential voltage. The substitution of the bipolar device with the PLDMOS transistor leads to several advantages such as a lower minimum operating voltage, higher efficiency operation and lower heat dissipation. In this case, the use of the n-channel lateral DMOS transistor would need some more circuitry and cannot be used in open loop conditions [2].

2 Experimental setup

The experimental setup was designed as flowchart in Fig.1 (b). Practically, the comparisons of the device degradation are performed by confrontment of the IV curve before and after stress time on the device structures. Thus, degradation trend for drain current saturation (IDsat) were calculated for different stress time until we will get 2% of IDsat degradation. Before that we have measured Vgmax from Ig-Vg curve at -40V of drain voltage and -5V of gate voltage. According to that we were selected V_{gmax} and the stress voltage -40V of V_{DD}. After stress, the drain current saturation calculated at 40V of drain and selected gate voltage (Vgmax from Ig-Vg curve).

Degradation, thermodynamic HCI and classical lucky electron models were invoked in the device simulation to

* Corresponding author: rickyyang121@asia.edu.tw

perform the interface trap generation due to HCI. A process of electrons tunnel through a barrier in the presence of a high electric field was taken into account by using Fowler-Nordheim model. While, the lucky-electron model provides an estimate of the probability that some carriers in silicon will be transmitted to the oxide by overcoming the local energy barrier at the Si-SiO_2 interface [5-7].

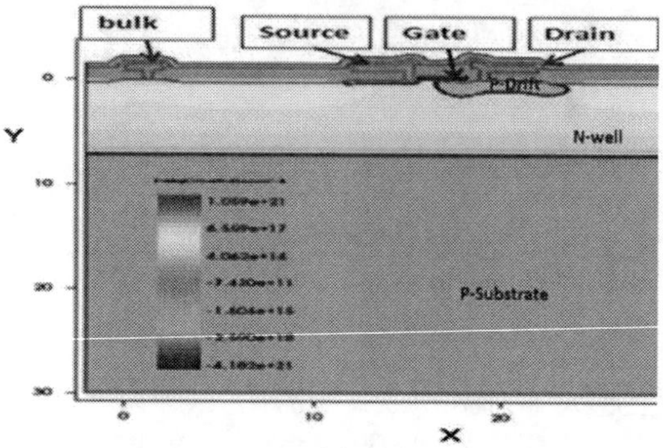

(a)

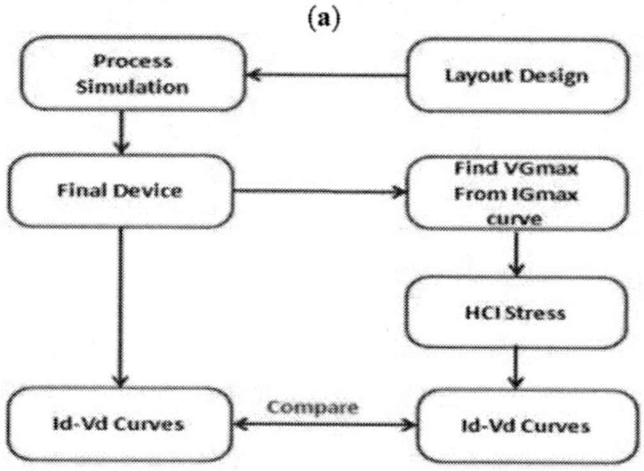

(b)

Fig. 1. (a) Simulated structure of new proposed PLDMOS structure (b) Flowchart of the experimental design.

3 Gate current model

Since, gate current is a better monitor than substrate current for device degradation in p-MOSFET's modelling of gate current is important. Unlike n-MOSFET's, p-MOSFET's exhibit the largest gate current when biased in the saturation region at low V. The gate current has a long mean free path. Also, the Si-SiO2 barrier height is lower for electrons and the vertical field at low VG favours electron injection [4].

4 Results and discussion

Simulations As we are shown in Fig 2, we have measured Vgmax from different devices and we have plotted Ig-Vg curves from different devices. The Vgmax was measured at V_{DD}=-40V and Vg=-5V. We have found lower Igmax for device4 as shown in Fig 2. This Igmax was better than other devices. From this Igmax curve, we have measured Vgmax. So, as we know HCI degradations is because of trapped charges into the oxide region of Si/SiO_2 interface and HCI degradation will be more with more traps that occurs in oxide regions. We perform HCI stress test for them until that device reaches 2% of IDsat the degradation and measured drain saturation current shift (ΔIDsat)at V_{DD}=-40V and selected gate voltage from gate current curve and we summarize all HCI results with different condition device performances. When we analyse the results, we can explain that the lower gate current device has very good HCI performance. We have proved our device lifetime, improved according to the gate current measurements. The comparison life time curves between device Life Time(Years) Curve Between Stress Time (Sec) and ID/ID (%) shown in Fig 3. It is possible for us to achieve this HCI performance because we put lots of effort to redesign the device so that impact-ionization hotspot should happen at a location away from the gate and below the surface so that the hot
carriers that generate and experience high lateral applied field should not reach or overcome the Si/Sio2 potential barrier and become trapped into gate-oxide region. So we kept this in mind and re-designed our device which helps to get better HCI performance and device can pass HCI life time reliability test.

The increasing rate of ΔID/ID with stress-time becomes small after extended stress. Extrapolating the short-term stress data to obtain device lifetimes can introduce large errors. To avoid this, we stress the devices long enough so that, ΔID/ID exceeds or nearly reaches the lifetime criteria. τ is defined as the time at which ΔID/ID reaches a certain percentage (2-4%). The devices were stressed with fixed VD, and varying VG. In both cases, the correlation can be expressed as $\tau \; \alpha \; IG^{-m}$ with m = 2.25 as shown in Fig 4.

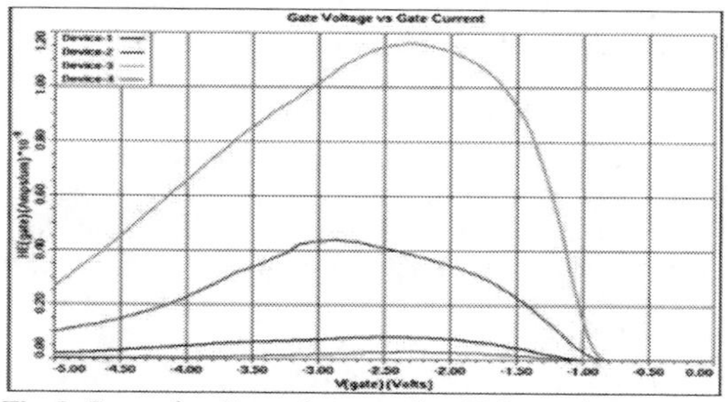

Fig. 2. Comparing Curves between Gate Voltage v/s Gate Current.

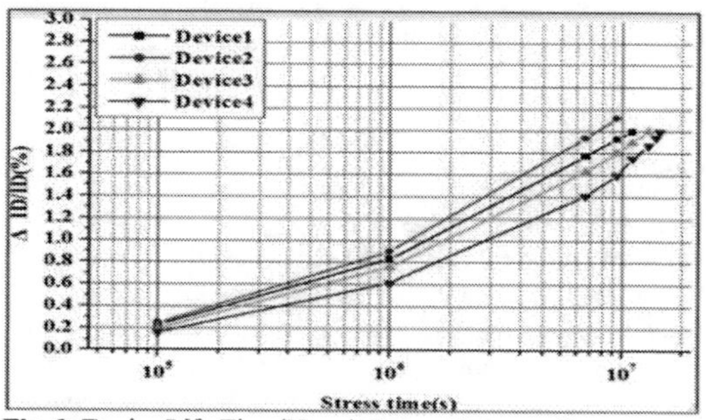

Fig. 3. Device Life Time(Years) Curves Between Stress Time(Sec) and ID/ID (%).

 https://doi.org/10.1051/matecconf/201820102001

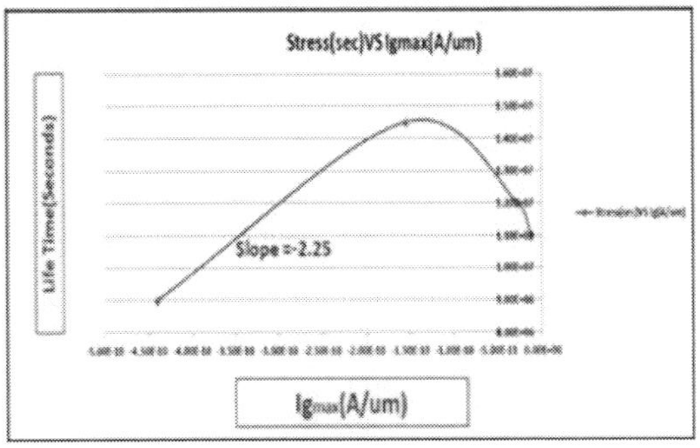

Fig. 4. Device Life Time(Years) Curves Between Stress Time(Sec) and Igmax

Table 2. Different Stress Time (Sec) and IDs at degradation shift (%)

	Device-1	Device-2	Device-3	Device-4
Stress Time (Sec)	ΔID/ID (%)	ΔID/ID (%)	ΔID/ID (%)	ΔID/ID (%)
1.00E+05	0.23	0.25	0.2	0.16
1.00E+06	0.83	0.90	0.76	0.614
6.93E+06	1.77	1.94	1.63	1.41
9.46E+06	1.93	2.12	1.80	1.60
1.10E+07	2		1.90	1.75
1.30E+07			2	1.87
1.40E+07				1.95
1.45E+07				2

It's clear from the table that the device with the lowest Ig current have the maximum life time. And as the Ig current increases the lifetime of the device degrades.

5 Conclusion

Some of the hot carriers generated in the bird's beak area are injected into the gate oxide and the others constitute the substrate current. The majority of hot carriers injected into the gate oxide is collected by the gate electrode and constitute the gate current. Both of the gate current and substrate current are a good monitor to predict device degradation. While gate current is a direct measurement of the injected carriers into the gate oxide, it is very sensitive to the trapping mechanism (during TCAD simulation) and is very low. In our present work, we measured gate current and it makes easier to measure. Although high- voltage LDMOSFETs have a large depletion area in the drift region (large part of the generation current by impact ionization in this region constitutes a gate current), gate current is an indirect way of measuring the hot carrier injection.

Acknowledgment: The authors would also like to thank National Center for High-performance computing, National Nano Device Laboratories, and the National Chip Implementation Center for supporting us.

References

1. P. Moens and G. Van den Bosch, *"Characterization of Total Safe Operating Area of Lateral DMOS Transistors"*, IEEE TED, pp. 340- 357 Vol. 6 (2006). Z. Li, Y. Chen, X. Li, T. I. Kamins, K. Nauka and R. S. Williams, Nano Lett. **4**, 245 (2004)
2. S. Aresu; R.P. Vollertsen; R. Rudolf; C. Schlünder; H. Reisinger; W. Gustin, *"Physical Understanding and Modelling of New Hot-Carrier Degradation on PLDMOS Transistor"*, Reliability Physics Symposium (IRPS), IEEE International, (2012)
3. T. -C. Ong; P. -K. Ko; C. Hu, *"Hot-Carrier Current Modeling and Device Degradation in Surface-Channel p-MOSFETs"*, IEEE Transactions on Electron Devices Year **37**, Issue: 7 Pages: 1658 – 1666 (1990)
4. T. -C. Ong; K. Seki; P. K. Ko; C. Hu, *"P-MOSFET Gate Current and Device Degradation"*, Reliability Physics Symposium, 27th Annual Proceedings., International, 178 – 182 (1989)
5. S. E. Rauch, III, and G. La Rosa, *"The Energy-Driven Paradigm of NMOSFET Hot-Carrier Effects,"* IEEE Transactions on Device and Materials Reliability, pp. 701-705, December (2005).
6. P.A. Cosmin, M. Badila, T. Dunca, *"Characterization of the Thin Oxides Degradation Through Fowler-Nordheim Current,"* International Semiconductor Conference **2,** (2003)
7. O. Penzin, A. Haggag, W. McMahon, E. Lyumkis, K. Hess, *"MOSFET Degradation Kinetics and Its Simulation,"* IEEE Transactions on Electron Devices, **50**, pp. 1445 - 1450, June (2003).
8. J. F. Chen; K.M. Wu; K.W. Lin; Y.K. Su; S. L. Hsu, *"Hot-Carrier Reliability in Submicrometric 40V LDMOS Transistors with Thick Gate Oxide"*, 2005 IEEE International Reliability Physics Symposium, Proceedings. 43rd Annual Pages: 560 – 564 (2005)

https://doi.org/10.1051/matecconf/201820102002

None Operational Amplifier (OPA) Based: Design of Analogous Bandgap Reference Voltage

Hao-Ping Chan and *Yu-Cherng* Hung*

Department of Electronic Engineering, National Chin-Yi University of Technology, Taiwan (ROC)

Abstract. By using 0.35-um CMOS process, this work achieves a design of analogous band-gap reference voltage circuit with low temperature coefficient. The proposed circuit operates at 3V and generates a reference current of 44 uA. The HSPICE simulation results show the temperature coefficient of this circuit is 23 ppm/°C at range of -10 °C to 100 °C, and the line regulation (the ratio of output current variation to supply voltage variation) is estimated as 1.95 uA/V from supply voltage variation of 3 V to 5 V. The experimental chip is fabricated and measured. The circuit provides adjustable capability for output voltage among temperature variation of -10 - 100 °C. The chip area is $534 \times 695\ \mathbf{um^2}$. In this new design, the operational amplifier is not necessary. The chip design effort can be great reduced.

1 Introduction

Because of the convenience and portability, more portable consumer electronic devices are frequently used today. There are always tens to hundreds of chips co-operation within these consumer electronic devices. In order to further shrink device size and toward lightweight continuously, more electronic elements are expected to be integrated into a chip to realize the system almost functions. As a result, the function of chip trends towards from single specific to system multiple functions. In general, a system-embedded-on-a-chip (SoC) has multiple voltage sources or voltage references within chip design. The capability of voltage reference is with low output voltage/current variation in spite of variety of temperature, supply voltage, and noise interfered. Therefore, the voltage reference circuit currently has been widely used in analog circuit, digital circuit and mixed-signal circuit, such as operational amplifiers, analog-to-digital converters (ADC), digital-to-analog converters (DAC), phase locked loop (PLL) circuits and power regulators. In open literature, many circuit schemes for voltage reference and its improved versions have been proposed [1-8] in recent years. The performance of voltage reference will dominate the system function. The design of internal voltage reference circuit becomes more important especially for in SoC era. Currently, the most popular circuit scheme is bandgap voltage reference.

The basic circuit for bandgap voltage reference is shown in Fig. 1. The bootstrapping circuit makes the potential voltage of nodes 'a' and node 'b' as equal as possible, to reduce the effects of channel length modulation and supply voltage variation. It uses emitter-base voltage difference between two bipolar junction transistors (BJTs) to generate a positive temperature coefficient (PTC) current. In conventional CMOS technologies, these BJTs are parasitic transistors. After that, it uses current mirror architecture (M3/M4/M5) to copy the PTC current to the output resistor R_L. The voltage drop V_{RL} is added to V_{EB} of BJT with negative temperature coefficient to generate a stable reference voltage output. Finally, the objective of the basic circuit is to form a precise and stable voltage reference in spite of temperature variations and supply voltage fluctuations. The output of bandgap reference circuit shown in Fig. 1 is given as

$$V_{ref} = V_{EB} + \Delta V_{EB}\left(\frac{R_L}{R_1}\right). \quad (1)$$

V_{EB} is with negative temperature coefficient, and ΔV_{EB} related to thermal voltage Vt (that is, kT/q) is with positive temperature coefficient. The temperature effects of V_{EB} and ΔV_{EB} are about -2.5 mV and +0.085 mV per centigrade degree respectively. According to the proper ratio settings of R_L, R_1, and the area matching in BJTs, temperature effect of output voltage can be canceled drift out each other. Therefore, output V_{ref} in theoretically can be obtained in independent of temperature.

However, the voltage on nodes 'a' and 'b' in Fig. 1 is not identical potential due to the channel length modulation and body effects. The temperature coefficient of basic scheme is a little bit large. Another conventional bandgap reference voltage circuit is shown in Fig.2. An operational amplifier is embedded in the circuit to provide nearly equal voltage between two input nodes. The output voltage of bandgap reference circuit is also given as Eq. 1. In despite of Figs. 1 and 2, the ratio of R_L and R_1 is always to set a proper value to keep the output voltage temperature insensitivity.

* Corresponding author: ychung@ncut.edu.tw

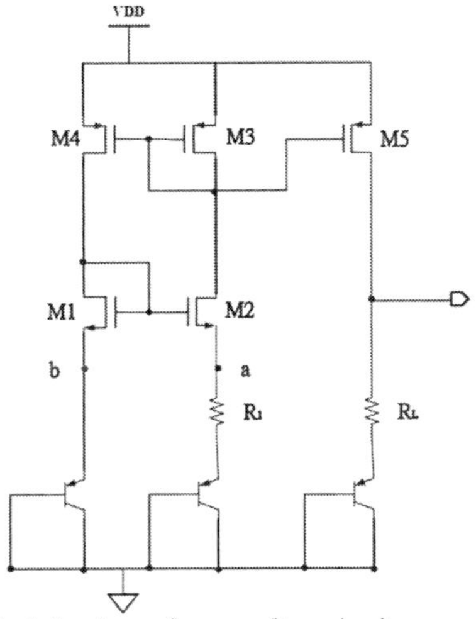

Fig. 1. Basic bandgap reference voltage circuit.

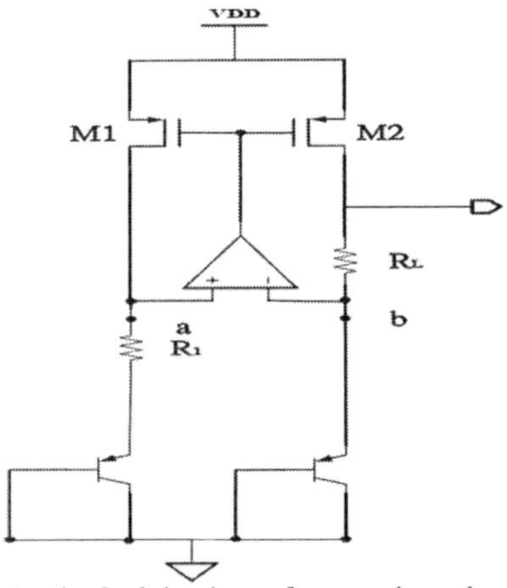

Fig. 2. Another basic bandgap reference voltage circuit (with opa)

Based on Fig. 2 scheme, an improved circuit for output voltage adjustable is achieved as Fig. 3 [1]. The circuit makes the output reference voltage can be altered by using various resistors ratios. In contrasting to Fig. 2, an additional operational amplifier and current mirror are extra used in Fig. 3. Due to high-gain operational amplifier, voltage on nodes 'b' and 'c' are equal. The current of M3 is V_{EB}/R_2 with negative temperature coefficient. By M3/M4 current mirror, the current of M4 is $(V_{EB}/R_2)(W/L)_{M4}/(W/L)_{M3}$. After M4/M5 current summation, the voltage of the output resistor R_L can be derived as

$$V_{ref} = R_L\left(\frac{V_{EB}}{R_2}\frac{(W/L)_{M4}}{(W/L)_{M3}} + \frac{\Delta V_{EB}}{R_1}\frac{(W/L)_{M5}}{(W/L)_{M2}}\right). \quad (2)$$

The desired output voltage Vref can be obtained by settings of various resistances and aspect ratio of transistors. However, two operational amplifiers are needed in this design. In general, the design of operational amplifier with high performance in chip realization is difficult by using conventional process.

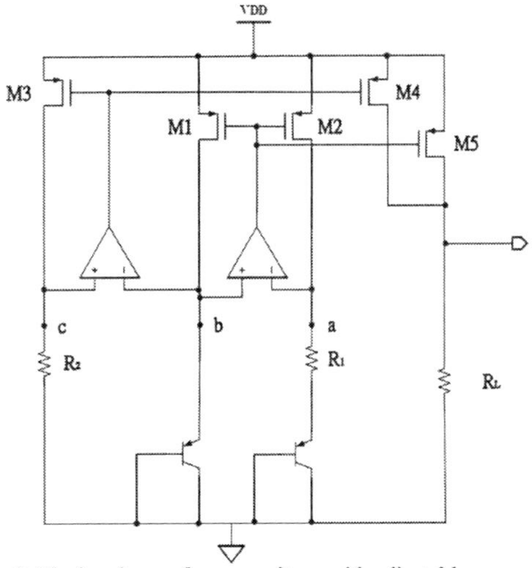

Fig. 3. The bandgap reference voltage with adjustable capability [1].

2 Circuit Design

In consideration of the following two issues: first, the output voltage of conventional band-gap reference circuit is always limited to around 1.25 V, due to the constant ratio of negative temperature coefficient of $\mathbf{V_{EB}}$ and positive temperature coefficient of $\mathbf{\Delta V_{EB}}$. The second issue, a high performance operational amplifier is not easily realized in chip. In addition, the overall circuit complexity and power consumption are resulted in increased due to these more electronic elements. In this study, bandgap reference voltage circuit without needing operational amplifier is redesigned and inspected. The new schematic diagram of the circuit is shown in Fig. 4.

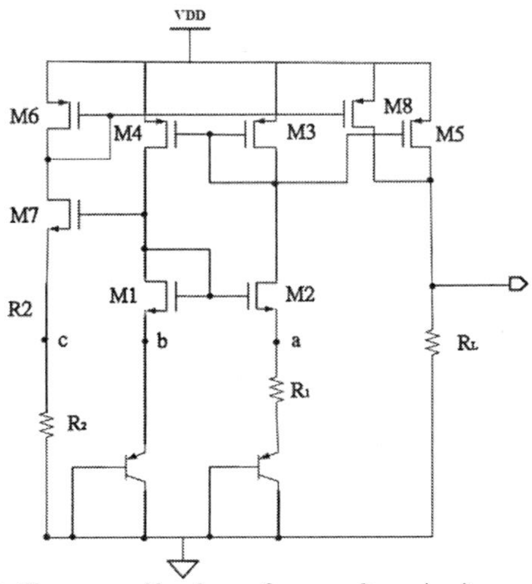

Fig. 4. The proposed bandgap reference voltage circuit without needing of operational amplifier.

 https://doi.org/10.1051/matecconf/201820102002

The current mirror function is achieved by M1/M4/M6/M7 to make nodes 'b' and 'c' voltage as equipotential as possible. Due to the equipotential, the current flows through resistor R_2, $I_{R2}=V_{EB}/R_2$, which is a negative temperature coefficient current. The current mirror of M6 and M8 is used to copy the current and addition of the positive temperature coefficient current I_{M5}. Finally, the output current with nearly zero temperature coefficient will be expected to arrive. The expression of the bandgap reference voltage is given as

$$V_{ref} = R_L\left(\frac{V_{EB}}{R_2}\frac{(W/L)_{M8}}{(W/L)_{M6}} + \frac{\Delta V_{EB}}{R_1}\frac{(W/L)_{M5}}{(W/L)_{M3}}\right). \quad (3)$$

A start-up circuit is needed to avoid a zero output current (another stable bias point) held in circuit initial phase. The whole circuit including start-up circuit is shown in Fig. 5. Transistors M9-M11 try to achieve a none zero current I_D in transistors M1 and M2 when the circuit is initially powered up.

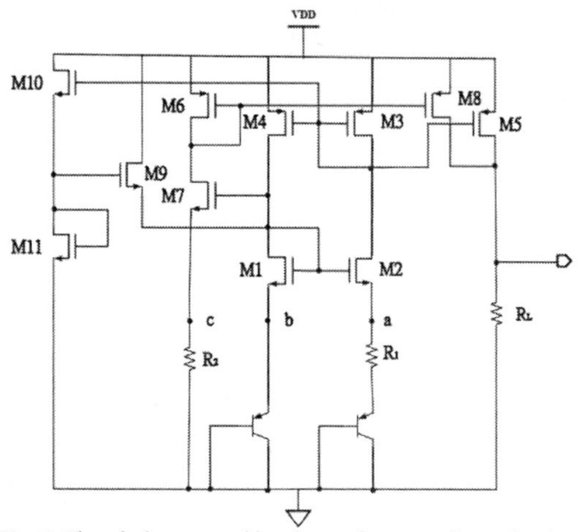

Fig. 5. The whole proposed bandgap reference voltage circuit.

3 Simulation and Chip Measured Results

Based on TSMC 0.35-μm CMOS process, the whole circuit shown in Fig. 5 is simulated by using HSPICE simulation program. HSPICE is a very popular circuit simulator in chip design, and nearly it is a de facto standard to verify circuit function. Figures 6 to 13 show the simulation results. Figure 6 shows the line regulation of output current when supply voltage varies from 3 V to 5 V. In Fig. 6, the output current of the circuit is 44.8 μA at 3-V supply voltage and 48.7 μA at 5 V. The line regulation for output current is estimated as 1.95 μA/V.

Another important factor for bandgap reference: temperature coefficient will be inspected. When the loading is altered and varied, the circuit is still function works within reasonable low temperature coefficients. We use various loading resistances of 1 Ω, 10 Ω, 100 Ω,1 kΩ, 10 kΩ, 20 kΩ and 30 kΩ to inspect the output voltage variation when temperature is varied from −10 ℃ to 100 ℃. Under R_L loading of 1-Ω, Fig. 7 shows the output voltage variation in temperature of −10 ℃ to 100 ℃. The maximum output reference voltage is 44.841 μV and the minimum output reference voltage is 44.728 μV. The temperature coefficient (TC) of the circuit for output voltage is evaluated as 23 ppm/℃.

In R_L loading of 10-Ω, Fig. 8 shows the maximum output reference voltage 448.411 μV and minimum reference voltage 447.276 μV. The TC also keeps 23 ppm/℃. Figs. 9-13 show the TC variations for loading resistances in 100 Ω, 1 kΩ, 10 kΩ, 20 kΩ and 30 kΩ respectively. In Fig. 9, the maximum reference voltage is 4.484 mV and the minimum reference voltage is 4.473 mV. In Fig. 10, the maximum reference voltage is 44.827 mV and the minimum reference voltage is 44.714 mV. In Fig. 11, the maximum reference voltage is 446.957 mV and the minimum reference voltage is 445.850 mV. In Fig. 12, the maximum reference voltage is 892.618 mV and the minimum reference voltage is 890.172 mV. In Fig. 13, the maximum reference voltage is 1.33V and the minimum reference voltage is 1.3266V. Obviously, Figs.7-13 shows the TC of the voltage reference almost keeps on 23 ppm/℃ in range of loading resistance of 1 Ω to 30 kΩ. Finally, according to these data, Fig. 14 shows the corresponding TC value.

The layout diagram and micro-photo of proposed circuit is shown in the top part and bottom part of Fig. 15 respectively, and the chip area is 534.55 × 694.85 $\mathbf{um^2}$. After layout phase, the parasitic effects are also extracted. The post-layout simulation in loading R_L of 1-Ω is shown in Fig. 16. Since the effects of parasitic resistance and capacitance, the TC of the reference voltage is raised from 23 to 26 ppm/℃. The chip fabrication is achieved already. The micro-photo of the chip is shown in right part of Fig. 15. When under temperature 25 ℃ and loading R_L 27 kΩ, the output of the voltage reference is 1.07 V (39.629 uA × 27 k) for 3-V supply voltage and 1.12 V (41.48 uA × 27 k) for 5-V supply voltage. The digital oscilloscope (TBS1052B-EDU) by Tektronix is used to measure the experimental chip for output voltage. Figures 17 (a) and (b) show the measured results for 3-V and 5-V supply voltage respectively. In addition, when temperature on the surface of the chip is risen to 100 ℃, the variation of output voltage is not revealed by using the digital oscilloscope due to 3% measurement accuracy of this instrument.

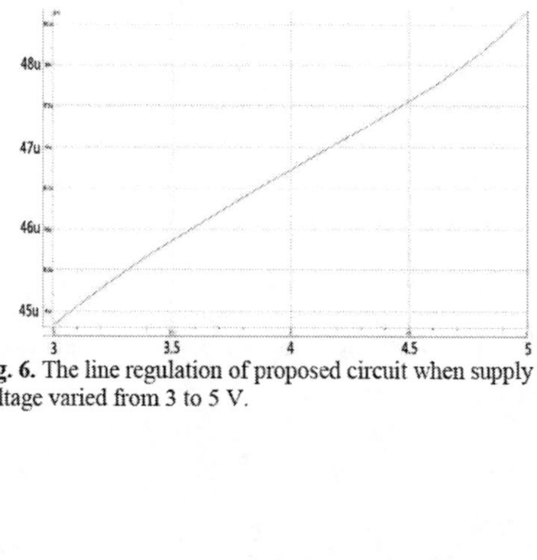

Fig. 6. The line regulation of proposed circuit when supply voltage varied from 3 to 5 V.

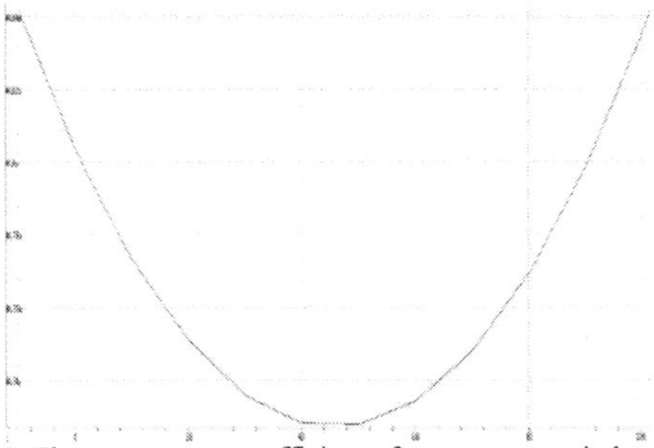

Fig. 7. The temperature coefficient of output current in loading resistance of 1 Ω.

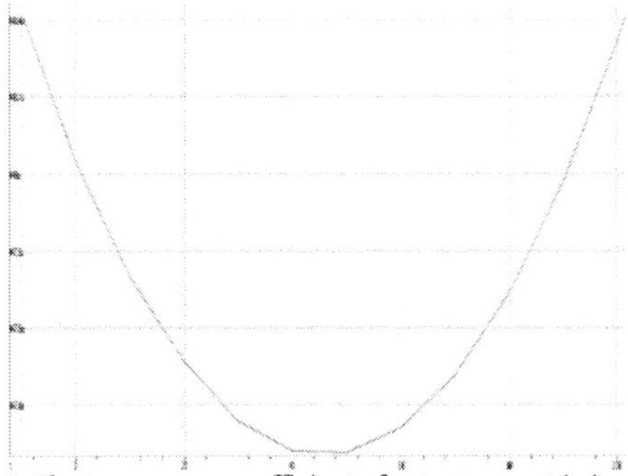

Fig. 8. The temperature coefficient of output current in loading resistance of 10 Ω.

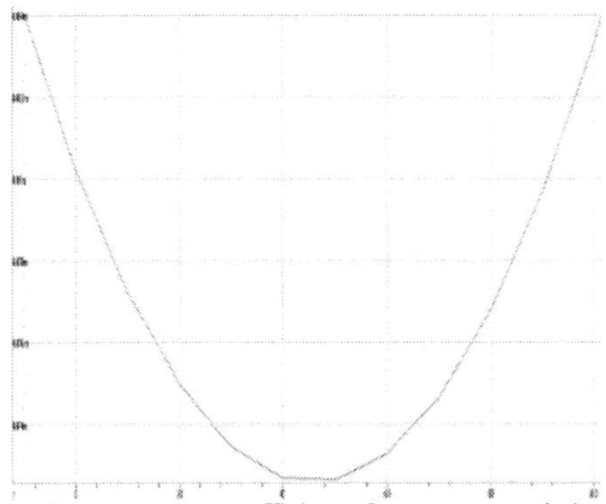

Fig. 9. The temperature coefficient of output current in loading resistance of 100 Ω.

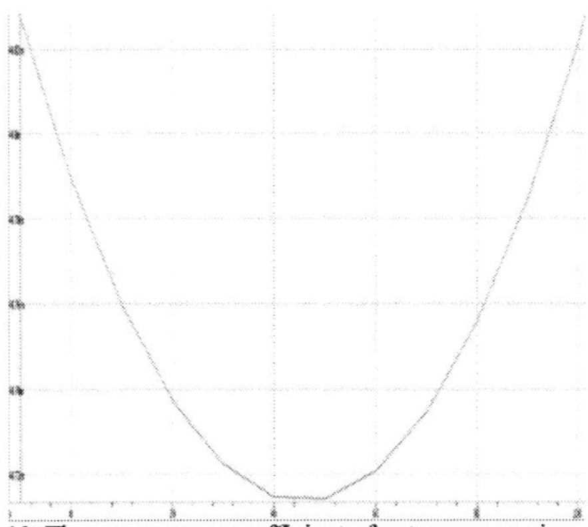

Fig. 10. The temperature coefficient of output current in loading resistance of 1 kΩ.

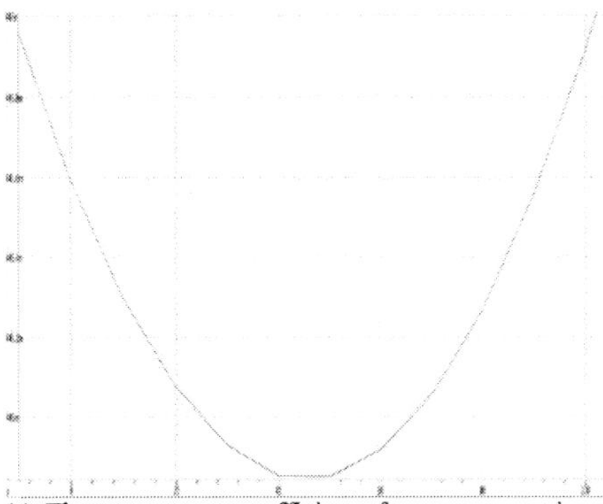

Fig. 11. The temperature coefficient of output current in loading resistance of 10 kΩ.

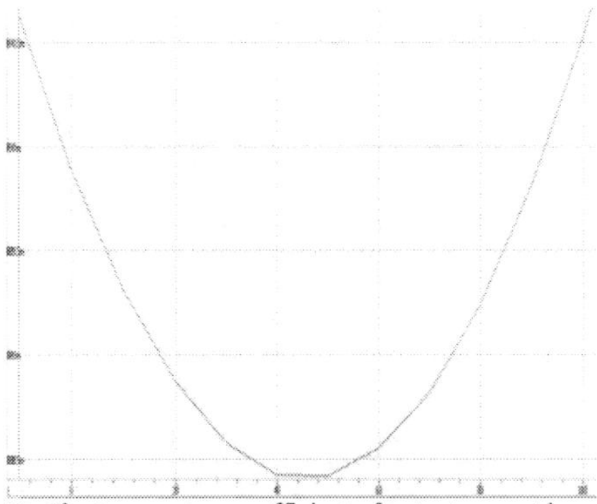

Fig. 12. The temperature coefficient of output current in loading resistance of 20 kΩ.

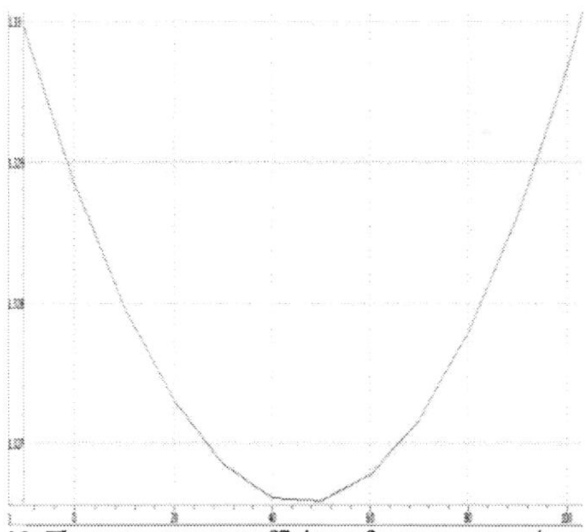

Fig. 13. The temperature coefficient of output current in loading resistance of 30 kΩ.

https://doi.org/10.1051/matecconf/201820102002

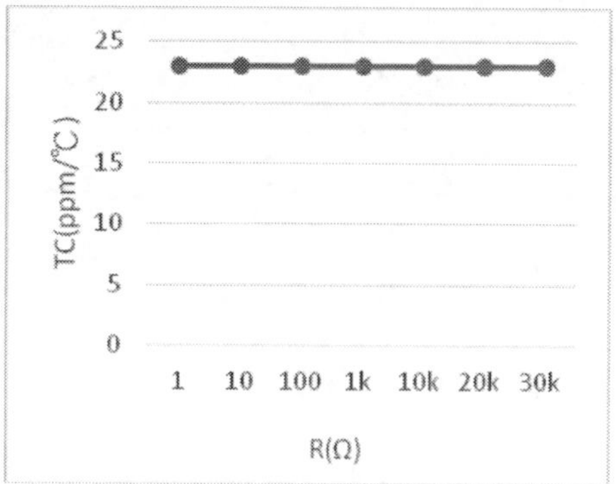

Fig. 14. The corresponding TC value under various resistance loadings.

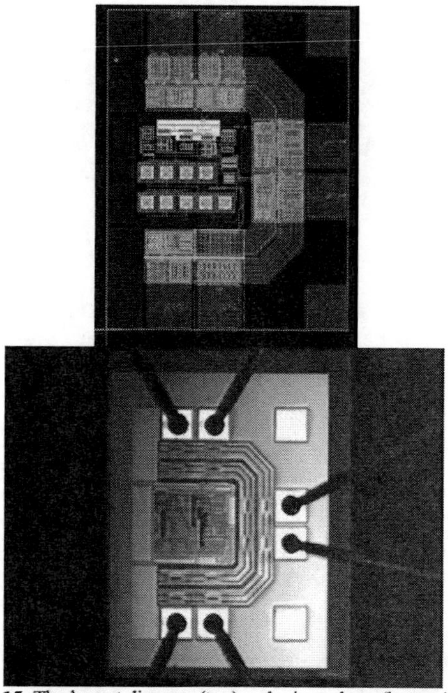

Fig. 15. The layout diagram (top) and micro photo (bottom) of the resembled bandgap reference circuit

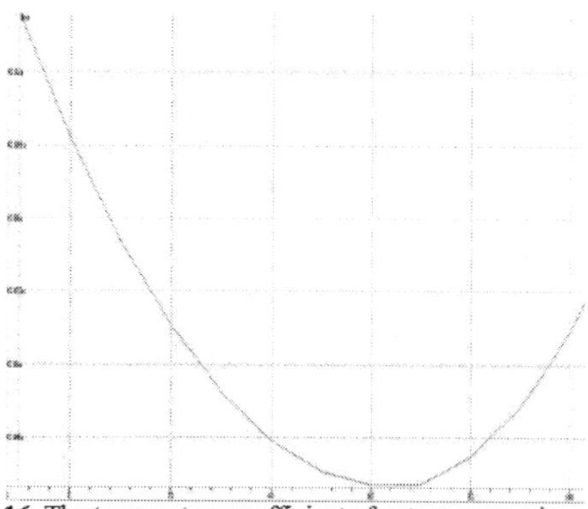

Fig. 16. The temperature coefficient of output current in loading resistance of 1 Ω (by post-layout simulation).

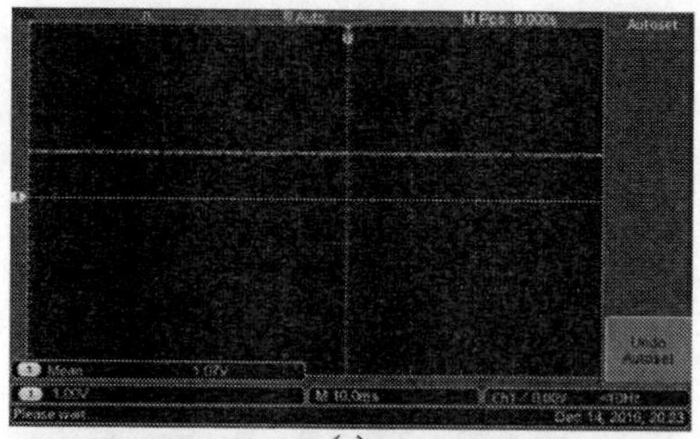

(a)

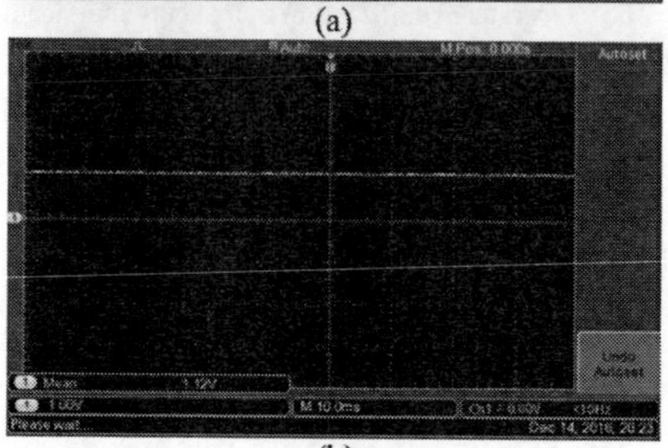

(b)

Fig. 17. The output voltage of the experimental chip for (a) 3-V and (b) 5-V supply voltage respectively.

The characteristics of the proposed circuit summarize and list in Table 1. The characteristics are also compared with reference [1]. The proposed has advantages of low complexity, less chip area, and wide range of output voltage.

Table 1. The characteristics summary and comparison

Characteristics	[1]	This work
Process	CMOS 0.35 μm	CMOS 0.35 μm
Operational Amplifier Required	Need Two OPAs	None
Power supply (V)	0.5	3
Temperature coefficient (ppm/℃)	13	26 (simulation)
Temperature range (℃)	-25 - 125	-10 - 100
No. of Transistor	23	11 MOS + 2 BJT
Circuit Complexity	High	Low

4 Conclusions

In contrast to conventional bandgap reference, the ratio of R_L and R_1 is almost constant value to fully eliminate the temperature effect. The output level of the bandgap reference in conventional design is always constant. In this work, we try to generate the current with positive temperature coefficient and a counterpart current with negative temperature coefficient. The two current then are summed at output terminal to cancel the temperature effect of each other. In addition, the output level will be adjustable by altered the loading resistance.

In this design, the complicated design for OPAs can be neglected to reduce the overall circuit complexity. By simulation, the TC was inspected for the loading of 1 Ω, 10 Ω, 100 Ω, 1 kΩ, 10 kΩ, 20 kΩ, and 30 kΩ. The TC will be kept around 23 ppm/℃ when temperature is varied from −10 ℃ to 100 ℃. Although the TC is not superior to other designs have been published in open literature which range of 10-15 ppm/℃, the chip area and chip design effort are both great reduced.

Acknowledgments: This work was funding part supported by the Ministry of Science and Technology Project (MOST 105-2221-E-167-022), and EDA tools support, experimental CMOS processes and chip fabricated, from the National Chip Implementation Center (CIC) and Taiwan Semiconductor Manufactory Corp. (tsmc).

Author Contributions: H.-P. Chan and Y.-C. Hung conceived and designed this study after co-discussion; H.-P. Chan performed CAD tool simulations and the experiments chip measured; Y.-C. Hung analyzed the data and wrote/organized the paper.

References

1. J. Sheng, Z. Chen, and B. Shi, "A 1 V supply area effective CMOS bandgap reference," Proceedings of the 5th International Conference on ASIC, **1**, pp. 619-622. (2003)
2. J. Chen, and B. Shi, "1 V CMOS current reference with 50 ppm/°C temperature coefficient," Electronics Letters, **39**, no. 2, pp. 209-210. (2003)
3. H. Banba, H. Shiga, A. Umezawa, T. Tanzawa, S. Atsumi, and K. Sakui, "A CMOS bandgap reference circuit with sub-1-V operation," *IEEE Journal of Solid-State Circuits*, **34**, pp. 670-674. (1999)
4. H.-M. Chen, C.-L. Huang, R. C. Chang, "A new temperature-compensated CMOS bandgap reference circuit for portable applications," *IEEE International Symposium on Circuits and Systems*, pp. 21-24, Greece. (2006)
5. J. H. Li, X. B. Zhang, M. Y. Yu, and L. Han,"A 10 ppm/°C 1.8V piecewise curvature-corrected bandgap reference in 0.5um cmos," *IEEE Microelectronics & Electronics*, pp. 416-419. (2009)
6. M. D. Ker, and J. S. Chen, "New curvature-compensated technique for CMOS bandgap reference with sub-1-V operation," *IEEE Trans on Circuits and Systems* II, **53**, no. 8, pp. 667-671. (2006)
7. H. J. Oguey, D. Aebischer, "CMOS current reference without resistor", *IEEE Journal of Solid-State Circuits*, **32**, no.7, pp. 1132-1135. (1997)
8. C. Azcona, B. Calvo, S. Celma, N. Medrano, M. T. Sanz, "Precision CMOS current reference with process and temperature compensation," *IEEE International Symposium on Circuits and Systems*, pp. 910-913. (2014)
9. P. E. Allen,"CMOS analog circuit design", Oxford University Press, New York, 2002
10. B. Razavi, "Design of analog CMOS integrated circuit", McGRAW-HILL. (2001)

An Innovated 80V-100V High-Side Side-Isolated N-LDMOS Device

Shao Ming Yangi[1,3*], *Gene* Sheu[1], *Ting Yao* Chien[2], *Chieh Chih* Wu[2], *Tzu Chieh* Lee[2], *Ching Yuan* Wu[1], *Chiu Chung* Lai[2]

[1]Department of Computer Science and Information Engineering, Asia University, 500, Lioufeng Rd., Taichung 41354, Taiwan.
[2]School of Software and Microelectronics, Peking University, Beijing, China.
[3]Department of Medical Research, China Medical University Hospital, China Medical University, Taichung, Taiwan.

Abstract. We used TCAD Synopsys 3D tools and device simulators to propose an innovative device structure of 80V-100V high-side NLDMOS by using the silicon to silicon-di-oxide ratio with side trench. The high-side can also be developed by placing an NBL structure which can deliver a high as over 200V isolation voltage. The 3D structure can clear see the optimized linear p-top and n-drift region have better charge balance with linear doping profile to get the benchmark breakdown voltage (BVdss) of 80V with on-resistance (Ron) as low as 130 mΩ -mm^2 and 100V with on-resistance as low as 175 mΩ -mm^2.The linear p-type buried layer using high dosage and lower energy to achieve the better SOA and higher isolation voltage. Optimized linear p-top and PBL can improve Ron by 32.5% compare to other 100V high side device which have done from reference.

1 Introduction

For 50V-140V smart power device is highly demanded by auto and motor driver's industry. In order to get high performance for ESOA and TSOA [1], some study use expensive technology for process and complication of structure that increase cost, such as silicon-on-insulator (SOI), double epitaxial layer [2], use n-well and p-well together etc. Kirk effect show NPN of β issue that is serious for on-state I-V curve and affect ESOA performance [3].

Comparison to low-side, high-side need a best junction isolation breakdown and also sustain the lateral breakdown which use NBL (n+ buried layer) between the source and the substrate. In this work, we propose a new innovated [4] high-side side-isolated n-channel LDMOS 3D device on both front and back edges of the extended drift region with thickness epitaxial layer. A double-RESURF concept incorporates an additional layer (linear p-top layer) [5] inside the n-drift extended region to get the charge balance, the net doping will clear see the linear profile curve, it can improve on-state resistance and keep high breakdown, the good charge balance not only get lower Ron and high breakdown also reduce the device length to cost down.

To avoid the transistor beta, cause the Kirk effect, we use linear p-type buried layer (PBL) [6] on top of n-type layer (NBL) inside the epitaxy layer, the balance between PBL and NBL need to consider the isolation BV can't be destroy, so the linear PBL give the small transistor beta and also make the good profile curve to sustain the high isolation breakdown. The device is 3D simulation. Each region is optimized by several experiments. The process was optimized using a simulation written in TCAD Synopsys 3D tools to determine.

2 Device structure and conditions

This NLDMOS High Side device in this study is using 0.35μ m process with shallow N-epitaxial drift region, simulated with TCAD Synopsys tools and device simulators.

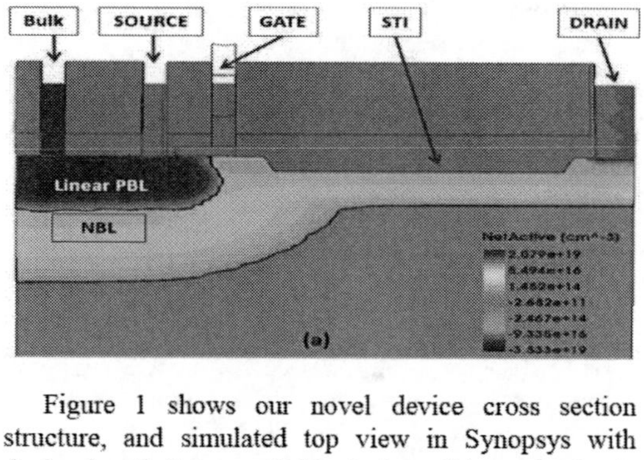

Figure 1 shows our novel device cross section structure, and simulated top view in Synopsys with device length 7.6μ m. Table 1 show this work simple condition. For this novel device, channel length of 0.35um is formed by p-body diffusion doped at 3× 10^{17}cm−3, drift region is doped at 4.65× 10^{16}cm−3, and source and drain contacts are all doped at 1×10^{19}cm^{-3}.

* Corresponding author: rickyyang121@asia.edu.tw

The gate oxide composed of SiO_2 is 120Å thick with a gate length of 0.75μ m.

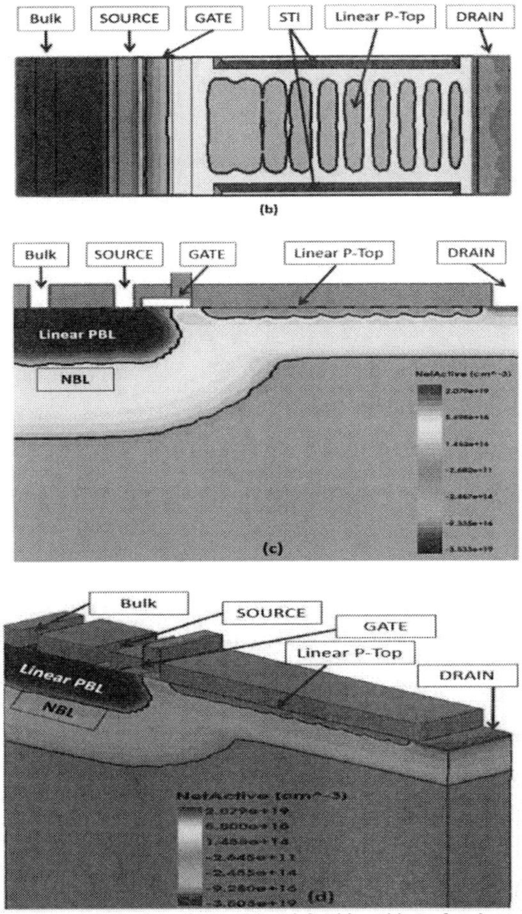

Fig. 1. Schematic of 3D (a) High-Side Side-Isolated N-LDMOS proposed structure; (b) top view; (c) front view; (d) rotation view.

Table 2. The parameters which using in the TCAD Synopsys 3D simulation.

Parameters	Unit	Values
Substrate	ohm-cm	100
N-epi	ohm-cm	0.145
Epi thickness	um	0.6
p-body	cm-2	$3e^{13}$~$3e^{14}$
n-type buried layer	cm-2	$5e^{12}$
n-type blanket	cm-2	$7e^{11}$~$9e^{11}$
Source contact	cm-3	$1e^{19}$
Drain contact	cm-3	$1e^{19}$

The key technique that implemented in this work are linear highly doped with lower energy of p-type buried layer and linear p-top region. The linear highly doped of p-type buried layer using high dosage and lower energy to get the charge balance in the deep n-type buried layer, the doping profile showed in figure 2, the linear curve can provide high isolation breakdown also make the better SOA.

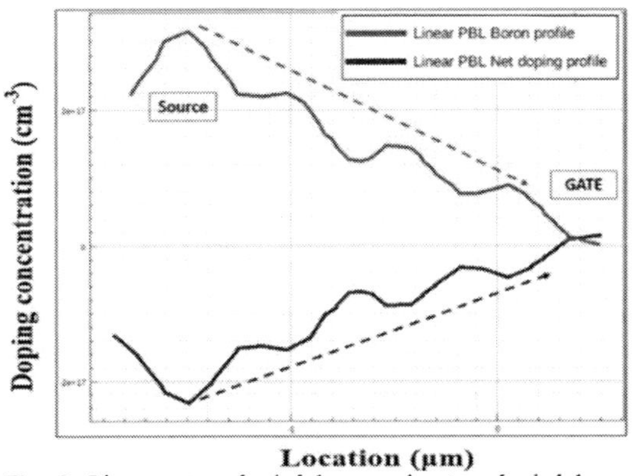

Fig. 2. Linear p-type buried layer and n-type buried layer doping profile, the curve present not only in boron profile also net doping profile have good linear trend.

The linear p-top made the good charge balance and present the linear doping profile in the n-drift region showed in figure 3, the linear trend curve redistribution the surface charge to make the high breakdown also improve R_{ON}.

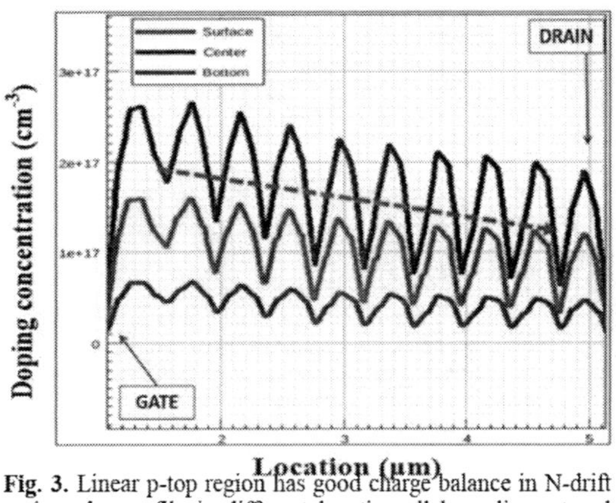

Fig. 3. Linear p-top region has good charge balance in N-drift region, the profile in different location all have linear trend curve.

3 Result and discussions

3.1 Device breakdown and SOA

From double RESURF concept, we put the p-top of shallow region in the n-drift region surface in our novel device. P-top region have a linear trend curve relationship with the n-drift region for charge balance. This linear trend curve not only get the high lateral breakdown but also have benchmark on-resistance.

For the High Side structure, we placed the N-buried layer under the source side. The shallow n-drift region cannot make a good sensitivity for P-buried layer and N-buried layer. In order to maintain a good isolation breakdown and reduce the beta of the parasitic NPN transistor, we innovate the linear p-buried layer. There by, the device has low leakage current and avoid on-state curves of Kirk effect. It not only can improvement the SOA curve but also have the good isolation breakdown as we can see in Figure 4.

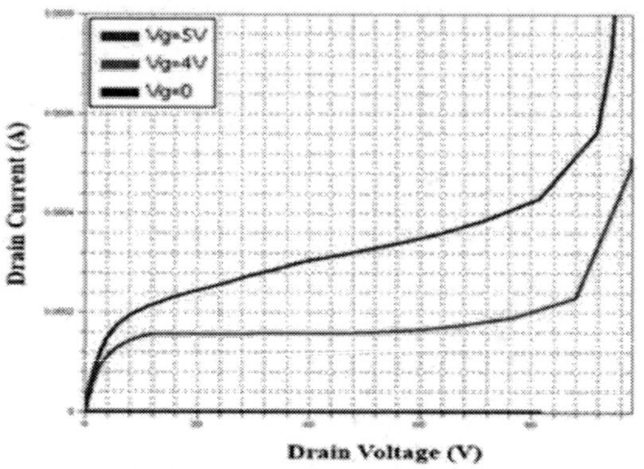

(a)

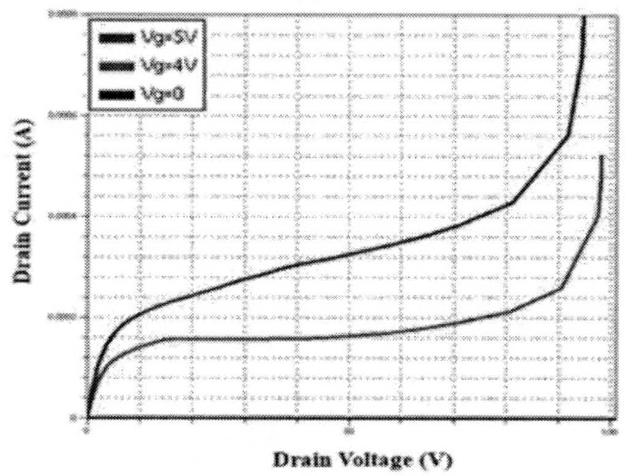

(b)

Fig. 5. Id vs. Vd characteristics of device for (a) 80V and (b) 100V High-Side Side-Isolated NLDMOS of off-state breakdown voltage at Vg=0 and on-state breakdown voltage at Vg=4V and Vg=5V in 3D simulation

3.2 Optimized characteristics of device

In order to consider the cost and charge balance, this paper of 80V-100V High-Side Side-Isolated NLDMOS device use the same size of device length, width and height. To analysis simulation of result, figure 6 shows that adjustment phosphorus dosage of n-blanket for our innovated 80V-100V High-Side Side-Isolated NLDMOS device design.

The curve of relationship can observe more phosphorus dosage of n-blanket that lateral breakdown voltage and Ron decreasing in direct proportion; otherwise increasing. In this work, for our 80V High-Side Side-Isolated NLDMOS use 9e11 of n-blanket dosage can get 81.8V of lateral breakdown voltage and Ron is 112 mΩ *mm^2. For 100V voltage use 7e11 can get 101V of lateral breakdown voltage and Ron is 118 m Ω *mm^2.

Figure 7 shows the result of breakdown voltage and on-resistance compare with some of the conventional high-side NLDMOS and this work has the best Ron for 80V-100V.

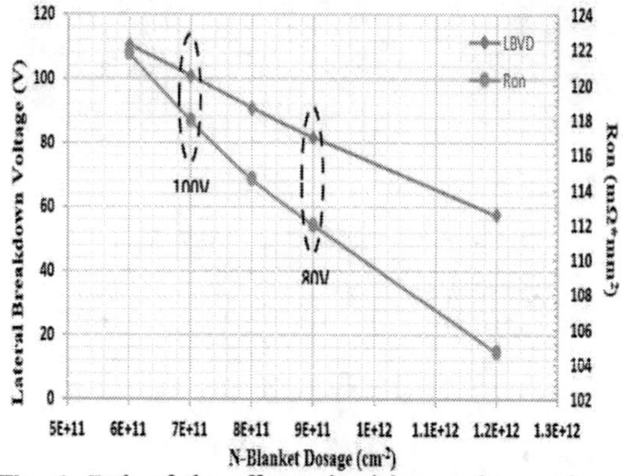

Fig. 6. Both of the off-state breakdown voltage and on-resistance curves as a different N-blanket dosage for innovation 80V-100V High-Side Side-Isolation NLDMOS device.

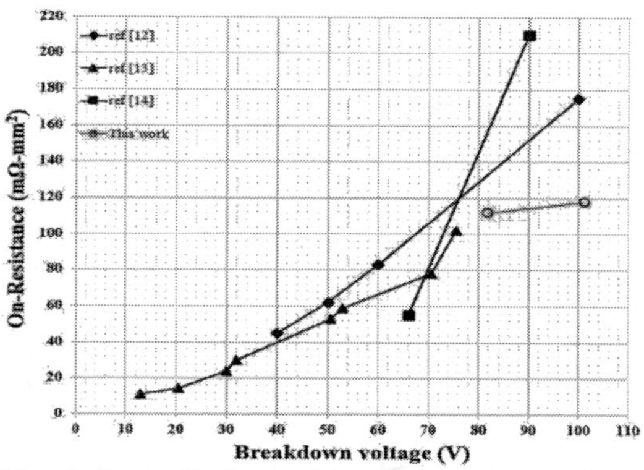

Fig. 7. Trade-off characteristics between the breakdown voltage and the specific on-resistance.

4 Conclusion

The 80V-100V High-Side NLDMOS with Sided-Isolated structure still produce high Ron due to the drift length limit. The newly invented device structure using short drift length with sided isolation can deliver high lateral breakdown and high isolation breakdown as well with low Ron. We implemented NBL (n+ buried layer) which to be located beneath the source region to prevent punch-through breakdown between the source and the p-substrate, also get high isolation breakdown without affecting other characteristics. In addition, the device with added linear p-type layer and linear p-top can reduce Kirk effect and get high breakdown with better low Ron.

Acknowledgment: The authors would also like to thank National Center for High-performance computing, National Nano Device Laboratories, and the National Chip Implementation Center for supporting us.

 https://doi.org/10.1051/matecconf/201820102003

References

1. P. Hower and S. Pendharkar, "Short and Long-Term Safe Operation Area Considerations in LDMOS Transistors", IEEE, (2005) pp 545-550.
2. P. Holland and P Igic, "A p+ /p-buffer/n-epi cmos compatible high-side RESURF LDMOS transistor for Power IC applications", Microelectronics Journal 38, 762-766 (2007)
3. R. Zhu, V. Parthasarathy, V. Khemka, A. Bose and T. Roggenbauer, "Implementation of High-Side, High-Voltage RESURF LDMOS in a sub-half Micron Smart Power Technology", IEEE, (2001)
4. J.A. Appels and H.M.J. Vaes, "High Voltage Thin Layer Devices (RESURF Devices)", IEEE, (1979)
5. S. Hardikar, M. M. De Souza, Y.Z. Xu, T.J. Pease and E.M. Sankara Narayanan, "A Novel Double RESURF LDMOS for HVIC's", Microelectronics Journal 35, Issue 3, 305–310 (2004)
6. P. Hower, J. Lin, S. Pendharkar, B. Hu, J. Arch, J. Smith and T. Efland, "A Rugged LDMOS for LBC5 Technology", in Proc. 17th Int. Symp. Power Semiconductor Devices & IC's, May 23-26, Santa Barbara, CA (ISPSD 2005), pp. 327–330

Design of a Low on Resistance High Voltage (120V) Novel 3D NLDMOS with Side Isolation Based on 0.35um BCD Process Technology

Shao-Ming Yang[1,3*], *Gene* Sheu[1], *Tzu Chieh* Lee [2], *Ting Yao* Chien [2], *Chieh Chih* Wu[2], *Yun Jung* Lin[1]

[1]Department of Computer Science and Information Engineering, Asia University, 500, Lioufeng Rd., Taichung 41354, Taiwan.
[2]School of Software and Microelectronics, Peking University, Beijing, China.
[3]Department of Medical Research, China Medical University Hospital, China Medical University, Taichung, Taiwan.

Abstract. High performance power device is necessary for BCD power device. In this paper, we used 3D Synopsis TCAD simulation tool Sentaurus to develop 120V device and successfully simulated. We implemented in a conventional 0.35um BCDMOS process to present of a novel high side 120V LDMOS have reduced surface field (RESURF) and Liner p-top structure with side isolation technology. The device has been research to achieve a benchmark specific on-resistance of 189 mΩ -mm^2 while maintaining horizontal breakdown voltage and vertical isolation voltage both to target breakdown voltage of 120V. In ESOA, we also proposed a better performance of both device without kirk effect.

1 Introduction

Recently, BCDMOS (Bipolar-CMOS-LDMOS) process is extensively used in variety of areas such like LED Driver, Switching Regulator, Battery IC, Audio Amplifier, Motor Drivers, large displays (TV and monitor), Power Management products, and storage controller chips [1]. One of the most common power switches used for Power IC technologies is the Lateral Double Diffused Metal Oxide Semiconductor (LDMOS) power transistor. The LDMOS provides the advantage of process compatible to VLSI process and is easy to integrate with logic IC or other devices. For power device, a lot of research on the specific on-resistance improvement of LDMOS device have been reported, because specific on-resistance is critical to device performance. Reduced Surface Field LDMOS (RESURF) has been proposed a better to optimize specific on-resistance. Double and multiple RESURF methods [2, 3] had been developed instead of single RESURF technology to highly utilize to improve the specific on-resistance and the junction/weak avalanche leakage at high electric field regions and reduce hot carrier injection into the dielectric in the aims of obtaining high breakdown voltage.

Since the source of a high-side LDMOS tied to the load, the source potential can be higher than the substrate potential while for a conventional LDMOS structure, the source electrode is always tied to the substrate. To implement high-side LDMOS in a conventional BCD process, the NBL (n+ buried layer) has to be located beneath the LDMOS source region to prevent punch-through breakdown between the source and the p-substrate [4]. The voltage capability of high-side LDMOS depended on junction isolation voltage of NBL junction. This design challenge was not only obtained the horizontal breakdown voltage, but also vertical isolation voltage maintained target breakdown voltage simultaneously.

2 Methods and simulations

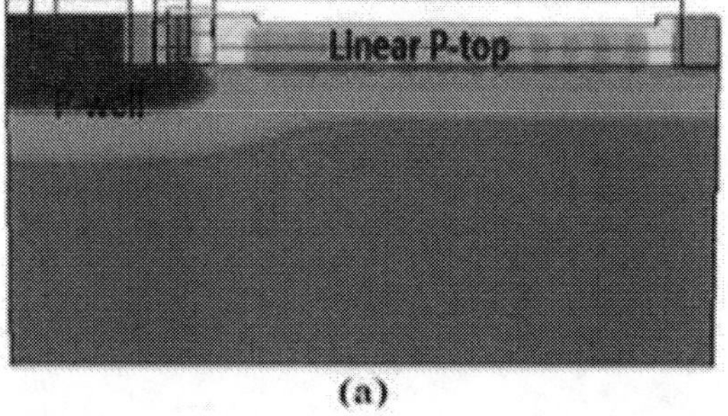

(a)

Figure 1(a) shows the schematic of a novel 3-dimensional and a single P-top layer NLDMOS structure with STI regions on both sides of the N-drift region which is performed by Sentaurus process simulation. In the cross-sectional view of the proposed high-side 120V n-LDMOS. The NBL should be used to prevent the

* Corresponding author: rickyyang121@asia.edu.tw

vertical punch-through breakdown between the source and the p-substrate. Because of the use of NBL, the breakdown voltage of the high-side LDMOS can endure higher than that of the low-side LDMOS when source tied to load. The main reason was built an isolation layer that provided punch-through breakdown more than 120V between the source and the p-substrate. Figure 2 (b) to (c) show the front and top views, respectively.

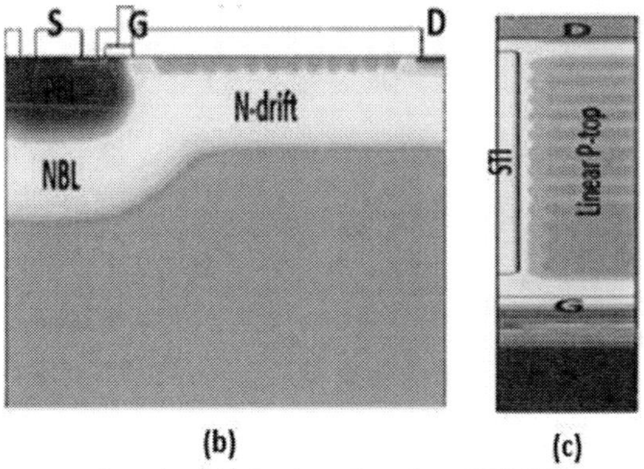

Fig. 1. Schematic of (a) 3D single P-top layer RESURF LDMOS (b) front view (c) top.

It clearly shows that a liner P-top layer is performed in the top of the N-drift region. The liner P- top layer is placed at the top centre of the N-drift in order to create more p-n junctions which will help increase the breakdown. LDMOS was integrated into the standard BCD process. Normal p-type silicon substrate with resistivity of 10-20 Ω -cm was used. For process conditions, the p-type background doping of about 1.3 × 10^{14} cm-3 was used in an oriented silicon substrate. An epitaxial process of 0.6-um-thickness N-type layer was performed on Si substrate with a doping concentration around 4.65 × 10^{16} cm-3. In addition, a variety of the width area ratio of WN-drift/WSTI were a crucial factor which applied to obtain the optimal performance.

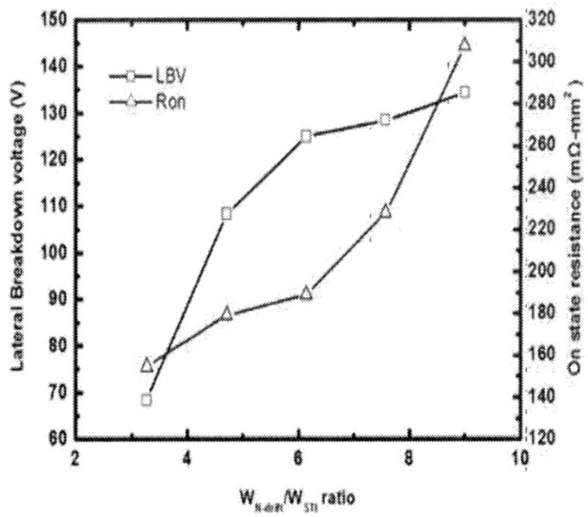

Fig. 2. LBV, Ron vs WN-drift/WSTI Curve.

Fig. 2 shows the off-state breakdown voltage and specific on-resistance curves as a function of different ratio of WN-drift/WSTI respectively. It is clearly seen the 6.14 ratio of WN-drift/WSTI has much better on-resistance and breakdown voltage compared to other ratios. The WN-drift/WSTI ratio significantly influences the device breakdown voltage and specific on-resistance. Because a large WN drift/WSTI ratio can obtain more breakdown voltage, but the specific on-resistance simultaneously degeneration velocity maybe faster than breakdown voltage. It led the device of poor performance.

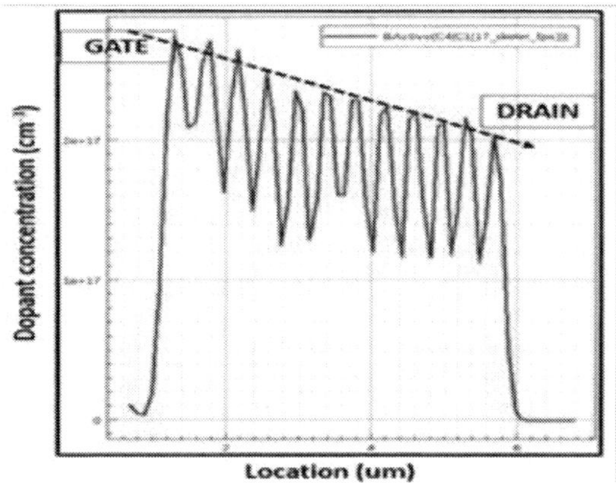

(a)

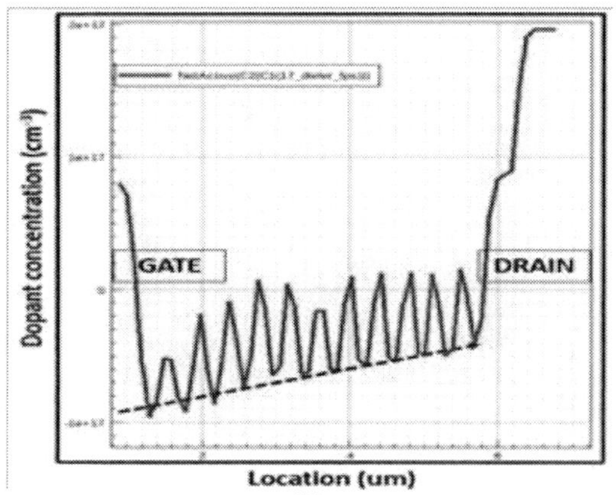

(b)

Fig. 3. The P-top linear profile (a) Boron doping profile (b) Net doping profile.

The mask design of linear P-top layer plays the crucial role in order to achieve target breakdown voltage and the lowest possible specific on-resistance. The P-top layer length, depth and doping concentration of the P-top layer are the key parameters in the Double RESURF LDMOS. The simulation result can be seen clearly in Fig. 3 which is demonstrating linear profile for boron impurity degraded gradually from source side to drain side. The appropriate linear variation of p-top layer can optimize both breakdown voltage and specific on-resistance values. The main purpose of this introduced P-top layer structure is to minimize the on-resistance while attain the desired breakdown voltage, meanwhile the conventional double RESURF and single RESURF structures are not able to achieve that technology value.

3 Results and discussion

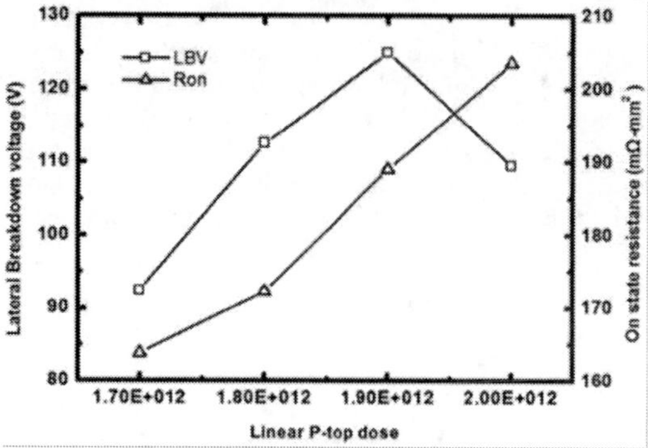

Fig. 4. LBV, Ron vs Linear P-top dose Curve

We fabricated the 120V high-side LDMOS transistors in our 0.35 μm BCD process. Simulations executed to obtain the desired breakdown voltage of 120V having lowest Ron possible without using any extra mask. One additional mask layer was used for the surface P-layer. Fig. 4 shows the characteristics of the breakdown voltage and the specific on-resistance are proportional from the linear P-top layer dosage variation. The proposed high-side LDMOS provides a breakdown voltage.

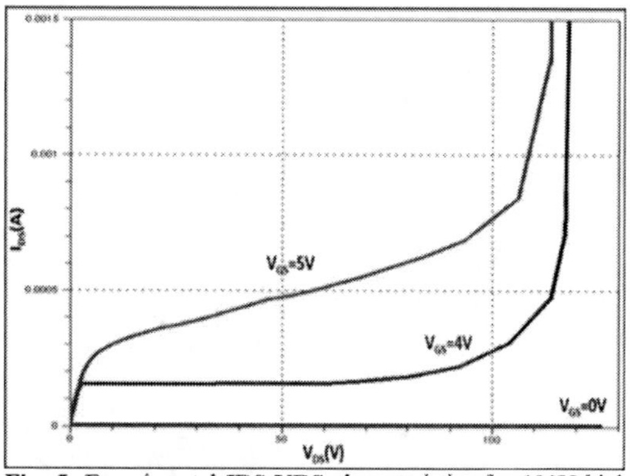

Fig. 5. Experimental IDS-VDS characteristics for 120V high side device

An ESOA of LDMOS device is very critical for power device performance. Fig. 5 shows the forward I_{DS}-V_{DS} characteristics and off-state breakdown voltage for the 120V high-side LDMOS transistors and the device shows a good ESOA performance when V_G=5V achieve high on-state breakdown voltages of V_{DS}=117V. Generally, the on-state breakdown voltage of the LDMOS is lower than the off-state breakdown voltage due to Kirk Effect [5]. However, the cause of the Kirk Effect problem mainly due to the high beta value of parasitic NPN transistor in the p-body. Therefore, we must have optimized beta of parasitic NPN transistor for reducing the kirk effect [6]. We can speculate the beta value of parasitic NPN transistor close to equal to 1 when off-state breakdown voltage near on- state breakdown voltages. It will obtain a good ESOA region and without kirk effect for On-state I-V curves.

4 Conclusion

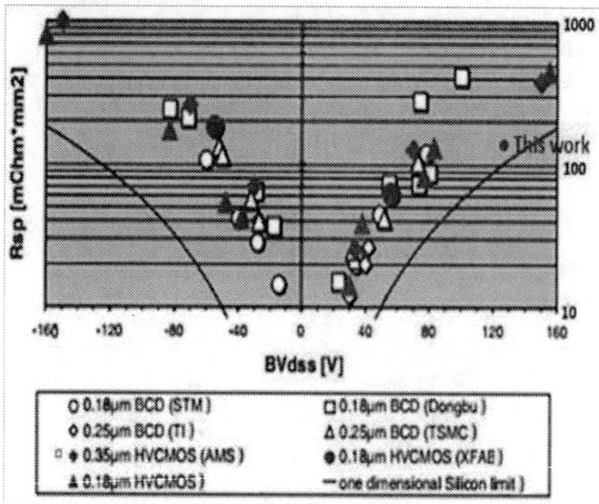

Fig. 6. Trade-off characteristics between the breakdown voltage and the specific on-resistance.

In this paper, 120V high-side LDMOS was implemented in a conventional 0.35 μm BCD process. The proposed LDMOS structure is very competitive to achieve breakdown and benchmark specific on-resistance. The proposed high-side LDMOS provides lateral BV 125V, vertical isolation voltage 135V and $R_{ON}sp$ = 1.89 mΩ-mm² with a wide region of ESOA. Based on Fig.6 [7] and these electrical performances, we believe that this novel device has sufficient potential in comparable with previous advanced LDMOS device.

Acknowledgment: The author would like to thank National Center for High-performance computing, National Nano Device Laboratories and National Chip Implementation Center for providing the MEDICI and TSUPREM-4 software.

References

1. B. Murari, F. Bertotti, and G.A. Vignola, *SMART POWER IC's*, Springer, New York, (1996)
2. A.W. Ludikhuize, *"A Review of RESURF Technology"*, Proceedings ISPSD, pp.11-18 (2000)
3. D.R Disney, A.K. Paul, M. Darwish, R. Basecki and V. Rumenik, *"A New 800V Lateral MOSFET with Dual Conduction Paths"*, Proceedings ISPSD, pp.399-402 (2001)
4. C. Contiero, et all, *"Characteristics and Applications of a 0.6μm Bipolar CMOS-DMOS Technology Combining VLSI Non-volatile Memories"*, IEDM, pp. 465-468, (1996).
5. P. L. Hower *"Safe Operating Area – a New Frontier in LDMOS Design"* Proc. of ISPSD, (2002) pp. 1-8.
6. S. K. Lee, Y. C. Choi, J. H. Kim, C. J. Kim, H. S. Kang, and C. S. Song, *"Extension of safe-operating-area by optimizing body-current in submicron LDMOS transistors"*, IEEE, (2001) pp. 67-68.
7. R. Minixhofer, *"A 120V 180nm High Voltage CMOS Smart Power Technology for System-on-Chip Integration"*, IEEE Trans. On ISPSD, pp. 75-78, (2010)

https://doi.org/10.1051/matecconf/201820102005

120V Low Side LDMOS Device with Sided Isolation of 0.35μm CMOS Compatible Process

Ravi Deivasigamani[1], *Gene* Sheu[1], *Chirag* Aryadeep[1], *S. Krishna* Sai[1], *S. Selvendran*[1], *Shao-Ming* Yang[1,2,*]

[1]Department of Computer Science and Information Engineering, Asia University, 500, Lioufeng Rd., Taichung 41354, Taiwan.
[2]Department of Medical Research, China Medical University Hospital, China Medical University, Taichung, Taiwan.

Abstract. In this paper, a novel 120V multiple RESURF lateral double-diffused MOS (LDMOS) transistor with shallow trench isolation (STI) structure in low side is developed and successfully simulated. The proposed multiple RESURF LDMOS is able to achieve better ESOA performance while maintaining a benchmark specific on-resistance with breakdown voltage over 120 Volts. The key feature of this novel device is linear p-top rings which are located in the n-drift region. Optimization of p-top mask design and n-drift region concentration is performed in order to achieve the lowest on-resistance possible with the desired breakdown voltage.

1 Introduction

LDMOS transistors are widely used in smart power technologies; Applications are mainly in display drivers, power switching, digital audio and power management devices etc. Now a day, the n-channel lateral DMOS transistor (NLDMOS) is one of the best choices for high voltage device. The focus is to optimize and improve the LDMOS device design to obtain power switches with very low specific on-state resistance (Rsp) while maintaining the high switching speed.

LDMOS can be easily integrated into a CMOS or a BiCMOS process which facilitates the fabrication of control, logic and power switches on a single chip [1,2]. Also, for this voltage range, an optimized LDMOS is much more efficient in terms of on-state voltage and switching losses compared to a power bipolar junction transistor (BJT) or other hybrid MOS bipolar devices [3]. Advantage of NLDMOS is that it can be easily integrated without significant process changes and within existing technologies [4]. In order to broaden the applicability of NLDMOS, it is necessary to enhance the electrical performances, such as breakdown voltage, low on-state resistance, and high current driving capability [5]. Since many years, experiments were carried out to improve Breakdown voltage and on-state resistance [6][7].

This paper discusses (how far NLDMOS can be used) with the limitation of the NLDMOS in terms of breakdown voltage and on-state resistance. In this paper, the NLDMOS structure is with the concept of multiple RESURF and linear P-top ring. Based on the simulation experiments 120V Low Side is obtained with Benchmark on-state resistance of 119.5 mΩmm2 (Rsp). Double and multiple RESURF methods [8] had been developed instead of single RESURF technology to improve the junction weak avalanche leakage at high electric field regions and additional layer of opposite conductivity (p-top layer) is incorporated inside the n-drift region. The main purpose of this structure is to increase the optimum charge in the drift region without reducing breakdown voltage for obtaining high breakdown voltage and low specific on-state resistance requirements in conventional NLDMOS devices. The P-top mask was optimized to get the highest breakdown with Lowest on-state resistance (Rsp) possible by increasing current-driving capability in the drift region [9–10]. Figure 1 shows the schematic view of new N-channel LDMOS structure with side isolations in front view and in top view.

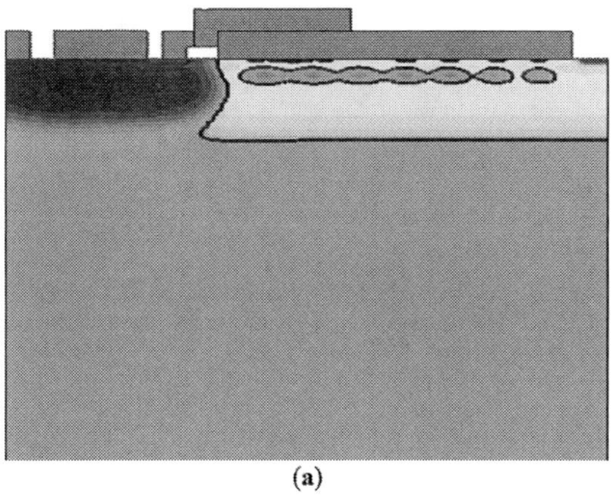

(a)

* Corresponding author: rickyyang121@asia.edu.tw

 https://doi.org/10.1051/matecconf/201820102005

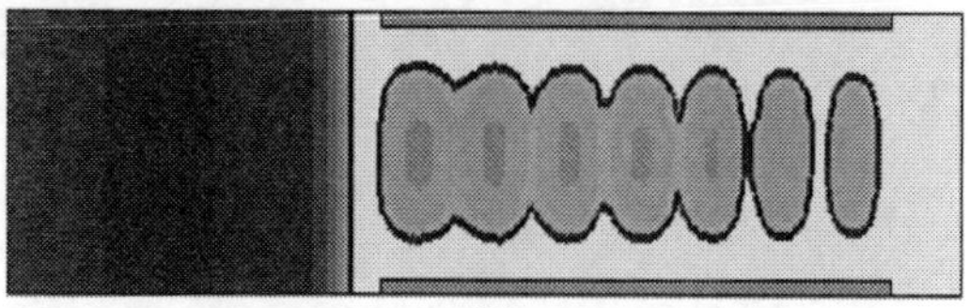

(b)

Fig. 1. Schematic view of new N-channel LDMOS Structure with side isolations (a) Front view and (b) Top view

2 Materials and methods

The device structure is designed with side isolation techniques to reduce the NPN beta, thereby to avoid the Kirk effect and reduce the leakage current.

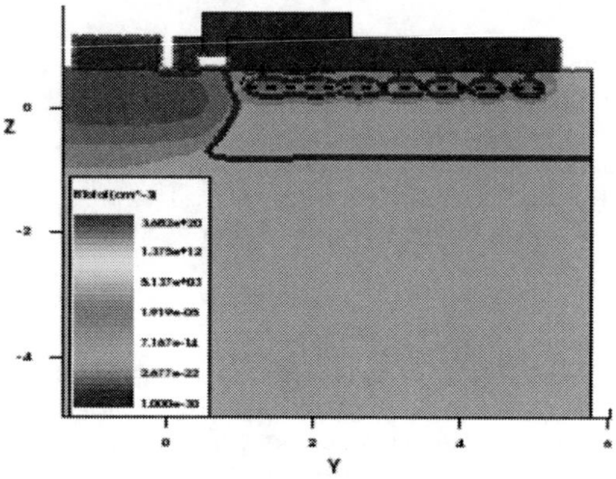

(a)

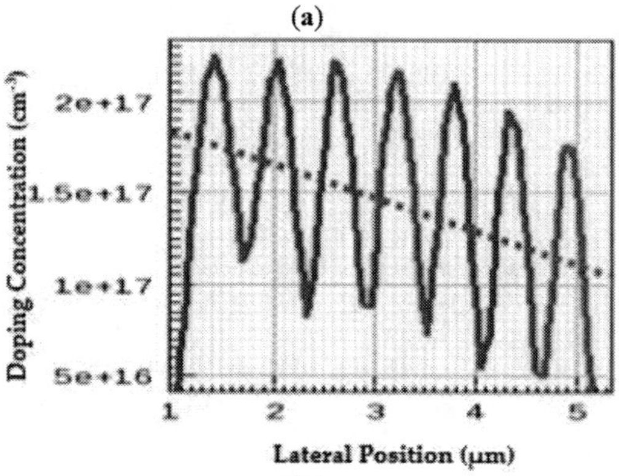

(b)

Fig. 2. Boron profile of proposed NLDMOS (a) Boron profile Front View (b) Cut line profile for Linear P-top

Figure 2(a) shows the Boron profile of proposed NLDMOS with STI regions and both sides of the N-drift region which is performed by Sentaurus process simulation. For lowering our NLDMOS on-resistance it is very important to improve doping in the n-drift region. Our proposed structure has optimized concentration in n-drift region and an additional layer of opposite conductivity (p-top layer) is included in the n-drift region. The RESURF LDMOS device with linear p-top is shown in figure 2. Linearity of p-top can be seen from the Figure 2(b). The main purpose of P-top in the n-drift region is to maintain the best charge balance in the drift region of the structure without reducing breakdown voltage. The Linearly Varying Doped (LVD) p-top layer with optimized mask and doping for a RESURF LDMOS has been utilized and proposed, which can improve the influence of inter-connection related breakdown better than conventional RESURF structure. It is clear from the figure that the P-top layer is placed in the n-drift region in order to create more p-n charge. For process conditions, the p-type <100>, background doping of about $6x10^{14}$ cm-3 was used in an oriented silicon substrate. An epitaxial process of 0.6 um thickness film in N-type layer was developed on Si substrate with a doping concentration around $5.17x10^{16}$ cm-3.

3 Results and discussion

Simulations were carried out to obtain the desired breakdown voltage of more than 120V for Low side NLDMOS device structure, which have the lowest on-state resistance possible. In order to obtain the desired breakdown voltage and the lowest specific on-resistance, the n-drift region and p-top rings mask and charges has been optimized in several conditions. Figure 3 shows the breakdown curves for the proposed NLDMOS devices. The on-state resistance of proposed structure is better than 0.13um, 0.18um, 0.25um technologies which were proposed before.

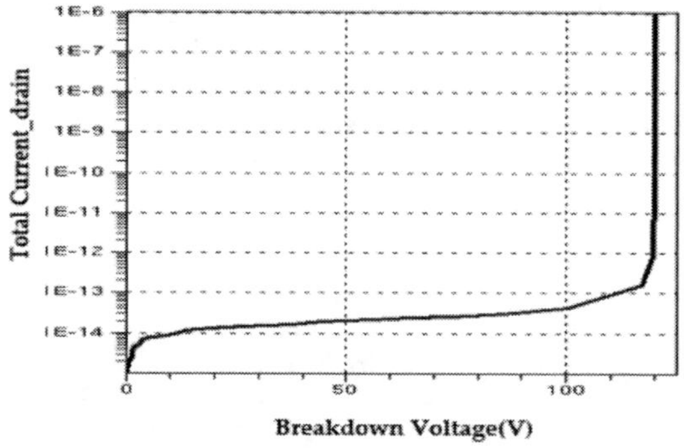

Fig. 3. Breakdown Curve for proposed Low Side NLDMOS device

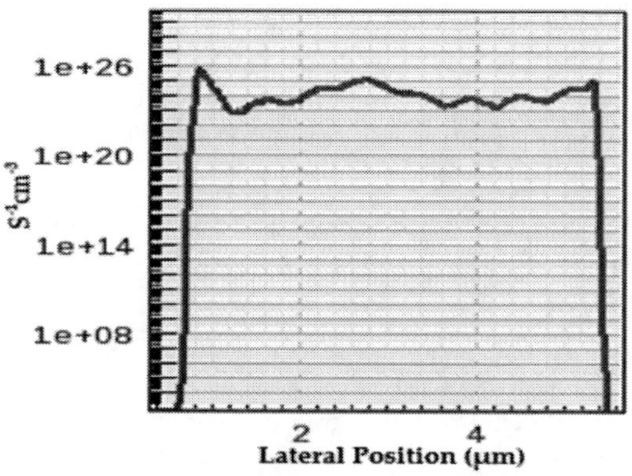

Fig. 4. Impact-ionization field of Low Side NLDMOS device

Figure 4 shows 3D simulation the surface impact-ionization field distributions along the drift region of the device. The structure has better SOA performance and there is no Kirk effect and saturation point. Figure 5 shows the SOA performance of our device, for gate voltage which justifies our result.

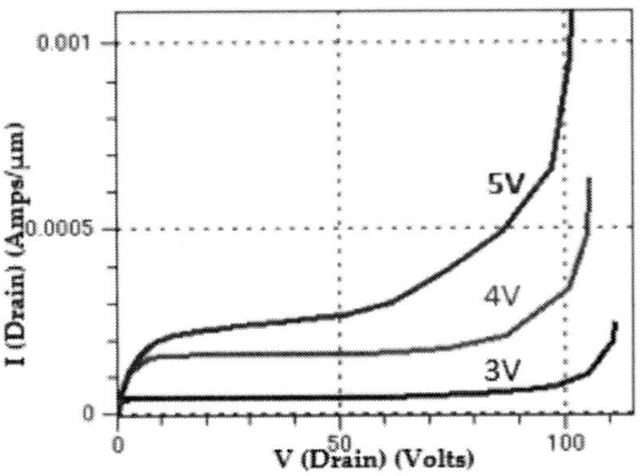

Fig. 5. I-V curves for our proposed NLDMOS structure for different gate voltage

Proposed NLDMOS structure is simple and cost-effective CMOS compatible process with side isolation, have 120V breakdown and better benchmark on-state resistance. By utilizing linear P-top in the n-drift region, we can able to achieve better charge balance in the drift region of the structure which help to reduce the on-state resistance.

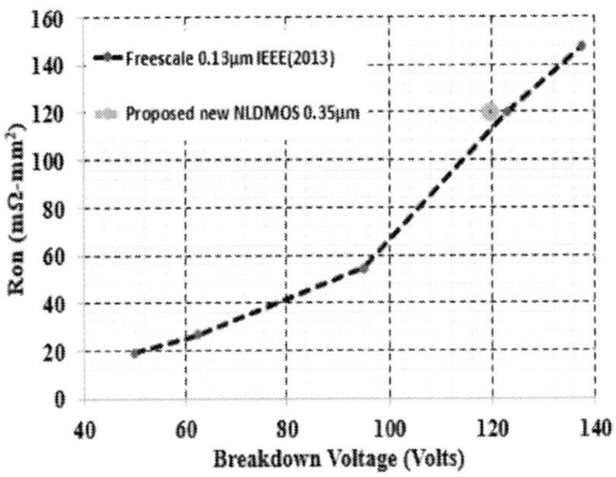

Fig. 6. Comparison of Benchmark curves of different technology

4 Conclusion

This device structure is very competitive to achieve the desired benchmark breakdown and on-resistance. This device structure has better impact-ionization, so hot carrier reliability life can be longer. So, we believe that this device structure can be used for future auto-electronics industries and applications.

Acknowledgment: The authors would also like to thank National Center for High-performance computing, National Nano Device Laboratories, and the National Chip Implementation Center for supporting us.

References

1. T. Efland, et. al., *"Optimized Complementary 40V Power LDMOSFET Use Existing Fabrication Steps in Sub-Micron CMOS Technology,"* IEEE IEDM Tech. Digest, pp. 399-402, (1994).
2. P. G. Y. Tsui, et. al., *"Versatile Half Micron Complementary Bicmos Technology for Microprocessor Based Smart Power Applications,"* IEEE Trans. on Electron Devices, pp. 564-570, March (1995).
3. B. J. Baliga, *"Power Semiconductor Devices"*, PWS Publishing Company.
4. D. Brisbin, P. Lindorfer, P. Chaparala, *"Substrate Current Independent Hot Carrier Degradation in NLDMOS Devices"*, National Semiconductor Corporation, (2006).
5. C. Contiero, P. Galbiati, M. Palmieri, Lodovica Vecchi, *"Characteristics and Applications of A 0.6μm Bipolar-Cmos-Dmos Technology Combining VLSI Non-Volatile Memories"*, IEDM, pp. 465- 468 (1996).
6. R. S. Wrathall, B. J. Baliga, K. Shenai, W. Hennessey, and T. P. Chow, *"Charge Controlled 80 Volt Lateral DMOSFET with Very Low Specific On-Resistance Designed for An Integrated Power Process"*, IEDM, (1990)
7. A. Kumar, E. Y. Hapsari, V. Kumar, A. Mrinal, G. Sheu, and S. M. Yang, *"Design of A Low on Resistance High Voltage (<100) Novel 3D NLDMOS With Side STI and Single P-Top Layer Based on 0.18um BCD Process Technology"*, (NMDC), (2013) IEEE 8th.
8. S. M. Yang, EP Hema, A. Mrinal, Md Amanullah, G. Sheu, and PA Chen, *"High Voltage NLDMOS with multiple-RESURF Structure to Achieve Improved On-resistance"*, (CSTIC, 2015) pp. 1-3.
9. A. W. Ludikhuize, *"A review of RESURF technology"*, (IEEE, 2000) pp. 11-18.
10. A. S. Kashyap, H. A. Mantooth, T. A. Vo, and M. Mojarradi," Compact *Modeling of LDMOS Transistors for Extreme Environment, Analog Circuit Design"*, (IEEE, 2010) pp. 1431-1439.

https://doi.org/10.1051/matecconf/201820102006

Building a Japanese MIDI-to-Singing song synthesis using an English male voice

Hung-Che Shen[1,*]

[1]I-Shou University, Digital Media Design Department, Kaohsiung, Taiwan

Abstract. This work reports development of a MIDI-to-Singing song synthesis that will produce audio files from MIDI data and arbitrary Romaji lyrics in Japanese. The MIDI-to-Singing system relies on the Flinger (**Festival singer**) for singing voice synthesis. Originally, this MIDI-to-Singing system was developed by English. Based on some Japanese pronunciation rules, a Japanese MIDI-to-Sing synthesis system was developed and derived. For a language transfer like Festival synthesized singing, two major tasks are the modifications of a phoneset and a lexicon. Originally, MIDI-to-Sing song synthesis can create singing voices in many languages, but there is no existing Japanese festival diphone voice available right now. We therefore used a voice transformation model in festival to develop Japanese MIDI-to-Singing synthesis. An evaluation of a song listening experiment was conducted and the result of this voice conversion showed that the synthesized singing voice successfully migrate from English to Japanese with high voice quality.

1 Introduction

The goal of this research is to synthesize natural singing Japanese song from an English Text-to-Speech voice. With the term MIDI-to-Singing, we mean the production of human-like singing voice based on a given MIDI format music. The MIDI-to-Singing system is an extension from a speech-to-singing synthesis, which converts a speaking voice reading the lyrics of a song to a singing voice given its musical score. Therefore, a different language singing can be easily derived by modifying the original speech features unique to them.

Singing voice synthesis enables computers to "sing" any song. Since 2007, it has become especially popular in Japan because of Yamaha's VOCALOID singing synthesizer [1]. There can be found a lot of original musical compositions in the video sites such as YouTube or Niko Niko Douga. There is now a growing demand for more flexible systems that can sing songs with various voices as evidenced by the many singer libraries being created and released on the Internet by users for UTAU [2] singing voice synthesis software.

Without a score editor environment for end-users, it should be noted that a concatenation-based singing synthesizer was already proposed by Macon et al. [3] in 1992. They finally released open source for this method that is called Flinger [4]. It is written by Mike Macon based on the Festival Speech Synthesis System [5], developed at the University of Edinburgh. Flinger needs the OGIresLPC plugin as the signal processing ``backend" that was developed at OGI [6]. This takes diphone waveform files, coded as residual-excited LPC parameters, and performs the necessary concatenation, pitch/duration change, and smoothing of the diphone waveforms.

* Corresponding author: shungch@isu.edu.tw

A MIDI-to-Singing system requires the integration of two major components. One is a MIDI sequencer with a lead-sheet view. The other is a singing voice synthesis (SVS). Based on a musical graphical interface such as a lead sheet, the users can compose music/lyrics in a MIDI sequencer.

In Festival, a new language is mainly comprised of constructing a phoneset and building a lexicon. The phoneset is basically a set of syllables and includes the linguistic characteristics of how vowels and consonants are pronounced. A lexicon is a database of words with their respective pronunciations, using the phones from the phoneset. During the past few years, we have been using songs for educational learning based on our previous MIDI-to-Singing system [7]. To extend the applications of singing voice synthesis, a language transfer will be needed. A language transfer refers to speakers applying knowledge from one language to another language. This paper assumes that a MIDI-to-Singing language transfer between English and Japanese is feasible. In order to demonstrate Japanese MIDI-to-Singing, some songs are available online as shown in Fig. 1.

Fig. 1. Japanese MIDI-to-Singing Demo Websites: http://sing.dmd.isu.edu.tw/en/.

This paper is organized as follows. In Section 2, we present Japanese syllable and word syntax which explains the language transfer in Festival Text-to-Speech. After that, a MIDI-to-Singing song synthesis is described in Section 3. Finally, experimental results are given in Section 4. Section 5 concludes this paper.

2 Derive a Japanese diphone voice

In Japanese, a syllable is formed by a vowel only or a combination of a consonant and a vowel. One syllable can only be one to three letters (Latin alphabet) long. A syllable cannot be a single consonant. In addition, a word can be formed by a series of syllables. Words may never end on a consonant, with the exception of consonant /n/. Once a word is broken into syllables it can be fed into a speech synthesis system, such as Festival, and then be pronounced. Japanese has five vowels. Vowels are the characters A, E, I, O, U. The vowels are pronounced roughly like these sounds in standard American English: "A" as in "father," "E" as in "set," "I" as in "bee," "O" as in "toe" and "U" as in "good". Vowels in Japanese may be long or short. Long vowels are held for twice as long as short vowels, but except for the length, there is no difference in pronunciation between short and long vowels. Japanese Vowels can be located in the initial, the medial and final part of words. Japanese also has what is called a "syllabic nasal." This sounds like the English "N" in "night" when it is followed by an "S," "Z," "T," "D," "N," or "R" sound.

Japanese Romanization (Romaji) is the standard way of transliterating Japanese into the Latin alphabet. Consonants and vowels are always broken up into the same "blocks" of sound allowing very easy parsing of words. This basic phonetic alphabet is known as hiragan as shown in the Table 1.

Table 1. Japanese Hiragana.

V\C	k	s	t	n	h	m	y	r	w
a	ka	sa	ta	na	ha	ma	ya	ra	wa
i	ki	shi	chi	ni	hi	mi	(y)I	ri	(w)i
u	ku	su	tsu	nu	hu	mu	yu	ru	(w)u
e	ke	se	te	ne	he	me	e	re	(w)e
o	ko	so	to	no	ho	mo	yo	ro	(w)o

There are a few oddities in the hiragana table. The blocks "(y)i", "(w)i", "(w)u", "(w)e", and "(w)o" are pronounced as the vowel components only, e.g., "(w)o" is simply "o"; (w) indicates the "w" is fully cut out from the sound. There is no "tu" sound. Instead we use the "tsu" sound. "Tsu" can give some people trouble, but using the notation above "tsu" would be pronounced as the ts in "cats" with a short "u" added to the end; (ca)ts-u. The Japanese Romaji consists of fourteen consonants—k, s, t, n, h, m, y, r, w, g, z, d, b and p. Japanese pronunciation follows a simple set of rules for syntax. Each vowel and basic consonant/vowel combination corresponds to a phonetic character in the Japanese alphabet. All syllables must end on a vowel. A syllable cannot be a single consonant.

Assuming that a voice set exists, constructing a language in Festival requires modifying a phoneset, building a lexicon, and adding prosody (defining the letter to sound rules). Because a word is usually broken into syllables in singing, when syllables are fed into a singing synthesis system, some considerations required in text-to-speech are ignored such as prosody. Two basic processes need to be addressed only contains:

• Modifying a phoneset,
• Modifying a lexicon,

2.1 Modifying a phoneset

A phoneme (or phone) is one of the units of sound that distinguish one word from another in a particular language. Syllables are considered the smallest unit of speech, while a phone is only a speech sound. For the Japanese language, there exists a 1-1, 1-2 and 1-3 relationship between syllables and phones. In Festival the phones are stored in the phoneset. A phoneset is a set of symbols which may be further defined in terms of features, such as vowel/consonant, place of articulation for consonants, type of vowel etc. This, like everything else in Festival, is a function-based structure in Scheme. The phoneset for a language has been defined in many cases, and it is wise to follow convention when it exists. For Japanese, that's probably ok as the Japanese phoneset is mostly a subset of the English phoneset. In Festival, the phones' features and their values must be defined with the phoneset. This, like everything else in Festival, is a function-based structure in Scheme. At synthesis time, each Japanese phone must be mapped to an equivalent (one or more or modified) US phone. This is done though phoneset members for the Japanese as shown in Table 2.

Table 2. Phoneset members for the Japanese.

Standard vowels	Long vowels	Unvoiced reduced vowels	Consonants
(a + s 3 3 - 0 0 0)	(a: + 1 3 3 - 0 0 0)	(I + a 1 1 - 0 0 0)	(k - 0 0 0 0 s v -)
(i + s 1 1 - 0 0 0)	(i: + 1 1 1 - 0 0 0)	(U + a 1 3 + 0 0 0)	(s - 0 0 0 0 f a -)
(u + s 1 3 + 0 0 0)	(u: + 1 1 3 + 0 0 0)		(sh - 0 0 0 0 f p -)
(e + s 2 1 - 0 0 0)	(e: + 1 2 1 - 0 0 0)	**Geminates**	(t - 0 0 0 0 s a -)
(o + s 2 3 - 0 0 0)	(o: + 1 2 3 - 0 0 0)	(Qk - g 0 0 0 s v -)	(ch - 0 0 0 0 a p -)
		(Qs - g 0 0 0 f a -)	(ts - 0 0 0 0 f a -)
		(Qsh - g 0 0 0 f p -)	(n - 0 0 0 0 n a +)
			(h - 0 0 0 0 f g -)
			(f - 0 0 0 0 f b -)
			(m - 0 0 0 0 n l +)

The description of phone features is shown in Fig. 2. The descriptions describe the following phone features, for vowels: length (short, long, diphthong, schwa), height (close, close-mid, mid, open-mid, open), frontness (front, central, back), and lip rounding (rounded, unrounded). For consonants: consonant type (stop, affricate, fricative, nasal, lateral, approximant), place of articulation (labial, alveolar, velar, palatal, post-alveolar, labio-dental, dental, glottal), and consonant voicing (voiced, unvoiced).

```
;;; Phone Features
(;; vowel or consonant
 (vc + -)
 ;; vowel length: short long dipthong schwa geminate (for consonants)
 (vlng s l d a g 0)
 ;; vowel height: high mid low
 (vheight 1 2 3 0)
 ;; vowel frontness: front mid back
 (vfront 1 2 3 0)
 ;; lip rounding
 (vrnd + - 0)
 ;; consonant type: stop fricative affricate nasal lateral approximant
 (ctype s f a n l r 0)
 ;; place of articulation: labial alveolar palatal labio-dental
 ;;                         dental velar glottal
 (cplace l a p b d v g 0)
 ;; consonant voicing
 (cvox + - 0)
 )
(
```

Fig. 2. Phone features.

However, scanning down the phoneset one will notice an arrangement of syllables. For example, "(a + l 2 2 – 0 0 0)" is the phone from the Radio phoneset included with festival. This phone represents the first 'a' can be the phone of a Japanese Romaji word "ai" or "au".

In the phone above, the “a” represents the name of the phone. This name is used in the lexicon to refer to which phones need to be uttered by the speech synthesis system to form words. Next comes a ‘+’ or ‘-‘ symbol where the positive affirms that the phone represents a vowel, and the negative indicates the phone represents a consonant. All of the remaining settings can take 0 for a value which indicates that that setting is not applicable. Next in the phone definition there is “l 2 2” which define three linguistic settings for vowels. The first entry corresponds to vowel length can be ‘s’ for short, ‘l’ for long, ‘d’ for diphthong, ‘s’ for schwa, or 0 for not applicable. Next, the second setting indicates vowel height and can be an integer from 0 for not applicable, 1 for high, 2 for medium, and 3 for low. Lastly for the vowel section, the third setting corresponds to vowel frontness and can have the values 1 for high, 2 for mid, and 3 for low. For the following setting, in the example above, “- “ represents lip rounding. When a human pronounces a phoneme the lip position can affect which phoneme is uttered. This setting can take the values “+” indicating that lip rounding is present, or “-“ which indicates the contrary. For the last three settings, the ones for consonants, we start with consonant type which can be ‘s’ for stop, ‘f’ for fricative, ‘a’ for affricate, ‘n’ for nasal, ‘l’ for lateral, or ‘r’ for approximant. Next, the second setting provides for the place of articulation and takes the values ‘l’, ‘a’, ‘p’, ‘b’, ‘d’, ‘v’, or ‘g’. The place of articulation represents how the mouth or throat says the consonant. Lastly, consonant voicing is represented by the final setting with values ‘+’ for its presence, or ‘- ‘ for its absence.

2.2 Modifying a lexicon

A lexicon is basically a large dictionary of words with the corresponding syllables to pronounce the word correctly. The lexicon had to be converted to the phonetic alphabet and to the format that is required by the Festival system. The lexicon format comes in three parts, a compiled lexicon, an addenda, and a rule system for handling unknown words. If any word appears that is not part of the lexicon, the pronunciation will be found by letter-to-sound-rules. Additionally, there exist many websites with examples of correct pronunciation of a subset of Japanese words. An addenda of words augment what is in the lexicon, but may not have been compiled and saved into the lexicon itself. This is useful for testing new additions to the lexicon. Some typical example entries of English are ("walkers" n (((w oo) 1) ((k @ z) 0))) for the word “walker” and ("present" v (((p r e) 0) ((z @ n t) 1))) for the word “present”.

A pronunciation in Festival requires not just a list of phones but also a syllabic structure. We already discussed about our phones with their features. The lexicon structure that is basically available in Festival takes both a word and a part of speech to find the given pronunciation. An example of an entry in the compiled lexicon is ("honda" nil (((h > n) 1) ((d ^) 0))). Note that this represents the word “Honda” and breaks it into the phones named “Hon,” and “Da.” Numbers next to the phone names can affect the duration of the phone pronounced. Explicit marking of syllables a stress value is also given (0 or 1). Lexicon entries of Japanese are shown in Fig. 3.

```
("a" nil (((A) 0) ((A A) 2)))
("i" nil (((j j) 0) ((i: i:) 2)))
("u" nil (((u) 0) ((u) 2)))
("e" nil (((E) 0) ((E) 2)))
("o" nil (((>) 0) ((oU) 2)))
("sa" nil (((s s) 0) ((A A) 2)))
```

Fig. 3. Lexicon entries of Japanese.

3 A MIDI-to-Singing song synthesis

Festival is a general-purpose concatenative text-tospeech (TTS) system that uses the residual-LPC synthesis technique, and is able to transcribe unrestricted text to speech. Assuming that a voice set exists, constructing a language in Festival requires creating a phoneset, building a lexicon, and defining the letter to sound rules. The voice set is the actual sounds that festival outputs. Since Festival provides some example voice sets, the focus of my research has been on the theoretical construction of the other components which have greater relevance to the Japanese language. Building a new voice set using a local Japanese speaker can be accomplished using the application FestVox.

3.1 OGI residual-LPC synthesizer (Festival plug-in)

This OGI residual-LPC synthesizer, which has to be considered as a plug-in for Festival, has been developed at OGI (Oregon Graduate Institute of Science and Technology, Portland, OR), and provides a new signal processing engine, and new voices, not included in the Festival distribution. Specifically, new pitchmark and LPC analysis algorithms, together with some scheme scripts that enable the creation of new voices in the OGIresLPC synthesizer are included. It is freely available for research and educational use. OGI has expanded its range of languages: there are TTS systems for English, Spanish and Welsh.

OGIresLPC is a drop-in module for the Festival TTS system created by CSTR at the University of Edinburgh (http://www.cstr.ed.ac.uk/projects/festival). This version of OGIresLPC has been designed to work with Festival version 1.2.0, released September 1997. It should work with any version 1.2.x newer than this, and can possibly be made to work with other versions of Festival, but this would require some changes to the code and knowledge of Festival internals. It provides waveform synthesis of speech with reasonable quality, but has not been extensively optimized in any way. It is meant to serve as a simple baseline synthesizer in the CSLU Toolkit and for other experiments.

3.2 Score editor

The Score Editor provides an environment in which the user can input notes, lyrics, and optionally some expressions. The Editor is designed especially for MIDI-to-Singing system. A lead sheet is a form of musical notation that specifies the essential elements of a MIDI song: the melody, lyrics and harmony. The melody is written in modern Western music notation, the lyric is written as text below the staff and the harmony is specified with chord symbols above the staff.

The user can type-in lyrics in normal writing and the Editor automatically converts the lyrics into phonetic symbols by looking into a built-in pronunciation dictionary. If the word consists of two or more syllables, the Editor automatically decomposes it into syllables. The user can easily add vibrato in the Editor. A screenshot of the MIDI-to-Singing process and score editor is shown in Fig. 4(a) and 4(b).

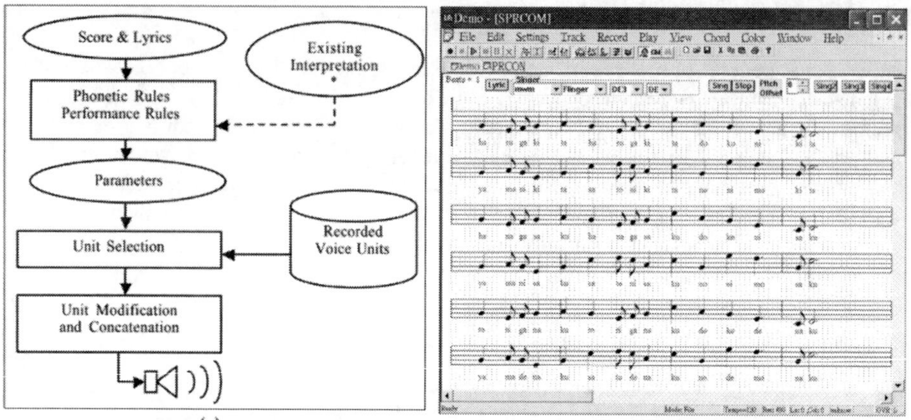

(a) (b)

Fig. 4. (a) Process of a MIDI-to-Singing system. (b) Score editor of MIDI-to-Singing.

4 Discussions

The task of synthesizing singing has, of course, a lot in common with that of synthesizing speech. For singing, the immense problems of reliably modelling intonation and syllable length are already solved (or rather by-passed) by the composer. In singing, Japanese provides relatively a greater ease for the English speaker learning Japanese than the English system would to Japanese singers. Not taking into account language variation (accent and dialect), there are five vowels and 17 consonant phonemes in Japanese while there are 20 vowels and 24 consonants in English language. Therefore, a Japanese MIDI-to-Singing system can be accomplished through an English MIDI-to-Singing system.

To evaluate the effectiveness of the proposed Japanese MIDI-to-Singing song synthesis, we conducted subjective experiments. Ten Japanese songs sung by MIDI-to-Singing system and sung by VOCALOID are used for evaluation. In order to evaluate the enhancement of modification strategies we adopted in singing synthesis, we scheduled a preference test to evaluate our system. The 10 kid MIDI songs are from Mama lisa's website: http://www.mamalisa.com/.

10 pairs of singing utterances were generated by 2 systems and 10 people took part in our experiment to judge which system got the better performance. These pairs of singing voices are played in a randomized order and the listeners gave their scores for each pair. The score is in 3 levels: the first is better, the second is better and they are almost the same. The result is listed in Table 3. As seen from Table 3, obviously the system with our proposed strategies got a lower performance than VOCALOID.

Table 3. Preference test score.

Prefer MIDI-to-Singing	Prefer VOCALOID
45%	55%

5 Conclusions

Japanese provides relatively a greater ease for the English speaker learning Japanese than the English system would to Japanese speakers. Not taking into account language variation (accent and dialect), there are five vowels and 17 consonant phonemes in Japanese while there are 20 vowels and 24 consonants in English language. Therefore, a Japanese MIDI-to-Singing system can be accomplished through an English MIDI-to-Singing system.

This paper outlines the theoretical issues that demonstrate that it is possible for English-to-Japanese transform of a singing synthesis project. Although the development of a Japanese MIDI-to-Singing system is still in working and far from complete. However, the project is likely to be an iterative process whereby the pronunciation of the system improves over time as the settings of the phones are made more precise, and the number of entries in the lexicon is increased. In the future, speech synthesis could also be fully integrated with singing synthesis. It will be challenging to develop new voice synthesis systems that could seamlessly generate any voice produced by a human or virtual singer/speaker.

We would like to thank Dr. Mike Macon for his invaluable contributions especially in developed Flinger to demo a MIDI-to-Singing synthesis. We would also like to thank Oregon Graduate Institute of Science and Technology for having made the OGIresLPC Plug-In for the Festival TTS.

References

1. H. Kenmochi, H. Ohshita, Proc. of Interspeech, (2007)
2. "UTAU," Available online: http://utau2008.web.fc2.com/, (2018)
3. M. Macon, Jensen-Link, Oliverio, Clements, Geourge, Proceedings of ICASSP 97, **435** (1997)
4. Flinger. Not available online: http://www.cslu.ogi.edu/tts/flinger URL (2007)
5. Festival Speech Synthesis, Speech Tools & documentation, http://www.festival.org/.
6. OGIresLPC PlugIn for Festival. www: http://cslu.cse.ogi.edu/tts/download/index.html (1997)
7. H. C. Shen, and C. N. Lee, 6th International WOCMAT & New Media Conference, Chungli, Taoyuan, Taiwan, (2010)

https://doi.org/10.1051/matecconf/201820102007

Application of a Hybrid Method for Power System Frequency Estimation with a 0.2-second Sampled Period

Chih-Hung Lee[1,*], and Men-Shen Tsai [2, 3]

[1]Graduate Institute of Mechanical and Electrical Engineering, National Taipei University of Technology, Taipei, Taiwan.
[2]Graduate Institute of Automation Technology, National Taipei University of Technology, Taipei, Taiwan.
[3]Research Center of Energy Conservation for New Generation of Residential, Commercial, and Industrial Sectors.

Abstract. The signal processing technique is one of the principal tools for diagnosing power quality (PQ) issues in electrical power systems. The Discrete Fourier Transform (DFT) is a frequency analysis technique used to process power system signals and identify PQ problems. However, the DFT algorithm may lead to spectral leakage and picket-fence effect problems for asynchronously sampled signals that contain harmonic, inter-harmonic, and flicker components. To resolve this shortcoming, a hybrid method for frequency estimation based on a second-level DFT approach and a frequency-domain interpolation algorithm to obtain the accurate fundamental frequency of a power system is proposed in this paper. This method uses a second-level DFT to compute the cosine and sine parts for the fundamental frequency components of the acquired signals. Then, a frequency-domain interpolation approach is adopted to determine the amplitude ratio for the cosine and sine parts of the system's fundamental frequency. A set of mixed signals with harmonic, inter-harmonic, and flicker components with the fundamental frequency deviation is used. The evaluation results demonstrate the superiority of the new method over other approaches for assessing asynchronously sampled signals contaminated with noise, harmonic, inter-harmonic, and flicker components.

1 Introduction

Power system signal analysis is a key step in PQ diagnosis. Effective extraction of power system signal features is helpful to understand the underlying physical nature of PQ's phenomena, and to evaluate its health condition, thereby providing convincing evidences for diagnosis. However, in both academic researches and engineering practices, power system signals are usually highly intricate. The vast increase usage in electronic devices may cause PQ problems such as harmonics, inter-harmonics, and voltage flickers in

[*] Corresponding author: t100669021@ntut.edu.tw

https://doi.org/10.1051/matecconf/201820102007

power systems. Such PQ problems may lead to power system, factory equipment, and public facility deviations or may even result in electrical equipment damage in severe cases.

The power system frequency is nonstationary. The degree of frequency change depends on the balance between power generation and load demand. Thus, the frequency is a key indicator for the safety and economy of the power system operation. A frequency below the nominal value represents an overloaded system; while a frequency above the nominal value represents a power oversupply. In general, the power system frequency is a critical indicator for power system monitoring, control, and protection [1-5]. Therefore, power system signal analysis is a key research topic and plays an important role in PQ diagnosis. International standards such as IEC-61000 have described the diagnosis of PQ.

In the past, several researches have successfully shown that the frequency assessment technology was able to detect the PQs of defects in power system. These technologies include Zero-crossing Algorithm [5-7], Discrete Fourier Transform (DFT) [8-13], Kalman Filter (KF) [14, 15], Phase-Locked Loops (PLL) [16, 17], Newton Algorithm [18, 19], Least squares Algorithm (LMS) [20, 21], Prony Algorithm [4, 22], Taylor Algorithm [23, 24], and Artificial-intelligence Algorithm [25, 26].

Among them, one of the two most popular techniques adopted is the Zero-crossing Algorithm, which has the least computational complexity and the fastest execution speed. However, this method is susceptible to noise and spikes, and can only provide an accurate frequency evaluation in noise-free and disturbance-free environments [5-7].

In [5], using the waveform construction method to combine the Time Domain Frequency Estimation Algorithm with the Newton Interpolation method was proposed. This approach can eliminate the leakage effect caused by the FFT (Fast Fourier Transform) calculation under asynchronous sampling conditions. In this paper, a Time Domain Zero-crossing Algorithm to evaluate the basic frequency is proposed. This algorithm uses the zero-crossing frequency detection method to calculate the basic frequency. Because this algorithm can be affected by non-basic frequency signals, a pre-filter must be used to eliminate the non-basic frequency signals. After the basic frequency has been obtained, Newton Interpolation method is applied to generate a new sample waveform that conforms to the FFT application conditions. As a result, the accurate basic frequency under asynchronous sampling conditions can be obtained.

In [6, 7], the authors proposed the digital filter and zero-crossing technique combination frequency evaluation method. They broke down the original sample signals into two orthogonal component waveforms using cosine and sine filters. These two waveforms and the zero-crossing technique are used to assess the basic frequency of the power system. The results indicated that the orthogonal filter and the zero-crossing technique can effectively reduce the noise and disturbance interferences.

The other technique that is popular used in calculating the fundamental frequency of a power system is DFT/FFT. In the IEC61000-4-30 standard, PQ measurement analysis is mostly based on DFT/FFT techniques. DFT/FFT can convert the periodic signals obtained via synchronous sampling into frequency domain data to help us learn more about the spectrum composition. However, the basic frequency of an actual power system will vary from time to time and become affected by noise, flickers, harmonic waves, inter-harmonic waves, and other disturbances. Therefore, it is unrealistic and impossible to achieve strict synchronous sampling without a special technique such as PLL (Phase Lock Loop). Asynchronous sampling would cause the DFT/FFT algorithm to create the spectral leakage and picket-fence effect problems and directly cause the FFT algorithm spectrum calculation accuracy to drop dramatically [8–13].

In [8], it was proposed to use the window method with DFT for frequency calculation, and to obtain the basic frequency parameter values according to the multi-point spectrum near the base frequency peak point as well as the Hanning window interpolation expressed as a function of the frequency domain itself. The results indicated that this multi-point frequency domain interpolation algorithm can effectively reduce the noise and disturbances.

Reference [9] adopted the pseudo-synchronization technique, Hanning window, and FFT combination for frequency calculation in order to improve the frequency estimation accuracy under the noise and disturbance effects. The author combined the original sample signals with the Hanning window function, performed FFT conversion for the new wave signals, and then assessed the basic frequency of the power system. The results indicated that the pseudo-synchronization technique combined with FFT can effectively reduce the noise and disturbances.

The PQ event detection algorithms require precise power system frequency which can be obtain using DFT-based frequency estimation algorithms under asynchronously-sampled signals that are contaminated with noise, flicker, and harmonic and inter-harmonic components. In this paper, we proposed a two-level DFT and frequency domain interpolation hybrid method to accurately calculate the basic frequency of a power system. This paper is divided into four chapters. Chapter 1 is the preface. Chapter 2 explores the two-level DFT and frequency domain interpolation hybrid method. Chapter 3 provides validation for the method. Chapter 4 concludes this paper.

2 Two-level DFT and frequency domain interpolation hybrid method

Frequency evaluation technology is the foundation of PQ analysis and monitoring. Therefore, excellent frequency assessment techniques can improve power system protection and monitoring. At present, the IEC61000-4-30 standard established by the International Electrotechnical Commission (IEC) for power quality-related measurement techniques is based on the DFT/FFT technique to analyze the PQ issues. To conform to the standard and facilitate development, numerous monitoring devices have adopted the fixed sampling frequency-based DFT technique in order to simplify device design. However, the basic electricity frequency changes may lead to asynchronous sampling problems for fixed sampling frequency devices, which may cause leakage effects during the DFT calculations. In addition, if the sampling frequency and calculation method window are not divisible, it would also cause the DFT method to obtain inaccurate basic frequencies.

The primary implementation steps of this paper are shown in Figure 1. First, we calculated the DFT orthogonal coefficient and amplitude ratio deviation coefficient based on the power signals captured. Next, we created two levels of orthogonal filtering based on the DFT orthogonal coefficients and power signals calculated. We then used the two orthogonal filtering signals and frequency domain interpolation to determine the amplitude ratio needed for the frequency calculation. Finally, we used the amplitude ratio and the amplitude ratio deviation coefficient to calculate the frequency more precisely.

https://doi.org/10.1051/matecconf/201820102007

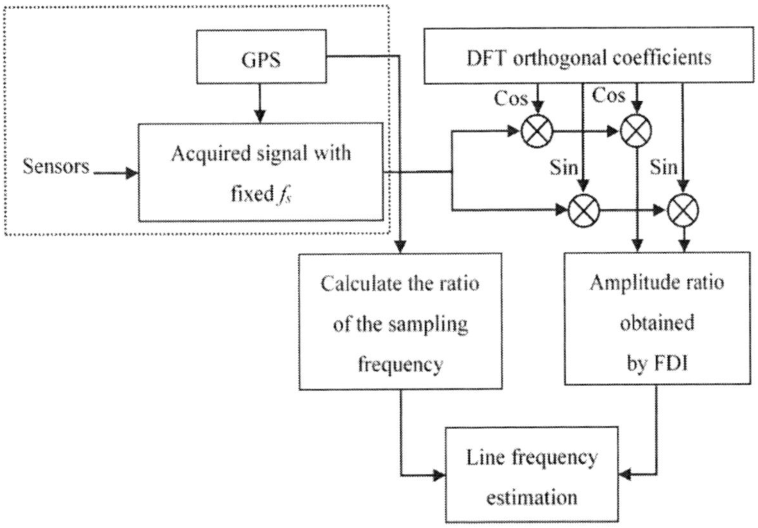

Figure 1. Proposed frequency assessment process.

2.1 DFT orthogonal filter coefficients

The actual power system signals (such as voltage and current) can be expressed in discrete time with three parameters: amplitude (A), frequency (f), and phase (θ), as shown in equation (1).

$$x(n) = A \cdot \cos\left(2\pi \frac{f_a \cdot n}{f_s}\right), n = 0,1,\ldots N-1 \tag{1}$$

$$f_s = f_0 \cdot N_0$$

$$X(i) = \frac{2}{N}[\sum_{n=0}^{N-1} x(n)\cos(2\pi \frac{f_a}{f_0 \cdot N_0} n) - j\sum_{n=0}^{N-1} x(n)\sin(2\pi \frac{f_a}{f_0 \cdot N_0} n)] \tag{2}$$

Assuming there is a single window with M-point samples, equation (2) can be expanded as follows:

$$\begin{aligned} \mathrm{X}(i) = &\frac{2}{M}\left(x(1)\cos(2\pi \frac{f_a}{f_0 \cdot N_0}) + x(2)\cos(4\pi \frac{f_a}{f_0 \cdot N_0}) + \ldots + x(M)\cos(2\pi \frac{f_a}{f_0})\right) \\ &+ j\frac{2}{M}\left(x(1)\sin(2\pi \frac{f_a}{f_0 \cdot N_0}) + x(2)\sin(4\pi \frac{f_a}{f_0 \cdot N_0}) + \ldots + x(M)\sin(2\pi \frac{f_a}{f_0})\right) \end{aligned} \tag{3}$$

Therefore, for the i-th data window, the sine and cosine components can be expressed as equations (4) and (5).

$$A(i) = \frac{2}{M}\sum_{n=i}^{M+i-1} x(i)\cos(2\pi \frac{f_a}{f_0 \cdot N_0} n) \tag{4}$$

$$B(i)=\frac{2}{M}\sum_{n=i}^{M+i-1}x(i)\sin(2\pi\frac{f_a}{f_0\cdot N_0}n) \tag{5}$$

If the fundamental signal frequency is equal to the assumed basic frequency ($f_a = f_0$), then equations (4) and (5) are orthogonal to each other. At this point, $A(t)$ and $B(t)$ represent pure cosine and pure sine wave forms, respectively. In Figure 2, the orthogonal filter has different amplitude responses for all frequencies other than the nominal frequency. Its different amplitude response results clearly indicated that, when the orthogonal filter conforms to $f_a = f_0$ (60 Hz), the amplitude response value is 1.

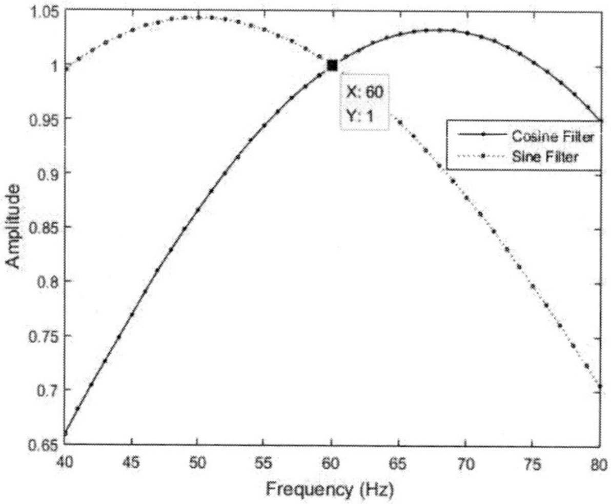

Figure 2. Frequency impact of the orthogonal filter.

2.2 Frequency estimation algorithm

In summary, we can derive the frequency change rules based on the amplitude response characteristics described above, and thus calculate the exact frequency. In practical applications, the usable vector lengths for the cosine and sine coefficients of the two orthogonal filters have the vector matrix of N_0 as expressed by equations (6) and (7).

$$CosWindow=\frac{2}{N_0}\left[\left(\cos(\frac{2\pi}{N_0}+\frac{\pi}{N_0}),\cos(\frac{4\pi}{N_0}+\frac{\pi}{N_0}),\text{K}+\cos(2\pi\frac{N_0-1}{N_0}+\frac{\pi}{N_0})+\cos(2\pi+\frac{\pi}{N_0})\right)\right] \tag{6}$$

$$SinWindow=\frac{2}{N_0}\left[\left(\sin(\frac{2\pi}{N_0}+\frac{\pi}{N_0}),\sin(\frac{4\pi}{N_0}+\frac{\pi}{N_0}),\text{K}+\sin(2\pi\frac{N_0-1}{N_0}+\frac{\pi}{N_0})+\sin(2\pi+\frac{\pi}{N_0})\right)\right] \tag{7}$$

Performing unilateral Z conversion for equations (6) and (7), their amplitude response functions can be expressed as equations (8) and (9) [10].

$$\left|H_{CosWindow}(f)\right|=\frac{4}{N_0}\cdot\frac{\cos\left(\frac{\pi}{N_0}\right)\sin\left(\frac{\pi}{N_0}\frac{f}{f_0}\right)\sin\left(\pi\frac{f}{f_0}\right)}{\cos\left(\frac{2\pi}{N_0}\frac{f}{f_0}\right)-\cos\left(\frac{2\pi}{N_0}\right)} \tag{8}$$

https://doi.org/10.1051/matecconf/201820102007

$$\left|H_{SinWindow}(f)\right| = \frac{4}{N_0} \cdot \frac{\sin\left(\frac{\pi}{N_0}\right)\cos\left(\frac{\pi}{N_0}\frac{f}{f_0}\right)\sin\left(\pi\frac{f}{f_0}\right)}{\cos\left(\frac{2\pi}{N_0}\frac{f}{f_0}\right)-\cos\left(\frac{2\pi}{N_0}\right)} \tag{9}$$

Equations (8) and (9) can be used to derive the amplitude ratio of the two filters, and this ratio can be expressed as equation (10).

$$R_{atio} = \frac{A}{B} = \frac{\left|H_{CosWindow}(f)\right|}{\left|H_{SinWindow}(f)\right|} = \frac{\tan\left(\frac{\pi}{N_0}\frac{f}{f_0}\right)}{\tan\left(\frac{\pi}{N_0}\right)} \tag{10}$$

Finally, the basic power signal frequency can be deduced using the amplitude value obtained using equation (10), and the basic power signal frequency is shown as equation (11).

$$f_a = f_0 \frac{N_0}{\pi}\tan^{-1}\left(\tan\left(\frac{\pi}{N_0}\right)\cdot R_{atio}\right) \tag{11}$$

However, the filtered signals can be affected by the amplitude responses and the frequency response effects. Therefore, the frequency evaluation using equations (10) and (11) will be subject to these factors. Equations (12) and (13) are phase response equations that can be used to deduce the 90° angle differences. Thus, we can resolve the phase angle differences and find the ideal amplitude ratios.

$$\angle H_{CosWindow}(f) = \pi - \pi\frac{(N_0-1)f}{N_0\cdot f_0} \tag{12}$$

$$\angle H_{SinWindow}(f) = \frac{1}{2}\pi - \pi\frac{(N_0-1)f}{N_0\cdot f_0} \tag{13}$$

To resolve the phase response effects, a DFT filter is used to determine the amplitude ratio of the filtered sine and cosine signals outputted during the first level. This method uses the phase response characters to offset the filtered signal by 90° to turn the signal phase difference into 180°. Thus, the two orthogonal signals will become symmetrical signals with only the positive and negative sign differences. The vectors of the second level DFT-filtered discrete signals are represented as Equations (14) and (15).

$$A = [A_1\ A_2\ A_3\ \ldots\ldots\ldots\ldots\ldots A_n]^T \tag{14}$$

$$B = [B_1\ B_2\ B_3\ \ldots\ldots\ldots\ldots\ldots B_n]^T \tag{15}$$

When equation (10) uses equations (14) and (15) to calculate the amplitude ratio, the amplitude ratio would have a significant deviation in the vicinity of the zero-crossover for the filtered values **A** and **B**, and the frequency calculation would produce an erroneous value. To resolve the zero-crossover problem, the frequency domain difference technique is adapted to verify the amplitude ratio because, in addition to the harmonic or inter-harmonic waves, real signals also contain voltage flickers and other noises. Although this frequency assessment method is based on the DFT filtering technique and can prevent harmonic and inter-harmonic wave interferences, the method still cannot prevent voltage flickers and other signal noise interferences. Thus, the interpolation technique is applied to further suppress the interferences and calculate the precise amplitude value.

2.3 Amplitude interpolation method

The discrete time sequence representation of a Hanning window is expressed as [8, 9]:

$$\mathbf{W}(n) = 0.5 - 0.5\cos\left(\frac{2\pi n}{N}\right), n = 0,1,..N-1 \tag{16}$$

The spectrum of the dot product of *x(.)* from equation (1) and the **W(.)** from equation (16) yields equation (17):

$$X(k) = -\frac{1}{2j}\left[Ae^{j\theta} \cdot W(\lambda - k) - Ae^{j\theta} \cdot W(\lambda + k)\right] \\ ,k = 0,1,...N-1 \tag{17}$$

where k is the frequency index of the DFT at the k-th spectral line; λ is the normalized frequency and can be written in two parts, as indicated in Equation (18) where l is the integer part of the frequency and δ is the fraction part of the frequency.

$$\lambda = \frac{f \cdot N}{f_0 \cdot N_0} = l + \delta, -0.5 \le \delta < 0.5 \tag{18}$$

Figure 3 shows the interpolation method of the Fourier transform spectrum where k is the largest index value in the X_k amplitude. When N is large enough, the amplitude can be expressed as:

$$V_k = |X_k| = \frac{N \cdot A \cdot \sin(\pi\delta)}{2\pi\delta} \tag{19}$$

δ is the largest frequency deviation for the true amplitude and the transformed amplitude in the spectrum, the value range of δ is between -0.5-0.5, the left and the right maximum amplitudes have the index values of k-1 and k+1, and its amplitude is expressed as:

$$V_{k\pm1} = |X_{k\pm1}| = \frac{N \cdot A \cdot |\sin(\pi\delta)|}{2\pi(1 - |\delta|)} \tag{20}$$

After the sampling signal is multiplied by the Hanning Window, the relationship between the largest amplitude frequency and the second largest amplitude frequency after the transformation—V_k and $V_{k\pm1}$—has the ratio of α which is expressed as:

$$\alpha = \frac{V_{k\pm1}}{V_k} = \frac{1 + |\delta|}{2 - |\delta|} \tag{21}$$

Through the Hanning Window relationship, the deviation ratio δ is expressed as:

$$\delta = \frac{2\delta - 1}{1 + \delta} \tag{22}$$

The amplitude correction value is thus expressed as:

$$V = \frac{2\pi|\delta|(1-\delta^2)}{N\sin(\pi\delta)}V_k \tag{23}$$

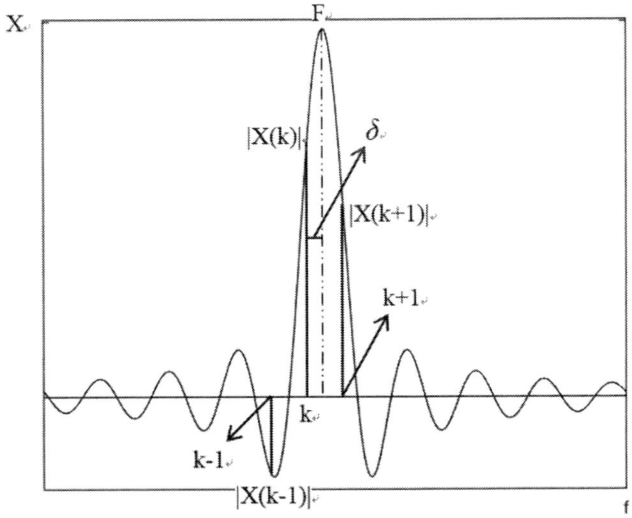

Figure 3. Interpolation algorithm diagram.

Finally, after the amplitude ratio has been incorporated into the frequency domain interpolation using equations (14) and (15), equation (23) is used to calculate the corrected orthogonal filter amplitude, and then incorporate the amplitude value into equation (11) to accurately evaluate the power system frequency.

3 Results

To verify the performance of the two-level DFT and frequency domain interpolation hybrid method proposed in this paper, we performed numerical simulations based on the various voltage signals encountered by the actual power system in a MATLAB simulation environment. They include harmonics, inter-harmonics, flickers, noises, and frequency offsets.

We used four frequency evaluation methods to compare all of the test results: the zero-crossing interpolation waveform reconstruction method (ZCIWR) [5], the frequency-domain interpolated (FDI) [8], the frequency-domain interpolated waveform reconstruction method (FDIWR) [9], and the method proposed in this paper. The objective of the comparisons is to understand the frequency deviations of the frequency estimation methods. The frequency absolute value proposed in [4, 26] is used to calculate the relative error as described in equation (24).

$$\text{Relative Error}(\%) = \frac{|\text{Actual Value - Estimated Value}|}{\text{Actual Value}} \times 100\% \tag{24}$$

3.1 Asynchronous sampling basic frequency evaluation

The IEC 61000-4-30 standard specifies the accuracy tolerance for measurements made by PQ analysis instruments. The basic frequency offset tolerance range for a power system with a rated frequency of 60 Hz is between 51 Hz and 69 Hz. To test whether the frequency evaluation method can effectively calculate the basic frequency, the simulated wave is represented using equation (25), where fa varies between 51 Hz and 69 Hz, and the with 1 Hz offset.

$$x(t) = \cos(2\pi f_a t) \tag{25}$$

Table 1 shows the results according to different frequencies under the various frequency evaluation methods. As anticipated, the proposed method is not affected by the a-th frequency offsets. Table 1 indicated that the deviations derived from the calculation method proposed by this paper are lower than 1e-14.

Table 1. Average relative frequency deviations for different basic frequency offsets.

Frequency Deviation(Hz)	Frequency evaluation deviation (%)			
	ZCIWR	FDI	FDIWR	Proposed method
51	9.174e-07	3.187e-04	1.087e-10	0
52	4.120e-07	5.431e-05	1.952e-11	9.455e-15
53	2.192e-07	4.192e-04	3.884e-08	8.097e-15
54	1.721e-06	3.191e-04	9.737e-12	1.315e-14
55	1.860e-06	0	1.991e-10	7.027e-15
56	1.649e-06	1.747e-04	4.488e-10	1.268e-14
57	1.934e-06	3.767e-04	1.166e-08	1.246e-14
58	1.784e-06	1.270e-04	6.679e-07	3.381e-15
59	2.671e-06	1.480e-04	2.492e-08	1.204e-14
60	9.852e-13	1.184e-14	0	0
61	1.987e-06	8.175e-05	4.386e-08	1.1648-14
62	1.530e-06	1.784e-04	9.756e-09	1.1460-14
63	2.278e-06	2.697e-04	1.982e-08	0
64	2.987e-06	6.740e-05	4.351e-09	0
65	4.387e-06	0	1.126e-10	0
66	4.756e-06	1.349e-04	2.862e-10	0
67	3.702e-06	1.203e-04	1.599e-09	0
68	3.198e-06	1.211e-04	1.607e-10	0
69	4.031e-06	1.233e-04	4.218e-07	0

3.2 Basic frequency evaluation under harmonic and inter-harmonic environments

In this paper, we referenced the IEC 61000-4-30 standard to propose the harmonic and inter-harmonic verification perimeters. The simulated waveform is represented using equation (26) where fa ranged from 51 Hz to 69 Hz and the offsets were made in 1 Hz increments.

$$x(t)=\cos(2\pi f_a t)+0.1\cos(3\times 2\pi f_a t)+0.05\cos(5\times \pi f_a t)+0.1\cos(7\times 2\pi f_a t+pi)+0.05\cos(13\times 2\pi f_a t) \\ +0.05\cos(25\times 2\pi f_a t)+0.05\cos(29\times 2\pi f_a t)+0.01\cos(3.5\times 2\pi f_a t)+0.01\cos(7.5\times 2\pi f_a t) \quad (26)$$

Table 2 indicates that all four techniques are affected by the harmonics and inter-harmonics in the harmonic and inter-harmonic environments. However, the average deviations derived from the frequency evaluation algorithm adopted by this paper under a variety of frequency offsets were all better than those of other methods.

Table 2. Average relative frequency deviation under harmonic and inter-harmonic environment.

Frequency Deviation(Hz)	**Frequency Evaluation deviation (%)**			
	ZCIWR	**FDI**	**FDIWR**	**Proposed method**
51	9.844e-07	3.781e-04	1.033e-04	3.602e-07
52	3.745e-07	4.233e-05	1.361e-05	4.119e-07
53	2.299e-07	4.126e-04	0.002	6.459e-07
54	1.601e-06	3.411e-04	4.764e-05	3.482e-07
55	1.513e-06	2.122e-06	1.565e-05	1.268e-08
56	1.414e-06	2.246e-04	2.939e-05	1.731e-07
57	1.964e-06	3.731e-04	3.879e-05	3.518e-07
58	1.894e-06	8.510e-05	4.630e-05	5.698e-08
59	2.760e-06	1.372e-04	4.218e-05	3.070e-08
60	9.971e-13	1.184e-14	0	0
61	2.025e-06	8.500e-05	4.233-05	4.798-09
62	1.504e-06	1.762e-04	3.616e-04	8.195e-08
63	2.169e-06	2.601e-04	7.604e-04	8.980e-08
64	2.906e-06	7.771e-05	3.063e-04	1.6156e-08
65	4.542e-06	5.025e-07	7.562e-07	1.372e-09
66	5.133e-06	1.456e-04	7.672e-06	1.004e-08
67	3.765e-06	8.755e-05	0.001	8.496e-08
68	3.364e-06	9.517e-05	0.004	3.193e-08
69	3.843e-06	1.318e-04	0.005	7.024e-08

3.3 Basic frequency evaluation under flickering environments

In addition to the harmonic and inter-harmonic frequencies, power system voltages usually also contain flicker frequencies. According to [27], human eyes are most sensitive to a flicker frequency of approximately 8.8 Hz. Thus, we added two flicker components of 5 Hz and 8.8 Hz to equation (26), with amplitudes of 0.05% and 0.1%, respectively.

Table 3 shows the frequency evaluation deviations of the four methods under the harmonic, inter-harmonic, and flicker interference environments. The relative deviation obtained using the method proposed by this paper was approximately 1e-4%, and was approximately 1e-1% using other methods. Thus, the method proposed by this paper has better performance under the harmonic, inter-harmonic, and flicker interference environments.

Table 3. Average relative frequency deviation under flicker environments.

Frequency Deviation(Hz)	**Frequency Evaluation deviation (%)**			
	ZCIWR	**FDI**	**FDIWR**	**Proposed method**
51	0.050	0.057	0.348	0.009
52	0.048	0.033	0.277	0.005
53	0.045	0.042	0.16	0.002
54	0.040	0.152	0.018	0.002
55	0.035	0.117	0.188	0.002
56	0.029	0.101	0.047	0.001
57	0.024	0.040	0.084	0.001
58	0.019	0.045	0.191	0.001
59	0.015	0.141	0.227	0.001
60	0.013	0.179	0.179	0.003
61	0.014	0.121	0.251	0.009
62	0.017	0.042	0.272	0.010
63	0.020	0.044	0.246	0.011
64	0.024	0.097	0.283	0.006
65	0.028	0.209	0.270	0.008
66	0.031	0.125	0.219	0.010
67	0.034	0.041	0.140	0.011
68	0.036	0.030	0.238	0.005
69	0.050	0.057	0.348	0.009

3.4 Basic frequency evaluation under noise environments

To test whether the frequency estimation algorithm can effectively calculate the basic frequency under a noise interference environment, a 60 dB of noise is added to the simulated waveform discussed in 3.3.

Table 4 shows the maximum relevant deviation from simulating all of the frequency estimation methods 500 times in mixed environments. The table indicates that when using the ZCIWR, FDI, FDIWR, and the method proposed by this paper in mixed interference environments with a steady-state evaluation frequency of between 51–69 Hz; the maximum average relative deviations were 5e-02%, 2e-01%, 3e-01%, and 1e-02%, respectively. The results indicate that all four algorithms had good responses in the 60 dB environment.

https://doi.org/10.1051/matecconf/201820102007

Table 4. Maximum relative frequency deviation in a mixed environment.

Frequency Deviation(Hz)	Frequency Evaluation deviation (%)			
	ZCIWR	FDI	FDIWR	Proposed method
51	0.050	0.058	0.347	0.009
52	0.048	0.033	0.278	0.004
53	0.045	0.042	0.160	0.003
54	0.040	0.152	0.019	0.002
55	0.035	0.116	0.181	0.001
56	0.029	0.102	0.047	0.001
57	0.024	0.040	0.083	0.001
58	0.019	0.045	0.191	0.001
59	0.015	0.141	0.227	0.001
60	0.013	0.178	0.175	0.003
61	0.014	0.121	0.251	0.009
62	0.017	0.042	0.272	0.010
63	0.020	0.044	0.246	0.012
64	0.024	0.096	0.282	0.006
65	0.028	0.208	0.269	0.008
66	0.031	0.125	0.219	0.010
67	0.034	0.041	0.140	0.011
68	0.036	0.030	0.238	0.005
69	0.037	0.111	0.166	0.008

4 Conclusion

In this paper, we adopted the classic spectrum analysis algorithm used by the majority of scholars—DFT—as the basis for frequency evaluation for the PQ analysis. A two-level DFT and frequency domain interpolation hybrid technique is used for basic frequency evaluation. This method used the DFT filter as the basis for the frequency calculation. This approach can reduce the harmonic and inter-harmonic interferences. The orthogonal characteristics and the frequency domain interpolation method were then used to further suppress the flicker components. The experimental results indicated that when the signals sampled using the method proposed by this paper contained harmonic, inter-harmonic, and flicker components, the method can obtain high-precision basic frequency that can be used to facilitate subsequent PQ spectrum analyses.

Acknowledgments

This research is supported by the Project of the Ministry of Science and Technology, Taiwan, under grant numbers MOST 104-2221-E-027-060-MY2 and MOST 106-3113-E-006-010.

References

1. Y. Luo, L. Kaicheng, Y. Li, D. Cai, C. Zhao, and Q. Meng, IEEE Transactions on Industrial Informatics, 1-1, 2017.
2. D. Camarena-Martinez, M. Valtierra-Rodriguez, C. A. Perez-Ramirez, J. P. Amezquita-Sanchez, R. d. J. Romero-Troncoso, and A. Garcia-Perez, IEEE Transactions on Industrial Electronics, **63**(4), 2369-2378, 2016.
3. U. Singh and S. N. Singh, IEEE Transactions on Industrial Informatics, 1-1, 2017.
4. I. C. Cheng, IEEE Transactions on Industrial Electronics, **60**(4), 1652-1658, 2013.
5. F. Zhou, Z. Huang, C. Zhao, X. Wei, and D. Chen, IEEE Transactions on Instrumentation and Measurement, **60**(8), 2804-2812, 2011.
6. M. B. Djurić and Ž. R. Djurišić, Electric Power Systems Research, 2008, **78**(8), 1407-1415.
7. Y.-C. Chen and T.-H. Chien: 'A Simple Approach for Power Signal Frequency Determination on Virtual Instrument Platform', 65-71; 2015,
8. D. Agrez, IEEE Transactions on Instrumentation and Measurement, **51**(2), 287-292, 2002.
9. G. Chang, C. I. Chen, Y. J. Liu, and M. C. Wu: 'Measuring power system harmonics and interharmonics by an improved fast Fourier transform-based algorithm', 193-201; 2008,
10. S.-R. Nam, S.-H. Kang, and S.-H. Kang, Energies, **8**(1), 79, 2015.
11. Y. Jun-Zhe and L. Chih-Wen, IEEE Transactions on Power Delivery, **15**(2), 494-499, 2000.
12. D. Belega and D. Petri, IEEE Transactions on Instrumentation and Measurement, **62**(5), 942-953, 2013.
13. D. Macii, D. Petri, and A. Zorat, IEEE Transactions on Instrumentation and Measurement, **61**(10), 2653-2664, 2012.
14. S. Reza, M. Ciobotaru, and V. G. Agelidis, IEEE Journal of Emerging and Selected Topics in Power Electronics, **4**(4), 1226-1235, 2016.
15. S. P. Talebi, S. Kanna, and D. P. Mandic, IEEE Transactions on Signal and Information Processing over Networks, **2**(4), 477-488, 2016.
16. S. Golestan, J. M. Guerrero, and J. C. Vasquez, IEEE Transactions on Power Electronics, 2018, **33**(2), 911-916.
17. S. Golestan, J. M. Guerrero, and J. C. Vasquez, IEEE Transactions on Power Electronics, **33**(1), 24-31, 2018.
18. M. S. Reza, M. Ciobotaru, and V. G. Agelidis, IEEE Transactions on Instrumentation and Measurement, **64**(3), 615-624, 2015.
19. S. Nanda and P. K. Dash, IEEE Transactions on Instrumentation and Measurement, **67**(1), 45-56, 2018.
20. Y. Xia, Z. Blazic, and D. P. Mandic, IEEE Transactions on Instrumentation and Measurement, **64**(3), 638-648, 2015.
21. Z. Ž, B. Krstajić, and T. Popović, IEEE Transactions on Power Delivery, **32**(4), 1809-1816, 2017.
22. T. Lobos and J. Rezmer, IEEE Transactions on Instrumentation and Measurement, 46(4), 877-881, 1997.
23. J. Khodaparast and M. Khederzadeh, IET Generation, Transmission & Distribution, **11**(18), 4406-4413, 2017.
24. L. Fu, J. Zhang, S. Xiong, Z. He, and R. Mai, IEEE Transactions on Smart Grid, **8**(2), 640-650, 2017.
25. D. V. Coury, A. C. B. Delbem, J. R. d. Carvalho, M. Oleskovicz, E. V. Simoes, D. Barbosa, and T. V. d. Silva, IEEE Transactions on Smart Grid, **3**(3), 1353-1361, 2012.

26. P. Gupta, R. S. Bhatia, and D. K. Jain, IEEE Transactions on Smart Grid, **6**(1), 26-35, 2015.
27. F. Bai, X. Wang, Y. Liu, X. Liu, Y. Xiang, and Y. Liu, CSEE Journal of Power and Energy Systems, **2**(3), 10-18, 2016.

https://doi.org/10.1051/matecconf/201820102008

A Study on the Application of Electronic Nose Coupled with DFA and Statistical Analysis for Evaluating the Relationship between Sample Volumes versus Sensor Intensity of Agarwood Essential Oils Blending Ratio

Sahrim Lias[1,*], *Nor Azah* Mohamad Ali[2], *Mailina* Jamil[3], *Mohd Shafik Yuzman* Tolmanan[4] and *Muhamad Afizzul* Misman[5]

[1-4] Natural Products Division, Forest Research Institute Malaysia (FRIM), 52109 Kepong Selangor, Malaysia
[5] Forestry and Environmental Division, Forest Research Institute Malaysia (FRIM), 52109 Kepong Selangor, Malaysia

Abstract. The exquisite agarwood oils are primary used for perfumery industries either as pure essential oils or in a perfume base. Commonly, Agarwood oils are extracted from low grade 100% agarwood chips via distillation processes and the extracted oil is called as pure agarwood essential oil which containing 100% of extracted material. In perfumery industry, the agarwood pure oils are often blend with other essential oils such as geranium, sandalwood, gurjum balsam, jasmine and Ylang ylang to create rich, complex and pleasant oils compared to pure Agarwood oils smell alone that may not suit all users preferences. To dates, agarwood oil quality assessment is typically carried out manually via human olfactory system which produces different results and inconsistency from traders and buyers. From the results, multiple linear regression analysis used to run the multiple regression prediction models using combination of 11 sensors shown better results by increasing the R^2 value from 0.674 to 0.915 and the RMSE value from 14.65% to 6.80% compared to single regression prediction models using sensor LY2/G. The sensors intensity values from multiple sensors are showing a strong correlation to the volume of the B1 in the blended samples (M11~M20) as the ratio of B1 is increased.

1. Introduction

Agarwood is originated from *Aquilaria* (Thymelaeceae) species, also known as Gaharu, Jin-Koh, Chim-Hyuang, oud and Kanankohis a highly valuable fragrant wood used for incense, perfume, traditional medicines and religious ceremony. In Peninsular Malaysia, five species of *Aquilaria* have been recorded and they are *A. malaccensis*, *A. microcarpa*, *A. hirta*, *A. beccariana* and *A. rostrate* [1]. Among this five species, *A. malaccensis* and *A. crassna* is the best known species which produced high quality and multipurpose used of gaharu resin.

Usually, Agarwood is distilled for essential oils using hydrodistillation, water distillation and supercritical fluid carbon dioxide extraction (SFE) techniques. The presence of complex chemical compounds can be identified using the headspace solid phase micro extraction (HS-SPME), Gas Chromatography Mass Spectrometry (GC/GCMS) and Gas Chromatography–olfactometry (GC-O) while Electronic Nose (EN) which mimic human nose is used to detect the strong and unique heavy scent of Agarwood oil [2]. Among them, combination of EN and HS-SPME-GCMS is also used to classify the quality of four agarwood oil into high and low grades [3]. Current study revealed that the presence of sesquiterpenes and its chromonederivaties such as 10-epi-γ-eudesmol, β-agarofuran, α-agarofuran and γ-eudesmol can be used as a standard in order to identify the high or low quality of agarwood oils [4]. High quality of agarwood oil contained major constituted of guaiene and eudesmanesesquiterpenes [5]. Two less known compounds: 9-11-eremophiladien-8-one and oxo-agarospirol always found in low quality of agarwood oil. β-agarofuran, α-agarofuran and 10-epi-γ-eudesmol were found less in low quality Agarwood oil. Some discovered compounds like β-agarofuran, 11-dien-9-one, camphor and (-)-selina-3 are major compounds contributing to the fresh and sweet aroma which represent the gorgeous and elegant character of agarwood oil [6].

The price range and quality of Agarwood oils are very reliant on its physical properties, color, odor and consumer perceptions. High quality oil commonly is dark color, long lasting odor, expensive and categorised as either supreme or deluxe oils with the price range between USD126 to USD633 per tola while the wood price for low qualities are USD19 per kg. Agarwood wood chips are traded according to its grade. Different countries graded or classified the Agarwood oil by their own methods. In Japan, Agarwood oil is categorized as high and low quality using its chemical profiles.

* Corresponding author: sahrim@frim.gov.my

https://doi.org/10.1051/matecconf/201820102008

KananKoh is categorized as the highest quality and Jinkoh is the lowest quality [7]. However, different grading techniques make the price of Agarwood oil fluctuates and not standardized in the market. Beside the grading techniques, agarwood oil itself is difficult to differentiate either it is pure or mixture oil.

Currently, there are many devices or instruments used to capture odor or scent and one of the equipment used is Electronic Nose (EN). EN is a device designed to mimic human nose functions which is to detect and differentiate smell with higher sample repeatability compared to human nose. EN being used widely for different usage such as for measurement for mango homogenate and whole fruit, mango fruit maturity, *saccharomyces cerevisiae* strains for alcoholic fermentation, milk self-life determination, virgin olive oil quality, zingiberaceae family oils [8-13]. DFA has been used to classify growing cell populations between the four groups defined in the learning cell population [14]. It is also used to classify Agarwood oils into pure and mixture clusters for easy observation [15] and compared to k-NN kfold classifier classification system [16].

This paper proposed a technique to observe significant data trend and to evaluate the relationship patterns between sample volume and sensor intensity from a set of Agarwood essential oil mixture samples. The blending process is based on the specific increment ratio of agarwood oil volume whereby the Gurjum balsam oil volume is fixed. All experiment and data analysis were conducted via EN experiments coupled with DFA and statistical analysis using R software.

2. Materials and Methods

This work is completed by conducting experiment using commercial FOX4000 EN from Alpha-MOS (Toulouse, France) bundled with AlphaSOFT version 12 data analysis software. Each of EN experiments are started with the samples preparation processes, EN parameters setup, sample heating using heating block, headspace generated manually injected to the EN using gas tight syringe and recording the sensors response data into the main database. Overall flows of this paper are as in Figure 1. The process is started with samples selection process whereby both sample were subjected to the chemical test using Gas chromatography–mass spectrometry (GCMS) equipment and chemical constituent detection technique. This test can identify each sample is Agarwood and Gurjum balsam essential oils because of each pure essential oils having only major significant chemical compounds known consisted in each oils. The process is continue with oils samples blending process, sample preparation process for EN experiments, features extraction process, data visualization and pattern recognition and classifier using DFA. Detail steps of each process are explained in the next subsection.

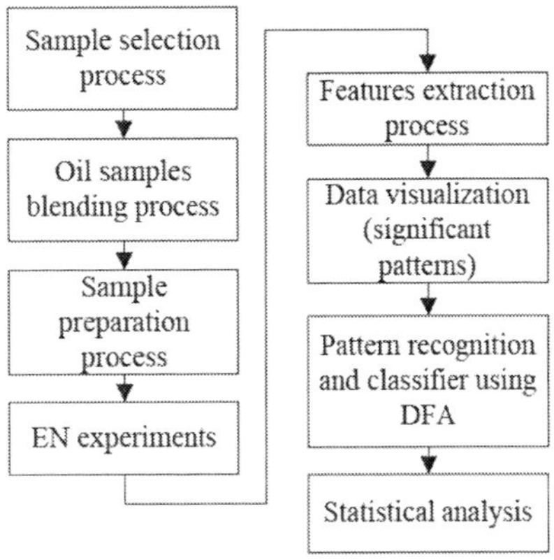

Figure. 1. Overall research flows.

2.1. Sample Preparation

Agarwood and Gurjum balsam essential oils samples were obtained from the Natural products division, FRIM essential oil collection whereby they were initially bought from trusted agarwood traders. 2 essential oils name as base B1 (pure agarwood) and base B2 (pure Gurjum balsam) were selected as reference essential oils. 10 mixture oils were blended from both base oils which are M11, M12, M13, M14, M15, M16, M17, M18, M19 and M20. The samples are names corresponding to the increment of B1 volume in the blended sample. Details samples preparation process, blending ratio, and pictures of blended oil samples are as in Table 1, Table 2 and Figure2.

Table 1. Sample preparation parameters.

Samples preparation	
Vial size and type	10 ml glass vial with magnetic clamp cap
Vial per sample	5
Sample volume	±10 µl per vial (no dilution)
Sample code	B1, B2, M11~M20
Sample blending ratio	10 samples: B1 varies 1~10 : B2 (fixed)

Table. 2. Pure Agarwood B1 and pure Gurjum B2 balsam sample blending ratio.

B1	B2	M11	M12	M13	M14	M15	M16	M17	M18	M19	M20
		B2 + B1	B2 + B1*2	B2 + B1*3	B2 + B1*4	B2 + B1*5	B2 + B1*6	B2 + B1*7	B2 + B1*8	B2 + B1*9	B2 + B1*10

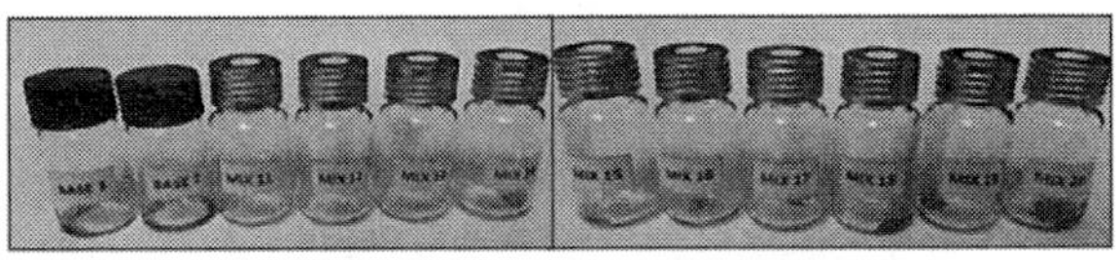

Figure 2. A set of 2 pure B1: pure Agarwood and B2: pure Gurjum balsam with 10 of blended oils (M11, M12, M13, M14, M15, M16, M17, M18, M19 and M20).

2.2. Electronic Nose Experiment

EN equipment comprised of 18 metal oxide semiconductors (MOSs) chemical sensors. The EN sensor chambers are divided into 3 type of high performance (HiP) chambers; Chamber A: doped metal oxide sensors (T30/1, P10/1, P10/2, P40/1, T70/2 and PA2) , chamber B: doped metal oxide sensors (P30/1, P30/2, P40/2, T40/2, T40/1 and TA2) and chamber CL2:undoped metal oxide sensors (LY2/AA, LY2/G, LY2/gCT, LY2/gCTl, LY2/Gh and LY2/LG) which can detect flammable gases, organic compounds, toxic gases and oxidizing gases. The carrier gas used is purified air grade (P = 5 psi). The complete EN system (manual injection configuration) consisted of heating block, main EN chamber and computer installed with AlphaSOFT software.

The internal EN hardware operations flows are illustrated as in Figure 3. The injection port is the main sample inlet to the EN hardware. Each headspace generated from the heated sample is injected into the injection port with special gas tide syringe. The system will allow the purified air as the headspace carrier gas to carry the sample headspace through all 3 chambers in the system and exit at the exhaust port. Simultaneously, the AlphaSOFT software will record all EN raw data for database establishment.

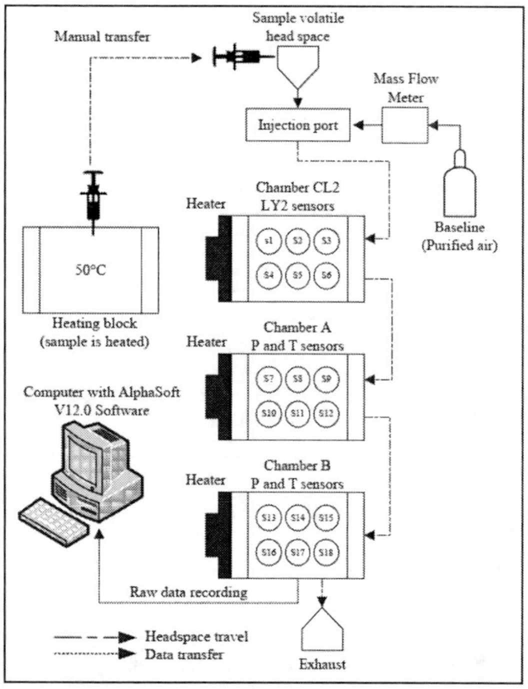

Figure 3. Alpha-MOS FOX4000 EN internal structures and sample injection flows.

EN was use to capture the uniqueness of agarwood essential oils samples scent and transform the information into sensor responses data. A total of 60 sample vials were used in the EN experiment for the database development process. A specific EN experiment protocol is optimized prior conducting the experiment. The optimized parameters used in the EN experiment are tabulated in Table 3.

Table 3. Electronic nose analytical conditions.

EN experiment parameters	
Injection type	Manual injection configuration
Sequence type	Interlace each sample
Acquisition duration (sec)	120
Acquisition period (sec)	1
Data sampling (sec)	1
Acquisition time (sec)	600
Flow (ml/min)	150
Gas tight syringe volume (ml)	2.5
Injection volume (μl)	500
Injection speed (μl/ sec)	500
Heating temperature (°C)	50
Heating time (sec)	300
Library construction option	Maximum (automatic selection of signal extrema). Delta (Ro – R)/Ro (R: resistance difference divided by the Ro: initial resistance). In this mode, the displayed value is relative resistance= (Ro-R)/Ro, where 0 R is the resistance at t = 0 (baseline resistance) and R is the resistance at time t

2.3. Data analysis (features extraction, DFA model and R statistical analysis)

All raw data were observed and extracted using AlphaSOFT version 12 data analysis software provided with the instrument. All experiment raw data were gathered from all 18 sensors responses. Each vial producing 120 continuous data corresponding to 120 seconds of acquisition duration with 1 s sampling rate. The "Delta R/R0" option displays the sensor values as relative resistance variation whereby R is sensor response correspond to the sample injected and RO is the initial resistance value as a baseline (no sample injected). For the main EN database, the "Maximum (automatic selection of signal extrema)" option criteria is selected. Therefore, with this selection, only the maximum peak data (+ve peak and –ve peak) from each sensor with a total of 18 data per vial were extracted. These databases comprised of 60x18 data size were then used for the development of DFA model.

Statistical analyses were performed using R software to test the relationship between sensor's sensitivity and volumes of Agarwood oils blending ratio. Mann-Whitney U test was tested on the maximum peak data to compare the diffferences between B1 and M11~M20 with 95% confident level for each sensor. The P-value is used as the main indicator and if the value is smaller than 0.05, it is indicates that the sensor can differentiate between B1 and M11~M20. Simple linear regression analysis was then applied to the maximum peak data of each sensor to find which sensor gave better result in predicting the volumes of Agarwood. Higher r-square (R^2) value indicates better result. For better prediction, multiple linear regression approach was also applied to the maximum peak data for the development of model, which combines several selected sensors to predict the volume of Agarwood in the blended oils. Finally, Analysis of Variance (ANOVA) was used to compare between the best models for single sensor with the model with a combination of several sensors.

3. Results

The raw data are extracted using maximum peak point from each sensor. All 18 sensor data are selected using library construction option: maximum for data library construction as one of example data in Figure 4 pointed as "Maximum response" which produced a total of 60x18 data matrix.

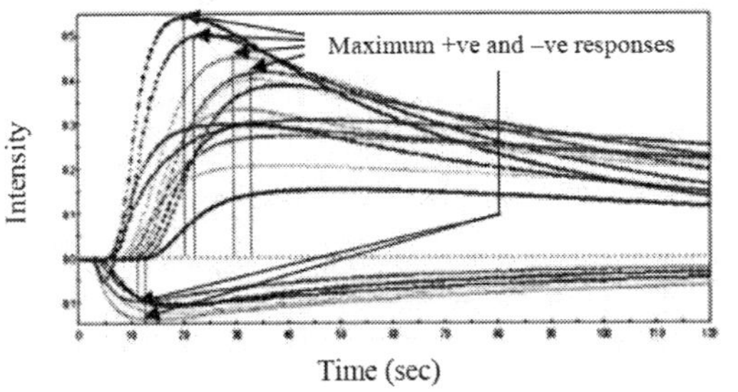

Figure 4. Total 120 seconds data recording time per sample with maximum response +ve and –ve points for each sensor extracted as raw data

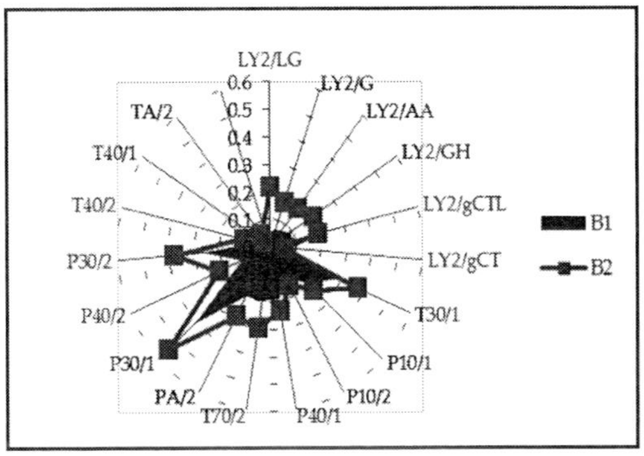

Figure 5. Radar view of 18 EN sensor data comparison between B1 and B2 samples.

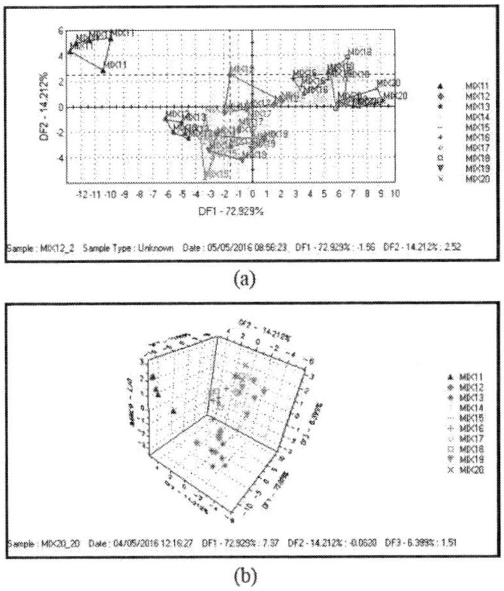

(a)

(b)

Figure 6. DFA model for 10 samples M11, M12, M13, M14, M15, M16, M17, M18, M19 and M20: (a) DFA1 and DF2 view and (b) DFA1, DF2 and DF3 view.

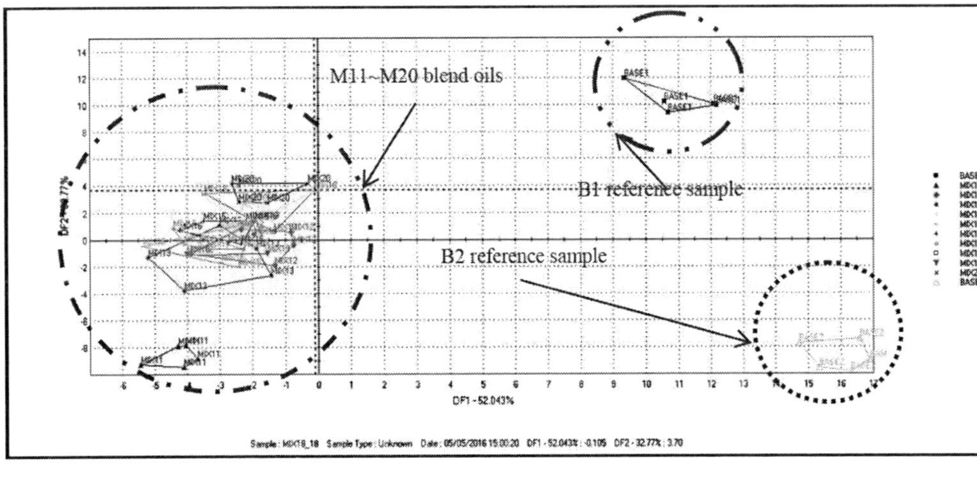

Figure 7. DFA model for 12 samples B1, B2, M11, M12, M13, M14, M15, M16, M17, M18, M19 and M20.

 https://doi.org/10.1051/matecconf/201820102008

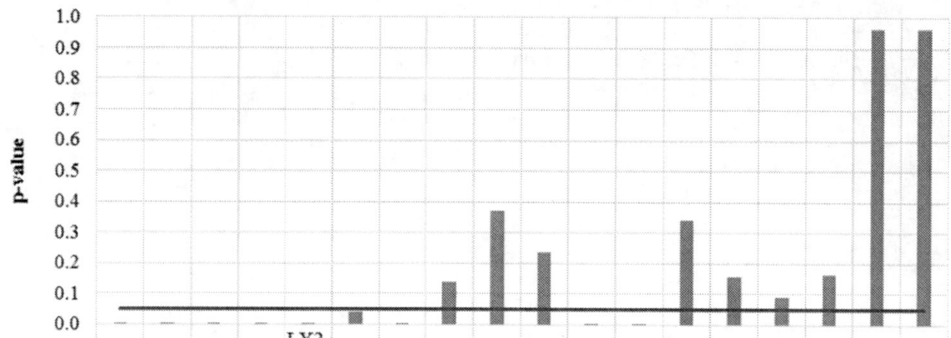

	LY2.LG	LY2.G	LY2.AA	LY2.GH	LY2.gCTL	LY2.gCT	T30.1	P10.1	P10.2	P40.1	T70.2	PA.2	P30.1	P40.2	P30.2	T40.2	T40.1	TA.2
p-value	0.00	0.00	0.00	0.00	0.00	0.04	0.00	0.13	0.37	0.23	0.00	0.00	0.34	0.15	0.09	0.16	0.96	0.96
sig.value	0.05	0.05	0.05	0.05	0.05	0.05	0.05	0.05	0.05	0.05	0.05	0.05	0.05	0.05	0.05	0.05	0.05	0.05

Figure 8. The p-value of Mann-Whitney U test tested on each sensor. Value over 0.05 indicates non-significant different between pure and mix Agarwood oils.

4. Discussion

Figure 5 shows that sample B1 and sample B2 are having a different EN sensors data response and patterns intensity whereby sample B2 is having higher sensors response value compared to sample B1. This proven that B1 and B2 are different samples and having a different fragrance. B1 and B2 then is blended with specific ratio into 10 blended samples (M11~M20). All 12 samples are then subjected into the DFA model constructed including B1 and B2 labeled as reference sample. There are 3 main group clusters (cluster 1: B1, cluster 2: B2 and cluster 3: M11~M20) can be observed in Figure 7 showing that each of group is having a different sensor response.

The observation is further done within the blended samples (M11~M20) for any sensors intensity differences. After they are subjected into constructed DFA model by excluding B1 and B2, they can be observed as different sample in 3D view (DFA1=72.929%, DF2=14.212% and DF3=6.399% view) much better compared to 2D view (DFA1=72.929% and DF2=14.212%) as in Figure 6 (b) and (a) respectively.

A statistical test, particularly Mann-Whitney U test has shown that 9 sensors including LY2/LG, LY2/G, LY2/AA, LY2/GH, LY2/gCTL, LY2/Gct, T30/1, T70/2 and PA/2 did pass the test at 95% confident level as shown in Figure 8. B1 and 10 blended samples (M11~M20) Agarwood oils at minimum concentration of 50 percent can be differentiate using these sensors. Other sensors, namely as P10/1, P10/2, P40/1, P30/1, P40/2, P30/2, T40/2, P30/2, T40/2, T40/1 and TA/2 have shown non-significant results. As for model development for the prediction of Agarwood volumes in mix oils, in overall most sensors gave low correlation values with an average R^2 of 0.20 and Root Mean Square Error (RMSE) of 22.45%. Only five sensors, which are LY2/LG, LY2/G, LY2/AA, LY2/GH, and LY2/gCTL gave moderate correlation values. LY2/G gave the best predictions of Agarwood volumes in mix oils with R^2 and RMSE of 0.674 and 14.65% respectively. The prediction of Agarwood volumes in mix oils using model developed by multiple regression analysis approach has shown a significant improvement with the combination of LY2/G, T30/1, PA/2, LY2/AA, LY2/LG, P30/1, P30/2, LY2/gCTL, LY2/GH, T70/2 and P40/2's sensors. The R^2 value of combined sensors has improved to 0.915. This model has also successfully reduced the RMSE to 6.80%. The result of ANOVA test was also shown the significant different between the best model using single sensor and combined sensors.

5. Conclusions

As a conclusion, from the EN experiments conducted, DFA model is enabled to differentiate B1 and B2 into two different clusters. Multiple linear regression analysis used to run the multiple regression prediction models using combination of 11 sensors had shown better results by increasing the R^2 value from 0.674 to 0.915 and the RMSE value from 14.65% to 6.80% compared to single regression prediction models using sensor LY2/G. From the results, it can be concluded that the sensors intensity values from multiple sensors are having a strong correlation to the volume of the B1 in the blended samples (M11~M20) as the ratio of B1 is increased.

Acknowledgments: All support from Forest Research Institute Malaysia (FRIM), Asia Pacific Association of Forestry Research Institutions (APAFRI) and Natural Products Division staffs are very much appreciated.

* Corresponding author: sahrim@frim.gov.my

References

1. Chang, Y.S., NorAzah, M.A. & Abu, S.A. Gaharu: A prized incense from Malaysia. *Malaysian Oil Science & Technology* **2001**, *vol. 9(2),* pp. 26-27.
2. Sahrim, L., Nor Azah, M.A., Mailina, J., Muhd Hafizi, Z., Abdul Majid, J. & Nurlaila, I. Classification of Agarwood Oils Using K-NN K-Fold. *Sensor Letters* **2014**, *vol. 12(6-7),* pp. 1038-1040.
3. Nurlaila, I., Nor Azah, M.A., Mailina, J., Mohd Hezri, F.R., SaifulNizam, T. &Mohd Nasir, T. A. review study of Agarwood oil and its quality analysis. *Jurnal Teknologi* **2014**, *vol. 68(1),* pp. 37-42.
4. Nor Azah, M.A., Nurlaila,I., Mailina,J., Mohd Nasir,T. &MohdHezri, F.R. Analysis of aroma compounds from Gaharu oil by Head-space solid phase microextraction and Gas chromatography-mass spectrometry. *In proceeding of the Seminar on Medicinal & Aromatic Plants: Translating natural products R, D& C initiatives in line with economic transformation programme* **2012**, Pp: 180-185.
5. Ishihara, M., Tsuneya. &Uneyama,K. Components of the Agarwood smoke on heating. *Journal of Essential Oil Research* **1993**, *vol. 5*, pp. 419-423.
6. Pripdeevech, P., Khummueng,W. &Park,S.K. Identification of odoractivecomponents of Agarwood essential oils from Thailand by Solid Phase Microextraction-GC/MS and GC-O. *Journal of Essential Oil Research* **2011**, *vol. 23*, Pp.46-53.
7. Ishihara, M., Tsuneya. &Uneyama,K, Components of the volatile concentrate of Agarwood. *Journal of Essential Oil Research* **1993**, *vol. 5*, pp. 283-289.
8. A. R. Paper Development of Electronic Nose Measurement for Mango (Mangifera Indica) Homogenate and whole fruit. *Proc. Fla. State Hort. Soc* **2004**, *vol. 51*, no. 7, pp. 421–425.
9. M. Lebrun, A. Plotto, K. Goodner, M. Ducamp, and E. Baldwin. Discrimination of mango fruit maturity by volatiles using the electronic nose and gas chromatography. *PostharvestBiology and Technology* **2008**, *vol. 48*, pp. 122–131.
10. P. Chalier, D. Chevalier-lucia, C. Ghommidh, and J. A. Ragazzo-sanchez, "Identification of Saccharomyces cerevisiae strains for alcoholic fermentation by discriminant factorial analysis on electronic nose signals", *Electron. J. Biotechnol* **2010**, *vol. 13*, no. 4.
11. S. Bazzo, S. Cade, and E. Chanie, "Shelf life determination by electronic nose: application to milk," *Sensor and Actuators* **2005**, *vol. 106*, pp. 199–206.
12. D. L. García-gonzález and R. Aparicio, "Coupling MOS sensors and gas chromatography to interpret the sensor responses to complex food aroma: Application to virgin olive oil," *Food Chem.* **2010**, *vol. 120*, no. 2, pp. 572–579.
13. Sahrim, L., Nor Azah, M.A., Mailina, J., Azrina, A., Siti Humeirah A.G. and Mohammad Faridz Z. P. Classification of selected essential oil from family zingiberaceae using e-nose and discriminant factorial analysis (dfa) techniques: an initial study. *Journal of Applied Mechanics and Materials (AMM)* **2015**, pp. 799-800: 932-936.
14. J. Savatier, J. Vigo, and J. M. Salmon, "Monitoring cell cycle distributions in living cells by videomicrofluorometry and discriminant factorial analysis," *Cytometry Part A* **2003**, *vol. 56A*, pp. 8-14.
15. Sahrim, L., Nor Azah, M.A., Mailina, J., Muhd Hafizi, Z. and Siti Humeirah A.G., "Classification of pure and mixture Agarwood oils by Electronic Nose and Discriminant Factorial Analysis (DFA)," *2015 International Conference on Smart Sensors and Application (ICSSA)* **2015**, pp.7-10.
16. Sahrim, L., Nor Azah, M.A., Mailina, J., Abdul Majid, J. and Mohd Fadhli, O. Discrimination of pure and mixture agarwood oils via electronic nose coupled with k-NN kfold classifier. *Procedia Chemistry* **2016**, *vol. 20*, p 63-68.

Comparison of bulk FinFET and SOI FinFET

Ying-Yu Chen[1] *and Yu-Hsien Lin*[*]

[1]National United University, Department of Electronic Engineering , 36063 Miaoli, Taiwan
[*]National United University, Department of Electronic Engineering , 36063 Miaoli, Taiwan

Abstract. In this study, we compare the differences and advantages between Bulk FinFET and SOI FinFET. The results are simulated by using the ISE TCAD software. By changing the parameters of the gate voltage, drain voltage and gate length to analysis which characteristic is better. Through the experiment results, we demonstrate that the SOI FinFET have the better characteristics than bulk FinFET[1].

1.INTRODUCTION

With the rapid development of technology, the device structure is very important. The main difference between the Bulk and SOI process is the different substrate, resulting in different process levels. A single-crystal silicon process have used on the SOI FinFET that the device must be deposited on the oxide layer is more difficult to control and the SOI Wafer is relatively more expensive; however, the bulk FinFET is difficult to control the values of parameters because of channel impurities[2]. The bulk FinFET has fewer steps of process and lower manufacturing costs. But, the process consumes high power and large leakage current ; SOI FinFET have the additional layer of oxide (BOX), the difference between the elements can be shortened by removing the n-well or p-well, and the BOX insulation reduces the device leakage[3]. As the results, in terms of the electrical simulation, SOI FinFET is better than Bulk FinFET.

2.Device Structure and Fabrication

The BULK FinFET consists of a diode and two adjacent PN junctions shown in Figure 1 (a), which is the most important circuit component in an integrated circuit with less process steps, lower manufacturing costs, and lower process costs high power, large leakage current. However, the SOI FinFET has more Buried Oxide (BOX) than the BULK FinFET shown in Figure 1 (b), the BOX insulation effect reduces the component leakage and consumes less power in the manufacturing process, but the manufacturing cost is higher.

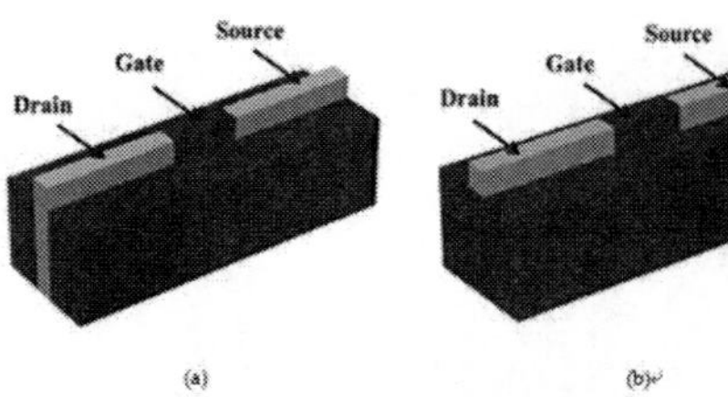

Figure 1. (a) It is the structure of BULK FinFET.(b) It is the structure of SOI FinFET.

3.Results

3.1 $I_D - V_G$ Characteristic diagram

In the simulation of $I_D - V_G$ characteristic curve shown in Figure 2, we choose different drain operating bias under the conditions of channel length (Lg) of 10um. We hope to observe that the current of BULK FinFET and SOI FinFET is on (I_{on}) and off (I_{off}) between the changes and observe the different curves of the swing and displacement to understand its characteristics. From the $I_D - V_G$ characteristic curve, it can be seen that when the drain bias is large, the circulating current is larger, the ratio I_{on} and I_{off} Ratio will be larger, and the sub-critical swing (SS) will be smaller. On the one hand, SOI FinFET also has better switching efficiency than BULK FinFET.

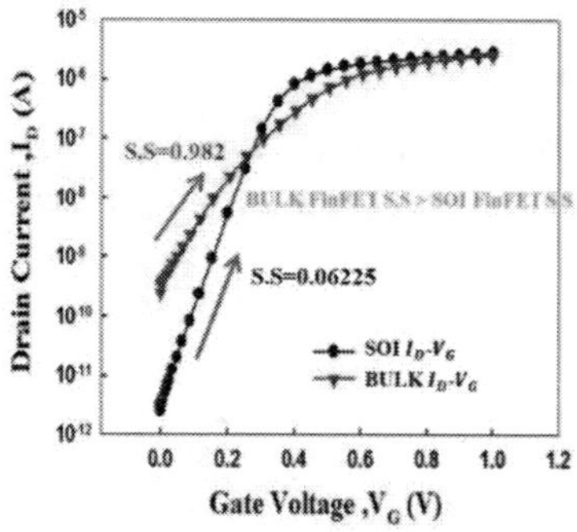

Figure 2. We can observe that the threshold swing (SS) characteristic of SOI FinFET is better than BULK FinFET.

3.2 $I_D - V_D$ Characteristic Diagram

It can be observed from Figure 3 (a) (b) that the electrical diagrams of the curves of the SOI FinFET and BULK FinFET at different voltages are shown in Figure 3. It can be clearly observed that the current of SOI FinFET is almost saturated at V_D = 1 V. It is higher than the saturation current of BULK FinFET shown in Figure 3 (c).

[*] Corresponding author: yhlin@nuu.edu.tw

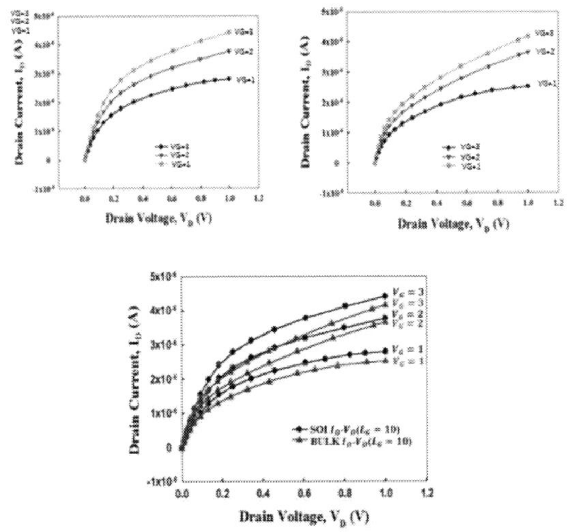

Figure 3. (a)(b) we can observe the characteristic of current when V_G is 1v, 2v and 3v.(c) When both components reach saturation current, it can be seen that the saturation current of SOI is larger than BULK.

3.3 Electronic Concentration Chart

Due to the experimental simulation I chose NMOS, and I capture the cross-section of the channel to observe the conduction of electrons turning on in the channel.When the channels of SOI FInFET and BULK FinFET are on, it can be observed from Figure 4(a) that the concentration of SOI FinFET is higher than BULK FinFET. In addition, the leakage current of BULK FinFET is more severe than SOI FinFET. However, when the channels of SOI FinFET and BULK FinFET are off, it can be observed from Figure 4(b) that the concentration of SOI FinFET is greater than BULK FinFET. Although BULK FinFETs are well-closed, the electron concentrations SOI FinFETs is higher than BULK FinFETs.

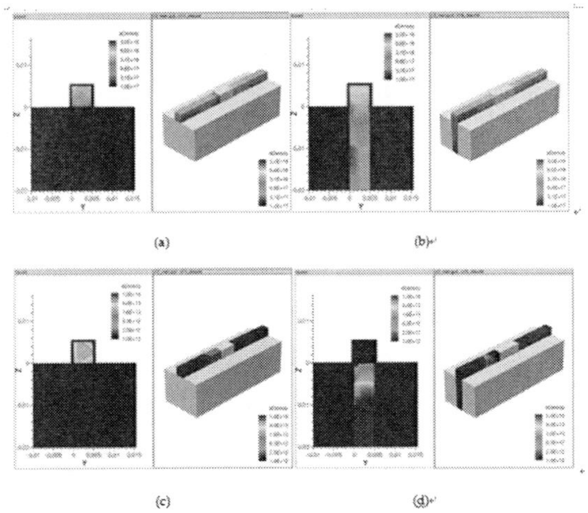

Figure 4. We can observe the electron density in SOI FinFET when(a) I_{ON} and(c) I_{OFF} . On the other hand, we show the electron density in Bulk FinFET when(b) I_{ON} and(d) I_{OFF}.

3.4 $I_D - V_G$ Characteristic Diagram (DIBL value)

When the off-state transistor has a high drain voltage, making the barrier between the source and the channel down, it results a nearly through phenomenon called DIBL (Reduced Induced Drain Barrier). Figure 5 shows that when I_D is fixed, there is no difference between $V_G = 1$ and $V_D = 0.05$ for the SOI FinFET shown in Figure 5 (a), but the difference between the K = 1 and $V_D = 0.05$ for the BULK FinFET varies greatly shown in Figure 5 (b). From this it can be found that DIBL of BULK FinFETs have more severe than SOI FinFETs.

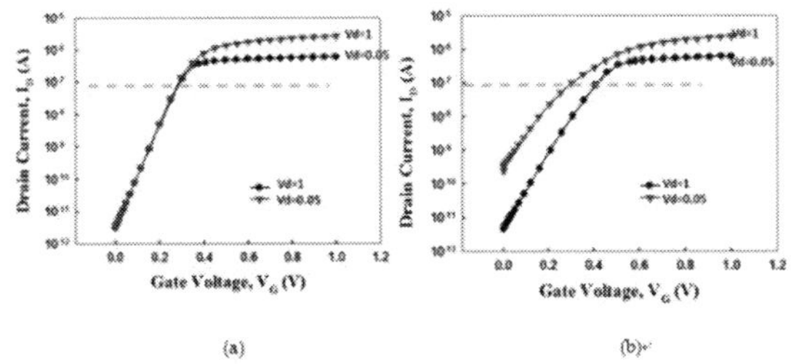

Figure 5. The $I_D - V_G$ characterization of SOI FinFET(a)is better than Bulk FinFET(b).

3.5 DIBL − L_G characteristic diagram

It can be observed from Figure 6 that as the channel length (L_G) changes, the DIBL value will also change. The longer the channel length, the smaller the DIBL value. Comparing the DIBL values of the SOI FinFET shown in Figure 6 (a) and BULK FinFET shown in Figure 6 (b), it can be observed that the DIBL value of the BULK FinFET is greater than that of the SOI FinFET for the same channel length.

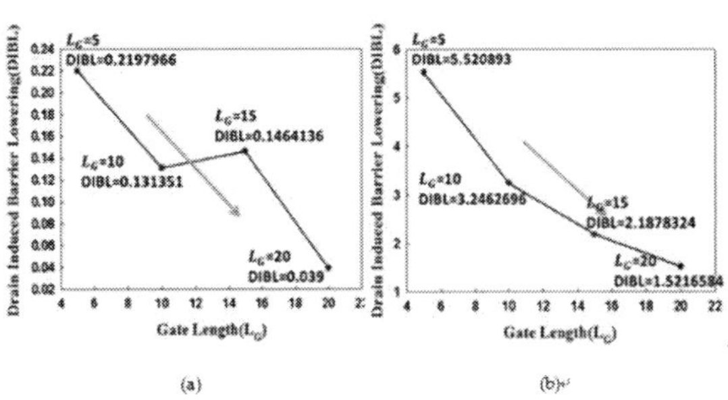

Figure 6. The DIBL of SOI FinFET(a) is better than Bulk FinFET(b).

4. Conclusion

In this study, the results are simulated by using the ISE TCAD software, and changing a variety of parameters to simulate in different situations. Then, we use the simulation diagram to compare the characterization between SOI FinFET and BULK FinFET. As a results, through the result of the simulation, we can observe that the characteristics of SOI FinFET are better than BULK FinFET.

Acknowledgments: The authors acknowledge the National Science Council of Taiwan for supporting this research under contract number MOST-106-2221-E-239-028 andthe National Nano Device Laboratories (NDL) for their technical support.

5.References

1. Anterpreet Gill; Charu Madhu; Pardeep Kaur, IEEE, " Investigation of short channel effects in Bulk MOSFET and SOI FinFET at 20nm node technology," 2015 Annual IEEE India Conference (INDICON), pp. 1-4, 2015.
2. D. Singh; S. K. Mohapatra; K. P. Pradhan; P. K. Sahu, IEEE, "Variation study of process parameters in Trigate SOI-FinFET," 2014 Annual IEEE India Conference (INDICON), Pages: 1 – 4, 2014.
3. Terence B. Hook; F. Allibert; K. Balakrishnan; Bruce Doris; Dechao Guo; Narasimha Mavilla; E. Nowak; G. Tsutsui; R. Southwick; J. Strane; Xin Sun, IEEE, 'SOI FinFET versus bulk FinFET for 10nm and below " 2014 SOI-3D-Subthreshold Microelectronics Technology Unified Conference (S3S), Pages: 1 – 3, 2014

Node-Gosper Island-Based Data Collection Method with Recharge Plan for Rechargeable Wireless Sensor Networks

Chi-Chang Chen[1]*

[1]Department of Information Engineering, I-Shou University, 84001 Kaohsiung, Taiwan

Abstract. Because of recent advances in wireless power transfer technologies, several key topics of wireless sensor networks (WSNs) need to be revisited. Traditional data collection methods for WSNs typically consider the balance of power consumption among sensors as a critical design criterion for avoiding uneven power depletion in the networks. I propose a solution for the uneven power consumption problem of data collection over WSNs. I designed a node-Gosper island-based scalable hierarchical cluster transmission method in conjunction with a wireless recharge plan for data collection over rechargeable WSNs. For the recharge plan, I used a mobile wireless charger to visit and recharge the batteries of sensors located on different levels of node-Gosper curves with various frequencies. The duration of each recharging process for each layer of sensors was calculated to verify the feasibility of the proposed recharge plan. The simulation results indicate that my proposed data collection method outperforms several well-known data collection methods in terms of energy consumption.

1 Introduction

A wireless sensor network (WSN) is a wireless communication network consisting of numerous automated devices that use sensors to cooperate in monitoring the physical or environmental conditions of designated locations, such as temperature, sound, vibration, pressure, movement, and contaminants. In recent years, the number of studies on WSNs has substantially increased. In such studies, the method of extending the lifetime of WSNs is always the key topic considered for designing protocols or algorithms for WSNs. Although previous efforts have provided several effective energy-saving methods, the ability to extend the lifetime of WSNs is still limited by the battery power configured in the sensors.

Wireless charging technology originated approximately 100 years ago with American scientist Nikola Tesla. In 2007, at the Massachusetts Institute of Technology (MIT), a group of theoretical physicists performed an electromagnetic resonance power transmission of 2 m to light a 60-W bulb [1], thereby bringing wireless power transmission into a new era.

In this work, I propose an energy-efficient data collection method for a rechargeable WSN (RWSN) based on the recursive structures of node-Gosper islands. In association with the proposed data collection method, I provide a novel recharge plan that uses a wireless charger travelling in different levels of node-Gosper curves to charge the sensors in the RWSN by using electromagnetic resonance power transmission technology. I simulated my proposed data collection method and compared the performance with several well-known data collection methods. The simulation results indicate that my proposed method outperforms those well-known data collection methods in terms of energy consumption.

2 Background and related works

A node-Gosper curve is a space-filling curve of fractal geometry generated by the continuous replacement of each vertex with the basic seven-segment curve. The resultant filled space is a node-Gosper island [2]. Figure 1 shows level-1 to level-3 node-Gopser islands, respectively, with their corresponding node-Gosper curves. Recently, the node-Gosper curve has been successfully applied to solve the mobile anchor localization problems of WSNs [3]. In the literature, a variety of hexagonal addressing methods for identifying hexagons in a hexagonal tessellated plane are described. In the present study, I used two addressing methods, namely the ring-based addressing scheme and base-7 addressing scheme, described in [3], both of which are suitable for addressing the hexagons in a node-Gosper island.

Generally, the data transmission methods of WSNs can be divided into three categories: direct transmission, multihop transmission, and cluster transmission. Direct transmission involves each sensor collecting and directly transmitting data to the base station. It is the simplest data transmission method. For multihop transmission, each sensor transmits data to neighboring nodes that are closer to the base station. This routing method can avoid mass energy consumption for the sensors that are far away from the base station. However, because data from

* Corresponding author: ccchen@isu.edu.tw

 https://doi.org/10.1051/matecconf/201820103001

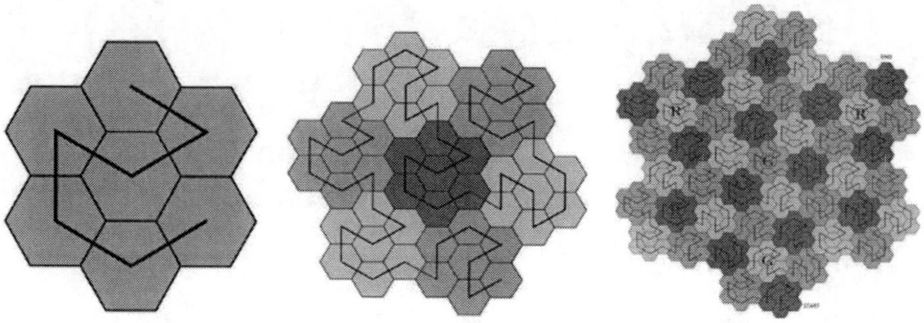

Fig. 1. Level-1, level-2, and level-3 node-Gosper islands and their corresponding node-Gosper curves.

all sensors are continuously transmitted to the base station, those that are close to the base station must transfer more information, resulting in the energy of these sensors being exhausted faster than that of others. Clustering transmission serves as a compromise between the previous two methods. First, the entire sensor network is divided into several clusters according to a specific topological relationship. Each cluster periodically selects its cluster head according to a protocol, and then all the sensors in the cluster transmit their collected data to the respective cluster head. Finally, the cluster head sends the aggregated data to the base station in a direct or multihop manner. Among all cluster transmission methods, the low-energy adoptive cluster hierarchy (LEACH) [4] is the most well-established.

Recent data collection methods for RWSNs, such as those proposed in [5], [6] and [7], usually performed wireless charging and data gathering functions over the same path for the same duration. However, for general WSNs, the durations for charging sensors and collecting data are typically different. The duration for data collection is typically measured in seconds and minutes and is much faster than that of charging the sensors in the network (possibly measured in months or years). Therefore, in this study, I separated these two functions, and performed them with different paths and different durations.

3 Proposed data collection method and recharge plan

In this section, I focused on the data collection methods of the RWSN and proposed a new method that uses the energy of the whole RWSN more efficiently. Additionally, in association with the data collection method, I provided an efficient recharge plan to charge all the sensors in the RWSN. I assumed that the RWSN contains two types of sensors, namely relay sensors and normal sensors, and that the base station was located at the center of the sensing area. Each relay sensor was installed with the long-range Zigbee communication chip, the communication range of which is over 1 km [8]. Each normal sensor was installed with the normal Zigbee communication chip, the communication range of which is 10–60 m depending on the environment of the sensing field. Both types of sensors were assumed to have the same amount of initial energy.

3.1 Proposed data collection method for the RWSN

In this subsection, I assume that the entire sensing area of the RWSN was covered by a sufficient level of the node-Gosper island and a relay sensor was deployed at the center of each sub-node-Gosper island. In my proposed data collection method, I adopted the hierarchical clustering approach based on the recursive structure of the node-Gosper island. I considered every seven basic hexagons (i.e., the first level node-Gosper island) as a basic cluster. Each sensor transmits its collected data to the center of the central hexagon in its cluster. In order to allow each normal sensor to send its collected data to its cluster head, the radius of the circumscribed circle of each basic hexagon is set to $r/3$, where r is the communication range of the normal sensors in the RWSN. Because the node-Gosper island has a recursive structure, the higher level node-Gosper island is composed of seven lower level sub-node-Gopser islands. Therefore, the sensor data can be transmitted to the central hexagon of the higher level node-Gosper island using the same method until all the data have been passed to the center of the central hexagon of the entire sensor network.

The proposed data collection method is summarized as the following two stages:

1) Setup Stage:

1. Cover the entire sensing area with the minimal level, say k, node-Gosper island, in which the radius of the circumscribed circle of each hexagon is set to $\frac{r}{3}$, where r is the communication range of the normal sensors in the RWSN.
2. Assign a base-7 address to each hexagon in the level-k node-Gosper island and calculate the Cartesian coordinates of the center of each addressed hexagon. Derive the node-Gosper curve of the level-k node-Gosper island by using the base-7 addressing sequence.

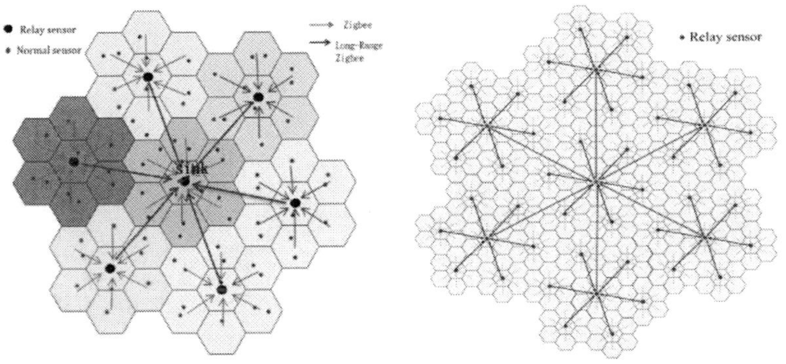

Fig. 2. Data collection paths in the level-2 and level-3 node-Gosper islands.

3. Localize all the sensors and separately identify the hexagons that they belong to. This can be achieved by programming a robot car equipped with a wireless communication chip and a GPS device to travel along the level-k node-Gosper curve obtained in Step 2. When the robot car reaches a turning point, it broadcasts its position message to all sensors within its communication range. Once a sensor has received more than three different position messages from the robot car, that sensor can estimate its coordinates by using the trilateration method, and subsequently identify the hexagon that the sensor belongs to based on the estimated coordinates.
4. A relay sensor is deployed at the center of each level-1 sub-node-Gosper island in the level-k node-Gosper island, either manually or by using a robot car (an example of a deployed level-2 node-Gosper island is shown in the left side of Figure 2).

2) Data Transmission Stage:

1. Each normal sensor sends its data to the relay sensor located at the center of the level-1 sub-node-Gosper island that the normal sensor belongs to based on the address of the hexagon it located.
2. Each relay sensor in the level-1 sub-node-Gosper island aggregates the collected data and sends the aggregated data to the relay sensor of the level-2 sub-node-Gosper island that it belongs to. Similarly, if applicable, each relay sensor of a lower level sub-node-Gosper island sends its collected data to the relay sensor of its immediate higher level sub-node-Gosper island until the base station located at the center of the level-k node-Gosper island is reached (Fig. 2 depicts the data collection paths of the level-2 and level-3 node-Gosper islands, respectively).

If the aforementioned method is used to transfer the collected data to the base station, the relay sensors of the higher level sub-node-Gosper islands must send more information with longer transmission distances, causing their power consumption levels to increase to levels higher than those of the lower level relay sensors. This phenomenon is restricted by the traditional data collection method in a WSN because the relay sensors of higher level sub-node-Gosper islands become invalid much earlier than do other sensors.

In the next subsection, I consider the aforementioned phenomenon and provide details of charging cycles for different sensors with different levels of power consumption to ensure that the power supply to all sensors in the sensor networks is sufficient and stable.

3.2 Recharge plan for the sensors in the RWSN

In this study, I outline the use of a wireless mobile charger called ChargerCar to charge the sensors in an RWSN. ChargerCar is a robot car equipped with a high-capacity battery, magnetic resonance power transmitter, wireless communication transceiver, and GPS.

According to the data collection method proposed in the previous subsection, I assumed that the sensing region of the RWSN is covered by a level-k node-Gosper island. The most power-consuming nodes are the relay sensors located at the center of the surrounding six level-(k–1) sub-node-Gosper islands, which I call layer-1 relay sensors. Considering the level-3 node-Gosper island in Fig. 8 as an example, the most energy-consuming nodes are the six layer-1 relay sensors located at the centers of the six level-2 sub-node-Gosper islands. Because I assumed that all the sensors in the RWSN have the same initial energy, the most energy-consuming sensors should be recharged earlier than the other sensors. For this purpose, we can use the path of the level-1 node-Gosper curve depicted in Fig. 9 as the routing path for ChargerCar to charge the layer-1 relay sensors located at the centers of the level-2 sub-node-Gosper islands.

Subsequently, the relay sensors in each level-(k–2) sub-node-Gosper island called layer-2 relay sensors can be arranged as the next charging nodes by using the level-2 node-Gosper curve. Fig. 10 illustrates the level-3 node-Gosper island and corresponding level-2 sub-node-Gosper curve as the charge path for layer-2 relay sensors. Similarly, for the other relay sensors in level-$(k - i)$, i = 3, .., (k – 1) sub-node-Gosper islands, called layer-i relay

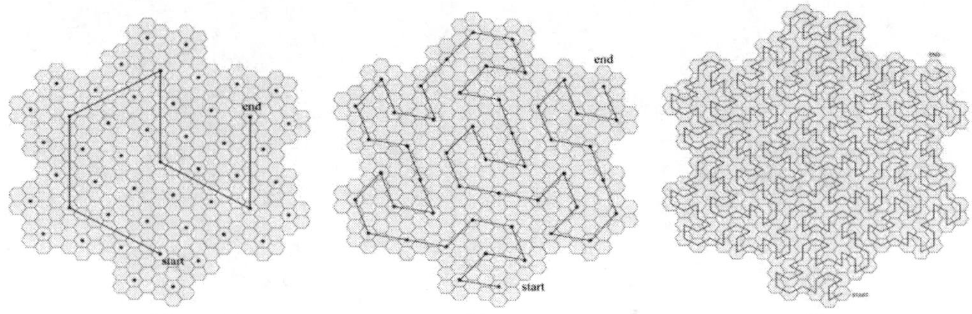

(a) (b) (c)

Fig. 3. Charge path of (a) layer1 relay sensors, (b) layer-2 relay sensors, and (c) normal sensors.

sensors, the node-Gosper curve of level-i can be used as the charge path for the relay sensors.

Finally, the charging path for all the normal sensors in the RWSN can follow the level-k node-Gosper curve. As shown in Fig. 11, ChargerCar can stay at the center of each hexagon to charge the sensors in a one-to-many manner in the hexagon. Because each normal sensor in the data collection method mentioned in the previous subsection transmits the sensing data directly and over a short distance to the relay sensor at the center of the level-1 sub-node-Gosper island to which it belongs, the power consumption is very low. Therefore, the energy of each normal sensor can last for an extended period before needing to be recharged.

If the sensing area is covered by a level-k node-Gosper island, the charge plan for the RWSN can be arranged as follows:

1. Estimate the cycles of recharge time for the relay sensors on each layer and the normal sensors according to the amount of data they have transmitted and received. Suppose that the cycles of recharge time for the relay sensors on layer-i are R_i days, where i=1,2,…,k−1, and for the normal sensors is N days.
2. For each i from 1 to k−1, identify the centers of the 7^i level-(k−i) sub-node-Gosper islands that constitute the level-k node-Gosper island. Every R_i days, send ChargerCar to visit and charge the layer-i sensors located at the 7^i center positions along the path of the level-i node-Gosper curve.

Every N days, send ChargerCar to travel along the level-k node-Gosper curve and stop at the center of each hexagon (i.e., the turning point of the node-Gosper curve) to charge the normal sensors in the hexagon in the one-to-many manner.

4 Simulation results

In this section, I simulate my proposed data collection method and compare its performance of various types of energy consumption with those of three other well-known data collection methods, namely direct transmission, the LEACH [4], and multihop routing with minimum hop counts [9].

The energy consumption model from the LEACH was applied to all sensors as follows:

$$E_{TX}(k,d) = \begin{cases} kE_{elec} + k\varepsilon_{fs}d^2, & d < d_0 \\ kE_{elec} + k\varepsilon_{mp}d^4, & d \geq d_0 \end{cases} \quad (1)$$

$$E_{RX}(k) = E_{elec} \times k \quad (2)$$

where E_{TX} and E_{RX} are the energy consumed when transmitting and receiving, respectively, k bits data from a source node to the anchor node. The sensors in the cluster used TDMA as the medium access control layer control protocol for communication. The simulation tool used was MATLAB R2013a. Simulations of 50 different deployments of sensors were performed and the mean values were taken for comparison. In the following, I showed the simulation results of different type of energy consumptions for my proposed method (node-Gosper) with aforementioned three well-known methods.

4.1 Accumulated energy consumption of all sensors

Figure 4(a) illustrates the simulation results of the accumulated energy consumption for the four data collection methods with 200 sensors. The figure indicates that my proposed method (node-Gosper) is superior to the direct transmission method, multihop routing with minimum hop count method, and LEACH. Fig. In the simulation, sensors are randomly distributed in the sensing field. Thus, many sensor nodes may locate far away from the base station. According to Equation (1) of the energy consumption model, when the transmission distance is greater than 87.7 m (i.e., d_0) [4], the transmission energy consumption is proportional to the fourth power of its distance. Therefore, if the direct transmission method is applied, these sensors consume very large amounts of energy and increase the total energy consumption to a very high level.

Regarding the LEACH method, a Voronoi diagram is used for clustering. Because the clusters vary in size, some of the sensor nodes may have communication distances greater than 87.7 m, despite data being sent to their cluster heads within their clusters. Additionally, the election of a cluster head for each round consumes a certain amount of energy from all sensors. These factors

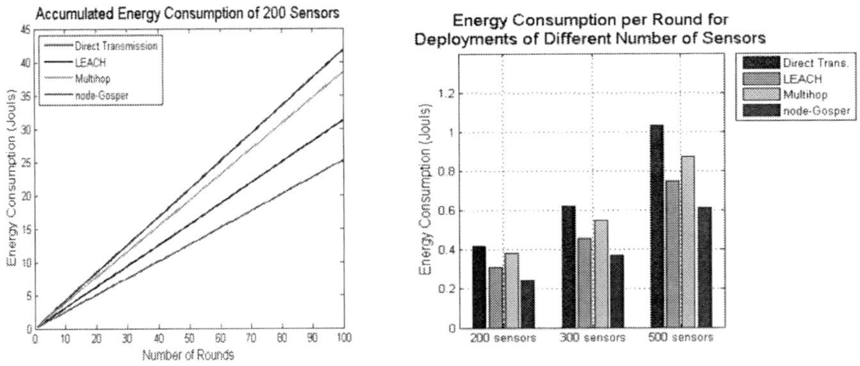

(a) (b)

Fig. 4. (a) Comparison of the accumulated energy consumption of 200 sensors for the four data collection methods. (b) Comparison of the average energy consumption per round for different number of sensors deployed in the sensing area for the four data collation methods

render the total energy consumption of the LEACH higher than that of my proposed method.

Regarding multihop routing with minimum hop count method, because sensors do not cluster, no data aggregation effect occurs. Although the distance between each hop is shorter, the total energy consumption of all sensors is still higher than that of my proposed method.

In my proposed method, the cluster size and the locations of cluster heads are fixed. Except for the lower layer relay sensors, almost all the transmissions between sensors occur over a short distance, and this conserves energy. Because my approach causes the lower layer relay sensors to consume excessive amounts of energy, this approach may not be suitable for traditional WSNs because of the uneven power consumption of sensors. However, in the RWSN, this problem can be resolved by shortening the recharging cycle for the lower layer relay sensors to achieve a sufficient energy provision environment.

4.2 Energy consumption for different node-densities

In this subsection, different number of sensors is deployed in the sensing area of each data collection method. I compared the average energy consumption of the sensors per round for the deployment of 200, 300, and 500 sensors in the same area of each method. The simulation result is shown in Figure 4(b), which indicates that my proposed method (node-Gosper) consumed less energy than the other three data collection methods for all the cases of different number of sensor deployments.

In my proposed method, as long as the topology of node-Gosper area is fixed, the number of relay sensors is fixed regardless the increase of the number of sensors. Therefore, as the number of sensors increases, the additional sensors are all normal sensors, which transmit sensing data in a very short distance, and they consume very little amount of energy. Due to the benefit of the data aggregation in the cluster head, the relay sensors only need to transmit 60% (the assumption in the simulation) of the data amount to their upper level. Therefore, the amount of energy consumption is less than the direct transmission method and multihop method, which do not have the clustering effect. For the LEACH method, the number of cluster heads (5% of the sensors in this experiment) increases as the number of sensors increases. Thus, there may be more cluster heads which have distance greater than 87.7 m, and these cluster heads consume a large amount of energy while they transmit collected data to the base station.

4.3. Average energy consumption of each sensor

In this subsection, I compare the average energy consumption of each sensor in the four data collection methods. In particular, I focus on the comparison of the normal sensor in my proposed method (node-Gosper) with the sensors in the other methods. In the simulation, I measured the average energy consumption of all the sensors. In my proposed method, I measured energy consumption of two types of sensors, namely relay sensors and normal sensors. Figure 5 indicates that the average energy consumption of the normal sensors in my method is much less than that of the sensors in the other methods. The reason is that the normal sensors, which the majority of the sensors, in my proposed method only need to send their sensing data to their corresponding cluster heads, and these transmissions are all within a short distance. On the other hand, most of the sensors in the multihop method not only need to send their sensing data, but also need to relay data for other sensors. In the LEACH method, although the non-cluster head sensors only need to send the sensing data for themselves, they may locate at a considerable distance to their cluster head due to the large size of the clusters.

As explained in the first subsection, the lower layer relay sensors in my proposed method may consume excessive amounts of energy. This problem can be resolved by shortening the recharging cycle for the lower

https://doi.org/10.1051/matecconf/201820103001

Table 1. Path lengths and number of stop stations required to charge all sensors in the RWSN

Charge path*	**Sensing Area (k×m^2)**	**Number of stop stations**	**Path length (m)**	**Number of stop stations per k×m^2**	**Path length per k×m^2**
SCAN (16×16 unit squares)	51.20	256	3606	**5.00**	**70.43**
Hilbert (order 4)	51.20	256	3606	**5.00**	**70.43**
S-curve(ad) (16×15 unit squares)	48.00	310	5063	**6.46**	**105.48**
Z-curve (order 4)	51.20	256	4188	**5.00**	**81.80**
Node-Gosper curve (level 3)	89.12	343	5923	**3.85**	**66.46**

* The radius of the circumscribed circle of each unit square (or hexagon) was 10 m.

layer relay sensors to achieve a sufficient energy provision environment in the RWSN.

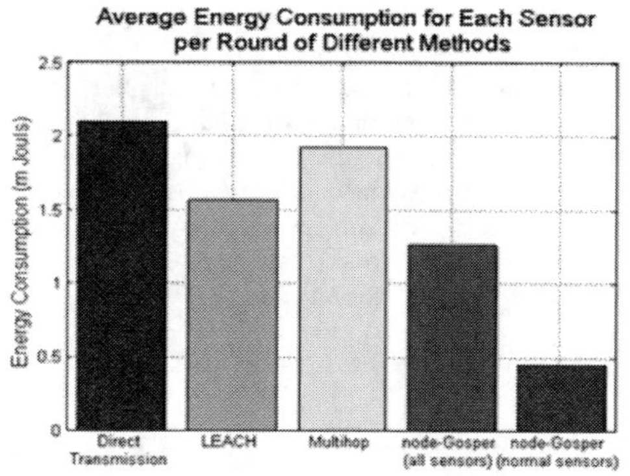

Fig. 5. Comparison of energy consumption of each sensor for the four data collection methods.

4.4 Comparison of various charge paths in the recharge plans

In [10] Han et al. used four well-known routing paths from traditional WSNs, namely the SCAN, Hilbert curve, S-curve(ad), and Z-curve, as charge paths for the RWSN. Table 1 compares the path lengths and number of stop stations of the node-Gosper curve, SCAN, Hilbert curve, S-curve(ad), and Z-curve, assuming that each unit regular polygon (square or hexagon) has the same radius (r = 10 m) of the circumscribed cycle. My proposed method has less number of stop stations and shorter path travel path than other charge paths over the same normalized area.

5 Conclusions

This paper presents a novel data collection method with a recharge plan for RWSNs. My method is based on the node-Gosper island in association with its corresponding node-Gosper curves. I compared my proposed method with three well-known data collection methods, namely direct transmission, the LEACH, and multihop routing with minimum hop count. My proposed method outperformed these three traditional data collection methods in terms of many respect of energy consumption, including the accumulated energy consumption of sensors, different densities of sensors, and average energy consumption of sensors.

I also compared the charge path lengths and the number of charge stops of the charge paths when separately using the node-Gosper curve, SCAN, Hilbert curve, S-curve(ad), and Z-curve for the RWSNs. The results in Table 1 indicate that the node-Gosper curve had the shortest charge path length and lowest number of charge stops among all the compared curves. This result implies that the node-Gosper curve is a suitable candidate for use as a charge path for RWSNs.

In recent years, wireless power transfer technologies have increased in popularity in many application domains such as electric vehicles and mobile phones. The cost of wireless power transfer modules is predicted to gradually decrease. Therefore, a rechargeable battery module is expected to soon become available for installation on sensor nodes in WSNs. In such a case, many existing solutions for WSNs from network protocols to working applications must be revisited and adjusted accordingly. I believe that more effort should be devoted to this newly derived research direction in the future.

Acknowledgments: This work was partially supported by the Ministry of Science and Technology, Taiwan, under contract MOST106-2221-E-214-010.

References

1. A. Kurs, A. Karalis, R. Moffatt, J. D. Joannopoulos, P. Fisher, M. Soljačić, Wireless power transfer via strongly coupled magnetic resonances. *Science*, 317(5834), 83-86 (2007)
2. J. Ventrella, "Root 7 Family." *Brainfilling Curves-A Fractal Bestiary*. Lulu.com (2012)
3. Chi-Chang Chen, Sheng-Bo Wang, Node-Gosper Curve-Based Unknown Sensor Localization Using Single Mobile Anchor in Wireless Sensor Networks. *International Journal of Distributed Sensor Networks*, 2016(7),13 pages (2016)

4. W. R. Heinzelman, A. Chandrakasan, H. Balakrishnan, Energy-efficient communication protocol for wireless microsensor networks. In System sciences, Proceedings of the 33rd annual Hawaii international conference on (pp. 1-10), IEEE (2000)
5. M. Zhao, J. Li, Y. Yang, A framework of joint mobile energy replenishment and data gathering in wireless rechargeable sensor networks. IEEE Transactions on Mobile Computing, 13(12), 2689-2705 (2014)
6. S. Guo, C. Wang C. Y. Yang, Joint mobile data gathering and energy provisioning in wireless rechargeable sensor networks. *IEEE Transactions on Mobile Computing*, *13*(12), 2836-2852 (2014)
7. B. H. Liu, N. T Nguyen,. V. T. Pham, Y. X. Lin, Novel methods for energy charging and data collection in wireless rechargeable sensor networks. *International Journal of Communication Systems* (2015)
8. Digi International Inc., XBee/XBee-PRO® S2C ZigBee® RF Module - Digi International, https://www.digi.com/resources/documentation/digidocs/pdfs/90002002.pdf, accessed on 2017/12/10.
9. I. F. Akyildiz, W. Su, Y. Sankarasubramaniam, E. Cayirci, Wireless sensor networks: a survey. *Computer networks*, *38*(4), 393-422 (2002)
10. G. Han, A. Qian, L. Liu, J. Jiang, C. Zhu, Impacts of traveling paths on energy provisioning for industrial wireless rechargeable sensor networks. Microprocessors and Microsystems, 39(8), 1271-1278 (2015)

 https://doi.org/10.1051/matecconf/201820103002

A Quality Discriminaton within Ultra Violet Spectrum using Optical Sensor for Selected Commercial Oils

Khadijah Ismail[1,*], and *Wardah* Abdul Razak[1]

[1]Department of Electrical & Electronics Engineering, Universiti Pertahanan Nasional Malaysia, 57000 Kuala Lumpur, Malaysia

Abstract. Nowadays ultra violet-visible (UV-Vis) spectrophotometers are widely used and is one of an important analytical instrument in modern day research. This work is conducted to determine oil quality discrimination of different selected oils using optical sensor, where the oil samples are analyzed within ultra violet (UV) spectrum, which ranges from 200nm to 400nm wavelengths. The oils extracted from five plants are analyzed based on the light absorption rate at different wavelengths. Different energy value is required for electron transition from lower level to the higher, due to different molecular structure of the main compound in the oil. The highest absorption rate at wavelength 393 nm is achieved from lemongrass oil, whereas the lowest absorption peak at 368 nm is observed from ginger oil.

1 Introduction

There are a lot of methods to analyze oil quality based on the compound content of the oil such as high-performance liquid chromatography (HPLC) [1], nuclear magnetic resonance (NMR) [2] and other chemometric and conventional methods [3]. Over a certain range of wavelength, every chemical compound absorbs, transmits or reflects [4]. By using optical sensor, the quality of oil are obtained in which the oil sample is placed between a light source and sensor detector, and then intensity of a beam of light is measured before and after passing through the oil samples as shown in Fig. 1. In this work, light absorption rate is measured within UV spectrum, which ranges from 200 nm to 400 nm.

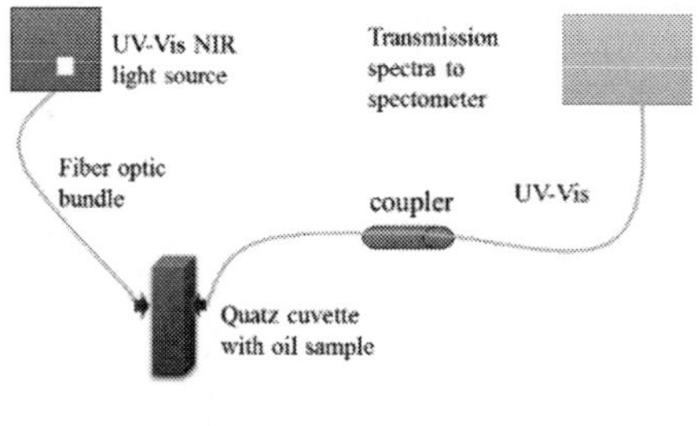

* Corresponding author: wardarazak@gmail.com

Fig. 1. UV-Vis spectrophotometer

Different type of oils comprise of different group of hydrocarbon bonding. These combination of H and C bonding has different type of bonding such as sigma (σ) bonding, pi (π) bonding, non (ŋ) lone pair bonding, π* anti-bonding and σ* anti-bonding [5]. In UV spectrophotometer only transition between pi bonding and non-bonding to anti bonding are occur because, the wavelength of that transition is in the range from 200 nm to 400 nm. The great deal of energy required during the transition bonding. Each bonding has different energy level as show in Fig. 2.

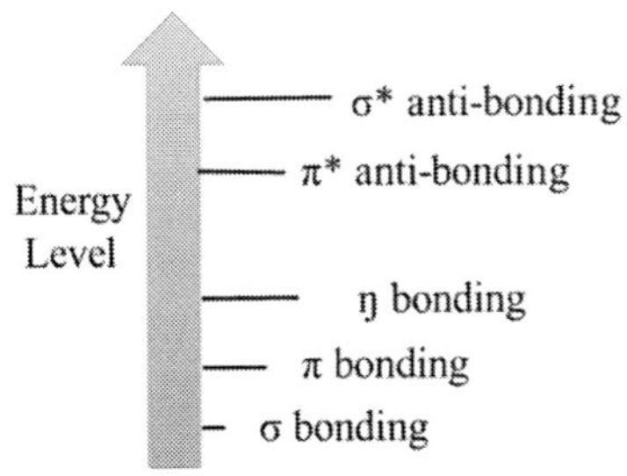

Fig. 2. Energy level of different types of bonding.

Energy is required in promoting the electron in molecules. The relationship between frequency of light absorbed and energy is

$$E = hv \quad (1)$$

where E= energy of light (J), h= plank's constant ($6.62607004 \times 10^{-34}$ m^2 kg / s) and v = frequency of light (Hz). On the other hand, the relationship between wavelength and frequency is

$$\lambda = c/f \quad (2)$$

where λ= wavelength (m), c= speed of light (3×10^{8} m/s) and f= frequency (Hz)
Therefore,

$$E = hc/\lambda \quad (3)$$

Thus, it shows that the greater the energy jump the higher the frequency of light absorb and the lower the wavelength. During the experiment, the intensity of light is measured by using equation of transmittance, T

$$T = I_t/I_o \quad (4)$$

where, I_t is the light intensity after the beam of light passes through the cuvette and I_o is the light intensity before the beam of light passes through the cuvette as shown in Fig. 3.

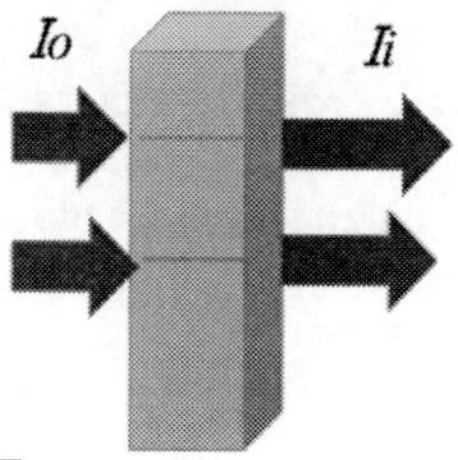

Fig. 3. The concept of transmittance, *T*.

The absorption, *A* and the transmittance, *T* is related by

$$A = -\log T \qquad (5)$$

where, absorbance is the amount of light that is absorbed by matter.

2 Experimental Set up

Five types of plant oils, derived from the plants which grow abundantly in South East Asia region, such as lemongrass, cinnamon, kaffir lime, ylang ylang and ginger are analyzed. The plants are chosen due to different medicinal properties [6]. Scientific names and main compound contents of the selected oils are tabulated in Table 1. The main compound contents are determined based on gas chromatography with mass spectrometry (GCMS) analysis.

Table 1. Scientific name and main compound content of the selected oils.

Plant	Scientific name	Main compound
Lemongrass	Cybopogon citratus DC [7]	Geranial
Cinnamon bark	Cinnamomum verum [8]	Cinnamaldehyde
Kaffir lime	Citrus hystrix [9]	Citronellol
Ylang ylang	Cananga odorata [10]	Benzyl acetate
Ginger	Zingiber officinale [11]	Curcumene

3 Results & Discussions

The absorption spectrum of ginger, ylang ylang, cinnamon bark, kaffir lime leaves and lemongrass are shown in Fig. 4. Based on the spectrums, absortion rates at lower wavelengths are achieved from ginger and ylang ylang oils at 368 nm and 371 nm respectively, whereas absorption rates at higher wavelength are seen for cinnamon bark and kaffir lime leaves oils, which are observed at 392 nm respectively, and the absortion of lemongrass oils are seen at 393 nm. More energy is required for light absortion at lower wavelength as in ginger and ylang ylang oils.

https://doi.org/10.1051/matecconf/201820103002

Lower energy is required for electron transition in the compound with more stable conjugated system, thus causing maximum absorption peak at higher wavelength. Based on the results, lemongrass oil which contains geranial as the main compound, and comprises of more stable conjugated system causes maximum absorption peak at longer wavelength, λ_{max} of 393 nm compared to other oils. On the other hand, more energy is required for electron transition in the energy band, for zingiberine of ginger oil, therefore maximum absorption peak is only observed at shorter wavelength of 368 nm.

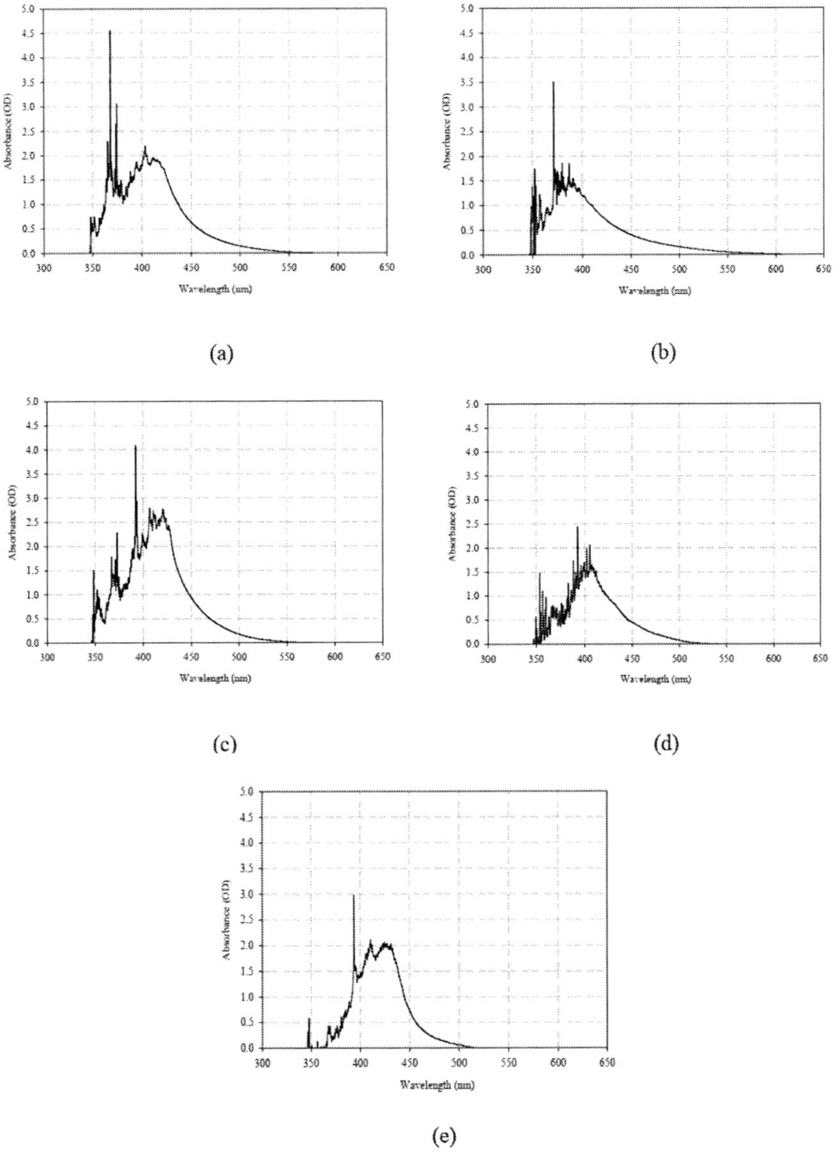

Fig. 4. Absorption spectrum of oils. (a) ginger (d) ylang ylang (c) cinnamon bark (d) kaffir lime leaves (e) lemongrass.

4 Conclusion

Analysis on the absorption of light in five plant oils proves that absorbance rate is related to the energy required for electron transition from lower level to higher energy level. Oils with more stable molecular conjugated system requires lower energy for electron transition, causing light to be absorbed at longer wavelenth. In this work, lemongrass oil absorbed light at longer wavelength of 393 nm, whereas ginger oil absorbed light at shorter wavelength of 368 nm.

References

1. F. N. A. Rashid *et al.*, "Aroma and optical absorption spectroscopy for quality assessment of vegetable cooking oils," *2014 2nd Int. Conf. Electron. Des. ICED 2014*, pp. 339–342, 2011.
2. D. S. Lee, E. S. Lee, H. J. Kim, S. O. Kim, and K. Kim, "Reversed phase liquid chromatographic determination of triacylglycerol composition in sesame oils and the chemometric detection of adulteration," *Anal. Chim. Acta*, vol. 429, no. 2, pp. 321–330, 2001.
3. M. T. Kimometik, "(Determination of Commercials Cooking Oils and Fats Using Chemometrics," vol. 17, no. 1, pp. 146–152, 2013.
4. F. M. Sanda, M. E. Victor, T. A. Monica, and C. Alina, "Spectrophotometric Measurements Techniques Fermentation Process (Part One): Base Theory for Uv-Vis Spectrophotometric Measurements," *Hungary-Romania Cross-Border Co-operation Program.*, p. 16, 2012.
5. Thermo Spectronic, "Basic UV-Vis Theory , Concepts and Applications Basic," *ThermoSpectronic*, pp. 1–28, 2013.
6. M. Shoeb, "Minireview Anticancer agents from medicinal plants," *Bangladesh J Pharmacol 2006;*, vol. 1, pp. 35–41, 2006.
7. G. Lv, H. Yang, N. Xu, and A. M. Mouazen, "Identification of less-ripen, ripen, and over-ripen grapes during harvest time based on visible and near-infrared (Vis-NIR) spectroscopy," *2012 2nd Int. Conf. Consum. Electron. Commun. Networks, CECNet 2012 - Proc.*, vol. 4000, pp. 1067–1070, 2012.
8. B. Adinew, "GC-MS and FT-IR analysis of constituents of essential oil from Cinnamon bark growing in South-west of Ethiopia," vol. 1, no. 6, pp. 22–31, 2014.
9. C. Paper, "Supercritical Fluid Extraction and Gas Chromatographic-Mass Spectrometric Analysis of Terpenoids in Fresh Kaffir Lime Leaf Oil," vol. 40, no. 2, pp. 240–247, 2013.
10. Aromatics international Sdn Bhd, "Aromatics International: Aromatherapy Pure, Organic Essential Oils," aromatics international Sdn Bhd, - april 2015. [Online]. Available: https://www.aromatics.com/products/essential-oils?search=ylangylang. [Accessed 3 January 2017].
11. J. Kizhakkayil and B. Sasikumar, "Characterization of ginger (Zingiber officinale Rosc .) germplasm based on volatile and non-volatile components," vol. 11, no. 4, pp. 777–786, 2012.

Design and development of a novel acoustic rain sensor with automated telemetry

Maria Leonora Guico [1,*], *Gemalyn Abrajano* [2], *Prince Aldrin Domer* [3], and *Jose Paulo Talusan*[4]

[1,2,3,4]Department of Electronics, Communications, and Computer Engineering, Ateneo de Manila University, Quezon City, Philippines

Abstract: This paper presents the recent results of the design of a novel acoustic rainfall sensing system that is low-cost, portable, and easily deployable, which makes use of the recorded sound produced by the impact of the raindrops on the sensor surface. The sensor design allows the gathering of acoustic signal power and sending it to a server after a specified time interval, either through SMS or mobile internet connection. It exists in a weather-proof, standard-conformant, standalone system with its own power supply and telemetric capabilities. These acoustic point sensors can gather rainfall data at high spatial and temporal resolutions. Such deployments can show the variations of rainfall intensities in sub-kilometer areas, particularly in the tropical regions. Since it is low-cost, it can also improve the density of rainfall measuring devices in an area. Moreover, the reliability is improved by providing near-real time data, as opposed to tipping buckets with manual data retrieval. The prototype sensor system was placed next to standard rain measuring devices and observed during the rainy season. The paper will discuss the design and deployment of the system, as well as initial results of data analysis and comparison with standard rain measuring devices.

1 Introduction

Intensities of rain events in tropical regions vary significantly in time and space. Gathering precipitation data for these events currently makes use of rainfall estimates in place of gauge observations, even when spatial localization and sub-kilometer rain measurements are significant. Satellite imagery, for instance, captures precipitation data at 100's of kilometers which cannot provide the resolution that tipping buckets or automatic weather stations can at sub-kilometer regions. Further, rain gauges in tropical countries are critical for facilitating the provision of an alarm or warning system for areas where phenomena such as flooding or landslide frequently occur. Placing these sensors at critical points detect if rain rates in high-risk areas - urban and rural, alike - are exceeding threshold levels. However, in a developing

* Corresponding author: mguico@ateneo.edu

country such as the Philippines, more economical measures for risk-mitigation in rain-induced calamities must be employed

A novel means of monitoring rain events was developed by the Department of Electronics, Computer and Communications Engineering of the Ateneo de Manila University. Through the use of standalone acoustic point sensor, shown in Figure 1(a), for rainfall data gathering,
the sound produced by the impact of the raindrops on the sensor surface captured by the microphone input can provide information on rain events, where levels of generated sound
corresponds to rain intensities. The research and development of this type of rain sensor started a few years back, and has not been performed by other research groups [1-2]. Similar efforts do exist but makes use of piezoelectric detectors to capture acoustic data [3]. Further, no data gathering from field deployments in actual weather observation sites has been done on the acoustic rain sensor. It has since undergone hardware and software design changes, from initial research prototypes [4], to improve reliability and operation to survive harsh weather and environmental field conditions.

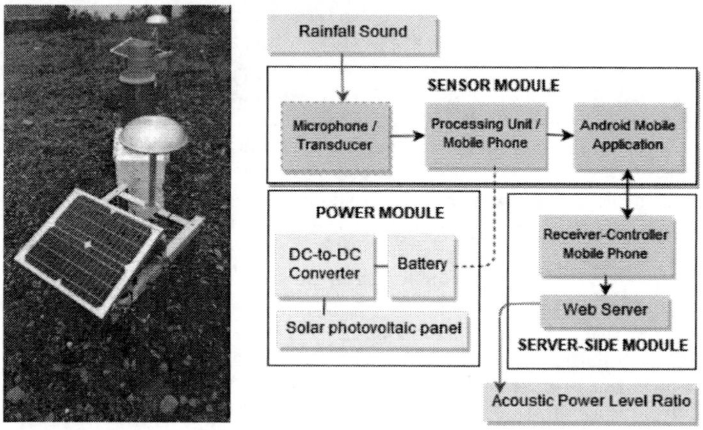

(a) (b)
Fig 1. (a) Acoustic rain sensor hardware setup, and (b) overview of its operation

2 Materials and Methods

2.1 Materials

The acoustic rain sensor presents a practical solution to rain monitoring that addresses problems related to cost-effectiveness, portability, and scalability. It works by recording the sound of the rainfall as it hits the metal sensor casing which doubles as an enclosure to the microphone input connected to the mobile phone (see Figure 1(b) for the operation overview). The metal enclosure is attached to a main frame which acts as a mounting platform and is composed of four legs made of aluminum metal bars for a sturdy and corrosion-resistant emplacement. A 12-Watt solar photovoltaic panel is placed atop the main frame at a 45-degree angle for maximized sun exposure. This doubles as waterproofing of the casing, reinforced by a silicone sealant, that houses the mobile phone and power supply elements (a 5-A DC-to-DC converter, and a 20000-mAh lithium-ion battery), which are responsible for the power supply, data processing, and data telemetry functions of the whole sensor setup.

The mobile phone in the acoustic rain sensor is an Android-based device which allows it to leverage high processing capacity using the Android software development kit (SDK). A 1.2-MB mobile application, shown in Figure 2, was developed to customize functions the phones can perform, both for the receiver and transmitter end, where managing the audio resource for the application to record audio from the microphone is handled by the AudioRecord public class. Deployed mobile phones in the field are labeled as 'transmitters' while a control phone in the laboratory functions as the 'receiver'. The transmitter and controller-receiver mobile phones are all identified by the numbers in the installed subscriber identity module (SIM) cards; all transmitter devices can be remotely controlled by the controller-receiver device through specific Short Message Service (SMS) messages. A list of instructions that the transmitter devices can recognize are listed below in Table 1.

Table 1. Control SMS messages from controller-receiver to transmitter devices

'Start-SMS'	Initiates operation of the transmitter device: recording of sound, audio processing and telemetry.
'Stop-SMS'	Stops the operation of the transmitter device.
'promo-<Message>-<Number>'	Allows SMS messages to be sent by the transmitter device to the specified number; used for registering to network provider's value-added service.

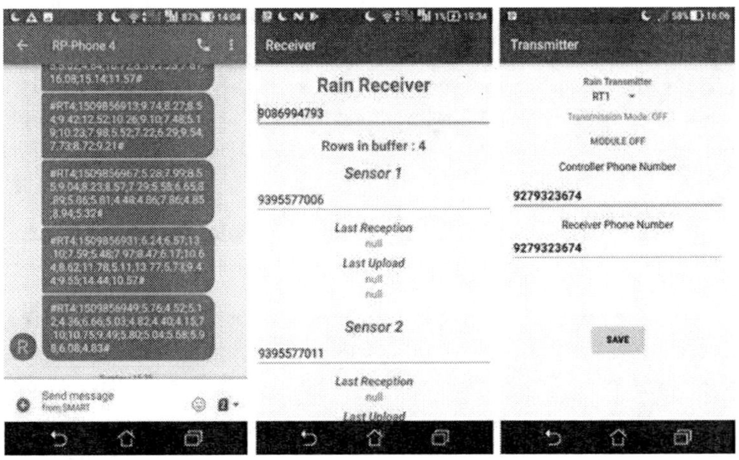

Fig 2. (left to right) Screenshots of (1) an acoustic rain sensor data sent as an SMS, the Android application in the (2) controller-receiver, and (3) transmitter end.

 https://doi.org/10.1051/matecconf/201820103003

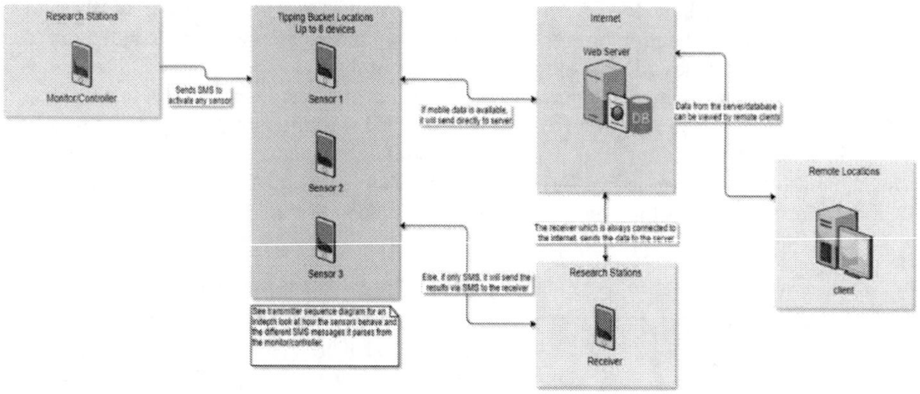

Fig 3. Outline of the telemetry system from the transmitter device in the sensor setup to the web server or the receiver phone.

2.2 Methods

The specific system used in this acoustic rain sensor is outlined in Figure 3. An SMS message is first sent to the transmitters to activate operation. From there, the transmitter will start accepting and processing audio input as triggered by a rain event. The sound is recorded as a 16-bit audio sampled at 44,100 Hz. The corresponding acoustic power level is then calculated as the variance of the samples, and is returned as a power ratio value in decibel (dB), available for every second. This value is sent directly to a web server and is stored in its designated transmitter cache, if mobile internet service is available. Otherwise, the data will be sent via SMS to a receiver phone that is always connected to the Internet, which will then be uploaded to the web server. Data sent through SMS is no longer queued for telemetry, once mobile internet service becomes available again.

Sending of data from the transmitter devices are enabled by SMS messaging and mobile internet services, which are availed to the transmitter devices by a special instruction (see Table 1). All the data stored in the server can then be accessed and viewed by remote clients, and can be downloaded as a comma separated value (.CSV) file. In one deployed sensor setup, the 16-bit pulse code modulation (.PCM) files are also saved to the mobile phone's internal memory, containing 5 minutes of raw audio recording for each file. The PCM files are to be used for digital signal processing to identify and investigate signal parameters.

Table 2. Deployment sites and their profile

Diliman, Quezon City	Situated near a residential area; possible source of ambient noise due to human activity.
Infanta, Quezon City	Situated near a rice farm; no nearby source of loud ambient noise.

Legazpi City, Albay	Situated near a major service road, and a local airport; with possible source of loud ambient noise.
Sasa, Davao del Sur	Situated near a local airport ; with possible source of loud ambient noise

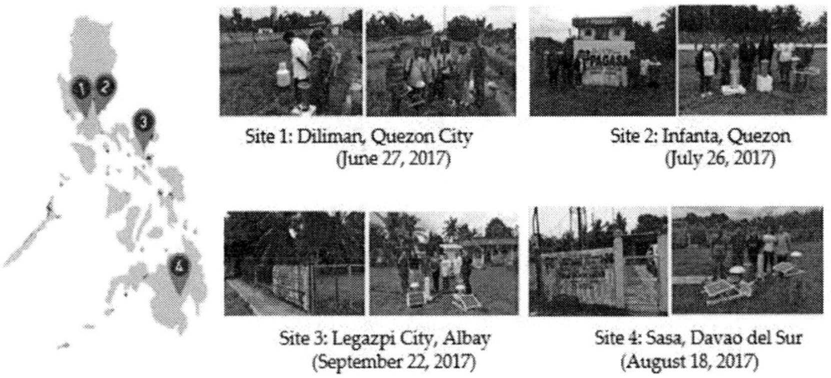

Fig 4. Location of Philippine Atmospheric and Geophysical Services Administration (PAGASA) weather observation sites where the acoustic rain sensors are deployed.

The rain sensors are deployed in four weather observation (Table 2, Figure 4) sites in the Philippines starting June 2017. For purposes of comparing with existing conventional rain gauges, the rain sensors are also placed side by side with tipping buckets with the main sensing element leveled with the brim of the rain gauge. Data retrieval from the tipping bucket data logger was likewise introduced in the data gathering setup using a Raspberry Pi with a real-time clock (RTC) that sends recorded tipping event to a server via Internet over a WiFi network. Recorded tipping events are to be used for mapping acoustic rain sensor output to tipping bucket rain gauge data.

3 Results and Discussion

The performance of the data gathering setup as deployed in the field are evaluated, which includes both the acoustic rain sensor and the tipping bucket data logger. Checking of gathered acoustic rain sensor data, and validation of rain events through the records in the tipping buckets data loggers allowed the evaluation of performance of the sensor telemetry system; whereas the validation of tipping bucket logger data was done in reference to weather observation data. Further, initial mapping of sensor output with the retrieved tipping bucket rain gauge output shows positive correspondence between rain intensities and computed acoustic power levels, especially for moderate to heavy rains.

3.1 Field Deployment Results

The aluminum frame and sensor casing deployed in the field experienced no rain-induced corrosion. No water leaks inside the circuit box and the microphone casing occured. Protection from foreign elements was likewise achieved proving the reliability of the sensor body design, and observed protocols in sealing sensitive sensor elements.

Additionally, the configuration of the power supply allowed for continuous charging of the battery in the setup thereby allowing continuous operation of the mobile phones. Except for one sensor setup where the Pulse Code Modulation (.PCM) files of the recorded sound are saved in the internal memory of the mobile phone; overloading and eventual crashing of the device is encountered, in which case, the PCM files were manually retrieved, and the Android application was re-activated. This sensor setup is located near the research laboratory to accommodate logistical constraints. Further, the status of phones - whether on or off - are validated through checking data transmitted in the server and by making a call to the transmitter device from the receiver.

Meanwhile, data reception is evaluated to be affected by the poor network performance of the selected cellular network service provider. Preparation of data summaries showed that acoustic rain sensor data for some rain events were not successfully or consistently sent to the web server. Additionally, occasional delays in data reception were encountered, in which case, chronological ordering of the received data were performed.

Lastly, the Raspberry Pi modules attached to the tipping bucket data logger was operational for the entire data collection period. Time-stamped tipping events were recorded and uploaded as a comma separated value (.CSV) file to a file hosting service. Sent files were grouped by day and were uploaded by the end of the day, including dates with no tipping events.

3.2 Acoustic Rain Sensor Output Versus Tipping Bucket Rain Gauge

Gathered acoustic rain sensor data from latest deployments returned values from 1 - 56 dB. To check trends or correspondence of returned values with the tipping bucket rain gauge, recorded tipping events were converted into rain rates using the novel International Atmospheric Physics (IAP) technique [5]. Rain rate extraction using the novel IAP technique, shown in equation (1) below, demonstrates that the time difference for two consecutive tipping events is taken into account, and where the sum of tips is defined for the time duration being considered. A unit tip is taken to be equivalent to 0.5 mm, as specified by the tipping bucket rain gauge collocated with the acoustic rain sensors. In general, there is a positive correspondence between the extracted rain rates and the gathered acoustic power levels for medium to heavy rain events.

$$Rain\ Rate = \frac{\Delta sum\ of\ tips}{\Delta time}\left(\frac{3600 * 0.5mm}{hr.}\right) \quad (1)$$

Figure 5 shows sample visualizations of gathered data for a 5-hour rain event in Infanta, Quezon weather observation site last November 24, 2017. The moving average with a window size of 60 is shown as the red trendline of the received acoustic power level ratio (dB), while the horizontal lines in the rain rate graph represent thresholds of different rain intensity levels specified by PAGASA (see Table 3). It can be observed

 https://doi.org/10.1051/matecconf/201820103003

that for periods of very intense rainfall, the acoustic rain sensor returns high dB values, with minimum dispersion. That is, the values are clustered at certain levels; whereas for lower intensities of rainfall, the dB values are generally more scattered, subject to the characteristic of the ambient noise in the environment, on top of intermittent man-made or biological noises present. In Figure 5, this is demonstrated after the 22:00 mark where the rain rate graph signifies very low-intensity rainfall where the dB values are evidently more dispersed. In general, it can be observed that the acoustic rain sensor plot prominently traces the trend of the computed rain rates.

It follows that when there is presence of strong rainfall, the impact of the rainfall drops on the sensor casing dominates the sound field that the microphone captures. This means that the ambient noise, during periods of strong rainfall is registered less. In the same logic, during periods of low intensity rainfall, the sound field is distributed across different sources of noise in the surrounding environment. Therefore, the sound captured by the microphone during these times is reliant on the sound profile of the selected deployment site (see Table 2).

Table 3. PAGASA Rain Rate Classification and Color Representation of Threshold Lines in the Rain Rate Plot

Rain Type	Intensity (mm/hr.)	Threshold (Color)
Torrential	>30	Red
Intense	15 - 30	Orange
Heavy	7.5 – 15	Green
Moderate	2.5 – 7.5	Blue
Light	0.01 – 2.5	-

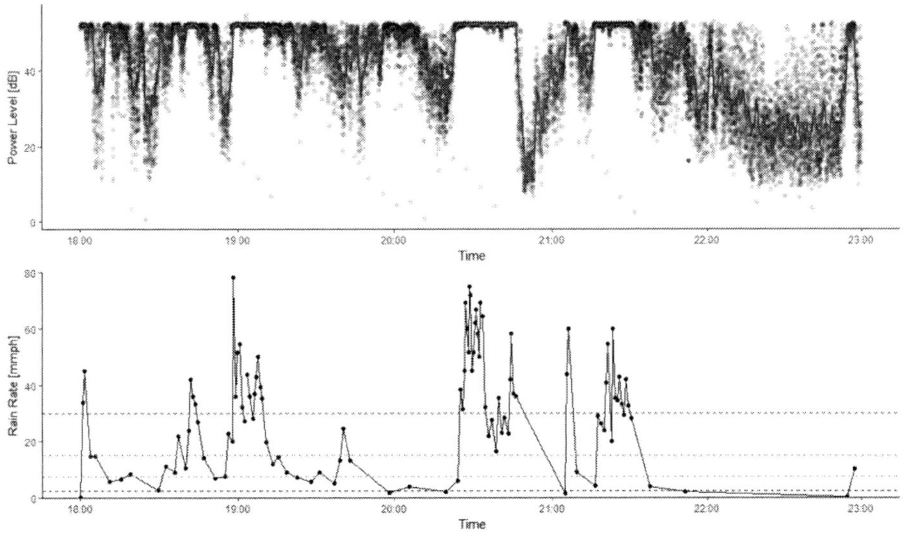

Figure 5. Sample rain rate and acoustic power level visualization for a 5-hour rain event in Infanta, Quezon weather observation site last November 24, 2017

4 Conclusion

The design of the acoustic rain sensor prototype is motivated by the need to lower the materials cost, without compromising reliability amidst harsh weather and environmental conditions the sensors are expected to be subjected to. Further, the decision to go with the implemented telemetry system stems from the need to come up with a way to integrate more readily available network service in the selected field deployment sites where Internet service through hardwired and wireless broadband access is limited or not present at all. Sending data through SMS messages proved to be an easy but not very dependable way to retrieve gathered data, owing to its reliance on the quality of service of cellular network service providers, alongside the degradation of service due to signal attenuation in the presence of localized heavy rain events. Further, while telemetry through mobile internet service has better performance than through SMS, it is still subject to the availability of the service, which can be quite unreliable at times.

Even so, successfully retrieved data showed positive correspondence with computed rain rate values. The acoustic rain sensor is capable of tracing the trend of rain rates computed from the tipping bucket rain gauges and is more prominent in rain events with higher intensity and in less noisy environments. In particular, periods of very intense rainfall correspond to high values of gathered power level ratio further characterized by minimum dispersion. With low-intensity rain events, the rain sensor picks up ambient noise more, as characterized by the profile of the environment generating different sound sources the microphone input can capture. In general, the gathered power level ratios are scattered across the whole range of available dB values. Findings in this research presents additional considerations that must be taken into account in the ongoing data analysis, and possible future deployments.

This research is a one-year partnership project between Ateneo de Manila University (ADMU) and the Philippine Atmospheric and Geophysical Services Administration (PAGASA) funded by the Department of Science and Technology (DOST) - Philippine Council for Industry, Energy and Emerging Technology Research and Development (PCIEERD) and partially funded by the Ateneo de Manila University. Acknowledgment also goes to Ms. Catherine Dela Cruz (ADMU), Engr. Juan Antonio Marinas, M.S. (ADMU), Mr. Chrisandro Favila (ADMU), Mr. Sonny Toledo (ADMU), Engr. Jeric Lim (ADMU), Ms. Danilyn Joy Orioste (ADMU), Mr. Francis Jerome Tiausas (ADMU), Engr. Ferdinand Barcenas (PAGASA), and Engr. Wilfredo Tuazon (PAGASA) for the rendered support in this research project.

References

1. G. Gu, R. Adler, G. Huffman and S. Curtis, *Long-Term Increase in Rainfall Seen in Tropics*, v. 20, no.**15**, Journal of Climate, (2007).

2. N. J. C. Libatique, G. L. Tangonan, R. Gustilo, et.al *Design of a Tropical Rain-Disaster Alarm System: A New Approach based on Wireless Sensor Networks and Acoustic Rain Rate Measurements*. International Instrumentation and Measurement Technology Conference 2009 (I2MTC), Singapore, (2009).

3. N. de Giesen, C. Degen, and R. Hut. *Affordable acoustic disdrometer: Design, calibration, tests*.Delft University of Technology. American Geophysical Union, Fall Meeting, (2009).

4. E. M. Trono, M. L. Guico, et.al. *Rainfall monitoring using acoustic sensors*. TENCON 2012 IEEE Region 10 Conference, Cebu, 2012, pp. 1-6, (2012)

5. O. Fiser and O. Wilfert. *Novel processing of tipping bucket rain gauge records*. Atmospheric Research, Volume **92**, Issue 3, (2009)

Positivity creation and its effect on idea patentability: a case of a new faucet invention

Chi-Hua Wu[1,*], and *Ding-Bang* Luh[1]

[1]Dpt. Industrial Design, National Cheng Kung University, Tainan, Taiwan

Abstract. Among criteria of patentability, concern of novelty is taking priority in comparing to non-obviousness and industrial applicability. However, novelty is difficult to be demonstrated before conducting a thorough research of the prior art after a proposal is been designed, which is time-consuming. Under such circumstance, 1) Positive creativity is applied in this research to enhance idea patentability by positively building it during a design process. 2) Start with elaborating idea of positive creativity, its conceptual tool is applied in this research to design a new faucet, and do actual patent application. 3) The result of patents obtained in several countries, including invention (Taiwan) and design patents (Taiwan, U.S., China), indicates that positive creativity is capable of producing patentable ideas. 4) Faucet manufacturing is a traditional industry within which theoretically more difficult to get invention patents. This further indicates that positive creativity (through positivity creation) should have similar effect in providing patentable ideas in highly-innovative industries.

1 Introduction

According to patent examining procedure announced in Taiwan and U.S., patentability consist of novelty, non-obviousness, and industrial applicability [1,2]. Novelty is taking priority in comparing to non-obviousness and industrial applicability, but it is difficult to be demonstrated before idea is developed into more feasible design proposal and conducted thorough research of prior art; the whole process requires a lot of efforts and could be time-consuming.

On the other hand, current creativity methods emphasis the role of divergent thinking and its effect on generating original business ideas which is the first step of the opportunity identification process [3], yet provide little guidance in developing non-obviousness and industrial applicability of an idea, not to mention making it patentable.

Considering the fundamental role of patent for companies, this article first revisits creativity researches; subsequently, positive creativity and its conceptual tool is introduced and articulated as new way of generating patentable ideas via actions of Positivity Creation. Case of a new faucet design that is actually applied for and patented is provided as demonstration.

2 Positive creativity and positivity creation

Most current researches illustrated innovation spaces via types of creative outcome by which they believe creativity processes can be largely represented. However, as creativity are referred to as '(ethically) positive' in literatures, they tend to ignore the dynamic essence of creativity as a kind of adaptability [4]. A second issue regarding current creativity typology is that they tend to presume creativity as 'positive'; although efforts were made in describing 'creativity with negative intentions' [5], it is not pragmatic in most situations where innovations are expected.

According to a parsimonious view of creativity, creativity and problem-solving should not be equated, while 'a person probably generates an idea and then react to it based on value. If the idea has some potential relative to the values, the person may explore that line of thought further. The person will not invest effort to do so unless it appears to be a valuable line of thought [6].' More specifically, creativity requires intent to achieve some goal; it is the intent and goal that were judged as positive or negative. The dynamic essence of creativity resides not in the creative outcome but in variation of outcomes, whereas properties of variation are yet to be determined.

2.1 Positive creativity

Positive creativity, as a philosophical thought of design, laid its foundation on innovation space illustrated by Creativity Mathematics [7]; as shown in Figure 1, innovation outcomes are divided into 'neutral solution (0)', 'negative solution (-X)' and 'positive solution (X)' that focuses on 'creating wishes and generating needs'. An imaginative mirror has been introduced as conceptual tool for visualization of positive creativity; philosophical

* Corresponding author: wu33000@gmail.com

thinking of Tai Chi in Taoism is introduced to makes the imaginative mirror function [8].

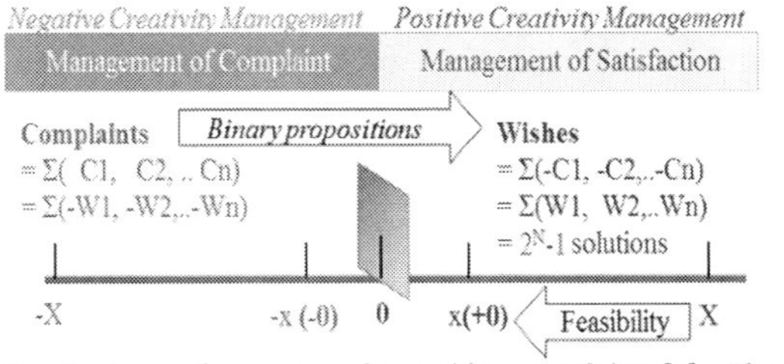

Fig. 1. Innovation spaces in positive creativity [8]. The mirroring function leads to wishful ideas that are not likely to be achieved by negative creativity. Feasibility is then built after ideas are assessed and selected.

Variation could only be observed through comparison; as motivation for comparing often stems from discontents toward current situation. Positive creativity and its mirroring function provides a way of generating alternative situations which take form of attribute sets. Comparisons are then made possible between original and new attribute sets before developing or testing idea feasibility as it is time-consuming.

2.2 Positivity creation as variations through positive creativity

Positive creativity can be viewed as an oriental conception of creativity that focuses more on the authenticity of the discovery process than the output of innovative products [9], and, like ancient Taoist and Confucian philosophers, ordinary modern Asians believe that things are constantly changing [10]. In this vein, 'state of existence (or presenting)' of individual attribute in attribute sets is brought into focus, as variations made by main actions of 'bring (attribute) into existence' in design process can be seen as Positivity Creation, in contrast to elimination, replacement or maintained as shown in Figure 2.

Original Attribute Set	Actions	New Attribute Set
	Positivity Creation	Attribute 0
Attribute 1	Elimination	
Attribute 2(a)	Replacement	Attribute 2(c)
Attribute 2(b)	Maintained	Attribute 2(b)
Attribute 3	-	Attribute 3
Attribute 4	-	Attribute 4
Attribute 5	-	Attribute 5

Fig. 2. Actions of positivity creation, elimination, replacement and maintained in design processes.

Consequently, there is a potential effect on enhancement on patentability with ideas generated through positive creativity and actions of positivity creation, as mirroring function has provided means in pursuing ideas that is non-obvious, selected idea would be develop into feasible proposal and made industrial applicable, and it is intuitively that new attributes lead to novelty.

3 Case of a new faucet invention

In this research, a new faucet design has been adopted as a case of positivity creation; it is designed and won Red dot concept award in 2011 [11]. Although constructions of positive creativity theory were in progress, its core ideas and mirroring function had already been developed and put to trial as early as 2010, while evolving constantly; on that account, newer formats in positive creativity process are used in this article to retrospectively describe the design itself and addressed design issues. The process can be simply divided into two stages as followed.

3.1. Mirroring customer journey (ordinary to ideal), building idea novelty.

An ordinary customer journey was retrieved from current faucets (both manual and automatic). Main problem and question in each step are then identified. Note that the main problem varies with different operators while it reflects underlying individual perspective towards value. Problem-free steps are then possible while some could be considered as rigid or mandatory steps for given activity.

Through mirroring function, main problems and questions lead to better situations in each customer journey steps, which aggregated into an ideal customer journey as shown in Table 1.

Table 1. Customer journey using traditional faucet, then turn into ideal customer journey with mirroring.

Ordinary Customer Journey	Ideal Customer Journey
Turn on the Faucet (*Difficult* to find the trigger)	Turn on the Faucet (*Easy/No need* to find the trigger)
Washing hands	Washing hands
Washing the handle (*Wasting* water and effort)	Do not wash the handle (*Do not waste* water and effort)
Turn off the faucet	Turn off the faucet

3.2 Looking for means in realizing ideal customer journey, building idea feasibility.

The ideal customer journey could be realized using different technologies and mechanical design, which can be translated into multiple ideas that correspond with different attribute sets. Theoretically speaking, every attribute set is more ideal than original one.

An idea (one attribute set) was then selected while its underlying actions were also identified in Table 2. Additional methods for idea selection can also be introduced while competition strategy of a company should be taken into account in more business settings.

Table 2. Attributes that users faced during original and new customer journeys.

Original Attribute Set	New Attribute Set	Actions
Trigger (Input) Water outlet (Output)	Trigger as Water outlet	Positivity Creation
Water outlet	Water outlet	Maintained
Trigger (Input) Water outlet (Output)	-	Elimination
Trigger (Input) Water outlet (Output)	Trigger as Water outlet	Positivity Creation

The selected idea was then turned into a design proposal with detailed design presentation, as shown in figure 3, and submitted for Red dot design competition.

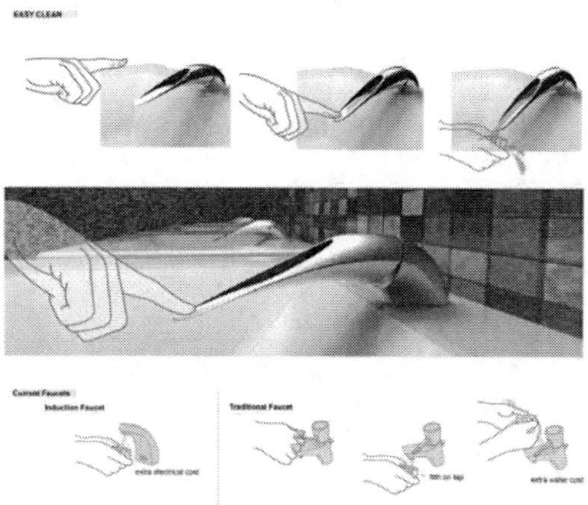

Fig. 3. Design presentation for selected idea

After the idea been awarded, a series of patents application were send with help from intellectual property departments; as a result, four patents were obtained internationally, including invention (Taiwan) and design patents (Taiwan, U.S., China) [12, 13, 14, 15].

4 Discussion and conclusions

On theory level, positive creativity is in line with a service centric thought which consider physical products as embodiments of service processes that promised and facilitates users in achieving certain goals, more specifically for goals that enhance users' subjective well-being. As subjective well-beings may never be truly understood as from Taoism perspective, research into and elaborates on situations and phenomena that constitute customer journey become a reasonable way of design, as it is done in positive creativity.

For positive creativity per se, it represents a possibility of harmony between users and artefacts; as indicated above that oriental creativity stressed the authenticity of discovery process, harmony presents more in actions of pursuing, rather than a still status which is difficult to persist in a more dynamic era as we are in now. Results of patents obtained in this case provide evidence for a way of development for companies to grow into future.

Faucet manufacturing, in this case, is a traditional industry within which theoretically more difficult to get invention patents as many works were accomplished and confining creativity simultaneously, which is not uncommon for most companies that were considered to be manufacturing industries or in product domains. This provides opportunity in amplifying impact of positive creativity while further indicates that positive creativity (through positivity creation) should have similar effect in providing patentable ideas in highly-innovative industries that are less confined and in essence more service-centric.

To summarize, positive creativity demonstrate a way of producing patentable ideas by sequentially develop idea novelty, non-obviousness and industrial applicability; it can be applied on product design and increase company competitiveness by potential patents, while its application in service industries are also foreseeable after intellectual property laws on service processes become more sophisticated.

This research is partially supported by Taiwanese Ministry of Science and Technology (project number 104-2221-E-006 -151 -MY2). Authors are also grateful toward Ms. Wang, Li-Hsin for assisted in design presentation and National Cheng Kung University for support in patent applications.

References

1. 國家衛生研究院電子報：如何避免自己的研究成果成為專利申請的前案[How to prevent one's research work from constituting prior art in patent application]. Available online: http://enews.nhri.org.tw/enews_list_new2_more.php?volume_indx=444&showx=showarticle&article_indx=8932 (Accessed August 7 2016).
2. 經濟部智慧財產局：現行專利審查基準彙編，第三章專利要件[Essentials of concurrent pattern laws in Taiwan, Ch3. Patentability]. Available online: https://www.tipo.gov.tw/ct.asp?xItem=422895&ctNode=6680&mp=1 (Accessed August 7 2016).
3. M. M. Gielnik, M. Frese, J. M. Graf, & A. Kampschulte, Creativity in the opportunity identification process and the moderating effect of diversity of information. J BUS VENTURING, **27(5)**, 559-576 (2012)
4. M. A. Runco, *Creativity: Theories and Themes: Research, Development, and Practice* (Elsevier Science, 2014)
5. K. James, K. Clark, & R. Cropanzano, Positive and Negative Creativity in Groups, Institutions, and

https://doi.org/10.1051/matecconf/201820104001

Organizations: A Model and Theoretical Extension. CREATIVITY RES J, **12(3)**, 211-226 (1999)
6. M.A. Runco, Creativity has no dark side. In D. Cropley, A. Cropley, J. C. Kaufman, & M. A. Runco (Eds.), *The dark side of creativity*, 15-32 (Cambridge University Press, 2010)
7. 陸定邦, *正創造：鏡子理論[Positive Creativity]* Tainan, Taiwan (De wind International, 2014)
8. D. B. Luh, "Design Management for Positive Creativity", *Innovation, Communication and Engineering* – Meen, Prior & Lam (Eds) © 2014 Taylor & Francis Group, London, pp.651-654 (2014)
9. T. I. Lubart, & A. Georgsdottir, Creativity: Developmental and Cross-Cultural Issues. In S. Lau, A. N. N. Hui, & G. Y. C. Ng (Eds.), *Creativity: When East meets West,* 23-54 (World Scientific, 2004)
10. R. Nisbett, *The Geography of Thought*, (Nicholas Brealey Publishing, 2011)
11. CLEAN V/S GREEN TAP. Available online: http://www.yankodesign.com/2012/06/13/clean-vs-green-tap/ (Accessed August 11st 2016)
12. 陸定邦; 吳啟華; 王俐心. 水龍頭[FAUCET]. I 443275 (Taiwan), (1st Jul. 2014)
13. 陸定邦; 吳啟華; 王俐心. 水龍頭[FAUCET]. ZL 2012 3 0212645.3 (China), (7th Nov. 2012)
14. D. B. Luh, C. H. Wu, & L. H. Wang, FAUCET. US D683,433 S (United States), (28th May 2013)
15. 陸定邦; 吳啟華. 水龍頭[FAUCET]. M 522285 (Taiwan), (21st May 2016)

Designing a video laryngoscope imaging system with a 7mm blade for neonatal patients

Ming-Ying Hsu[1], *Wen-Tse* Hsiao[2], and *Han-Chao* Chang[2*]

[1]National Synchrotron Radiation Research Center, Experimental Facility Division, 30076 HsinChu, Taiwan
[2]National Applied Research Laboratories, Instrument Technology Research Center, 30076 HsinChu, Taiwan

Abstract. When a newborn infant has been pushed from the birth canal due to ventilation failure while using a resuscitation mask, the doctor must implement infant intubation and other emergency steps to keep the baby alive. However, due to the excessively small mouth area of a newborn or premature infant, the doctors are unable to view the glottis entrance, which can lead to either a failed intubation or longer intubation time, thereby resulting in either a drop in oxygen levels or a rise in intrathoracic pressure. Although the normal video laryngoscope with a 12mm metal blade certainly improves this type of difficult intubation, nevertheless, doctors often complain that the depth of field (DOF) is insufficient and the width of the blade is too wide when performing intubation on neonatal patients. Therefore, this study aims to develop two modules of infant's video laryngoscope, an ultra-thin 7mm metal blade and an optical imaging system, the core technology of which includes an optical design of a 2.5mm lens and verifications of imaging quality. In order to allow physicians to determine the infant's airway position immediately and to avoid the binocular disparity from a physician while giving intubation, this study has simulated the optical properties of monolithic lenses while designing the imaging system, allowing the doctor to have a clearer and undistorted image within the field of view.

1 Introduction

Annually, anaesthetists or emergency physicians perform more than a million tracheal intubations. Neonate and premature infant tracheal intubation is the most challenging task for physicians prior to surgery or emergency treatment; babies and their mouth ranges are so small, that doctors are unable to view the glottal entrance, which can lead to intubation failure or an excessive intubation time, resulting in a delayed treatment or declined oxygen concentration.

The video laryngoscope is an indispensable tool for performing endotracheal intubation. The video laryngoscope is divided into three parts, the monitor, the handle and the blade. A light source is positioned at the front of the blade for illumination to assist the doctor with the intubation. In conventional clinical laryngoscope intubation, the patient is laid head up, the laryngoscope is inserted into the mouth from the left to the right and the tongue is then flipped; according to the patient's mouth size, the corresponding blade size is selected [1], the laryngoscope is inserted manually until it reaches the patient's epiglottis cartilage, and then the patient's head is moved to the intubation posture. According to the anatomy and the export of the hypopharyngeal position, the "Sniffing Position" [2] is considered the optimal intubation posture in which to place the patient (Figure 1). After that, the endotracheal tube is inserted through the mouth, then through the glottis into the trachea to form an airway, allowing air or oxygen to pass through the channel to and from the lungs. Depending on whether the soft palate, uvula, throat, and glottis are visible, the difficulty of endotracheal intubation can be divided into Mallampati I~IV grades [2] (Figure 2). According to Caplan [3] and Lambert [4], there are still 30% to 40% of cases of surgical anesthesia deaths resulting from difficult intubations. In recent years, even though doctors have been using German or American-made video laryngoscopes, the blade size (12mm) [1, 5] is too big for Asian newborns, the image's depth of field (DOF) is insufficient, as well as other clinical problems. Therefore, for this study, 7mm ultra-thin blades were designed and a set of 2.5mm image acquisition modules were completed to solve the DOF problem, in order to provide a new imaging optical system for improved neonatal intubations.

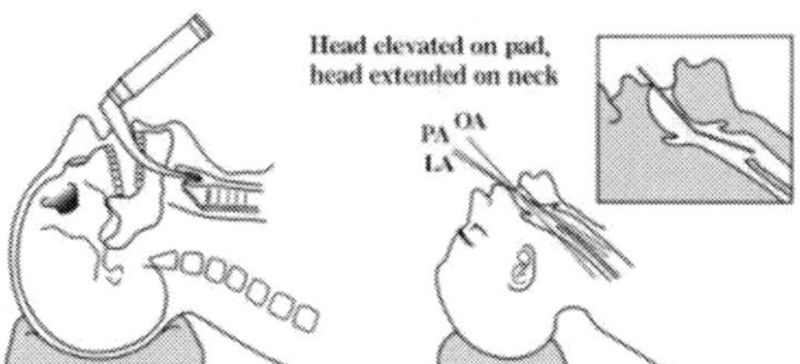

Fig. 1. Best intubation posture "Sniffing Position".
Source: Kim et al [2]

* Corresponding author: roman@narlabs.org.tw

https://doi.org/10.1051/matecconf/201820104002

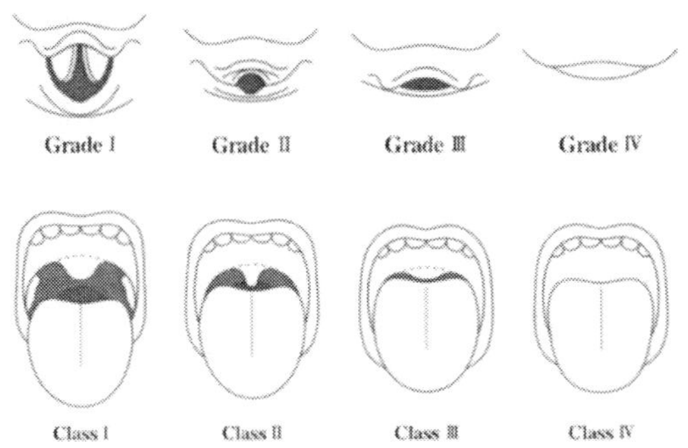

Fig. 2. Mallampati I~IV
Source: Kim et al [2]

2 Materials and Methods

In order to allow the doctor to immediately observe the position of the trachea and thus avoid any misjudgments; the study used 7mm short thin metal blades, as well as a single-lens optical design to correspond to neonatal oral size, which allow doctors to obtain a larger field of view (FOV) to clearly see the blade tip and the baby's glottis position (Figure 3).The largest diameter of the video laryngoscope in this study was 3.0 mm, so the lens shape had to be less than 2.5mm to insert into the machine system. When a physician presents innovative ideas for an optical video laryngoscope system, it is necessary to consider whether it is technically and physically feasible. The aperture must be proportional to the DOF, the aperture diameter also must be proportional to the input light intensity to satisfy the conditions of the optimal imaging quality while the number of lenses is less. In order to obtain high-quality optical imaging, the design of the system size calculation, the initial structure of the calculation, aberration correction and image quality evaluation must all be considered. Therefore, the decision-making process of an optical design is as follows: shape size calculation, initial structure calculation, aberration correction and image quality evaluation.

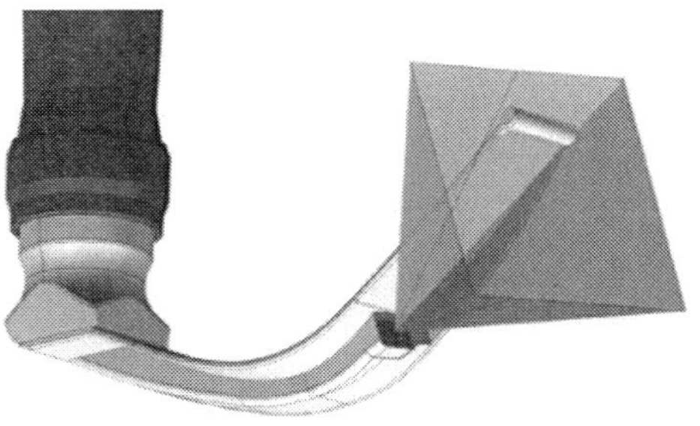

Fig. 3. Optical Design of FOV for video laryngoscope

2.1 Shape Size Calculation & Initial Structure Calculation

First of all, this study had to determine the basic optical properties, to meet the requirements of product technology, which determine the magnification ratio or the focal length, FOV, numerical aperture, working distance from light bar position and shape size. Therefore, this stage is often referred to as the shape dimension calculation. The general concern is calculated according to the theory and a formula of the ideal optical system in this dimension. In the calculation, the mechanical structure and the arrangement of electronic components must be considered to prevent the mechanism from being realized. The initial structure is usually confirmed by following two methods: 1. the first is calculated by the size according to the primary aberration theory. 2. Secondly, mining from the database to select the initial structure, a more practical and easier way to succeed and, as a result, one that has been widely adopted by many optical designers. It requires designers to have a deep understanding of optical theories and thorough experience in the design selection. As the task of choosing the initial structure directly affects the design of follow-up light-machine components, this will consequentially affect the overall image quality of video laryngoscopes.

2.2 Aberration Correction and Image Quality Evaluation

After the initial structure had been selected, this study used an optical calculation program to calculate all aberrations and light path aberration curves. From data analysis, this study was able to find out the aberration factors which affect the imaging quality of the optical system, and find ways to improve the quality and also to conduct aberration correction. Aberration analysis and light paths' balance is a repeated process, until it meets the quality of imaging (Distortion <0.05%). The imaging quality of optical systems is related to the size of aberrations, and the optical design aims at correcting aberrations in optical systems. However, in any optical system, it is impossible to correct all other aberrations to zero, there is always a residual aberration. Of course, for different sizes of residual aberration, the image quality is not the same. Hence, the designer must understand the value of optical aberration and tolerance for a variety of the optical system's residual aberrations, so that the design can correspond with the size of residual aberration of the optical system's imaging quality. The evaluation method of optical system imaging quality [6, 7, 8] includes modulation transfer function (MTF), the chief ray angle (CRA) and tolerance analysis.

This study used the MTF evaluation method. An object is composed of a spectrum of various frequencies, when light irradiates the object, the light source is imaged in the plane. After that, the image energy distribution map of the light source is used, and the optical system's MTF is ascertained using the Fourier transform. An optical imaging system is treated as being a linear system with non-sinusoidal frequencies under the transmission. The object is imaged by the optical system and can be regarded as a sinusoidal distribution of linear transmission at different frequencies. The frequency of the transmission feature remains the same, but the contrast changes, the phase goes and stops at a certain frequency. The reduction in contrast and the change of the bit phase vary with frequency, and the functional relationship between them is called MTF. As the optical transfer function and aberration, it can be used to evaluate the optical system imaging quality. It has an objective and reliable advantages, and is easy to calculate and measure. Not only can it be used for the evaluation of optical design results, but also for controlling the optical system design process, lens inspection, optical design and other aspects. After the optical design has been completed, the optical path diagram is combined with the mechanical design, and the stray light and ghost phenomenon are analysed by the optical machine simulation software. According to the situation of the light machine, the analysis slightly adjusts the optical design, in order to minimize the stray light.

3 Results

In this study, Zemax® software was used to simulate the through-focus MTF with a spatial frequency of 42 lp/mm and 83 lp/mm, to conform to Omni Vision's CMOS sensor (OV6930, 400 x 400 pixels, pixel size 3μ m) and an imaging distance of 30mm. Research results show that in the same 30mm as the distance, on axis MTFs were 84% and 65%, which became 78% and 55% respectively when simulated in a 70% field (Figures 4&5).

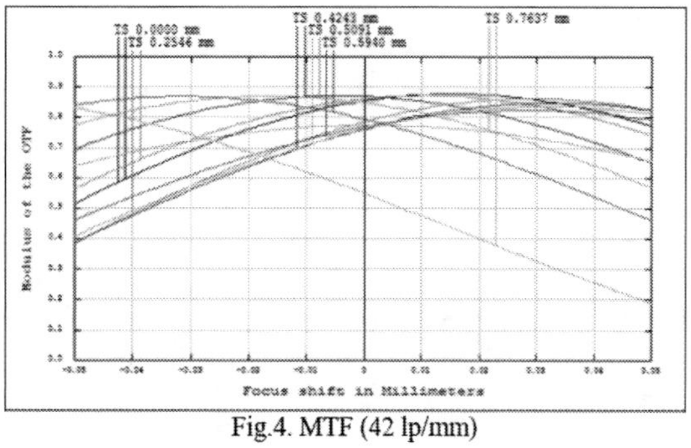

Fig.4. MTF (42 lp/mm)

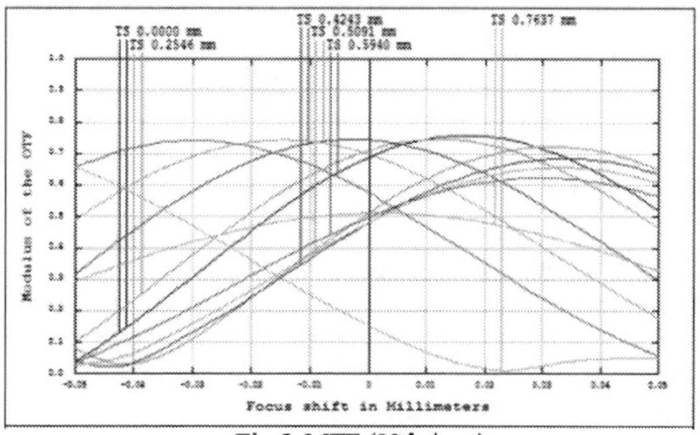

Fig.5. MTF (83 lp/mm)

Therefore, this study adopted a through-focus MTF of 42 lp/mm, and its EFL was 1.47mm, and the F. No was 3.90. In the calculation of through-focus MTF 42 lp/mm (MTF> 25%), the DOF value in the 100-10000nm near field position was within the 25-33mm range, thereby satisfying the DOF requirements for a video laryngoscope. Relative illumination is the percentage by which the image moves away from the middle of the image to the corner, as this affects the overall system resolution. In this study the point of highest transmission was defined as 100% when the field was 0.00 (image height=0.00 mm), and finally the Relative illumination became 58.3% when the field was 1.00 (image height=0.850) (Figure 6).

Finally, after having analysed the tolerance, all the MTF values were larger than 0.2, meaning this optical design is practicable for video laryngoscopes (Figure 7). the figure as close as possible after the point where it is first referenced in the text. If there is a large number of figures and tables it might be necessary to place some before their text citation. If a figure or table is too large to fit into one column, it can be centred across both columns at the top or the bottom of the page.

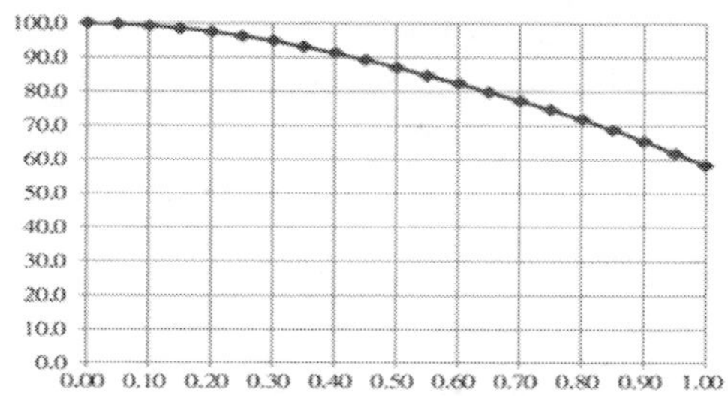

Fig.6. Relative Illumination

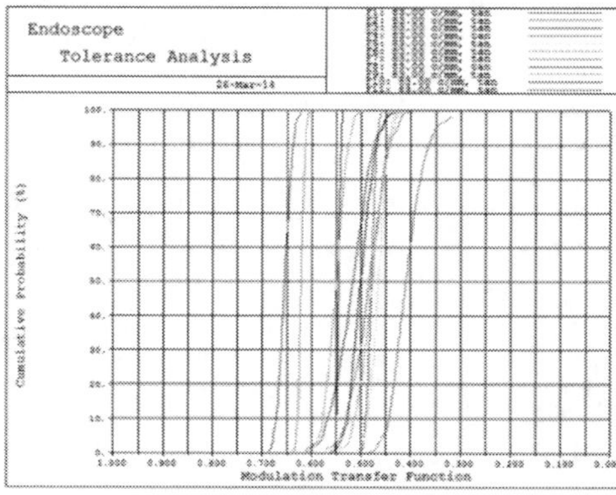

Fig. 7. Tolerance analysis

4 Conclusions

The specifications of the optical components of medical devices often require a balance between the other commercially available components (e.g., CMOS sensor) and clinical requirements (7mm blades), and furthermore, to achieve the basic need for optical quality. In this study, the OV 6930, small and with a low power demand, was selected as the main CMOS sensor for 7mm video laryngoscopes. In order to see the top of blade and neonatal glottis position simultaneously on the screen, this study had to choose an inferior MTF design (42 lp/mm) with a smaller FOV, and was unable to select a better MTF value with FOV design (83 lp/mm). However, these two still exceed the basic 0.2 MTF requirement. After the completion of the imaging system, this study will continue with colour adjustment, 7mm ultra-thin Ti-6Al-4V metal blade production and mechanical testing.

Acknowledgments: The authors are grateful for the research support from the Ministry of Science and Technology of Taiwan under grant numbers MOST 105-2622-E-492-016-CC3 and MOST 106-2221-E-492-021.

References

1. R. Singh, N. Kumar, A. Jain, Asian J Anesthesiol **55**, 2 (2017)
2. H. Kim, J.E. Chang, S.W. Min, J.M. Lee, S. Ji, J.Y. Hwang, Am J Emerg Med **34**, 9 (2016)
3. R.A. Caplan, K.L. Posner, R.J. Ward, F.W. Cheney, Anesthesiology **72**, 5 (1990)
4. R.C. Lambert, C. Ban, A.U. Rivera, G.J. Eckert, D.G. Krishnan, J.D. Bennett, J Oral Maxillofac Surg **73**, 7 (2015)
5. L.B. Mellick, T.Edholm, S.W. Corbett, Pediatr Emerg Care **22**, 4 (2006)
6. K. Baker, E. Tremblay, J. Karp, J. Ford, N. Finer, W. Rich, J Biomed Opt **15**, 6 (2010)
7. H.S. Yang, Y.G. Jo, G.U. Kim, Y.W. Lee, Opt Rev **18** (2011)
8. Y.Y. Liu, F.S. Xue, H.X. Li, G.Z. Yang, Eur J Anaesthesiol **34** (2017)

Applying Design Thinking Process in Student's Project: A case of EGF Products

Chun-Ming Yang[1,*] , and *Hong-Thien T.* Man[1]

[1]Industrial Design Department, Ming Chi University of Technology, Taiwan

Abstract. Design thinking process is best known as an effective, human-centred approach to more creative problem solving. This method has been applied as an innovative solution generation technique not only for designers but in other disciplines as well. While Epidermal Growth Factor (EGF) is an important growth factor in human body. It plays a crucial role in recent biological researches for many health-care applications. This study incorporated the design thinking process in EGF application products, aims to encourage student designers to embark on this freshly new problem-solving methodology in biological application, and hope to help introduce new medical products in daily life. Two cases as the results came out from the hands-on class project were also presented.

1 Introduction

Design Thinking has been growing as a central point in the contemporary design world with a variety of applications not only focusing on just a single product but more becoming a methodology to practice for innovations. From a large scale of the design industry, this human-centred approach results in innovative impacts, to a smaller scale of academic environments, applying design thinking also helps design students build up with creative confidence and transform them into design thinkers [1].

In the journal "Notes on the Evolution of Design Thinking: A Work in Progress", Craig M. Vogel emphasized on the progression of design thinking within multidisciplinary programs that could bring out a new model for innovation not just in universities but companies to approach all of the unmet global human need [2]. Design Thinking has been taught in successful design education at d.school, the Institute of Design at Stanford University as a methodology for innovating routinely [3] with feasibility, viability, and desirability to approach the real needs and desires of the human. Roger Martin also believed that design thinking could bring potential effects on education when design thinking was about the mental processes through a project-based workflow for problem-solving solutions [4]. Moreover, Design Thinking might help students become empowered agents on their own way of self-developing because of possessing both the tools and the confidence to change the world [5].

There are three typical spaces in Design Thinking Process: inspiration, ideation, and implementation [6] while Carroll and other researchers [5] proposed a conceptual

* Corresponding author: cmyang@mail.mcut.edu.tw

framework with six key steps of Design Thinking Process: Understand, Observe, Point of View, Ideate, Prototype, and Test. This study integrated the three-space model with six-step framework to introduce a Design Thinking process to design student with hands-on practice within a industrial design class project. This assignment is designed to bring the fundamental concept of Design Thinking to unlock students' potential abilities and creative confidence. This paper begins with reviewing relevant literature, followed by Design Thinking process conducted in this class project and then demonstrating results with the cases from the EGF application project.

2 Literature Reviews

Design Thinking has a rich history in the academic environment from Bauhaus time to Stanford's d.school. And one of the reasons that coined Design Thinking as a valued methodology is human-centeredness. In 1955, Dreyfuss also expressed the idea of human-centred approach in his book, Designing for People [2]. Human-centeredness is not just about emerging field of human factors and ergonomics but needs for logical approaches to produce innovative solutions by focusing on making people the source of inspiration and direction for solving design challenges [5]. Design Thinking Process is human-centred, not technological or business-centred, and about the idea "need-finding" [7].

In the book "The Design of Everyday Things" by Don Norman, the human-centred design process was introduced with four different activities: Observation, Ideation, Prototyping, and Testing. These four activities are iterative to get closer to the desired solution [8]. Tim Brown in his book "Change by Design" also pointed out three mutual elements, which could bring success to any design program: insight, observation, and empathy [1]. Carroll and other researchers mentioned that empathy, which comes from observing, is the intellectual identification of the feelings and thoughts of others [5]. The empathy could enable design thinkers to uncover people's deep insights and implicit needs. And with empathy, designers could stand in others' shoes to connect with the people they observed fundamentally [1]. For that reason, prototypes and drawings, scenario design, storytelling, and role-playing are methods to bring potential solutions back into an imagined situation to address users' experience and emotional response for useful feedbacks and an idea forward [1]. Especially, the culture of prototyping is really important in Design Thinking Process when it focuses on being highly experimental to engage people with artifacts for a better solution [5].

Carroll and other researchers believed that collaboration is essential to Design Thinking Process [5]. The collaborative process in a class project was influenced by students' willingness to listen to other's ideas to take risks and to share their ideas with others. The ability to work collaboratively is also one of the important factors in a design thinker's personality [9]. The best design thinkers need to work along together with other disciplines to collaborate their own significant experience. Instead of working only with your own knowledge or background, a problem or quest would be described on an open and innovative site so that designers could get help from the creative minds of all over the world to solve that problem or quest [3].

One of the important spaces in Design Thinking Process is Ideation – the process of generating ideas to approach potential solutions [9]. There has been an increasing attention on developing more effective methods for idea generation. However, among many methods such as Brain-sketching, C-Sketch, 6-3-5, and Gallery Method [10], C-Sketch is considered as a progressive idea generation method, especially in design related fields. C-Sketch Method, a.k.a. Collaborative Sketching, is shown to be more effective in performing the quality and variety of designs (Kulkarni et al., 2001). Design Thinking Process with C-Sketch as an idea generation tool could encourage an environment to cut through traditional structure and mindset barrier to create an innovative mixture of new ideas. Responsibility for the final outcome is not on any person but from the team's contribution, so there will be no "my idea" in a multidisciplinary team. Collaboration, therefore works much more effective when team members are from different backgrounds or perspectives (Kelly, 2013).

3 Process & Methods

This research generated three spaces in design thinking process (Brown & Wyatt, 2010) (inspiration, ideation, and implementation) with six design thinking phases proposed by Carroll et al. (2010) (understand, observe, point of view, ideate, prototype, and test) to develop a systematic framework for solving design problem. There were different creativity activities and tools introduced as hands-on practices in different phases in order to help students approach design-thinking concept and achieve specific tasks in each phase.

In Phase 1 – Understand, students conducted pre-research with data collection and presentation to the expert in order to understand the fundamental relevant knowledge. In Phase 2 – Observe, students were required to do a market survey to comprehend deeper customers' behaviors and needs as well as contemporary technologies and products on the commercial market. In Phase 3 – Point of View, students with data analyzing figured out the customers' needs as well as narrowing down the design problem. In Phase 4 – Ideate, students were instructed to use a various collection of hands-on practices with creativity tools such as: Lotus Blossom Method, C-Sketch, AEIOU & 5W1H, Scenario & Storytelling, to diverge and develop conceptual idea solutions. Finally with Phase 5 – Prototype and Phase 6 – Test, students were required to come out either virtual or physical prototype for testing to help students ensure if their design solutions could meet customers' needs. Figure 1 demonstrates the framework of this research, which is based on three main spaces of design thinking:

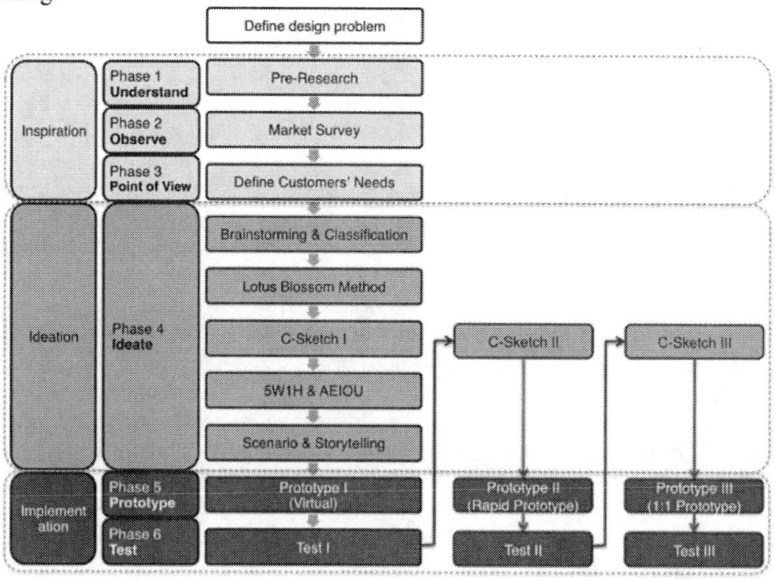

Fig. 1. Framework of this study

3.1 Phase 1: Understand

After the design problem had been assigned, students were required to (1) conduct a research for fundamental knowledge based on three questions: What is it? What can it help? Is there any application in our daily life? So the students could get the general comprehension about the technology with its background as well as the limitations; (2) present the pre-research before an expert in that industry for a deeper understanding of the problem.

3.2 Phase 2: Observe

With the fundamental understanding from Phase 1, students conducted a market survey with a quick field trip to several commercial supermarkets in order to ensure if there is any application with that technology available on the real market. Moreover, they interviewed some potential customers to understand their using behaviours. This was also one of the important characteristics of design thinking: human-centred approach.

3.3 Phase 3: Point of view

Students analyzed the data from two previous phases to narrow down the design problem and define the customers' needs.

3.4 Phase 4: Ideate

3.4.1 Brainstorming & Classification

After conducting the market survey, students were asked to write down all keywords relating to products, technologies in the industry on post-it notes. After that, they categorized them in groups of issues (Figure 2). This activity helped students focus on the potential group of issues, which could meet the customers' needs and be applied in the industry.

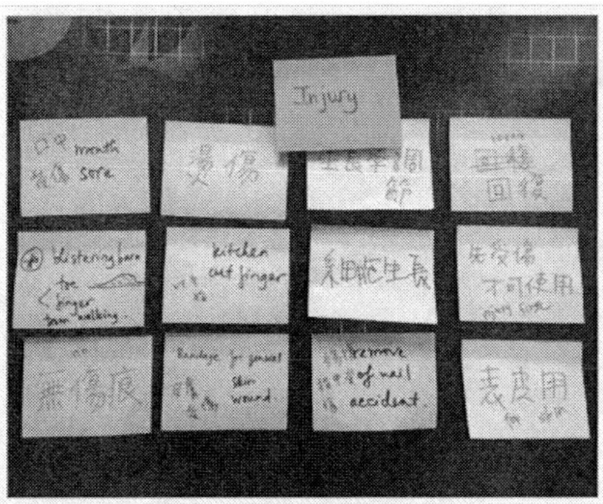

Fig. 2. Post-it notes with keywords and issue groupings

3.4.2 Lotus Blossom Brainstorming Method

Students set design topic in the centre of Lotus Blossom Map, and then fill the first layer of boxes with main keywords from the previous phase (3.4.1). Those main keywords in the first layer of boxes would be set as main topics in the centre of the second layer for divergence. Following those new central keywords, students figured out more keywords to expand the map until it was completed (Figure 3). Finally, the convergence of the Lotus Blossom Map would be started from the outmost layer towards the centre. With the central keywords of each layer, two other keywords would be chosen for the idea combinations. There would be 8 idea combinations from the final map. They would be written in the format: "Design topic = Keyword 1 + Keyword 2 + Keyword 3 +...+ Keyword n." Lotus Blossom Brainstorming Method could help students generate a much broader collection of different ideas in a free-flowing and impulsive way (Chen, Yang & Lai, 2016).

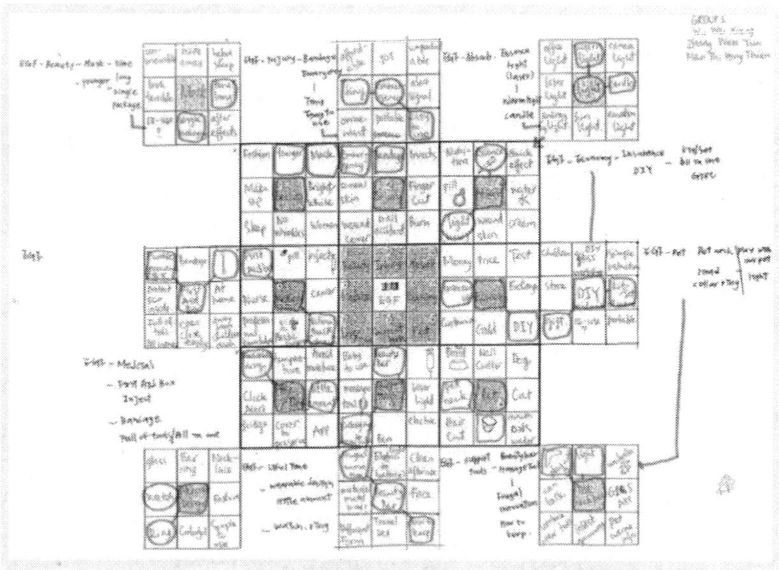

Fig. 3. Lotus Blossom Brainstorming Map

3.4.3 Collaborative Sketch (C-Sketch)

From the idea combinations got in the previous phase (3.4.2), students would write down that idea combination on the top of the sketch paper and performed a three-round collaborative sketching. (1) The group conducted the first round to select the most potential concept for proposal with experts' discussion to dig into a deeper level on technical solution of the conceptual idea. (2) Getting the experts' feedbacks from the first round, students continued on developing the conceptual idea and proposed again for the second round of experts' discussion. (3) In the final round, students focused on finishing the conceptual idea according to the second round feedbacks from experts. Collaborative Sketch could help students generate conceptual design solutions in a technological way, which could meet customers' needs. Moreover, sketching helps conceptual design solutions visualized for much dynamic group discussion and idea generation [11].

3.4.4 5W1H & AEIOU

From the conceptual idea chosen in the first round of C-Sketch (3.4.3), students would use 5W1H (standing for Who, What, When, Where, Why, and How) and AEIOU (standing for Activities, Environments, Interactions, Objects, and Users) methods to define the environment, target customers, and activities when using the products etc. These two methods incorporated with Lotus Blossom Map and C-Sketch Method were to help establish meaningful and appropriate design concepts to potential customers [12]. Moreover, these methods also helped the conceptual idea solutions more detailed, completed, and constructive for the later phase of scenario-based design.

3.4.5 Scenario & Storytelling

From the potential customers created in the previous phase (3.4.4), students developed the personas with more detailed characteristics (name, gender, occupation, education, hobby, and personality). The scenario framework was also created with a brief description (who, where, what, and when). And then students developed storyboards to visually establish the potential persona's interaction with the conceptual design solution. Scenario Design & Storytelling play important roles in developing the design concepts in which human-centred approach was focused [12].

3.5 Phase 5: Prototype

Prototyping is an essential phase of design thinking even if it is created virtually or physically. The power of prototyping is to generate results faster because the faster a designer make an idea tangible, the sooner he/she would be able to evaluate it, refine it for a better solution [1]. This phase was conducted with three times: (1) Students were asked to create a virtual prototype with sketching or 3D modelling images. (2) After the discussion with experts, students made a rapid prototype usually with paper at the scale 1:1 to ensure whether the form would be suitable for the function and applied technology. (3) Finally, the prototype would be refined again with details, usage instructions, and real material, still at the scale 1:1, to improve the better image of conceptual solutions. Prototyping encouraged students to interact with their own conceptual solutions to make sure if the design meets potential customers' needs.

3.6 Phase 6: Test

Following three times of prototyping, there were also three times of testing. (1) The first time was to check if the conceptual sketches from phase 1.4.3 could be developed after the discussion with experts about the possibilities and limitations. (2) Getting the experts' advice from the first round, the design was developed and improved with a rapid prototype at the scale 1:1. In this second testing, the conceptual design would be check if it could be developed in the real commercial market. (3) At the final testing, with the feedbacks from experts' second testing, the conceptual product at the scale 1:1 with real material and completed packaging design were ready to persuade the potential customers' needs. Testing ensures that students learned what would be possible and that might not work for target customers. That required them to go back to their prototype and modify it based on experts' feedbacks [5].

4 Results

This study, incorporated the design thinking process in epidermal growth factors (EGF) application products as the design problem, aims to encourage student designers to embark on this new problem-solving approach to introducing solutions for EGF application. The research was conducted during ten weeks of the Industrial Design course in the first semester of the 2016-2017 academic years with first-year master students at the Department of Industrial Design in Ming Chi University of Technology as the participants. There were 12 students who were divided into four groups and instructed by one industrial design expert and one biochemistry expert. The results of this applying design thinking process were displayed as the flow of previous process and methods above.

4.1 Phase 1: Understand

Students conducted a research for fundamental knowledge about EGF as well as presented their pre-research with the biochemistry expert (Figure 4). The experts would discuss more on their research to help students understand deeper the reality of this technology and industry, such as: EGF history, production method, applicable wounds, economic cost and value, and impacts in life, etc.

4.2 Phase 2: Observe

Students conducted a market survey to learn if there is any application with EGF technology available on the commercial market, especially in beauty care and wound care products. With human-centred spirit, they also interviewed potential customers to understand their behaviours in using skincare products. This observation encourages students to develop a sense of empathy [5].

4.3 Phase 3: Point of view

After students learned from Phase 1. Understand and Phase 2. Observe they developed a point of view that focused on potential customers' needs and insights [5]. In this case with EGF applications, the design problem was narrowed down through their research: (1) there were no skincare or wound care product with EGF application technology in the commercial market, (2) how does EGF work when applying onto the wounds as a healing factor?

Fig. 4. One slide from students' pre-research about EGF before discussion with experts.

4.4 Phase 4: Ideate

4.4.1 Brainstorming & Classification

With new knowledge after the market survey and defined design problem from previous steps, students wrote down all relevant keywords on post-it papers and categorized into groups. They came out totally 33 keywords and grouped into 4 themes: Economy, Absorb, Injury, and Beauty (Table 1).

Table 1. Categorized 33 keywords into 4 themes of ideas

Economy (5)	Absorb (3)	Injury (12)	Beauty (13)
Economy	Absorb	Burn	Repair
Expiration date	Metabolism	Repair	Moist
Different species	Osmosis	For skin	Beauty
Keep something		No scar	Woman
High price		Mouth sore	Elasticity
		Cut finger	Anti aging
		Cell growth	Essence
		Injury first	Reduce the wrinkle
		Relative growth rate	Dark lips brightening
		Remove of nail accident	Support instrument
		Bandage for general skin wound	Bandage for facial spots
		Blistering burn (toe, finger) from walking	Eye dark circles brightening
			Skin on head hair care after being dyed

4.4.2 Lotus Blossom Brainstorming Method

Students set EGF – the design topic – in the central box of Lotus Blossom Map, then fill 4 main keywords from the previous categorized groups (Economy, Absorb, Injury, and Beauty). They need 4 more to complete the very first layer of the 9-window-map, so they added 4 more keywords: Medical, Life/Time, Support Tools, and Pet from their previous brainstorming phase. These 8 keywords would be the central keywords of the second level 9-window-map to be continued for divergence. After fulfilling the whole map of 3 level of 9-window-map, they came out 8 idea combinations (Figure 5a & 5b).

4.4.3 Collaborative Sketch (C-Sketch)

From 8 idea combinations got from the previous phase (4.4.2), students performed a three-round collaborative sketching with 6 idea combinations. After finishing 2 rounds, they came out 42 sketches (7 sketches for each idea combinations) in which they chose 6 final conceptual sketches for the next phase of Design Thinking Process. Figure 6a & 6b would show the process of Collaborative Sketch through 3 rounds of one example of an idea combination: EGF = Economy + DIY + Insurance + All in One + Gift.

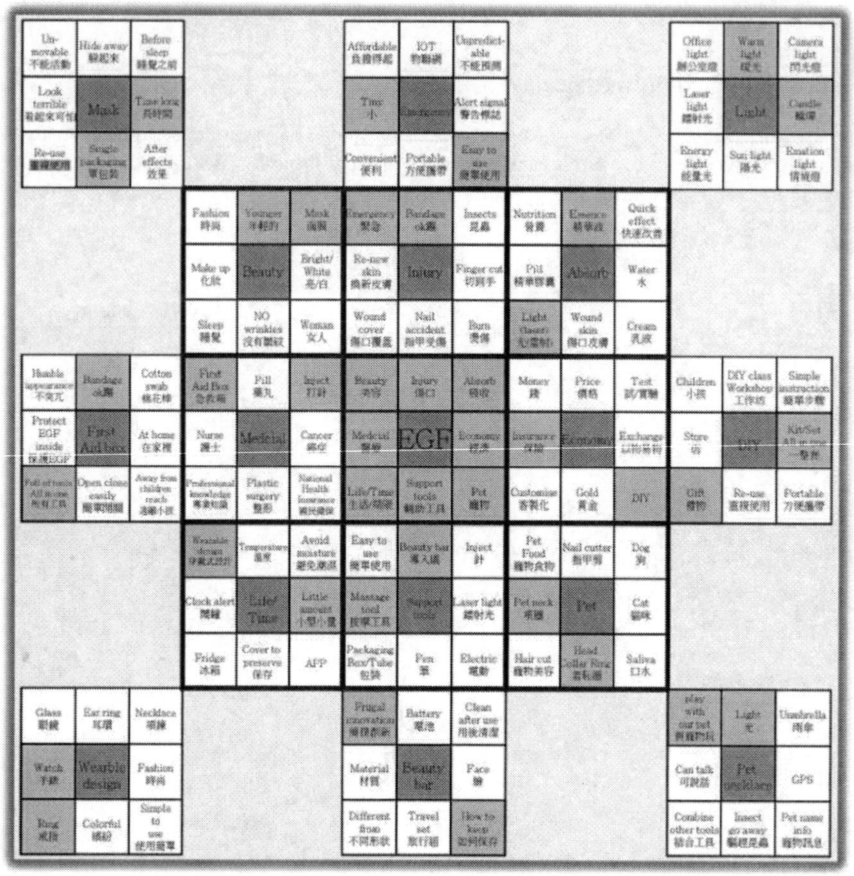

Fig. 5a. Fulfilling the whole Lotus Blossom Map

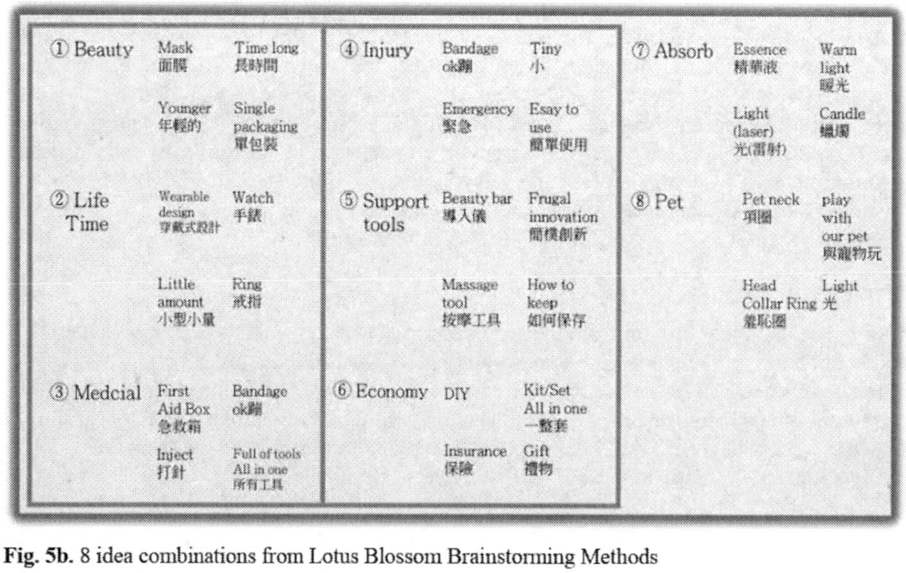

Fig. 5b. 8 idea combinations from Lotus Blossom Brainstorming Methods

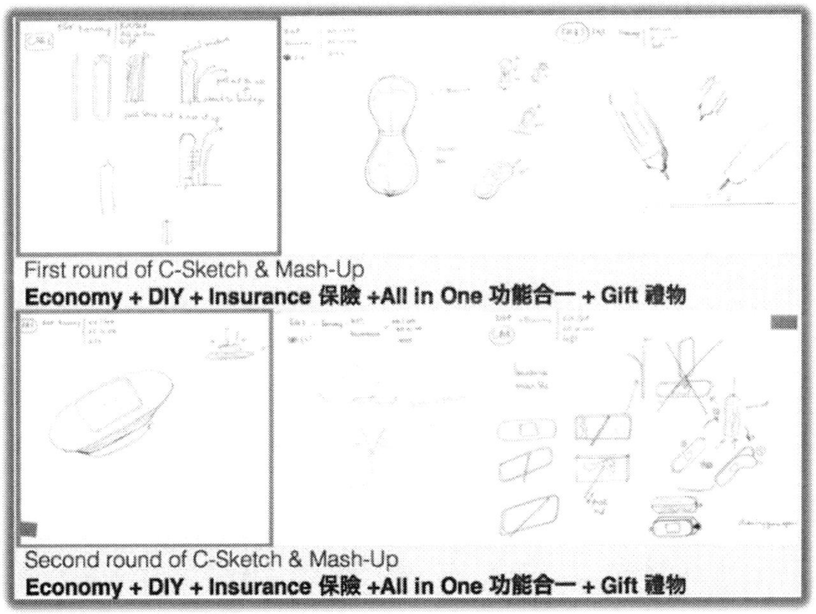

Fig. 6a. The first round and the second round of C-Sketch

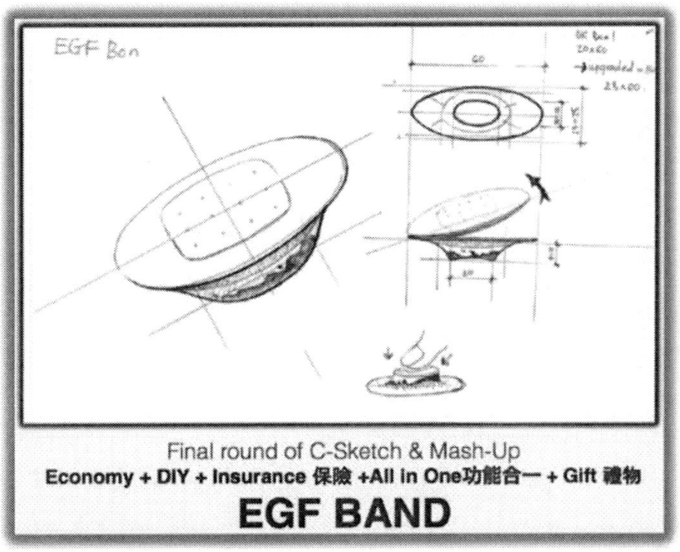

Fig. 6b. The final round of C-Sketch

4.4.4 5W1H & AEIOU

From the final conceptual idea from the three-round collaborative sketching (4.4.3), with the case EGF Band, students used 5W1H and AEIOU to get the detailed and imaginative approach to potential customers who might use the product in some situations. In this case, these methods could help students understand more about the possibility and convenience of using EGF Band with a purpose of an intensively fast healing solution (Figure 7).

4.4.5 Scenario & Storytelling

With detailed and contributive information from the previous phase (4.4.4), students carved more clearly with the personas that would be potential customers of their product design by developing storyboards visually (Figure 7). In this case with EGF Band, they described the scenario in which a teenager named Lufy (who) got into a fight at school (where) after class (when) then used EGF Band (what) to heal the wound on his face (why).

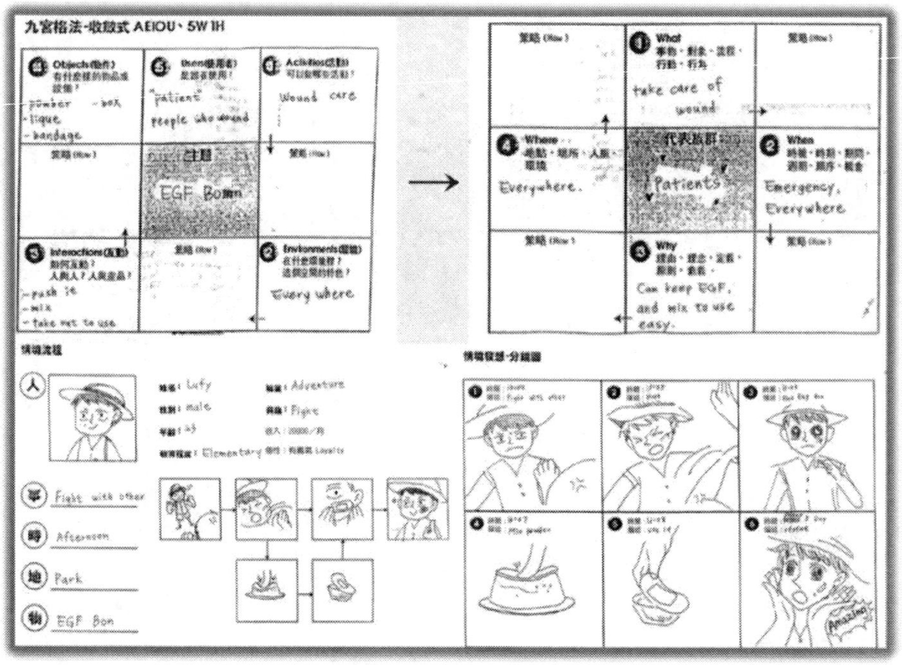

Fig. 7. Using 5W1H & AEIOU with Scenario & Storytelling

4.5 Phase 5: Prototype

Students conducted this phase three times to refine the conceptual product whether it could fulfil the customers' needs or requirements as a medical daily product which is easy to use and bring along. Figure 8 would show more about the EGF Band with virtual prototype and 1:1 one also.

4.6 Phase 6: Test

Students took testing with expert's feedbacks by presentations through three times to ensure the possibility of conceptual product EGF Band that was persuaded as a both user-and-environment-friendly product (Figure 9).

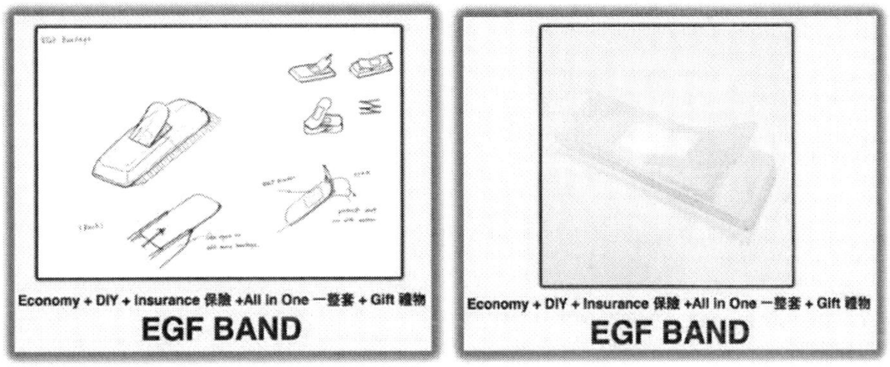

Fig. 8. Virtual prototype (2D sketching) and 1:1 prototype (3D model)

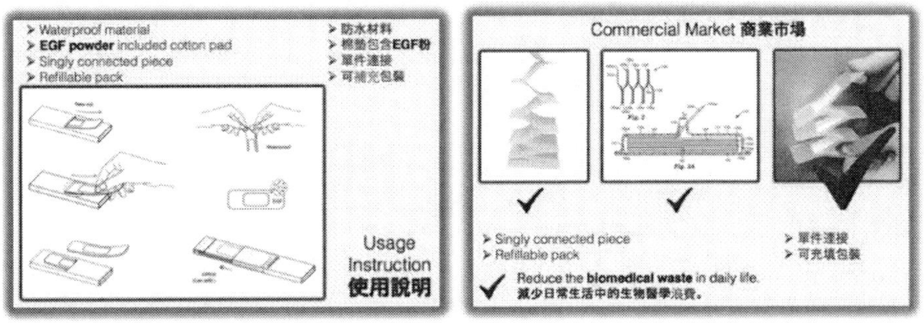

Fig. 9. Testing the conceptual product by presentation with expert

5 Discussion & Conclusion

This design thinking process was conducted with six-phase framework that was proposed by group researchers of Carroll: Understand, Observe, Point of View, Ideate, Prototype, and Test [5]. In spite of time constraint, students were instructed to follow completely the process with some idea combinations to come out conceptual solutions, some of which were commented by experts as good ideas to develop in reality for the design problem. With EGF Band, EGF Nurse was also a potentially conceptual design, which the group of students chose to develop until the last phase (Figure 10). However, these conceptual designs still need to be considered with more factors (trial manufacturing, material costing, user testing, and business marketing, etc.) for higher potential products.

In conclusion, this study demonstrated how we applied three spaces in design-thinking process: inspiration, ideation, and implementation) [6] with six design thinking phases proposed by group researchers of Carroll [5] (understand, observe, point of view, ideate, prototype, and test) to generate a systematic framework within the environment of an industrial design class project. We believed with this new framework, design students could learn more about the human-centred approach, collaborative design, and divergent and convergent thinking to achieve new experiences in solving a design problem. This study with different creativity activities and tools instructed as hands-on practices in separate phases could help design students build up their creative confidence and encourage them to become design thinkers in future.

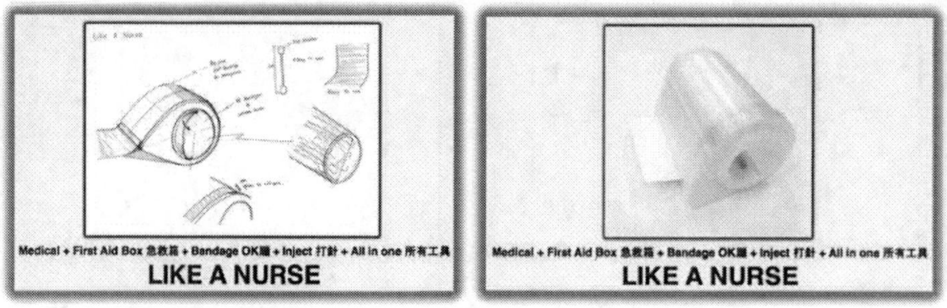

Fig. 10. Another conceptual design in the same Design Thinking Process

Acknowledgments: The authors are grateful for support of the Ministry of Science and Technology, R.O.C. under grants MOST105-2221-E-131-024- and MOST106-2221-E-131-017-. The authors also gratefully acknowledge the helpful comments and suggestions of the reviewers, which have improved the presentation. Furthermore, the authors are grateful for Professor Liang-Jung Chien and all students, especially Wen-Yun Zhang and Wei-Xiang Wu, participated in the design thinking workshop in Industrial Design Course of Fall September, 2016, Industrial Design Department, Ming Chi University of Technology, Taiwan.

References

1. T. Brown, *Change by Design: How Design Thinking Transforms Organizations and Inspires Innovation* (2009)
2. C. M. Vogel, DMR, **20**, 15-27 (2010)
3. T. Kelly, D. Kelly, *Creative Confidence* (2013)
4. D. Dunne, R. Martin, AMLE, **5**, 512-523 (2006)
5. M. Carroll, S. Goldman, L. Britos, J. Koh, A. Royalty, M. Hornstein, IJADE, **29**, 37-53 (2010)
6. T. Brown, J. Wyatt, SSIR, **8**, 30-35 (2010)
7. M. Camacho, TJDEI, **2**, 88-101 (2016)
8. D. A. Norman, *The design of everyday things*, 217-257 (2013)
9. T. Brown, HBR, **86**, 84-92 (2008)
10. J.S. Linsey, E. F. Clauss, T. Kurtoglu, J. T. Murphy, K. L. Wood, A. B. Markman, JMD, **133** (2011)
11. S. Kulkarni, J. D. Summers, N. Vargas-Hernandez, J. J. Shah, JCB, **35**, 168-198 (2001)
12. M. F. Chen, C. M. Yang, W. Y. Lai, *Proceedings of the SIGGRAPH ASIA Symposium on Education* (2016)

MATEC Web of Conferences **201**, 04004 (2018) https://doi.org/10.1051/matecconf/201820104004
ICI 2017

Smart Learning of Porn Fake News in the Family-Friendly Filters

Meiling Jow[1,*], and *Yaojung* Shiao[2]

[1]Department of Information and Communication, Tamkang University, Taipei, Taiwan
[2]National Taipei University of Technology, Taipei, Taiwan

Abstract. The proliferation of fake news on Facebook and Google has been a hot-button topic after the 2016 US presidential election. Fake news phenomenon is not limited in the political sphere. The porn industries have been using affiliate marketers to send fake news to reach more consumers, even children. Easy availability of pornography for children on the internet has been an issue. In US, the average age of exposure to porn is 11 to 12. Frequent exposure to pornography may lead to normalization of harmful behaviors. Starting late 2013, internet service providers in Britain made "family-friendly filters," which block X-rated websites, the default for customers, because kids are exposed to pornography at a young age. Google banned pornographic ads from its search engine from July 2014. Prostitution and escort services extend its market despite these efforts for the sake of the upsurge porn fake news. Porn fake news is produced purposefully to click, share, react, and comment. To mitigate the damage caused by porn fake news, designing a fully automated fake news detector is currently infeasible, because the problem at hand is too complex for technology alone. Even the subproblem of defining the criteria under which to classify news as "fake" creates ambiguity that requires human judgment. The ability to determine whether an article is real or fake requires more than just information about the article; it requires an understanding of cultural factors, for example "tea" maybe used by prostitution and escort services in Taiwan. This paper suggests one way to use artificial intelligence and human judgment to make it more valid to quarantine porn fake news.

1 Introduction

Fake news currently plagues the world. The proliferation of fake news on Facebook, Twitter and Google has been a hot-button topic after the 2016 US presidential election. Fake news is fueled in part by advances in technology. Wonder Woman star Gal Gadot's face was pasted onto a porn actress's body [1]. According to the Reuters report: "*from bots that automatically fabricate headlines and entire stories to computer software that synthesizes Donald Trump's voice and makes him read tweets to a new video editing app that makes it possible to create authentic-looking videos in which one person's face is stitched onto another person's body.*" The war to fight fake news is not going to be easy.

Fake news phenomenon is not limited in the political sphere. The porn industry has long been using affiliate marketers to send porn fake news to reach more consumers, among them even young children. Average age of first internet exposure to pornography is 11 years old, according to research. Dissemination of obscene material to children regardless of its form from traditional broadcasting is outlawed by almost every nation in the world. Criminal Offences relating to the publication of obscene material have long existed in England. But the distribution and marketing of porn industry evolves wisely along with the advance of communication technologies to avoid regulation, while age-verification requirements for online porn is not effectively working.

Kids are exposed to pornography at a young age on the internet because of its easy accessibility. There are 4.2 million pornographic websites, 12% of all websites. Some porn sites get more traffic than news sites like CNN. According to the website Paint Bottle, 30 percent of all data transferred online is porn. Pornhub is the 63rd most visited site on the Internet according to Alexa [2]. All kinds of people can access it, whether they are minors, adults, or people with psychological problems. Children are particularly vulnerable.

Easy availability of pornography for children on the internet has been an issue worth worrying. A lot of online pornography is violent. Frequent exposure to pornography may lead to normalization of rape, risky sexual behavior, or sex at a young age among other effects. The easy availability of pornography is creating a dangerous situation where kids get caught up in sexually addictive behavior at an early age. Mental health professionals are fearful of the impact on future generations, comparing internet pornography to "crack cocaine" because of its highly addictive nature [3].

2 Banning from countries, search engines, and social media

* Corresponding author: meilingj@mail.tku.edu.tw

The first defense against child exposure to pornography and exploitation is to use a good internet filter, or subscribe to a filtered internet service. The internet regulation has relied on the system of user reporting, a "notify and take down" basis, to tackle the problem of online porn. In the United Kingdom the blacklist is open and available through institutions such as Internet Watch Foundation.

To better crack down on online pornography and make the internet safer for children, internet service providers in Britain were asked to make "family-friendly filters," which block X-rated websites, the default for customers starting from 2013, because kids are exposed to pornography at a young age. Instead of letting people choose what filtering they want, the "Yes" option for filtering was pre-ticked. However, the policy was been challenged over its censorship. Studies of filters on some UK ISPs have shown that well-known porn sites go unblocked while education sites about sexually transmitted diseases or sexual health are inaccessible [4].

At the same time, ISPs and search engines were under the pressure from the advocacy groups to tackle illegal pornography. Google changed its advertising policy in March 2014 to ban pornographic ads from its search engine, including ads promoting underage and non-consensual sexual content, as well as prostitution and escort services.

Facebook restricts the display of nudity and sexual activity because of their audiences cultural background or age. Machine learning is used to see if something in a photo violates the company's "Community Standards." The social media gave people the option to block mature and suggestive content from their News Feeds from August in 2016.

Although YouTube has systems in place to take swift action on obscene material both through machine learning and by increasing human and technical resources, a BBC Trending investigation has discovered a flaw in a tool that enables the public to report abuse. Part of YouTube's system for reporting sexualized comments left on children's videos has not been functioning correctly for more than a year [5].

3 Fighting back from the porn industry

After the banning of pornographic ads and blocking mature contents, porn industries tried to utilize key influencers and embedded marketing in which references to porn websites or videos are incorporated into another work, such as a newspaper or television news, with a specific intent to promote porn websites or videos. Event marketing is entering a guerrilla era where the physical and the virtual cross paths, offering new options for marketing professionals who create buzz over a service or product. The created event is called pseudo-event in journalism. For example, the porn industry might create a seemingly newsworthy information to distribute a news, like an Irish reporter discovered the secret to use the keyword of "scannáin" being able to search for a lot of hidden pornographic videos on the YouTube [6].

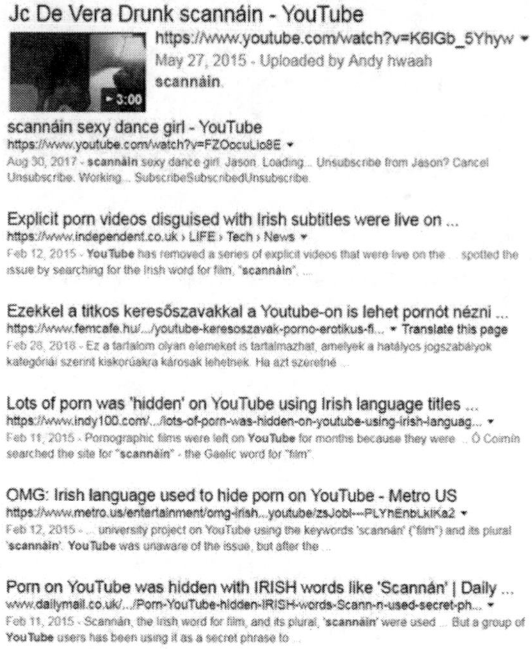

Fig. 1. Google search result. This is a figure showing how the news was reported not in 2015 but also till 2018.

The news would then be reported all over the world to give information to people, even children, how to find pornography and come along with other true news again and again like the hotnews below (Figs. 2 & 3). Even in 2018, YouTubers will stumble upon what is really porn when searching for the keyword "scannán."

Fig. 2. Type of product placement. This is a figure showing how the porn sponsored news repeatedly appears on the webnews of a mainstream newspaper of Taiwan in 2018.

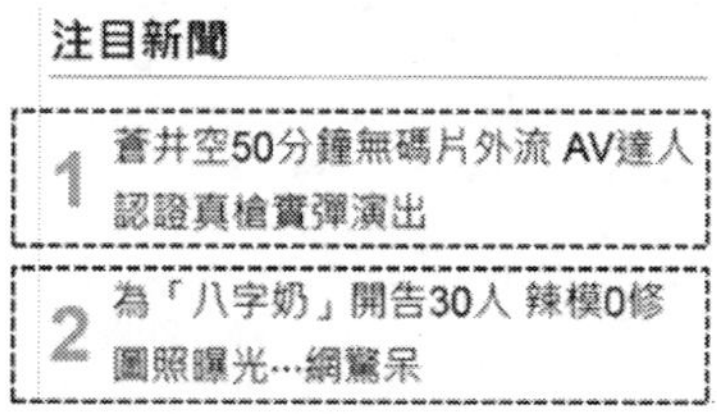

Fig. 3. Type of product placement. This is a figure showing how porn promoted stories repeatedly appears on the webnews of a mainstream newspaper of Taiwan in 2018.

Porn fake news is produced purposefully to click, share, react, and comment just like political fake news. Unlike a political fake news aiming to disrupt an election or provoke civil unrest, porn fake news is not an issue of what news sources to trust or whether the information is accurate or not. It is an event marketing by interactively hiring online key influencers to create fictional or make-up news stories with clickbaiting headlines geared to travel on social media to click on and share as propaganda, which is spread even more widely by placement marketing of newspaper and television news broadcasting and will last long after the reporting by way of PR promotion as advertising (sponsored news you may like) to come along with other true news again and again to be clicked and to promote their porn websites or videos in the nature.

Fig. 4. Type of product placement. This is a figure showing how porn fake news appears on the webnews of a mainstream newspaper of Taiwan in 2018 without marking as promoted.

To overcome the issue of age-appropriateness and general decency, the pictures are carefully processed, as above, not to reach the level of obscenity or sexually explicit, so that volunteer moderators can not report it to the regulative body. PornHub is especially good at making porn fake news without violating age-appropriateness and general decency. It launched its first US advertising campaign, a crowdsourcing competition to require entrants to submit a G-rated, suitable for work ad (print or multimedia) that clearly promotes the brand in 2014. The event received worldwide broadcasting and publication, and the winning advertising then was widely spread out in news and shared among social media on Christmas.

Hence, a particular event coming from a legitimate site of news sources cannot guarantee the event is not a porn fake news. For example, CNBC had aired specials on prostitution and a documentary called "Porn: Business of Pleasure." Viewers can see a pornographic product placement on TV and newspaper's interviews with a series of porn-makers or porn star [7].

Production of the fake news is to spread out the information about a porn website, prostitution, porn related services, videos or products to attract maximum attention of people. According to Pornhub, nearly 92 billion videos were watched over the course of 23 billion visits to the site by many millions of very horny visitors in 2016. That's 64 million visitors per day, or 44,000 every minute.

4 How AI and machine learning fight fake news.

After coming under heavy public criticism for not taking full responsibility for fake news affecting the outcome of the 2016 presidential election, the technology tycoons such as Google, Facebook, and Twitter now plan to crack down on fake news. There are four ways commonly used by AI and machine learning [8]:

1. Score Web Pages: Google takes the accuracy of facts presented to score web pages. The technology has grown in significance as it makes an attempt to understand pages' context without relying on third-party signals.
2. Weigh Facts: A Natural Language Processing engine can go through the subject of a story along with the headline, main body text, and the geo-location. Further, artificial intelligence will find out if other sites are reporting the same facts. In this way, facts are weighed against reputed media sources.
3. Predict Reputation: Using predictive analytics backed by Machine Learning, a website's reputation can be predicted through considering multiple features like domain name and Alexa web rank.
4. Discover Sensational Words: When it comes to news items, the headline is the key to capturing the attention of the audience. Artificial Intelligence has been instrumental in discovering and flagging fake news headlines by using keyword analytics.

These might be ways to combat political fake news, but they are not good ways to mitigate the damage caused by porn fake news for children.

AI systems are used to fill the gaps left by online fact-checking outlets, whose human fact-checkers lack the bandwidth to evaluate every article that appears online. Designing a fully automated fake news detector is currently infeasible, because the problem at hand is too complex for technology alone.

There are many different categories misinformation can fall into. Even the subproblem of defining the criteria under which to classify news as "fake" creates ambiguity that requires human judgment. The ability to determine whether an article is real or fake requires more than just information about the article; it requires an understanding of cultural factors, for example "tea" maybe used by prostitution and escort services in Taiwan, and "John" is prostitute's client in US slang. Algorithms will be helpful, but real progress on understanding or controlling the fake news phenomenon is ultimately about humans not machines. Current forms of AI can look at the style of the language, and the topic that the text is discussing, but it can't figure out the meaning behind statements [9].

Even though an AI-based system like Enterra would be able to interpret the phrase "seeing red" in context as referring to a high level of frustration, because it can perform human-like reasoning and analyze the report contextually [10], it might not be able to detect the fraudulent stories disguised in the form of product placement in journalism.

The way that Facebook polices mature content is using AI to monitor video on Facebook Live and flag it, if offensive content is found. But the study doesn't recommend the machine learning to make a model to flag news content as porn fake news. Using a red banner to highlight that a story is fake to prevent it going viral is even worse for decreasing children's accessibility to porn fake news by alerting their attention.

Trying to predict whether a news site is a fake news site or not is one possible way to solve the porn fake news problem if these stories come from the bloggers or key influencers of social media who constantly produce porn fake news. But this way is not realistic for the porn fake news produced as an event marketing by the porn industry on the mainstream media.

The study suggests one way to solve the problem: beyond predicting a website's reputation and discovering sensational words, researchers need to create a database according to cultural codes and to use a Natural Language Processing engine to go through the message to find the websites or the keywords mentioned in the news, and then to follow and check the websites or the keywords. If they lead to an age-verification sign like Fig. 5 or obscene pictures or videos, then they must be a news to be filtered away from children.

Fig. 5. Age-verification sign. This is a figure showing that an age-verification sign used in Taiwan, which can be easily cheated by children under 18 years old to click the "I'm over 18 years old" button and pass age-verification.

5 Conclusions

The study points to a fact which needs equal attention when the world is focusing on the political fake news after the 2016 US presidential election. That is porn fake news which has much impact on children. To protect children from viewing inappropriate adult material, United Kingdom is going to activate the Age Verification for Online Pornography (clauses 15-25) on the Digital Economy Bill from 2018, which asks anyone who makes pornography available online on a commercial basis must ensure under 18s in the UK cannot access it. If machine learning can do a better job to combat the war by building a better family-friendly filter, government regulation can be loosen. The researcher observed different types of porn fake news and how they appear on different media to spread. These observations might provide researchers in machine learning or other AI tools some thoughts to build a more useful model to mitigate the danger of porn fake news to children.

References

1. P. Perry, Available online: http://bigthink.com/philip-perry/these-ai-tools-could-lead-to-the-next-generation-of-fake-news (accessed on 2017).
2. L. Gilkerson, Available online: http://www.covenanteyes.com/2013/02/19/pornography-statistics/ (accessed on 22 Sep. 2013).
3. Available online: http://coheargroup.com/services/sexual-recovery-services/pornography-addiction-in-adolescents/ (accessed on 2017).
4. Available online: http://www.bbc.com/news/technology-23403068 (accessed on 2017).
5. BBC, Available online: http://citifmonline.com/2017/11/24/flaw-youtubes-obscenity-tracking-tool/ (accessed on 2017).
6. T. Lee, Available online: http://www.ubergizmo.com/2015/02/porn-uploaded-and-disguised-on-youtube-using-irish-language-titles/ (accessed on 2017).
7. CNBC Available online: https://www.mrc.org/articles/cnbc-mainstreams-gross-out-porn (accessed on 2017).
8. R. Akiwatkar, Available online: https://channels.theinnovationenterprise.com/articles/how-can-artificial-intelligence-combat-fake-news (accessed on 2017).
9. Available online: https://towardsdatascience.com/i-trained-fake-news-detection-ai-with-95-accuracy-and-almost-went-crazy-d10589aa57c (accessed on 2017).
10. A. Wolk, Available online: https://www.forbes.com/sites/alanwolk/2018/01/17/can-enterras-advanced-ai-systems-stop-the-fake-news-epidemic/#6d264af92049 (accessed on 2018).

Analysis of Anti-JFET for 600V VDMOS and HCI Reliability

Shao-Ming Yang [1,3*], *Gene* Sheu[1], *Chiu-Chung* Lai[2], *Ravi* Deivasigamani[1]

[1]Department of Computer Science and Information Engineering, Asia University, 500, Lioufeng Rd., Taichung 41354, Taiwan.
[2]School of Software and Microelectronics, Peking University, Beijing, China.
[3]Department of Medical Research, China Medical University Hospital, China Medical University, Taichung, Taiwan.

Abstract. In VDMOS device the anti-JFET concentration has important role for determining the breakdown voltage and on-resistance of the device. Because higher N-drift doping concentration can provide the very best on-resistance of the device but also decrease breakdown voltage. It also has a proportional relationship with threshold voltage degradation. In this paper, we report the anti-JFET implantation energy influence effect electric potential distribution, the highest impact ionization shifted from the silicon surface to deeper. It will have less hot carrier impact, and we have found higher breakdown voltage. The anti-JEFT implantation is critical for on-resistance off-state breakdown voltage optimization. However the high field and high impact ionization near the gate region will cause severe hot carrier Injection problem. The general expectation of high voltage VDMOS transistor is to have higher breakdown voltage, less degradation due to hot carrier injection and better on-resistance.

1 Introduction

This device structure is fabricated by starting with an N-type epitaxial layer grown on a heavily doped N type substrate. The channel is formed by the difference in lateral extension of the P-base and N type source regions produced by their diffusion cycles. Without the application of a gate bias, a high voltage can be supported by the VDMOS structure when a positive bias is applied to the drain. The general VDMOS device has high breakdown voltage, lower on-resistance and less hot carrier impact. In this study objective of reducing the efficiency of the junction field effect transistor by mean of introducing an anti-JFEF implant in the fabrication process.

The present work is a continuation of that described in, with the objective of reducing the efficiency of the junction field effect transistor by mean of introducing an anti-JFE implant in the fabrication process. The optimization of the implanted dose leading to the optimum trade-off between the on-state resistance and the breakdown voltage.

The contribution of the Junction Field Effect Transistor resistance R_{JFET}, the resistance of the region between the p-base diffusions, depends on the spacing and depth of the p-base diffusions and the doping concentration of the drift region.

The resistance of the epi layer R_{Epi} is dependent on its doping concentration and its thickness. Its value can be lowered by increasing the doping concentration or by decreasing the thickness of the epi layer. The resistance of the epitaxial layer dominates R_{on} for high voltage devices.

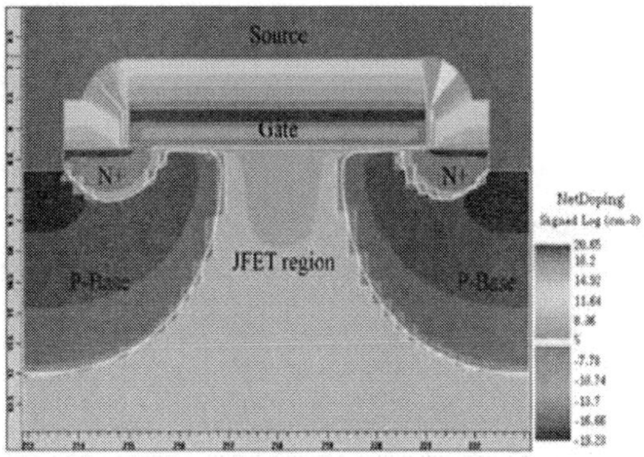

Fig. 1. Net doping profile of the anti-JFET region 3.5E12 at 360kev implanted.

This article summarizes the TCAD and experimental results of this technique when applied for the improvement of device stability and lifetime.

2 Simulation methodology

The simulations are done by using Synopsys software. The VDMOS transistor device is virtually fabricated using tsuprem4 and characteristics are simulated by using Medici. In this paper, we work done by varying the doping concentration and energy of anti-JFET region,

* Corresponding author: rickyyang121@asia.edu.tw

https://doi.org/10.1051/matecconf/201820105001

and study the result based on the threshold voltage degradation caused by hot carrier injection.

In order to optimize the dose and energy of the anti-JFET implant. The difference distribution of electric potential in line with anti-JFET implanted dose (a) high dose (3.5E12) (b) low dose (1.5E12) at 360kev as shown Fig.2.

These simulations show a reduction of the on-state resistance 15.4% and breakdown voltage only losing 4.75% at energy 360kev. For VDMOS transistor a high equipotential under the gate is the major reason of the device. In this paper, we simulated portion of the VDMOS transistor for the JFET implant of dosage and energy variation. The anti-JFET implanted dose trade-off between the breakdown voltage and on-resistance as shown Fig.3. The on-state resistance of the VDMOS transistor can be significantly reduced by introducing a blanket anti-JFET implant without a major impact on the voltage capability.

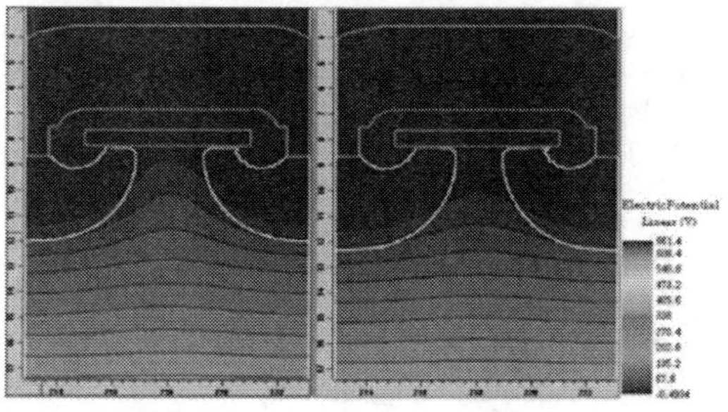

(a) (b)

Fig. 2. The equipotential lines have lower and also had better HCI reliability. (a) High dose (b) Low dose

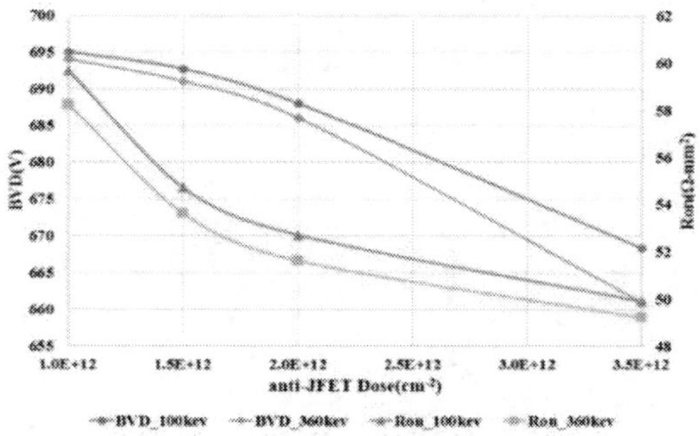

Fig. 3. Variation of off-state breakdown voltage and on-state resistance with anti-JFET implant process.

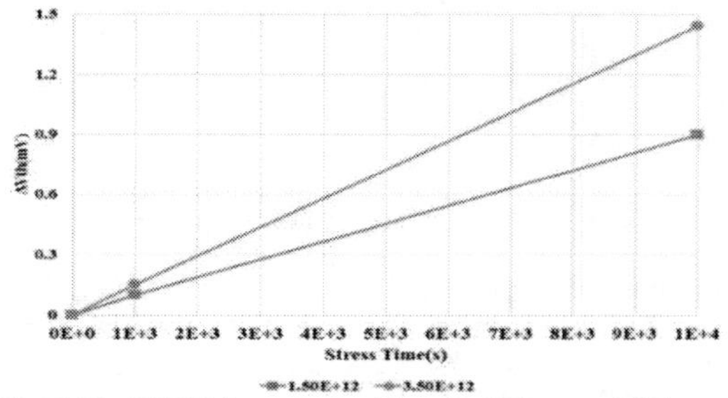

Fig. 4. The VDMOS transistor with anti-JFET energy 360kev measured up to stress 1E4 seconds and after that we have measured Vth degradation of the device.

Carriers generated by impact ionization can themselves gain enough energy (call hot carriers) to be injected into the gate oxide. We observed if equipotential line crowding then HCI reliability is worse. In this paper, thermodynamic HCI were invoked in the device simulation to perform the interface trap generation due to HCI. For VDMOS transistor a high field under the gate region is the major source of the device degradation.

Hot carrier stress experiments were performed under Vgs=5V and V_{DD}=600V, the simulation of reliability based on anti-JFET implantation energy at 360kev. On the other hand, electron injection and trapping at the SiO2/Si interface in the gate oxide and the major cause of the degradation of threshold voltage which increases constantly throughout stress time as shown Fig.4.

We found threshold voltage degradation reduced 37.5% from 3.5E12 to 1.5E12 at 1E4 stress times.

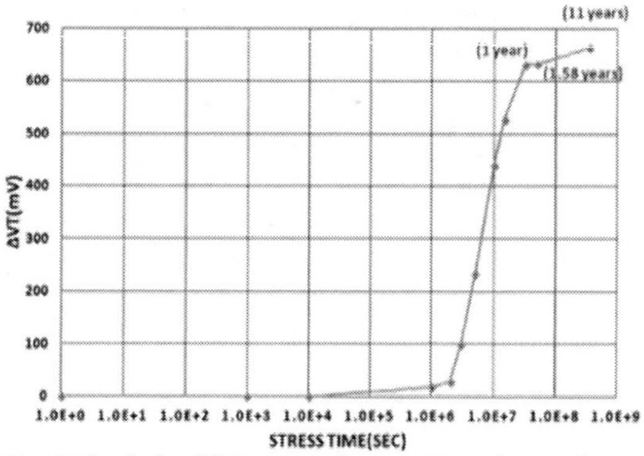

Fig. 5. The device lifetime curve between V_{th} and stress time

We have stressed this cool device for almost 11 years and found as shown in Fig.5. Only a small amount of ΔVth after 1 year is observed throughout the rest of stress time. Assuming donor and acceptor traps (pre-existing prior to stress) at the JFET field region (near to the channel), Vth increases with electron injection (or trapping at the acceptor states), and it finally starts to decrease by new donor type interface traps, which correspond that the negative charge by electron injection is compensated by the positive charge build-up at the Si/SiO2 interface and in the oxide.

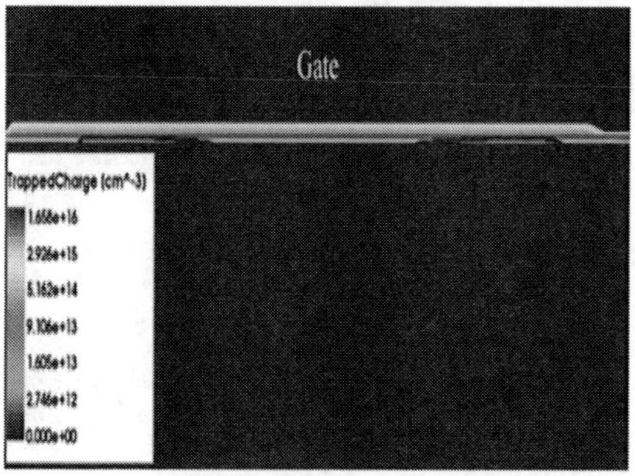

(a)

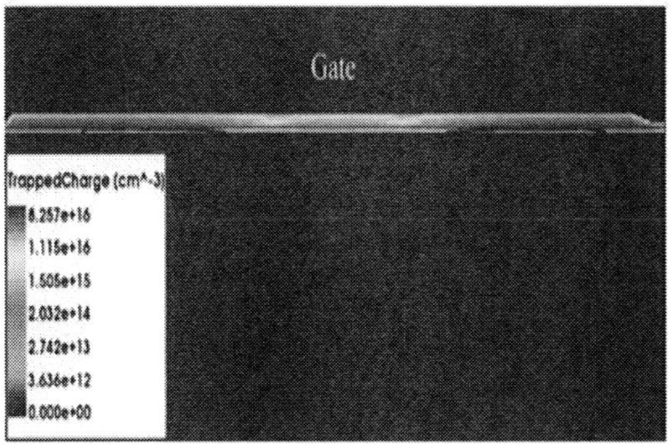

(b)

Fig. 6. Trapped charge distribution of the anti-JFET 1.5E12 at 360kev implanted after (a) 0 second (b) 3.5E8 seconds of HCI stress.

In this reliability test, we can observe that trapped charge distribution after HCI stress 0 second and 3.5E8 seconds. From Fig.6 the trapped charge in the order of 1.658E16 but after 3.5E8 seconds HCI stress time it is in the order of 8.257E16. It is approximately 5 times more traps for 0 second compared to 3.5E8 seconds.

3 Conclusion

The paper proposed vertical DMOSFET transistor, the JFET doping concentration has a relation with the threshold voltage degradation. The effects of anti-JFET implant on the on-resistance, blocking capability and the reliability of the VDMOS have been studied. Experimental results show that the anti-JFET implant can reduce the threshold voltage degradation by moving higher field region to the surface channel region. It's highly influence the breakdown voltage and on-state resistance, and less hot carrier induced device degradation. Optimized dose and energy, improve the trade-off between the breakdown voltage and on-state resistance with a good device lifetime.

From our experiments we proved the device after 10 years stress, the breakdown voltage still holds. Therefore, this device has very good HCI performance.

Acknowledgment: The authors would also like to thank National Center for High-performance computing, National Nano Device Laboratories, and the National Chip Implementation Center for supporting us.

References

1. B. Jayant Baliga, "*Fundamentals of Power Semiconductor Devices*", 279-285 (2008)
2. H. Hakim; D. Bolognesi; F.D. Pestel, "*Integrated VDMOS Transistor with Reduced JFET Effect*", European Solid-State Device Research Conference, 278-281 (2006)
3. W.S Tam, "*Off-State Drain Breakdown Mechanisms of VDMOS with Anti-JFET Implantation*", *Microelectronics Reliability*, 51:2064-2068 (2011)
4. M. Knaipp, "*Investigations on An Isolated Lateral High-Voltage N-Channel LDMOS Transistor with A Typical Breakdown of 150V*", IEEE, 266-269 (2006)
5. S. Manzini, "*Hot-Electron-Induced Degradation in High-Voltage Submicron DMOS Transistors*", IEEE, 65-68 (1996)
6. H.H.M. Yusof, "*Design Consideration of N-Drift Region Doping Concentration in High Voltage VDMOS Transistor*", IJSRET, 3(4):764-766 (2014)
7. U. Heinle, "*Vertical High-Voltage Transistors on Thick Silicon-on-Insulator*" (2003)
8. C. Lombardi, "*A Physically Based Mobility Model for Numerical Simulation of Non-Planar Device*", IEEE, (1988)
9. S. Manzini and C. Contiero, "*Hot-Electron-Induced Degradation in High-Voltage Submicron DMOS Transistors*", IEEE, (1996)
10. S.M. Sze, "*Semiconductor Devices Physics and Technology*", (1985).

A Novel Approach to Improve Quality Control by Comparing the Tagged Sequences of Product Traceability

Jing-Doo Wang[1,⋆]

[1] *Dept. of Computer Science and Information Engineering, Asia University, Taiwan.*

Abstract. Quality control is an essential issue for manufacture, especially when the manufacture is towards intelligent manufacturing that is associated with "Internet of thing"(IOT) and "Artificial Intelligence"(AI) to speed up the rate of product line automatically nowadays. To monitor product quality automatically, it is necessary to collect and monitor the data generated by sensors, or to record parameters by machine operators, or to save the types (brands) of materials used when producing products. In this study, it is assumed that the sequences of the traceability of unqualified products are different from that of qualified ones, and these different values (or points) within the sequences result in these products qualified or unqualified. This approach extracts maximal repeats from the tagged sequences of product traceability, and meanwhile computes the class frequency distribution of these repeats, where the classes, e.g. "qualified" or "unqualified", are derived from the tags. Instead of inspecting all of the sequences of product traceability aimlessly, quality control engineers can filter out those maximal repeats whose frequency distributions are unique to specific classes and then just check the corresponding processes of these repeats. However, from the practical point of view, it should be estimated as a big-data problem to extract these maximal repeats and meanwhile compute their corresponding class frequency distribution from a huge amount of tagged sequential data. To have this work practical, this study uses one previous work that is based on Hadoop MapReduce programming model. and has been applied for an U.S.A patent (US Patent App. 15/208,994). Therefore, it is expected to be able to handle a huge amount of sequences of product traceability. With this approach that can narrow down the range for identifying false points (processes) within product line, it is expected to improve quality control by comparing tagged sequences of product traceability in the future.

1 Introduction

To speed up the processes of producing products and to reduce the cost of human labors, nowadays manufactories are toward to industry 4.0 [1] that adopt robots and combine with internet of things (IOT) [2]. It is predictable that the increasing rate of producing products in industry 4.0 will overwhelm the ability of quality control engineers to handle the problem in time when defective products occur and they need to identify what factors result in that products. To promote the ability of quality control [3] to meet the requirement of industry 4.0, it is necessary and essential to set up sensors

⋆e-mail: jdwang@asia.edu.tw

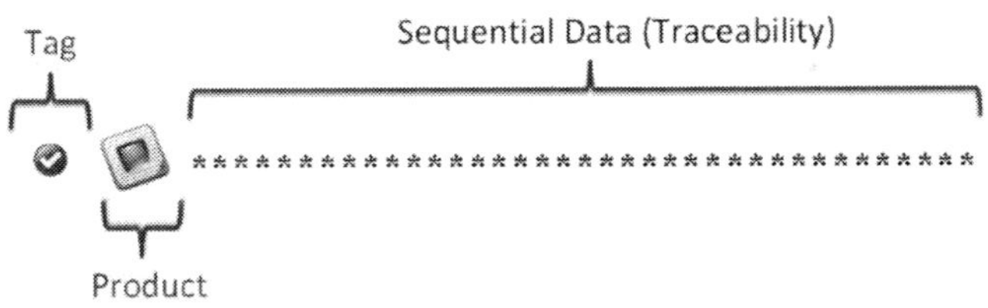

Figure 1. The traceability of one product attached with a tag.

to collect automatically the parameters from both environment and machines. That is, quality control (assurance) engineers can use these data to trace back the producing processes of those defective products and to identify false steps within the product line if abnormal products are detected or reported. Due to the increasing rate of producing products using robots, it is beyond the ability of quality control engineers to identify the false processes that result in these abnormal (false) products efficiently without extra analysis tools. It is desired to have novel approach to overcome above big data computational problem [4] to promote the power of quality control of industry in the future.

To improve quality control for reducing the response time of false points identification within the product line, in this study, the sequences of the traceability of products are collected first of all. The traceability of one product, as shown in Fig.1, is a ordered list (sequence) of elements or records that consist of data generated by sensors, or parameters of machines, or the types of materials collected sequentially when that product is produced. In this study it is assumed that the tag (class) of one product, given by quality control, is certainly concerned with its traceability. In other words, all of the sequences of traceability of those false or abnormal products with the same tag are supposed to contain some specific subsequences, called "markers", that result in of those products. Intuitively, the sequence of product traceability of one product determines the outcome of one product; the makers, some subsequences hidden within its traceability, are the keys to decide its tag that is the same as the quality control labels with. One class marker, therefore, is expected to be highly correlated with its own class (tag) such that it can provide clues to quality control engineers to inspect and identify false points from the subsequence representing that markers, instead of scanning the whole sequence of its traceability.

The goal of this paper is to extract class markers by comparing the class frequency distribution of maximal repeats extracted from the tagged sequences of product traceability via the scalable approach in the previous work[5]. The approach proposed in this study is to reduce the range of searching factors that result in unqualified products by comparing the tagged sequences of product traceability, where the traceability of one product is the sequential data generated while that product is produced, e.g. values collected by sensors, machine parameters, materials or components used or the identifier of operators; the tags are labels given by quality control staff. It is believed that these class markers, if they can be extracted efficiently, are valuable to quality control engineers because they can focus on inspecting those steps that are corresponding to these markers within the sequences of product traceability to speed up the processes of locating the false points within product line, instead of surveying the whole steps aimlessly.

The remainder of this paper is organized in the following. Section 2 describes how to generate the tagged sequences for experiments and the method to extract class markers. Section 3 shows experimental results. Section 4 has discussions and Section 5 gives conclusions and future works.

2 Materials and Methods

This study assumes that each of products is labeled with a tag (ClassID), e.g. one of these five classes as "normal", "abnormal I", "abnormal II", "abnormal III" or "abnormal IV" by quality control (assurance) engineers, and there is a sequence of traceability generated and collected when that product is produced. Most important of all, for simplicity, one "abnormal" tagged sequence of product traceability is expected to contain one specific subsequence, called "marker" in this study, that result in the same class labeling as quality control engineers do. That is, whenever one product is generated and its traceability sequence contain one of these markers, then its class labeling is determined according to which one of these markers. In this following, section 2.1 shows how to generate tagged sequences for experiments and section 2.2 describes the approach to extract maximal repeat briefly.

2.1 Tagged Sequences of Product traceability

To have the sequences of product traceability as experimental resource for demonstration in this study, there are 50 sequences of product traceability generated randomly and then each of these sequences is inserted with one class marker manually. Table 1 shows, for example, 50 sequences (N=50) of product traceability containing 20 steps (k=20) in which each of steps can be one of five symbols as "a", "b", "c", "d" and "e". For example, the value of the 2nd step in the sequence of traceability for first product "P1" is "S2,b". Each of these sequences is associated with one "ClassID" of "C1", "C2", "C3" and "C4", and is hidden with one marker, as shown in Table 2. For example, the "C3" contains 10 products and all of these products are hidden with the marker "S2,b S3,a S4,a". Note that these markers are supposed to be unknown and hidden within the sequences of product traceability in advance and the lengths of markers are not fixed but variable.

2.2 Extracting Class Markers from Tagged Sequences

A maximal repeat[8] is estimated to be a marker of one class if that repeat is with highly biased class frequency distribution, e.g. appearing in only that class and most of the sequences belonging to that class contain that marker. In other words, a marker of one specific class is a representative pattern for that class. In this study, the sequences of product traceability for experiments are generated randomly, and the markers are inserted into these sequences manually according to their corresponding tags individually.

To extract these distinctive markers hidden in classes that are derived from the tags, this study adopts a scalable approach developed in the previous work[5] that based on Hadoop MapReduce programming model [6, 7]. That approach has been proved to be capable to handle a huge amount of maximal repeat extraction from sequential data[9, 10] and is applying for a patent [11]. To have discussion systematical, there are definitions given in the section 2.2.1 and the approach of maximal repeat extraction is described briefly in the section 2.2.2.

2.2.1 Definition: Class Marker

In this study, products with their sequences of traceability are divided into k classes Ci, $1 \leq i \leq k$, where the types of classes are derived from the tags according to what kind of frequency distribution of subsequences is expected to be biased among these classes. Let the length of the sequence of one product traceability is "k". Let $CF(MR_j)$ be the number of classes that contain the maximal repeat MR_j. The number of product traceability in class Ci is defined as n_{Ci} and the total number of product traceability is $N = \sum_{i=1}^{i=k} n_{Ci}$. Let $df(MR_j, Ci)$ be the number of product traceability of class Ci that

	ClassID	ProductID	Product Traceability																			
			1	2	3	4	5	6	7	8	9	10	11	12	13	14	15	16	17	18	19	20
1	C3	P1	S1,e	S2,b	S3,a	S4,a	S5,b	S6,b	S7,d	S8,d	S9,d	S10,a	S11,c	S12,b	S13,a	S14,d	S15,e	S16,a	S17,d	S18,e	S19,c	S20,a
2	C1	P2	S1,a	S2,e	S3,d	S4,a	S5,b	S6,d	S7,e	S8,c	S9,e	S10,b	S11,c	S12,c	S13,c	S14,c	S15,a	S16,c	S17,a	S18,b	S19,c	S20,b
3	C4	P3	S1,a	S2,c	S3,b	S4,a	S5,a	S6,b	S7,e	S8,c	S9,d	S10,d	S11,b	S12,d	S13,b	S14,c	S15,e	S16,c	S17,a	S18,e	S19,d	S20,c
4	C2	P4	S1,d	S2,d	S3,e	S4,a	S5,b	S6,a	S7,a	S8,d	S9,d	S10,b	S11,c	S12,c	S13,d	S14,e	S15,b	S16,b	S17,a	S18,e	S19,e	S20,c
5	C1	P5	S1,a	S2,e	S3,d	S4,a	S5,c	S6,d	S7,c	S8,e	S9,d	S10,d	S11,d	S12,c	S13,c	S14,d	S15,e	S16,b	S17,a	S18,b	S19,b	S20,c
6	C2	P6	S1,c	S2,d	S3,c	S4,c	S5,c	S6,e	S7,e	S8,a	S9,c	S10,d	S11,e	S12,d	S13,e	S14,e	S15,b	S16,b	S17,a	S18,c	S19,d	S20,a
7	C2	P7	S1,a	S2,d	S3,b	S4,e	S5,c	S6,a	S7,a	S8,d	S9,d	S10,a	S11,a	S12,d	S13,d	S14,e	S15,b	S16,b	S17,a	S18,a	S19,d	S20,c
8	C4	P8	S1,b	S2,e	S3,b	S4,c	S5,d	S6,e	S7,a	S8,a	S9,e	S10,d	S11,b	S12,d	S13,b	S14,c	S15,e	S16,c	S17,b	S18,c	S19,b	S20,a
9	C2	P9	S1,a	S2,a	S3,a	S4,c	S5,e	S6,b	S7,d	S8,c	S9,a	S10,d	S11,a	S12,d	S13,b	S14,e	S15,b	S16,b	S17,a	S18,a	S19,a	S20,d
10	C3	P10	S1,d	S2,b	S3,a	S4,a	S5,a	S6,c	S7,d	S8,a	S9,a	S10,d	S11,e	S12,e	S13,b	S14,c	S15,d	S16,b	S17,b	S18,b	S19,c	S20,a
11	C4	P11	S1,d	S2,a	S3,d	S4,a	S5,b	S6,b	S7,a	S8,e	S9,c	S10,a	S11,d	S12,d	S13,b	S14,c	S15,e	S16,c	S17,c	S18,c	S19,c	S20,c
12	C2	P12	S1,a	S2,e	S3,c	S4,e	S5,a	S6,c	S7,a	S8,b	S9,b	S10,b	S11,b	S12,c	S13,c	S14,e	S15,b	S16,b	S17,a	S18,e	S19,a	S20,a
13	C1	P13	S1,a	S2,e	S3,d	S4,a	S5,b	S6,a	S7,b	S8,d	S9,a	S10,e	S11,d	S12,d	S13,d	S14,c	S15,b	S16,b	S17,a	S18,e	S19,c	S20,e
14	C1	P14	S1,a	S2,e	S3,d	S4,a	S5,a	S6,e	S7,a	S8,a	S9,c	S10,b	S11,c	S12,a	S13,a	S14,e	S15,a	S16,c	S17,b	S18,d	S19,d	S20,d
15	C3	P15	S1,e	S2,b	S3,a	S4,a	S5,c	S6,c	S7,a	S8,b	S9,c	S10,d	S11,c	S12,c	S13,e	S14,d	S15,d	S16,b	S17,b	S18,c	S19,d	S20,c
16	C1	P16	S1,a	S2,e	S3,d	S4,a	S5,e	S6,e	S7,e	S8,d	S9,b	S10,d	S11,b	S12,a	S13,c	S14,d	S15,d	S16,b	S17,d	S18,c	S19,d	S20,c
17	C2	P17	S1,a	S2,d	S3,c	S4,d	S5,c	S6,d	S7,b	S8,c	S9,d	S10,a	S11,e	S12,d	S13,e	S14,e	S15,b	S16,b	S17,a	S18,b	S19,d	S20,b
18	C1	P18	S1,a	S2,e	S3,d	S4,a	S5,c	S6,e	S7,a	S8,c	S9,b	S10,e	S11,b	S12,c	S13,d	S14,c	S15,e	S16,b	S17,b	S18,d	S19,e	S20,a
19	C4	P19	S1,c	S2,b	S3,b	S4,b	S5,d	S6,c	S7,a	S8,c	S9,e	S10,d	S11,d	S12,d	S13,b	S14,c	S15,e	S16,c	S17,e	S18,a	S19,d	S20,b
20	C1	P20	S1,a	S2,e	S3,d	S4,a	S5,a	S6,c	S7,a	S8,c	S9,d	S10,a	S11,e	S12,d	S13,b	S14,e	S15,b	S16,e	S17,e	S18,c	S19,d	S20,d
21	C4	P21	S1,a	S2,e	S3,b	S4,b	S5,e	S6,a	S7,b	S8,b	S9,d	S10,e	S11,b	S12,d	S13,b	S14,c	S15,e	S16,c	S17,b	S18,e	S19,b	S20,d
22	C3	P22	S1,c	S2,b	S3,a	S4,a	S5,b	S6,c	S7,c	S8,c	S9,c	S10,c	S11,b	S12,e	S13,a	S14,e	S15,a	S16,e	S17,c	S18,a	S19,e	S20,c
23	C4	P23	S1,a	S2,b	S3,e	S4,e	S5,e	S6,e	S7,e	S8,e	S9,b	S10,d	S11,c	S12,d	S13,b	S14,c	S15,e	S16,c	S17,a	S18,a	S19,c	S20,a
24	C4	P24	S1,e	S2,e	S3,b	S4,c	S5,b	S6,b	S7,e	S8,c	S9,a	S10,e	S11,c	S12,d	S13,b	S14,c	S15,e	S16,c	S17,c	S18,d	S19,a	S20,e
25	C1	P25	S1,a	S2,e	S3,d	S4,a	S5,e	S6,e	S7,c	S8,c	S9,a	S10,a	S11,b	S12,b	S13,a	S14,b	S15,d	S16,d	S17,a	S18,c	S19,c	S20,e
26	C1	P26	S1,a	S2,e	S3,d	S4,a	S5,b	S6,a	S7,d	S8,e	S9,d	S10,e	S11,d	S12,e	S13,a	S14,a	S15,b	S16,e	S17,b	S18,b	S19,d	S20,d
27	C2	P27	S1,e	S2,a	S3,e	S4,a	S5,b	S6,b	S7,d	S8,d	S9,e	S10,a	S11,b	S12,d	S13,c	S14,e	S15,b	S16,b	S17,a	S18,d	S19,e	S20,b
28	C4	P28	S1,b	S2,c	S3,e	S4,e	S5,a	S6,b	S7,e	S8,b	S9,a	S10,e	S11,e	S12,d	S13,b	S14,c	S15,e	S16,c	S17,e	S18,a	S19,d	S20,d
29	C2	P29	S1,a	S2,a	S3,d	S4,d	S5,b	S6,b	S7,d	S8,d	S9,c	S10,d	S11,a	S12,d	S13,a	S14,e	S15,b	S16,b	S17,a	S18,a	S19,d	S20,c
30	C4	P30	S1,d	S2,a	S3,a	S4,e	S5,e	S6,e	S7,a	S8,c	S9,b	S10,e	S11,c	S12,d	S13,b	S14,c	S15,e	S16,c	S17,a	S18,c	S19,e	S20,c
31	C4	P31	S1,c	S2,c	S3,d	S4,a	S5,b	S6,d	S7,a	S8,a	S9,a	S10,c	S11,b	S12,d	S13,b	S14,c	S15,e	S16,c	S17,d	S18,e	S19,b	S20,b
32	C1	P32	S1,a	S2,e	S3,d	S4,a	S5,e	S6,a	S7,d	S8,a	S9,d	S10,d	S11,a	S12,d	S13,b	S14,a	S15,b	S16,c	S17,d	S18,a	S19,c	S20,c
33	C4	P33	S1,c	S2,c	S3,a	S4,c	S5,b	S6,c	S7,a	S8,c	S9,d	S10,e	S11,a	S12,d	S13,b	S14,c	S15,e	S16,c	S17,c	S18,d	S19,b	S20,c
34	C3	P34	S1,e	S2,b	S3,a	S4,a	S5,c	S6,a	S7,d	S8,d	S9,d	S10,e	S11,a	S12,e	S13,d	S14,b	S15,d	S16,a	S17,b	S18,e	S19,e	S20,b
35	C4	P35	S1,d	S2,e	S3,b	S4,d	S5,d	S6,e	S7,e	S8,a	S9,e	S10,c	S11,e	S12,d	S13,b	S14,c	S15,e	S16,c	S17,d	S18,d	S19,a	S20,d
36	C2	P36	S1,b	S2,d	S3,b	S4,e	S5,d	S6,a	S7,b	S8,a	S9,c	S10,e	S11,a	S12,a	S13,a	S14,e	S15,b	S16,b	S17,a	S18,b	S19,a	S20,c
37	C3	P37	S1,b	S2,b	S3,a	S4,a	S5,e	S6,c	S7,b	S8,e	S9,a	S10,d	S11,e	S12,c	S13,b	S14,b	S15,a	S16,d	S17,e	S18,c	S19,d	S20,c
38	C2	P38	S1,c	S2,d	S3,c	S4,a	S5,b	S6,c	S7,c	S8,e	S9,d	S10,c	S11,a	S12,e	S13,e	S14,e	S15,b	S16,b	S17,a	S18,c	S19,c	S20,b
39	C4	P39	S1,e	S2,b	S3,c	S4,d	S5,c	S6,c	S7,a	S8,e	S9,e	S10,c	S11,d	S12,d	S13,b	S14,c	S15,e	S16,c	S17,c	S18,c	S19,a	S20,a
40	C1	P40	S1,a	S2,e	S3,d	S4,a	S5,d	S6,d	S7,d	S8,c	S9,c	S10,a	S11,a	S12,e	S13,a	S14,e	S15,d	S16,c	S17,d	S18,a	S19,e	S20,c
41	C3	P41	S1,a	S2,b	S3,a	S4,a	S5,d	S6,a	S7,e	S8,a	S9,b	S10,b	S11,a	S12,e	S13,a	S14,d	S15,b	S16,e	S17,e	S18,e	S19,d	S20,b
42	C3	P42	S1,c	S2,b	S3,a	S4,a	S5,d	S6,a	S7,c	S8,a	S9,e	S10,a	S11,e	S12,d	S13,c	S14,b	S15,d	S16,e	S17,c	S18,d	S19,c	S20,d
43	C3	P43	S1,c	S2,b	S3,a	S4,a	S5,b	S6,a	S7,d	S8,b	S9,b	S10,a	S11,d	S12,a	S13,d	S14,a	S15,e	S16,c	S17,b	S18,d	S19,b	S20,a
44	C4	P44	S1,b	S2,e	S3,e	S4,c	S5,e	S6,d	S7,d	S8,e	S9,c	S10,e	S11,a	S12,d	S13,b	S14,c	S15,e	S16,c	S17,a	S18,b	S19,a	S20,b
45	C2	P45	S1,a	S2,b	S3,b	S4,e	S5,e	S6,b	S7,b	S8,b	S9,d	S10,a	S11,e	S12,d	S13,a	S14,e	S15,b	S16,b	S17,a	S18,a	S19,c	S20,e
46	C4	P46	S1,e	S2,b	S3,b	S4,c	S5,a	S6,a	S7,b	S8,b	S9,e	S10,e	S11,b	S12,d	S13,b	S14,c	S15,e	S16,c	S17,c	S18,e	S19,c	S20,c
47	C2	P47	S1,b	S2,d	S3,d	S4,a	S5,c	S6,c	S7,d	S8,d	S9,a	S10,a	S11,c	S12,e	S13,e	S14,e	S15,b	S16,b	S17,a	S18,d	S19,e	S20,e
48	C1	P48	S1,a	S2,e	S3,d	S4,a	S5,b	S6,e	S7,d	S8,b	S9,c	S10,c	S11,e	S12,e	S13,e	S14,d	S15,b	S16,c	S17,d	S18,c	S19,a	S20,b
49	C2	P49	S1,c	S2,e	S3,a	S4,b	S5,b	S6,a	S7,e	S8,d	S9,c	S10,e	S11,e	S12,c	S13,a	S14,e	S15,b	S16,b	S17,a	S18,c	S19,d	S20,b
50	C3	P50	S1,d	S2,b	S3,a	S4,a	S5,c	S6,a	S7,c	S8,b	S9,e	S10,b	S11,a	S12,d	S13,e	S14,a	S15,d	S16,d	S17,c	S18,c	S19,a	S20,e

Table 1. 50 products with their traceability and tags (ClassID)

ClassID	# of Product	Class Marker	Length
C1	12	S1,a S2,e S3,d S4,a	4
C2	13	S14,e S15,b S16,b S17,a	4
C3	10	S2,b S3,a S4,a	3
C4	15	S12,d S13,b S14,c S15,e S16,c	5
Total	50		

Table 2. The statistics of four classes with markers hidden in their corresponding traceability

contains the MR_j; let $tf(MR_j, Ci)$ be the number of the MR_j appearing in the product traceability of class Ci. Note that it might happen that the MR_j appears more than twice in one product traceability if there exists repeat processes within the product line.

Let $WC(MR_j, Ci) = \frac{df(MR_j,Ci)}{n_{Ci}}$, the coverage of one maximal repeat MR_j within class Ci, be the percentage of the number of traceability within the Ci that contain the MR_j. Let $DF(MR_j) = \sum_{i=1}^{i=k} df(MR_j, Ci)$ and $TF(MR_j) = \sum_{i=1}^{i=k} tf(MR_j, Ci)$. Intuitively, the MR_j is representative for class Ci when the value of $CF(MR_j)$ is "1" and the value of $WC(MR_j, Ci)$ is as high as possible. That is, the MR_j appears only in one class Ci and the majority of product traceability in Ci contain the MR_j. In this study, for simplicity, one maximal repeat MR_j is estimated as one "marker" of class Ci if $CF(MR_j) = 1$ and $WC(MR_j, Ci) = 100\%$. That is, the MR_j appears only in class Ci and all of the sequences of traceability in Ci contains the MR_j.

2.2.2 Maximal Repeat Extraction

To identify these markers from a huge amount of the sequences of product traceability attached with ClassID, this paper adapts the previous work in [5] that is a scalable approach based on Hadoop MapReduce programming model [7]. This approach can extract the maximal repeats [8] from a huge amount of tagged sequential data, and meanwhile compute the class frequency distribution of these repeats within these sequential data, where the types of classes are derived from the tags specified by the users or observers for comparison on purpose. To mine for specific subsequences, called markers in this study, that can be used to distinguish one class from another, this study filter out the maximal repeats that only appear in one class and meanwhile happen in the majority of product traceability of that class.

To have this study more self-contained, the approach of maximal repeat extraction are described briefly in the following. Based on Hadoop MapReduce programming, the input of tagged sequences are split into several fixed-size partitions and are distributed to mappers by Hadoop system evenly and automatically. First of all, each of mapper generated all of suffixes of each sequences and have each of these suffixes attached the same tag as that sequence it derived from. Secondly, the mappers output the pair of "key-value" to the reducers, where the "key" is the fixed-length prefix of each suffix and the "value" is the tagged suffix. According to the feature of MapReduce programming, each of reducers will receives the values, some tagged suffixes, with the same key while these suffixes are sorted in lexicographical order. Finally, the reducers scan the sorted suffixes and extract candidate maximal repeats with "right" boundary validation; meanwhile compute the class frequency distribution of these repeats via a stack with push/pop operations[5]. To have maximal repeats with "left" boundary validation, it is similar with the same processes as described above, but with the reversed sequences as the input. The maximal repeats are those candidate maximal repeats pass both of "right" and "left" boundary validation.

3 Results

In this study, there are 50 sequences of product traceability generated and are tagged with specific markers manually for experimental resources. Table 3 gives the distribution of 413 maximal repeats extracted from these 50 tagged sequences in Table 1 according to the values of "CF" and the length of maximal repeats. It is observed that there are 99 maximal repeats whose "CF" values are 1 and the length of these repeats ranges from 1 to 8.

To further inspect the WC values of these 99 maximal repeats ("CF=1") for one class they appear, Table 3 sorts the WC values of and selects the top 18 maximal repeats whose WC values of one class

CF	The Length of Maximal Repeat	The Number of Distinct Maximal Repeat
1	1	3
1	2	33
1	3	14
1	4	8
1	5	17
1	6	13
1	7	9
1	8	2
2	1	16
2	2	127
2	3	39
2	4	9
2	5	3
3	1	33
3	2	31
3	3	4
4	1	46
4	2	6
Total		413

Table 3. The statistics of maximal repeats extracted from the tagged sequences in Table 1

	Maximal Repeat	DF	TF	CF	Length	Class Frequency Distribution (ClassID#df#tf)	Class Frequency Distribution (Coverage within one class)			
							C1	C2	C3	C4
1	S1,a S2,e S3,d S4,a	12	12	1	4	(C1#12#12)	100.0%			
2	S14,e S15,b S16,b S17,a	13	13	1	4	(C2#13#13)		100.0%		
3	S2,b S3,a S4,a	10	10	1	3	(C3#10#10)			100.0%	
4	S12,d S13,b S14,c S15,e S16,c	15	15	1	5	(C4#15#15)				100.0%
5	S2,d	7	7	1	1	(C2#7#7)		53.8%		
6	S1,a S2,e S3,d S4,a S5,b	4	4	1	5	(C1#4#4)	33.3%			
7	S11,b S12,d S13,b S14,c S15,e S16,c	5	5	1	6	(C4#5#5)				33.3%
8	S12,d S13,b S14,c S15,e S16,c S17,c	5	5	1	6	(C4#5#5)				33.3%
9	S13,a S14,e S15,b S16,b S17,a	4	4	1	5	(C2#4#4)		30.8%		
10	S13,e S14,e S15,b S16,b S17,a	4	4	1	5	(C2#4#4)		30.8%		
11	S14,e S15,b S16,b S17,a S18,a	4	4	1	5	(C2#4#4)		30.8%		
12	S1,c S2,b S3,a S4,a	3	3	1	4	(C3#3#3)			30.0%	
13	S1,e S2,b S3,a S4,a	3	3	1	4	(C3#3#3)			30.0%	
14	S2,b S3,a S4,a S5,b	3	3	1	4	(C3#3#3)			30.0%	
15	S2,b S3,a S4,a S5,c	3	3	1	4	(C3#3#3)			30.0%	
16	S2,e S3,b	4	4	1	2	(C4#4#4)				26.7%
17	S2,c	4	4	1	1	(C4#4#4)				26.7%
18	S1,a S2,e S3,d S4,a S5,e	3	3	1	5	(C1#3#3)	25.0%			

Table 4. Examples: the statistics of 18 maximal repeats whose CF values are equal to 1 and WC values of one class are ≥ 25%

are greater than or equal to 25%. It is observed that the four class markers as shown in Table 2 are extracted and are the same as the first four repeats whose WC values are 100%. That is, experimental results as described above shows that the previous approach[5] did extract and identify these class markers that are hidden within the sequences of product traceability.

4 Discussion

There are still room to make this study more robust and practical in the future. First of all, in this study, one class marker is defined as a consecutive (continuous) subsequences. Indeed, this assumption may be too restricted in real cases because the false points may be not consecutive to form only one complete segment but several short segments. It needs more efforts or another strategy to overcome this problem. On the other hand, the *WC* condition of one marker that appears in only one class in which all of sequences contain that marker can be relaxed by selecting the markers whose values of the entropy[13] of class frequency distribution is lower than a given threshold.

Secondly, the values generated in each of steps in the sequence of product traceability are set to be one of five symbols as "a", "b", "c", "d" and "e". When dealing with real practical data, these values may be numeric but not just several symbols. It is necessary to learn how to partition these numeric values into symbols precisely [14] because different transformation might have totally different results.

Thirdly, the experimental resource used in this study only contains 50 sequences of product traceability and the markers are created and inserted manually. From the practical point of view, it is expected to have these tagged sequences for experiments from the factory in real world. Furthermore, the approach proposed in this study do improve the quality control to reduce the searching ranges of the candidate false points that results in abnormal product in this future.

5 Conclusions

This study provides a novel approach to speed up the processes of locating the false points within the product line via comparing the tagged sequences of product traceability. These class markers extracted can provide clues to locate false point in the product line more efficiently and furthermore can be stored in database as false patterns for quality assurance analysis in the future. As the time of industry 4.0 combined with internet of things (IOT) and artificial intelligent (AI) is coming, it is worth of embedding this approach into quality control services as a package or tool such that monitoring the product line and searching the false points can be done automatically in the future. It is expected that this approach proposed in this study can provide modern industry with new research or direction about quality control (assurance), especially in drug and semiconductor manufacturing.

Acknowledgments

This study is supported by Ministry of Science and Technology, Taiwan under project *MOST 106-2632-E-468-002*.

References

[1] A. Gilchrist, *Industry 4.0: The Industrial Internet of Things*, 1st edn. (Apress, Berkely, CA, USA, 2016), ISBN 1484220463, 9781484220467

[2] P. Waher, *Learning Internet of Things*, Community experience distilled (Packt Publishing, 2015), ISBN 9781783553549, `https://books.google.com.tw/books?id=auRrBgAAQBAJ`

[3] J. Jain, *Quality Control and Total Quality Management* (McGraw-Hill Education (India) Pvt Limited, 2001), ISBN 9780070402140, `https://books.google.com.tw/books?id=8Q3sRWAAP74C`

[4] B. Marr, *Big Data in Practice: How 45 Successful Companies Used Big Data Analytics to Deliver Extraordinary Results* (Wiley, 2016), ISBN 9781119231387, `https://books.google.com.tw/books?id=wAOmCgAAQBAJ`

[5] J.-D. Wang, *Extracting significant pattern histories from timestamped texts using mapreduce, The Journal of Supercomputing*, pp. 1–25, 2016. [Online]. Available: `http://dx.doi.org/10.1007/s11227-016-1713-z`
[6] R. McCreadie, C. Macdonald, I. Ounis, *MapReduce indexing strategies: Studying scalability and efficiency Information Processing & Management* **48**, 873 (2012), large-Scale and Distributed Systems for Information Retrieval
[7] F. Li, B.C. Ooi, M.T. Özsu, S. Wu, *Distributed Data Management Using MapReduce* ACM Comput. Surv. **46**, 31:1 (2014)
[8] D. Gusfield, *Algorithms on Strings, Trees, and Sequences : computer science and computational biology* (Cambridge University Press, 1997), ISBN 0-521-58519-8
[9] J.D. Wang, M.C. Hwang, *Extracting significant pattern histories from timestamped texts using mapreduce,Applied Sciences*, **7** (2017). [Online]. Available: `http://www.mdpi.com/2076-3417/7/9/878`
[10] J.D. Wang, Y.C. Wang, R.M. Hu, J. Tsai, *Extracting the Co-occurrences of DNA Maximal Repeats in both Human and Viruses*, in *The 17th annual IEEE International Conference on Bioinformatics and Bioengineering (BIBE2017)* (2017)
[11] C.T. Wang, *Method for extracting maximal repeat patterns and computing frequency distribution tables* (2017), US Patent App. 15/208,994, `https://www.google.com/patents/US20170255634`
[12] J.D. Wang, W.L. Chan, C.C. Wang, J.G. Chang, J.J. Tsai, *Mining Distinctive DNA Patterns from the Upstream of Human Coding&Non-Coding Genes via Class Frequency Distribution*, in *2016 IEEE Conference on Computational Intelligence in Bioinformatics and Computational Biology (CIBCB 2016)* (2016)
[13] E. Alpaydin, *Introduction to Machine Learning* (The MIT Press, 2004)
[14] I.H. Witten, E. Frank, *Data Mining: Practical Machine Learning Tools and Techniques (Third Edition)* (Elsevier, 2011), ISBN 0120884070

A Nnumerical Study of Drag force for Optimist Dinghy on Flat Water

Chien-Nan Lin[1,*] and *Jong-Ming* Chou[1,2]

[1] Department of Mechanical Engineering, Far East University, Tainan, Taiwan
[2] Simen Elementary School, Tainan, Taiwan;

Abstract. This study investigates numerically the drag force on the Optimal dinghy, which is one of the official classes of international sailing regatta. The drag force is affected by the forward and backward tilt angles and the heels angles. The results revealed that the minimum drag force on the dinghy occurred under the flat dinghy and zero tilt angle condition. The drag force decreases with increasing backward tilt angle. Meanwhile the minimum drag force occurred at the 10 degree of the heeling angle under low velocity condition, and it occurred at the 5 degree while the sailing velocity exceeded 2 m/s. The correlation of the drag force and the sailing velocity can be expressed as $F_D = 13.87V^2$ for flat dinghy sailing.

1 Introduction

The Optimal dinghy is one of the official classes of international sailing regatta. It is also the most popular sailing within all classes. The sailing power come from the transform of air pressure and flow velocity as described by the Bernoulli's equation but not the reaction force impacting on the sail sheet. Therefore, the relative speed of the sail boat and the pressure difference caused by the sailing sheet can drive the boat sails in slightly up-wind and cross-wind direction. The resulting wind force is divided into two perpendicular direction that is parallel to the longitude length of boat and the transverse width of the boat. The former force drive the boat forward, and the later force pull the sideward. Modern Optimal dinghy equipped with a central panel, which suppress the side force to avoid the boat capsizing. Curry [1] firstly discussed the flow dynamic of the sailing boat. Then, many literature studied on the aerodynamic performance of sailing operation [2-5]. Recently, the complex fluid dynamic characteristics are discussed as the progress of computational technique. Akimoto [6] considered the flow dynamics with the free surface between water and the air, and compared the complex shape of sailing boat. Parolini and Quarteroni [7] studied the flow characteristic of sailing boat for competition in America's Cup, and obtained useful information for racing. The Optimist dinghy has the dimensions of 231cm

*Corresponding author: lincn@mail.feu.edu.tw

in length, 113cm in width, and its weigh is 35 kg, the area of sail sheet is $3.5m^2$. The photo and sketch of the Optimal dinghy are shown as Figure 1. This study aims to analyze the variation of dragged force resulting from water resistance under the various operating condition of the sailing Optimal dinghy, owing to the viscosity of water is much greater than that of air.

2. Theory Analysis

2.1 Governing Equations

A three-dimensional numerical model is performed to examine the flow characteristic of the Optimal dinghy by utilizing the software ANSYS. Thus, the continuity and momentum equations are described as follows.

$$\frac{\partial \overline{u_i}}{\partial x_i} = 0 \qquad (1)$$

$$\frac{\partial}{\partial x_j}\rho(\overline{u_i}\,\overline{u_j}) = -\frac{\partial \overline{p}}{\partial x_i} + \frac{\partial}{\partial x_j}\left[\mu_{eff}\left(\frac{\partial \overline{u_i}}{\partial x_j} + \frac{\partial \overline{u_j}}{\partial x_i}\right) - \rho\overline{u_i' u_j'}\right] \qquad (2)$$

The k-ε turbulent model is adopted to couple with the Navier-Stokes equation. The forward tilt angle and side tilt angle affects significantly the contact area and perimeter shape, and resulting in the change of water resistance. The tilt angle is defined as the angle of the gunwale and the water plane. Owing to the center of gravity is depended on the position of the sailor, the boat experience forward when the sailor moving forward and moving to the left or right sides as the sailor changer the position. The resistance of water drag is composed of the pressure drag and the friction drag. The pressure drag is occurred while the flow along a varied shape surface, In contrast the friction drag is due to the viscosity induced shear fore on the interface of fluid-solid. They are defined as $D_p = \int p \cdot \cos\theta \cdot dA$ and $D_f = \int \pi_w \cdot dA$, respectively

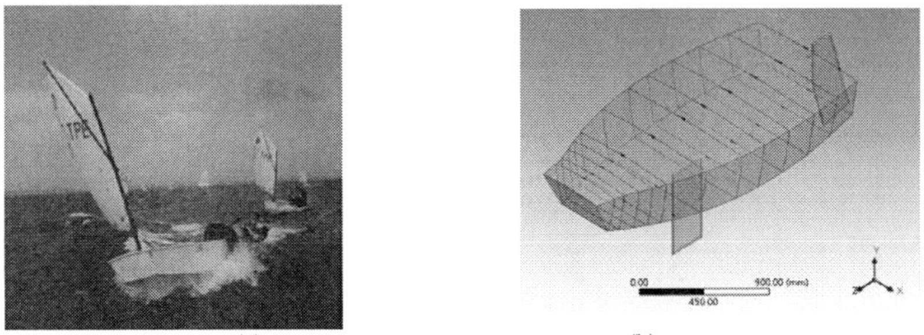

(a) (b)
Figure 1. (a) The photo and (b) the sketch of the Optimal dinghy

2.2 Boundary Conditions

This study focus on the dragged force resulting from water resistance under the various operating condition of the sailing Optimal dinghy The computational domain of the water and the numerical grids of the boat is sketched in Figure 2. The boundary conditions are assumed as follows: The surfaces of the boat is considered as non-slip boundary

 https://doi.org/10.1051/matecconf/201820105003

condition. The front plane (positive z plane) is a velocity inlet boundary, along negative z direction, to simulate the velocity of the boat. In contrast, the rear plane (negative z plane) is considered a pressure outlet boundary. The other planes are considered as symmetric planes to simulate the water flow in this simulation, owing to the limited computational domain in the study.

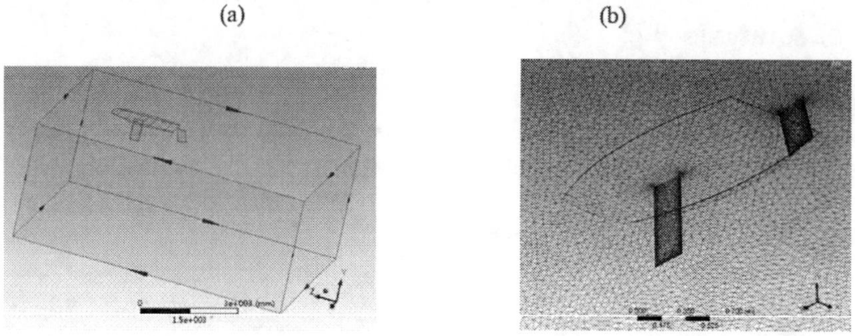

Figure 2. (a) The sketch of the Optimal dinghy and (b) the computational domain

3. Results and Discussions

Figure 3 displays the total water resistance exerted on the Optimal dinghy surface under horizontal sailing condition, i.e. zero forward and side tilt angle. The surface of boat comprises the surface of forward, aft, bottom, port, starboard, rudder, and centerboard. The centerboard and the bottom have the equivalent effect on the drag force; they contribute about total 70% of the resistance, owing to the greater surface area than the others. The total drag force is 15.6 N, 56 N, and 121N, for the 1 m/s, 2 m/s, and 3 m/s of sailing velocity, respectively. The drag force increases rapidly with an increase of the sailing velocity, the correlation can be expressed as $F_D = 13.87V^2$. Besides, the dray on forward surface is zero, owing to it is not wetted for this sailing condition.

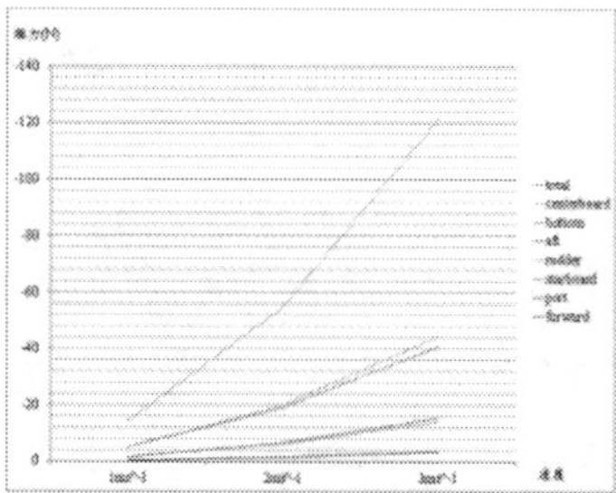

Figure 3. The variation of drag force with the sailing velocity

Note that the drag force shown in Figure 3 considers the full immerged length of 700 mm of centerboard, which is a movable device used in the Optimal dinghy to control the sailing direction against the wind. Therefore the immerged length of centerboard is varied from 7 mm through 700 mm. Figure 4 shows the variation of drag force with the immerged length of centerboard for 1 m/s of sailing velocity. The drag force increased linear with the immerged length, owing to the centerboard is shaped in rectangular. A turning point occurred at the length of 175 mm, however, the influence of the immerged length increases on the weighting of total drag force, it varied from 0% to 35%.

Figure 4. The variation of drag force with the sailing velocity

The variation of the drag force along the sailing direction (z- direction) with the forward tilt angle is displayed in Figure 5(a)-(c). The minimum total drag force occurred at the 0

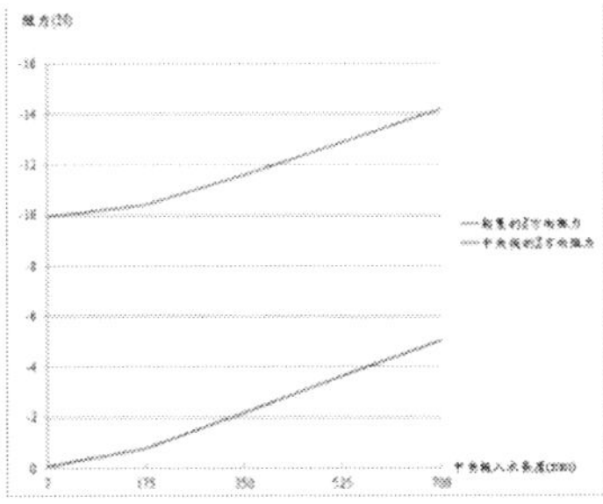

degree of tilt angle whatever the sailing velocity is, it increase linear with the both forward and backward tilt angle as shown in Figure 5(a). The total drag forces are 125N, 305N, and 345N, for the tilt angle are 0, forward 10 degree, and backward 10 degree, respectively. This yields a 140 % and 175% incensement of total drag force, respectively. The total drag force is composed of the pressure drag and friction drag as mentioned, which are displayed

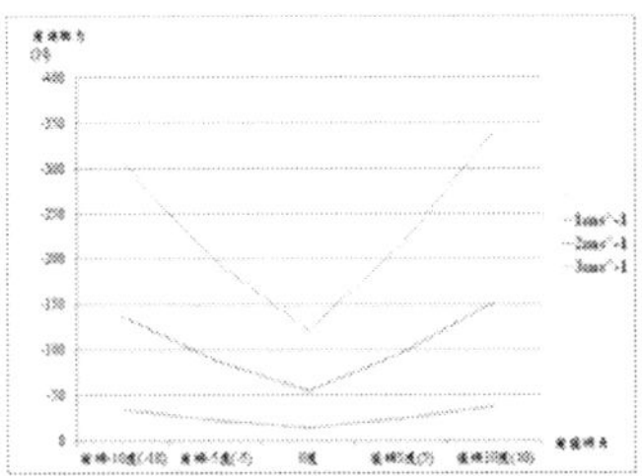

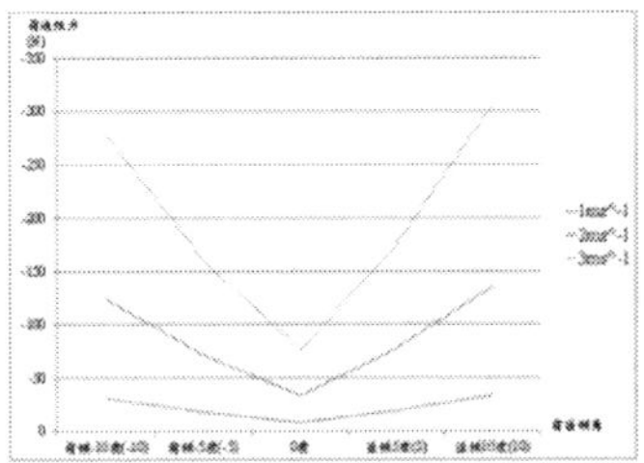

in Figure 5(b) and (c), It depicts that the increased total drag force is resulted from the pressure drag, moreover, the friction drag decreases while increase the forward or backward tilt angle. As shown in Figure 1, the bottom surface of the Optimal dinghy is a smooth streamline surface while sailing in horizon. The premiered surface is varied with the tilt angle; therefore, the pressure drag increases. The influence of the backward tilt angle is greater than that of forward tilt angle. That mean while the sailor move backward causing the smooth streamline surface changed and resulting in more drag force exerted on the boat. Besides, the decrease in friction drag is owing to the decrease of the immerged surface as shown Figure 5(d)

(a) (b)

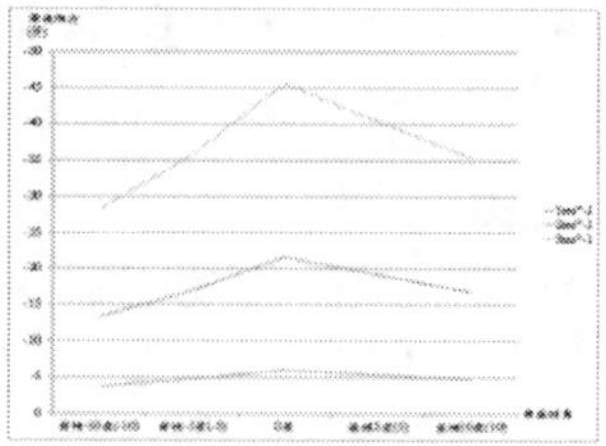

(c)

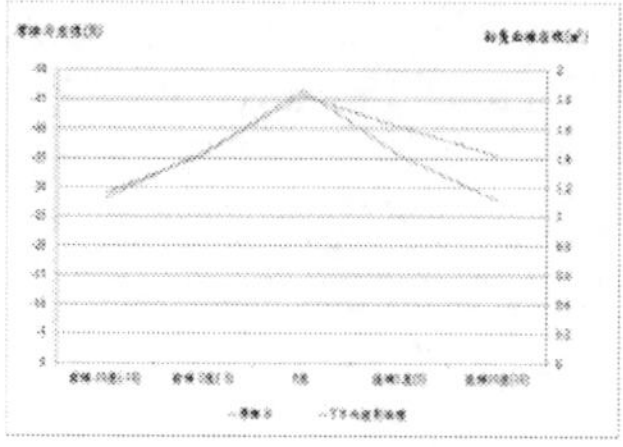

(d)

Figure 5. The variation of drag force with the forward and backward angle (a) the total drag force, (b) the pressure drag force, (c) the friction drag force (d) the friction drag force and the projected area of y-axis

The velocity contour and the streamline for 1 m/s of sailing velocity with the 10 degree of backward tilt angle are displayed in Figure 6. The low velocity region appeared behind the centerboard and the rudder is obvious, as the flow circulation appeared behind the rudders, which affect the pressure drag significantly.

The total drag force for various side tilt angle under 0 degree of forward tilt angle is shown in Figure 7. The drag force decreases with an increasing of side tilt angle, the minimum drag force occurred around at 5-10 degree of side tilt angle. Reversely, the drag force increase as the tilt angle greater than 10 degree. Besides, the angle of the minimum drag force is slightly shifted from about 5 degree to 10 degree, while the sailing velocity increases from 1 m/s to 3 m/s. It is similar to the suggestion of Slater [8] for the Optimal racing.

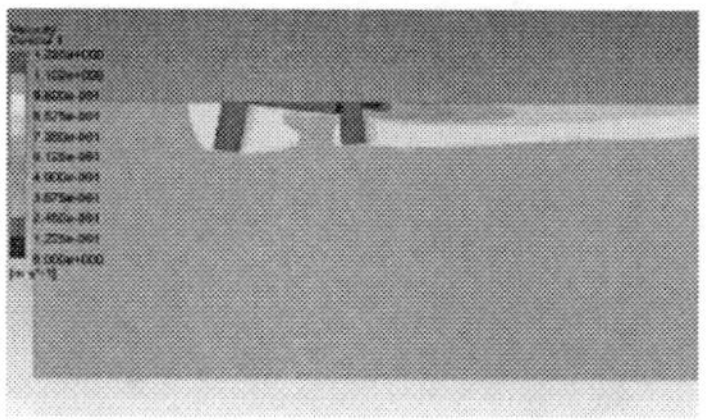

(a)

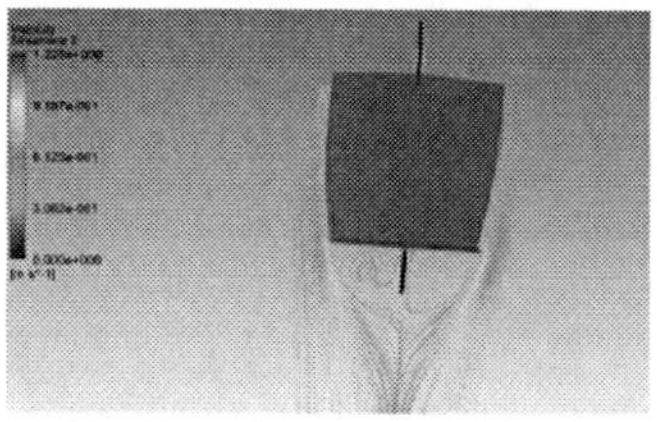

(b)

Figure 6. (a) Velocity contour and (b) streamline for1 m/s of sailing velocity and the 10 degree of backward tilt angle

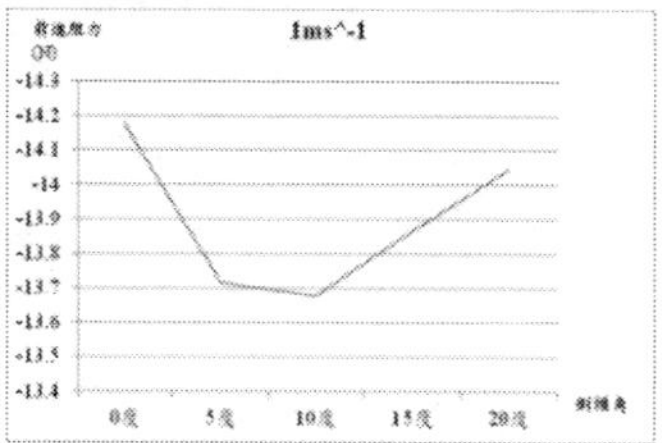

Figure 7. (a) Velocity contour and (b) streamline for1 m/s of sailing velocity and the 10 degree of backward tilt angle

4. Conclusions

The drag force of water resistance for the Optimal dinghy has been performed. Based on the above results: The drag force increases rapidly with an increase of the sailing velocity, the correlation can be expressed as $F_D = 13.87V^2$. Besides, the dray on forward surface is zero, owing to it is not wetted for this sailing condition, the influence of the immerged length increases on the weighting of total drag force, it varied from 0% to 35%. The tilt angle of forward 10 degree, and backward 10 degree, yields a 140 % and 175% incensement of total drag force, respectively. The Figure revealed that the minimum drag force occurred about 10 degree of side tilt angle for 1 m/s of velocity. It shifted to about 5 degree of tilt angle while the velocity increased to 2 m/s and 3 m/s.

References

1. Curry, M., Yacht Racing, The Aerodynamics of Sails and Racing Tactics, New York, Holt, 1925.
2. Davidson, K., Some Experimental Studies of the Sailing Yacht, SNAME Transactions, 1936.
3. Hammit, A.G., Sailboat Rudders, Ancient Interface 3, AIAA Symposium on the Aero/Hydrodynamics of Sailing, AIAA, 1971.
4. Gerritsma, J., Course Keeping Qualities and Motions in Waves of a Sailing Yacht", Ancient Interface 3, AIAA Symposium on the Aero/hydrodynamics of sailing, AIAA, 1971.
5. TiTlowt, J.D., A Dynamic Model for Downwind Sailing", Ancient Interface 8, AIAA Symposium on the Aero/Hydrodynamics of Sailing, AIAA, 1977.
6. Akimoto, H., Finite Volume Simulation of the Flow around a Sailing Boat with Unsteady Motion, Journal of the Society of Naval Architects of Japan. 1997, Vol. 181, pp. 35-44.
7. Parolini, N., Quarteroni, A., Mathematical models and numerical simulations for the America's Cup, Computer Methods in Applied Mechanics and Engineering. 2005, Vol.194 pp. 1001-1026.
8. Slater, P., Optimist Racing, fernhurstbooks, UK, 2001

Using AdaBoost-based Multiple Functional Neural Fuzzy Classifiers Fusion for Classification Applications

Jyun-Yu Jhang[1] Chin-Ling Lee[2] Cheng-Jian Lin[3*] Chin-Teng Lin[4,5] Kuu-Young Young[4]

[1] Institute of Electrical and Control Engineering, National Chiao-Tung University, Hsinchu 300, Taiwan
[2] National Taichung University of Science and Technology, Taichung 411, Taiwan
[3] Department of Computer Science and Information Engineering, National Chin-Yi University of Technology, Taichung 411, Taiwan
[4] Department of Electrical and Control Engineering National Chiao Tung University, Hsinchu 300, Taiwan
[5] Faculty of Engineering and Information Technology University of Technology Sydney, Sydney 2007, Australia

Abstract. In this study, two intelligent classifiers, the AdaBoost-based incremental functional neural fuzzy classifier (AIFNFC) and the AdaBoost-based fixed functional neural fuzzy classifier (AFFNFC), are proposed for solving the classification problems. The AIFNFC approach will increase the amount of functional neural fuzzy classifiers based on the corresponding error during the training phase; while the AFNFC approach is equipped with a fixed amount of functional neural fuzzy classifiers. Then, the weights of AdaBoost procedure are assigned for classifiers. The proposed methods are applied to different classification benchmarks. Results of this study demonstrate the effectiveness of the proposed AIFNFC and AFFNFC methods.

1 Introduction

The object classification methods, as stated in [1]-[2], are to divide the initially undefined entities into classes. In each class the individuals are close to one another in some sense. These methods can be used to determine the particular symptoms of the diseases in medical science, to classify the species in biology, and to solve common classification problems in engineering and other fields. Most traditional statistical classification approaches, such as discrimination analysis, are built on the Bayesian decision theory [3], and each method generally has its own explicit probability model, but it works well and performs effectively only when the underlying assumptions are correct. For measurement of the similarity, twelve similarity structures were listed in the work of [4]. In supervised machine learning for classification, about 126 relative works are summarized in recent literature [5], which works are based on logical/symbolic techniques, perceptron-based techniques, and Statistics.

The boosting approaches are meta-algorithms for supervised learning, which are originally proposed to improve the accuracy of classification and prediction problem. Derived from machine learning, Valiant [6] presented the probably approximately correct (PAC) architecture and defined the notation of learnability. Furthermore, Kearns and Valiant [7] introduced the idea of weak learnability, and claimed the minimum performance of an algorithm should be better than a random guess. The above guess was proved by Schapire [8]. Schapire stated that the original classification results of dealing with the 2-class classification problem can be improved if a weak classifier could be divided into two new classifiers via a specific process of data filtering and grouping. Such approach was named as Boosting by Schapire. Later, Freund [9] developed a more efficient approach, but it suffered from some practical drawback. Afterwards, Freund and Schapire [10] proposed the AdaBoost algorithm and claimed the method can reduce the learning error and continuously decrease the testing error without over-fitting phenomenon. The traditional AdaBoost approach is hard to deal with the multi-class problems, and its performance highly depends on the design of weak classifiers. Consequently, the general solution for multi-class problem is to deploy hundreds or thousands weak classifiers for the traditional AdaBoost method.

Vast researches in neural classification have shown that neural networks [11-12] are promising alternatives to conventional classification methods. However, the meaning of each neuron and the decision of each weight are difficult to understand in the neural networks. Fuzzy entropy measure [13] is employed to partition the input feature space into decision regions and to select relevant features with good separability for the classification task. Neural fuzzy networks [14] integrate the advantages of both neural networks and fuzzy systems, which bring the low level learning ability, optimization capability and computational power of neural networks into fuzzy systems and give the high-level human-like thinking and

* Corresponding author: cjlin@ncut.edu.tw; Tel.: +886-953-002-825

reasoning of fuzzy systems to neural networks. Besides, the fuzzy inference systems can be adapted into with the ability of self-tuning and getting closer to neural networks.

The rest of this paper is organized as follows. In section 2, we introduce the traditional Adaboost method, functional neural fuzzy classifier proposed early, and our proposed AdaBoost-based approaches, and section III to their performance applying on three classification benchmarks. Finally, conclusions are drawn in Section 4.

2 The Proposed AdaBoost-based Approaches

This section describes the proposed AdaBoost-based incremental functional neural fuzzy classifier (AIFNFC) and AdaBoost-based fixed functional neural fuzzy classifier (AFFNFC). Besides, the AFFNFC can be divided into two different models, named the AFFNFC-1 and AFFNFC-2, based on the influence factor c. The general architecture of the proposed classifiers is shown in Figure 1.

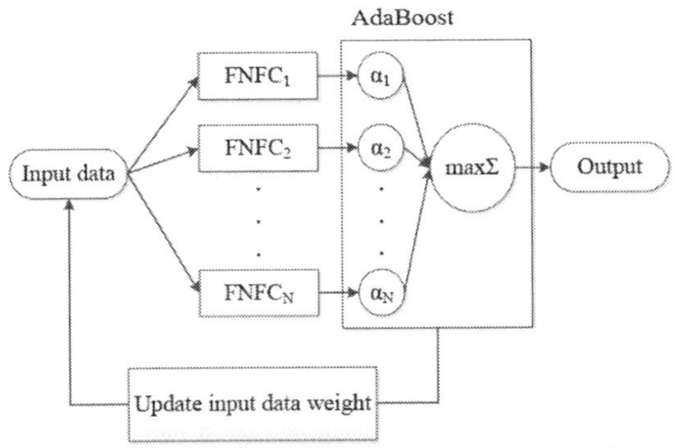

Figure 1. General architecture of the proposed classifiers

2.1. The Original AdaBoost Method

The AdaBoost method constructs a complex nonlinear strong classifier as a linear combination of M simpler weak classifier. In every epoch, the method assigns the weights to the weak classifiers for committee voting, and a weak classifier with lower error rate will be assigned a larger weight. In the following, we show the details of the AdaBoost algorithm in the form of pseudo codes [15].

Algorithm: AdaBoost

1. Given N input examples $\{(X_1,Y_1),\ldots,(X_N,Y_N)\}$, with labels $y_i \in Y = \{0,1\}$.
2. Initialize the observation weights $w_i = \frac{1}{N}$, for $i = 1,2,\ldots,N$.
3. For $t = 1,\ldots,T$
   (1) Fit a classifier $h_t(x)$ to the training data using weights w_i;
   (2) Calculate the training error
   $$\varepsilon_t = \sum_{i=1}^{N} w_i I(h_t(x_i) \neq y_i) / \sum_{i=1}^{N} w_i$$
   (3) Calculate hypothesis weight
   $$\alpha_t = log\frac{1-\varepsilon_t}{\varepsilon_t}$$
   (4) Update the observation weight
   $$w_i \leftarrow w_i \cdot exp\big(\alpha_t \cdot I(h_t(x_i) \neq y_i)\big), i = 1,2,\ldots N$$
   (5) Renormalize w_i
4. Output:

$$H(x) = arg\max_k \sum_{t=1}^{T} \alpha_t \cdot I(h_t(x_i) = k)$$

In step 3, $I(h_t(x_i) \neq y_i)$ represents an identical function, when $h_t(x_i) \neq y_i$ it returns 1, otherwise is 0; ε_t is the error rate, α_t is the log-odds rate of ε_t and the weighted value of weak classifier at the tth epoch. It can be easily observed that a smaller ε_t will increase the value of α_t; while ε_t is closed to 1/2, α_t will approach to zero.

2.2 The Functional Neural Fuzzy Classifier

Before introducing the proposed AdaBoost-based classifiers, the weak classifiers - functional neural fuzzy classifier (FNFC) [16], is briefly reviewed in this subsection. The FNFC was a traditional TSK-type functional neural fuzzy network integrated with the functional-link neural network (FLNN) [17] generating complex nonlinear combinations of input variables to the consequent part of the fuzzy rules. As shown in Figure 2, the network architecture can be divided into five layers.

The FNFC implements a fuzzy IF-THEN rule as following,

Rule-j:
IF x_1 **is** A_{1j} **and** x_2 **is** A_{2j} **...and** x_i **is** A_{ij} **...and** x_N **is** A_{Nj}

$$\textbf{THEN}\ \hat{y}_j = \sum_{k=1}^{M} w_{kj}\Phi_k$$

where x_i and $\hat{y}_j$ are the input and local output variables, respectively; N is the number of input variables; Rule-j is the jth fuzzy rule; A_{ij} is the linguistic term of precondition part with Gaussian membership function; w_{kj} is the link weight of the local output; Φ_k is the basis trigonometric function of input variables and M is the number of basis function.

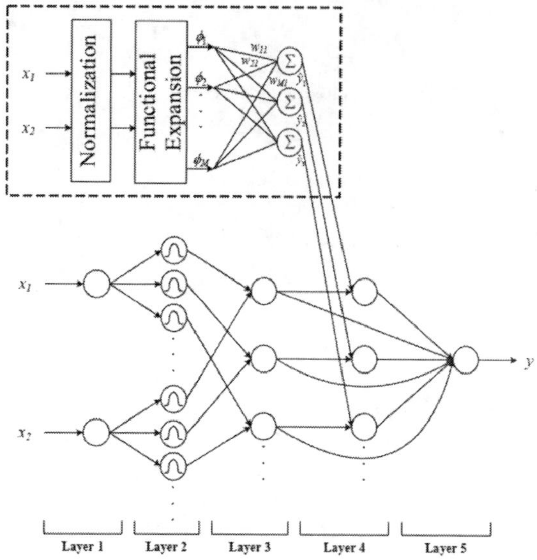

Figure 2. General Architecture of the FNFC classifier.

Layer 1: Each node in this layer only transmits input values to layer 2 without computation.

$$u_i^{(1)} = x \quad (1)$$

Layer 2: The calculated membership value represents the degree which an input value belongs to a fuzzy set $\mathbf{A_{ij}}$ in layer 2. We use the Gaussian membership function here, which is defined as

$$u_{ij}^{(2)} = exp\left(\frac{-[u_i^{(1)} - m_{ij}]}{\sigma_{ij}^2}\right) \quad (2)$$

where m_{ij} and σ_{ij} are the mean and variance of Gaussian membership function, respectively.

Layer 3: The product operator is adopted to perform the precondition part of the fuzzy rules. The corresponding equation of each inference node is presented as,

$$u_j^{(3)} = \prod_i u_{ij}^{(2)} \quad (3)$$

Layer 4: Node in layer 4 received the output from layer 3 and the FLNN output. As a result, the equation can be summarized as following,

$$u_j^{(4)} = u_j^{(3)} \cdot \sum_{k=1}^{m} w_{kj} \cdot \Phi_k \quad (4)$$

where w_{kj} is the corresponding link weight of the FLNN

and Φ_k is the functional expansion of input variables. The functional expansion uses a trigonometric polynomial basis function, given by

$x_1 \sin(\pi x_1) \cos(\pi x_1) x_2 \sin(\pi x_2) \cos(\pi x_2)$ for two-dimensional input variables. Therefore, M is the number of basis functions,

$\mathbf{M = 3 \times N}$, where N is the number of input variables.

Layer 5: The out node in layer 5 acts as a defuzzifier with

$$y = u^{(5)} = \frac{\sum_{j=1}^{R} u_j^{(4)}}{\sum_{j=1}^{R} u_j^{(3)}} = \frac{\sum_{j=1}^{R} u_j^{(3)}(\sum_{i=1}^{M} w_{ij}\Phi_i)}{\sum_{j=1}^{R} u_j^{(3)}} \quad (5)$$

where R is number of fuzzy rules and y is the output of FNFC model.

The learning algorithm of the FNFC includes the structure learning phase and parameter learning phase. The division of input space and the establishment of fuzzy rules are performed automatically in structure learning phase; meanwhile, the link weights in consequent part and the parameters of the membership function are adjusted in the parameter learning phase. The details of the FNFC can be found in [16].

2.3 The Proposed AIFNFC Approach

When handling the multi-class classification problem, most boost-based methods restricted the problem into multiple two-class problems. Without this restriction, we proposed a new AdaBoost-based incremental functional neural fuzzy classifier (AIFNFC), which uses the FNFCs as the weak classifiers. By using the FNFC as the weak classifier, AIFNFC approach improves the disadvantage of boost-based methods for multi-class classification. In each epoch, the weights will be updated by AdaBoost approach; the better classifier is assigned a higher weight to improve the final classification result. The pseudo code of AIFNFC is listed in the following.

Algorithm: *AIFNFC*

1. With *C* classes, given *N* training examples, $\{(x_1, y_1, z_1), \ldots, (x_i, y_i, z_i), \ldots, (x_N, y_N, z_N)\}$, where x_i represents the given input attribute, label y_i, $y_i \in Y = \{1, 2, \ldots, C\}$, is the desired class, and the label z_i, $z_i \in Z = \{0, 1\}$, is the predicted outcome.
2. Initialize the data weights $w_i = \frac{1}{N}$, $z_i = 0$ for i=1,2,…,N, where N is amount of the training data amount, T for amount of the epoch amount, and t for epoch index.
3. For $t = 1, \ldots, T$;
   (1) If $z_i = 0$, create a weak classifier $h_t(x_i)$ by FNFN;
   (2) Calculate the classification error with all data by
   $$\varepsilon_t = \sum_{i=1}^{N} w_i I(h_t(x_i) \neq y_i) / \sum_{i=1}^{N} w_i \quad (6)$$
   where $I(\cdot)$ represents an identical function
   (3) If $\varepsilon_t > 0.5$, go to step 4;
   (4) Calculate the weight of this weak classifier by
   $$\alpha_t = log\frac{1-\varepsilon_t}{\varepsilon_t} \quad (7)$$
   (5) Update the ith data weight by
   $$w_i \leftarrow w_i \cdot exp(\alpha_t \cdot I(h_t(x_i) \neq y_i)) \quad (8)$$
   (6) Update the predicted outcome label by

$$z_i = \begin{cases} 1, if \ \ h_t(x_i) = y_i \\ 0, if \ \ h_t(x_i) \neq y_i \end{cases} \quad (9)$$

(7) Renormalize w_i;

4. Output the resulted strong classifier by

$$H(x) = arg \max_k \sum_{t=1}^{T} \alpha_t \cdot I(h_t(x_i) = k) \quad (10)$$

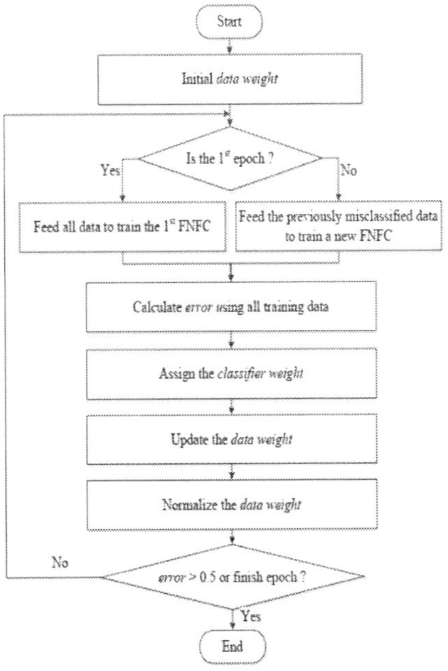

Figure 3. Flowchart of the proposed AIFNFC approach

2.4 The Proposed AFFNFC Approach

We observe that the poor classifier in the AIFNFC approach is generally followed by a relatively better classifier. Hence, one modification of AIFNFC is needed to force all classifiers on contributing themselves with greater effectiveness. The proposed AdaBoost-based fixed functional neural fuzzy classifier (AFFNFC) is characterized by a customized amount of weak classifiers, and the AdaBoost method is used to update the weight of these weak classifiers that lastly contribute the final outcome via their weights. In addition, the amount of weak classifiers should be defined before executing the epoch process. The pseudo code of AIFNFC is listed in the following.

Algorithm: *AFFNFC*

1. With C classes, given N training examples $\{(x_1, y_1), \dots, (x_i, y_i), \dots, (x_N, y_N)\}$ where x_i represents the given input attribute, label $y_i \in Y = \{1, 2, \dots, C\}$ the desired class.
2. Initialize the data weight $w_i = \frac{1}{N}$ for $i = 1, 2, \dots, N$, epoch amount *T*, epoch index *t*, the amount of classifiers *M*, and the ratio *c*.
3. Train *M* FNFN classifiers.
4. For $t = 1, \dots, T$

   (1) For $m = 1, \dots M$

   Fit a classifier $h_m(x_i)$;

   Calculate the classification error by

$$\varepsilon_t = \sum_{i=1}^{N} w_i I(h_m(x_i) \neq y_i) / \sum_{i=1}^{N} w_i \quad (11)$$

   (2) Calculate the weight of this weak classifier by

$$\alpha_{t,m} = log \frac{1-\varepsilon_{t,m}}{\varepsilon_{t,m}} \cdot c \quad (12)$$

   where the influence factor $c = (M - r)/M$

   (3) Update the ith data weight by

$$w_i \leftarrow w_i \cdot exp(\alpha_{t,m} \cdot I(h_m(x_i) \neq y_i) \cdot c) \quad (13)$$

   (4) Re-normalize w_i

5. Calculate the sum of T weights for the mth classifier by

$$\beta_m = \sum_{t=1}^{T} \alpha_{t,m} \quad (14)$$

6. Output the resulted strong classifier by

$$H(x) = arg \max_k \sum_{m=1}^{M} \beta_m \cdot I(h_m(x_i) = k) \quad (15)$$

After a certain training epoch conducted, all error rates of classifiers are sorted in descending order, and the number of order is used to determine the influence factor c. The factor c is defined as $(M-r)/M$, where M represents the amount of fixed classifiers, and positive integer $r \in [0, M-1]$ represents the ranking order of the classifier. A specific classifier with $r = 0$ means this classifier is with the lowest error rate among all the classifiers.

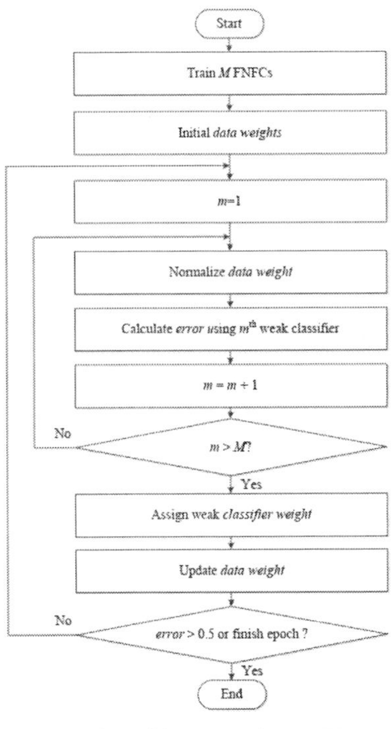

Figure 4. Flowchart of the proposed AFFNFC approach

There are two design schemes in this paper for different influence factor c. When there are some classifiers of the same error rate, the ranking factor r would be set according to their processing order, and this scheme is named AFFNFC-1. The other design scheme, called the AFFNFC-2, will assign the same ranking factor r to all the classifiers of the identical error rate.

3 Experimental Results

In this study, three benchmark dataset, Iris, Wine, and Breast Cancer are measured to evaluate the performance of the proposed methods. These three datasets come from the Donald Bren School of Information and Computer Science University of California at Irvine (UCI), the well-known Machine Learning Repository website [18]; Iris classification is a low-dimensional problem, and Breast Cancer and Wine classifications are multi-dimensional problems. Table 1 summarizes the amounts of samples, attributes and classified classes. Since this website recoded many benchmark datasets for machine learning, researchers can easily apply these benchmarks to verify their classification approaches, and conduct the necessary comparison of the corresponding training and testing results. In the rest of this section, we compare the performances of AIFNFC, AFFNFC-1, AFFNFC-2, and other methods combined with FNFC model, such as voting method with multiple FNFCs and single FNFC.

Table 1. Statistics of the chosen benchmark datasets.

Dataset	#Samples	#Attributes	#Classes
Iris	150	4	3
Wine	178	13	3
Brest Cancer	683	9	2

To compare with other methods, all the commonly used parameters are set identical initially, the learning rate η is set to 0.01, the entropy is set to 0.3, the amount of training epochs is set to 100 times, and the numbers of weak classifiers FNFCs are respectively set to 5, 10 and 15 for different experiment. In these experiments, half patterns of dataset are selected randomly as the training set, and the other patterns are used as testing data. For example, 75 instances of original 150 examples in Iris dataset will be used as training data and the rest 75 instances are applied for the testing. In addition, the randomized selecting process will be carried out five times for each benchmark dataset.

Example 1: Classification of the Iris Data

The Iris dataset is by Fisher [19], which is frequently chosen to verify newly designed algorithms in machine learning. The classification of the iris dataset is to differentiate the species based on the iris sepal (length and width) and petal (length and width). The Iris data comprises 150 actual instances that are distributed into three species: Iris Setosa, Iris Versicolout and Iris Virginica. Each iris dataset has four input features and one predicted attribute, , shown in Table 2.

Table 2. Attribute information of the Iris data

Attribute Type	No.	Attribute Description
Input	1	Sepal Length
features	2	Sepal Width
	3	Petal Length
	4	Petal Width
Predicted Attribute		Class of Iris Plant: (1) Iris Setosa (2) Iris Versicolout (3) Iris Virginica

We repeated the experiment on 5 different training-testing datasets that were obtained via a random selecting process from the original Iris data. Table 3 summarizes the five-run averaged experimental accuracy rates of the AIFNFC, AFFNFC-1, AFFNFC-2, single FNFC, and voting method with multiple FNFCs. Compared to the other approaches, the proposed AFFNFCs are generally with better performances.

Table 3. Average Accuracy on Iris Data

	Classifiers Number	Training (%)	Testing (%)
AIFNFC	-	97.60	92.27
AFFNFC-1	5	98.67	95.20
	10	99.47	96.27
	15	99.73	96.53
AFFNFC-2	5	98.93	96.53
	10	99.47	96.27
	15	99.73	96.53
Voting method with multiple FNFCs	5	97.60	93.87
	10	98.67	96.27
	15	98.93	95.73
FNFC (single)	-	95.36	92.96

Example 2: Classification of the Wine Data

The Wine dataset [20] is the results of a chemical analysis of 178 wines which are brewed in the same area in Italy but derived from three different cultivars. The classification of wine type is based on 13 constituents found in the wines. The information of constituents and predicted attribute are presented in Table 4.

Table 4. Attribute information of the wine data

Attribute Type	No.	Attribute Description
Input Attribute	1	Alcohol
	2	Malic Acid
	3	Ash
	4	Alcalinity of Ash
	5	Magnesium
	6	Total Phenols
	7	Flavanoids
	8	Nonflavanoid Phenols
	9	Proanthocyanins
	10	Color Intensity
	11	Hue
	12	OD280/OD315 of Diluted Wines

	13	Proline
Predicted Attribute		Class of Wine Identifier (1-3) (1)Barolo(2) Grignolino (3) Barbera

Table 5 lists the five-run averaged accuracy rates experimented on the Wine dataset. In this experiment, the AIFNFC method with fewer classifiers is a bit weak on performance since the applied number of AIFNFC classifiers is not fixed. Therefore, there are fluctuations of accuracy rate in classification results of the AIFNFC method. But, the proposed AFFNFCs still have better performance than other methods.

Table 5. Average accuracy on wine data

Algorithms	Classifiers Number	Training (%)	Testing (%)
AIFNFC	-	95.96	87.19
AFFNFC-1	5	98.65	91.69
	10	**100.0**	**93.48**
	15	100.0	93.26
AFFNFC-2	5	98.65	91.69
	10	**100.0**	**93.48**
	15	100.0	93.26
Voting method with multiple FNFCs	5	98.43	91.24
	10	99.10	93.03
	15	99.33	93.48
FNFC (single)	-	94.65	85.71

Example 3: Classification of the Breast Cancer Data

This breast cancer dataset was created by Dr. William H. Wolberg at the Wisconsin University [21]. The total number of the original samples is 699. Since there are 16 samples contain missing values, only 683 patterns were used in this experiment. The columns of sample id and class label in original dataset are removed, so each pattern only consists of nine input features and one predicted attribute, as shown in Table 6.

Table 6. Attribute information of the breast cancer data

Attribute Type	No.	Attribute Description
Input Attribute	1	Clump Thickness
	2	Uniformity of Cell Size
	3	Uniformity of Cell Shape
	4	Marginal Adhesion
	5	Single Epithelial Cell Size
	6	Bare Nuclei
	7	Bland Chromatin
	8	Normal Nucleoli
	9	Mitoses
Predicted Attribute		Class of Breast Cancer: (1) Benign (2) Malignant

Better testing classification results are with the AIFNFC method, since the AIFNFC is great at improving the best classifier which finally influences the final classification results. The AFFNFC always has good results in training phase, but it did not conduct a superior performance in this case. The experimental results are listed in Table 7.

Table 1. Average accuracy on breast cancer data

Algorithms	Classifiers Number	Training (%)	Testing (%)
AIFNFC	-	97.94	**96.51**
AFFNFC-1	5	98.34	96.06
	10	98.40	96.00
	15	**98.45**	96.06
AFFNFC-2	5	98.34	96.06
	10	98.40	96.00
	15	98.40	96.11
Voting method with multiple FNFCs	5	98.05	95.89
	10	97.77	95.43
	15	97.94	95.89
FNFC (single)		98.09	95.45

When massive voting decisions are applied, the experimental results show that the wrong decisions of most of the classifiers will increase the misclassification rate for the voting method with multiple FNFCs. On the other hand, the proposed AdaBoost-based approaches have the benefit of arranging larger associated weights for the classifiers of higher accuracies, which release the influence of low-accuracy classifiers. Besides, if a training instance is misclassified by a classifier of greater weight, the final classification result can be improved with the other classifiers when the summation of their weights is bigger than the one of misguided classifier. For example, for the 34th instance in Iris dataset, both the AFFNFC and voting method are with 7 misclassified classifiers, then the voting method makes a wrong decision, but the final classification of the AFFNFC remained correct.

4 Conclusions

In this paper, we propose two intelligent AdaBoost-based approaches, AIFNFC and AFFNFC, for the classification applications. The AIFNFC approach will increase the amount of functional neural fuzzy classifiers based on the corresponding error during the training phase; while the AFNFC approach is equipped with a fixed amount of functional neural fuzzy classifiers. Then, the weights of AdaBoost procedure are assigned for classifiers. Experimental results show that the proposed AIFNFC and AFFNFC approaches can effectively improve the classification performances.

References

1. R. M. Cormack, "A Review of Classification," Journal of the Royal Statistical Society (Series A), Vol. 134, No. 3, pp. 321-367, 1971.
2. J. M. CAMIN and R. S. SOKAL, "A Method for Deducing Branching Sequences in Phylogeny," Evolution, Vol. 19, No. 3, pp. 311-326, 1965.
3. P. O. Duda and P. E. Hart, "Pattern classification and scene analysis," Wiley, NY, USA, 1973.
4. J. A. Hartigan, "Representation of Similarity Batrices by Trees," Journal of the American Statistical Association, Vol. 62, No. 320, pp. 1140-1158, 1967.

5. S. B. Kotsiantis, "Supervised Machine Learning: A Review of Classification Techniques," Informatica, Vol. 31,pp. 249-268, 2007.
6. L. G. Valiant, "A Theory of the Learnable," Communications of the ACM, Vol. 27, pp. 1134-1142, 1984.
7. M. Kearns and L. Valiant, "Learning Boolean Formulae or Finite Automata is as Hard as Factoring," Technical Report, TR-14-88, Aiken Computation Laboratory, Karrard University, Cambridge, MA.
8. R. E. Schapire, "The Strength of Weak Learnability," Machine Learning, Vol. 5, pp. 197-227, 1990
9. Y. Freund, "Boosting a Weak Learning Algorithm by Majority," Information and Computation, Vol. 121, pp. 256-285, 1995.
10. Y. Freund and R. E. Schapire, "A Decision-Theoretic Generalization of On-Line Learning and an Application to Boosting," Journal of Computer and System Sciences, Vol. 55, No. 1, pp. 119-139, 1997.
11. G. Peter Zhang, "Neural Networks for Classification: A Survey," IEEE Transactions on Systems, Man, and Cybernetics:Applications and Reviews, Vol. 30, No. 4, pp. 451-462, Nov. 2000.
12. K. Devulapalli, "Neural Networks for Classification and Regression. Biom. Biostat. Int. J.,Vol. 2, Issue 6, DOI: 10.15406/bbij.2015.02.00046S, 2015.
13. L. A. Zadeh, "Fuzzy Sets," Information and Control, Vol. 8, pp. 338-353, 1965.
14. C. J. Lin and H.-Y. Lin, "Mobile Robot Wall-following Control Using a Fuzzy CMAC with Group-based Strategy Bacterial Foraging Optimization," International Journal of Advanced Robotic Systems, Vol. 14, Issue 4, DOI: https://doi.org/10.1177/1729881417720872, July 14, 2017.
15. J. Zhu, H. Zou, S. Rosset and T. Hastie, "Multi-class AdaBoost," Statistics and Its Interface, Vol. 2, pp.349–360, 2009.
16. C. H. Cheng, M. T. Su, C. J. Lin, and C. T. Lin, "A Hybrid of Bacterial Foraging Optimization and Particle Swarm Optimization for Evolutionary Neural Fuzzy Classifier," International Journal of Fuzzy Systems, Vol. 16, No. 3, September 2014, pp. 422-433.
17. J. C. Patra, R. N. Pal, B. N. Chatterji and G. Panda, "Identification of Nonlinear Dynamic Systems Using Functional Link Artificial Neural Networks," IEEE Transactions on Systems, Man, and Cybernetics, Vol. 29, No. 2, pp. 254-262, 1999.
18. UCI Machine Learning Repository, 2013, Available from URL: http://archive.ics.uci.edu/ml/
19. R. A. Fisher, "The Use of Multiple Measurements in Taxonomic Problems," Annual Eugenics, Vol. 7, No.2, pp. 179-188, 1936.
20. M. Forina, R. Leardi, C. Armanino, and S. Lanteri, "PARVUS - An Extendible Package for Data Exploration," Journal of Chemometrics, Vol. 4, No. 2, pp. 191-194, 1990.
21. W. H. Wolberg and O. L. Mangasarian, "Multisurface method of pattern separation for medical diagnosis applied to breast cytology," Proceedings of the National Academy of Sciences of the United States of America, Vol. 87, pp. 9193-9196, 1990.

Effects of regular exercise on functional fitness of community elderly

Tsui-Er Lee*

Office of Physical Education, Asia University, 41354 Taichung City, Taiwan

Abstract. This study aims to discuss the effect and the retention effect of regular exercise on functional fitness of community elderly. Total 65 community elderly aged above 65 (77.03±6.41 years old) who voluntarily participate in this study are selected as the research subjects. Functional fitness pretest is practiced before the regular exercise intervention, the posttest is preceded in the 12th week, and the retention test is preceded in the 24th week. The results show that the functional fitness test, after the 12-week regular exercise intervention, reveals that males make significant progress in upper/lower limb strength, cardiorespiratory endurance, static balance, upper limb flexibility, agility and dynamic balance and females appear remarkable progress in upper limb strength, cardiorespiratory endurance, static balance, upper limb flexibility, agility and dynamic balance. Regular exercise could remarkably promote functional fitness of the elderly. In this case, designing community fitness programs as long-term continuous activity would promote and maintain fitness.

1 Introduction

The advance of technology and the change of societies result in large changes of population structure. The 2012-2060 Population Projection report, proposed by National Development Council, stated that aged population above 65 years old in 2060 would largely increase 2.9 times more than it in 2012 and the ratio of total population would increase from 11.2% in 2012 to 39.4% in 2060, in which the ratio of aged population above 80 years old would largely increase from 25.4% in 2012 to 41.4% in 2060. Moreover, the aging index was 76.3% in 2012, i.e. the proportion of aged population and young population was about 1:1.3; aged population in 2016 would exceed young population and the aging index would exceed 100%; and, the aging index would be up to 401.5% in 2060 when aged population was about 4 times more than young population [1]. It proves the increasing aged population structure in Taiwan that aging becomes the inevitable trend.

The elderly are facing the threat of chronic degenerative diseases. Past research indicated that regular physical activity could effectively improve physical and mental health and prevent cardiovascular diseases and chronic diseases from occurrence. Health promotion therefore is the trend developed from the global strategy to cope with national health. The so-called health promotion refers to applying various educational, organizational, economic, and environmental supports to facilitate the public practicing behaviors good for health. One or more lifestyle-related behaviors is generally selected as the objective, such as smoking, drinking and drug abuse, nutrition, exercise, stress adaptation, and safe protection [2]. Li-juan Chen & Chin-yi Wu proceeded 20-week walking intervention [3] and found out the similar effects of improving cardiovascular risk factors and reducing the risk of coronary heart diseases. The cultivation of regular exercise habits and the promotion of physical fitness standards to establish healthy lifestyles therefore are the primary issues at the moment.

Functional fitness refers to a body being able to independently and safely complete daily physical activity, without over-fatigue [4]. It contains strength, aerobic endurance, flexibility, agility/dynamic balance, and body mass index. Accordingly, functional fitness combines health physical fitness and exercise physical fitness to form functional fitness. For the elderly, vitality and independent life are necessary; and, functional fitness is the comprehensive ability to enhance the elderly adapting to various stimuli. The demand for and the importance of functional fitness for the elderly therefore are far larger than physical fitness. In consideration with the physical function degeneration of the elderly [5], Mei-ling Lu pointed out an important course for health promotion to promote the quality of life of the elderly by testing the functional fitness standard of the elderly and providing suitable exercise prescription and programs. Apparently, functional fitness is critical for the health promotion of the elderly.

This study aims to discuss the effect of the 12-week regular exercise intervention on the functional fitness of community elderly.

* Corresponding author: vivian@asia.edu.tw

2 Methodology

2.1 Research subject

With purposive sampling, total 65 healthy community seniors aged above 65 (33 females and 32 males) with independent daily behaviors in Nantou City (Taiwan) are selected as the research subjects. All participants are requested to sign the agreement before the experiment and fill in the questionnaire.

2.2 Experiment procedure

The participants are proceeded the 12-week integrated exercise training and cognition course, including weekly group course and twice-a-week home-based independent exercise. Functional fitness tests are preceded before and after the intervention. The participants are requested to maintain normal lifestyles except participating in the courses and tests and not to additionally engage in other exercise. They have to fully participate in the weekly group course and fill in exercise records about the physical activity. The examiners in this study have the national physical fitness examiner certificate approved by Sports Administration, Ministry of Education, to ensure the test accuracy.

3 Result

Table 1 reveals notable differences in lower limb strength (chair stand) and upper limb strength (musculus biceps brachii left arm curling, musculus biceps brachii right arm curling), cardiorespiratory endurance (high knees in place) and static balance (open-eye single leg standing), as well as upper limb flexibility (scratching), but not lower limb flexibility (chair sit-and-reach) of male elderly. The agility and dynamic balance (chair stand detour) also present remarkable differences ($p < 0.5$).

Table 2 show significant differences in upper limb strength (musculus biceps brachii left arm curling, musculus biceps brachii right arm curling), but not lower limb strength (chair stand), of female elderly. The cardiorespiratory endurance (high knees in place) and static balance (open-eye single leg standing) also achieve notable differences. The upper limb flexibility (scratching) reaches remarkable differences, but not the lower limb flexibility (chair sit-and-reach); and, the agility and dynamic balance (chair stand detour) also reveal significant differences ($p < 0.5$).

Table 1. Male functional fitness pretest/posttest difference (n = 32).

Item	Pretest	Posttest	t	p
Chair stand	15.16 ± 3.90	16.57 ± 4.16	-2.83	0.008 *
Musculus biceps brachii arm curling (left)	19.03 ± 4.16	20.19 ± 4.49	-3.97	0.000 *
Musculus biceps brachii arm curling (right)	18.97 ± 4.29	20.72 ± 3.96	-6.09	0.000 *
High knees in place	89.38 ±16.39	91.00 ±15.81	-3.32	0.002 *
Chair sit-and-reach	-7.39 ±11.99	-5.06 ±10.42	-1.92	0.065
Open-eye single leg standing	14.58 ±15.28	16.75 ±14.64	-4.07	0.000 *
Scratching test (left)	-19.22 ± 9.58	-16.66 ± 8.84	-3.80	0.001 *
Scratching test (right)	-9.51 ±12.21	-7.66 ±11.59	-4.90	0.000 *
Chair stand detour	7.93 ± 2.35	7.33 ± 2.26	5.55	0.000 *

*p < .05

Table 2. Female functional fitness pretest/posttest difference (n = 33).

Item	Pretest	Posttest	t	p
Chair stand	16.18 ± 4.10	17.28 ± 5.05	-1.97	0.057
Musculus biceps brachii arm curling (left)	20.12 ± 3.74	21.48 ± 4.05	-4.43	0.000 *
Musculus biceps brachii arm curling (right)	20.24 ± 4.56	22.21 ± 4.87	-5.28	0.000 *
High knees in place	83.82 ±23.36	88.55 ±24.71	-4.18	0.000 *
Chair sit-and-reach	-0.27 ± 6.79	1.04 ± 6.63	-1.42	0.165
Open-eye single leg standing	12.64 ± 7.21	14.46 ±14.10	-4.32	0.000 *
Scratching test (left)	-16.00 ±10.35	-13.58 ± 8.38	-3.80	0.018 *
Scratching test (right)	-5.12 ± 9.18	-2.64 ± 7.81	-4.36	0.001 *

*p < .05

4 Discussion

This study reveals the remarkable improvement of the functional fitness of the elderly after the physical fitness exercise training and cognition courses. Both male and female elderly present notable progress on upper limb strength, cardiorespiratory endurance, static balance, upper limb flexibility, and agility and dynamic balance. Such a result is similar to several studies. Tsung-ching Lin, Li-ying Chang, Yun-dai Ling, Yin-hsin Li & Tzu-yuan Hsiang proved that the 12-week hydraulic resistance intervention could remarkably promote the physical fitness of female elderly [6]. Aiming at the elderly in nursing homes, Grönstedt et al. preceded 3-month individual physical activity intervention [7], covering the balance, physical activity, and muscles of the elderly. The experimental group appeared significant improvement on walking and wheelchair pushing speed and leg muscle strength. Nevertheless, the lower limb flexibility of both males and females and the lower limb strength of females did not reach the significance, but revealing the improving trend. It might be the reason that distinct exercise would enhance physical fitness differently. From the literature, continuous 40~60min Taiji exercise for 2~3 times a week could effectively promote the lower limb strength and flexibility of the elderly after 8-12 week training [8]. Taiji exercise therefore could be arranged in the exercise course to achieve better training benefit. In terms of static and agility/dynamic balance, Shimada, H., Uchiyama, Y., & Kakurai, S. preceded 12-week balance training and gait exercise for the elderly [9] and found out the remarkable improvement on static and agility/dynamic balance. The result conforms to this study. The functional fitness improvement could enhance the daily physical activity ability, promote the functional fitness performance of the elderly, and improve the health condition.

Acknowledge

We are grateful for the project funding support of Ministry of Science and Technology (MOST 104-2629-E-468-002) and would like to show our appreciation.

References

1. National Development Council of the Executive Yuan of Taiwan, *The report of Republic of China from 2012 to 2060 census* (National Development Council of the Executive Yuan, Taiwan, 2014)
2. S.Z. Huang, Taiwan Journal of Public Health **18(1)**, 55-63 (1991)
3. L.L. Lin, Z.I. Wu, Sports & Exercise Research **12(4)**, 90-98 (2010)
4. C.J. Jones, R.E. Rikli, Journal of Aging and Physical Activity **7**, 129-161 (1999)
5. M.L. Lu, The Associations of Health, Physical Activity and Functional Fitness among Older Adults. Master, National Taiwan Normal University, Taipei, Taiwan, 2003. (In Chinese)
6. T.C. Lin, L.Y. Chang, Y.T. Lin, Y.H. Lee, T.Y. Shiang, Taiwan Geriatr Gerontol **9(1)**, 15-27 (2014)
7. H. Grönstedt, K. Frändin, A. Bergland, J.L. Helbostad, R. Granbo, L. Puggaard, M. Andresen, K. Hellström, Gerontology **59(3)**, 220-229 (2013)
8. H.Y. Chang, Y.P. Lin, I.P. Cheng, S.H. Lin, Macau Journal of Nursing **10(2)**, 48-52 (2011)
9. H. Shimada, Y. Uchiyama, S. Kakurai, Clinical Rehabilitation **17(5)**, 472-479 (2003)

* Corresponding author: vivian@asia.edu.tw

Effect of scaling on thermal properties and switching operation of phase change memory devices

Jie Zhu[1], *Changcheng Ma*[1], *Jing He*[1], *Jingjing Lu*[1], *Zuoqi Hu*[1,*]

[1]School of Optical and Electronic Information, Huazhong University of Science and Technology, Wuhan, 430070, China

Abstract. Phase change memory (PCM) is one of the most promising emerging non-volatile memory technologies. This paper simulates phase change memory devices (PCMDs) with careful attention to the scaling and its resulting impact on programming current during the switching operation, while Thomson heating within the phase change material and Peltier heating at the electrode interface are considered. The simulation results show that the device scaling has an influence on temperature distribution, volume of the molten region, heat diffusion and switching operation of PCMDs. The programming current decreases with smaller electrode size, greater thickness of phase change material and deeper isotropic scaling. The heat diffusion becomes more serious when the thickness of phase change materials decreases and the size of PCMD is isotropically scaled down. The scaling arguments also indicate that the impact of thermoelectric phenomena weakens with smaller dimensions due to the influence of programming current, heat diffusion and action area. This simulation provides useful insights to understand the switching operation of the PCMDs under the impact of thermoelectric effects. The process is instrumental for a complete understanding of device operation and hence provides valuable feedback for fine-tuning the device design so as to enhance its efficiency.

1 Introduction

To date, phase change memory (PCM) is one of the most promising emerging non-volatile memory technologies due to its fast programming speed, exceptional endurance and capability of scaling [1-3]. In terms of a phase change memory device (PCMD), with the application of bias voltage the information can be programmed by a non-volatile phase transition of phase change materials, especially some chalcogenide materials like GST [2,4]. In a set operation, the phase change material can be switched from a low-resistance crystalline state, set state as well, to a high-resistance amorphous state, namely reset state, because of the Joule heating [5]. On the other hand, during a reset operation, the reset state

* Corresponding author: hu_zuoqi@hust.edu.cn

turns back to the set state when the current is extremely high that the temperature of phase change material is above the melting point [6].

However, the reset operation is considered as a Gordian knot for research of PCM, owing to the requirement of a relatively high current, which is limited by the minimal size of devices and the possibility of parallel programming in an array. Therefore, recently great efforts have been made to analyze the relationship between programming current and scaling [3-4, 6-11]. In addition, with the size of PCMD scaled down, the thermoelectric effects in phase change material becomes more predominated [12-14]. Hence, it is essential that thermoelectric heating should be considered in studying the switching operation in PCM devices. This paper simulates PCMD aiming at studying the relationship between the scaling and its resulting impact on programming current during the switching operation, while thermoelectric effects are considered.

2 Model

In our study, the PCMD is designed as a mushroom-shaped structure, a widely utilized structure in PCMDs, containing a TiN top electrode, a 200 nm thick GST phase change layer and a 200 nm thick TiN pillar-type bottom electrode with a diameter of 250 nm, while top and bottom electrodes are respectively contacted with W electrode contacts, and the whole structure is surrounded by SiO2 electrical passivation. During the switching operation, the top electrode is biased while the bottom electrode is grounded.

In our simulation, based on the finite difference method [15-16], the model contains electrical, thermal, phase-change and percolation sub-models for a total demonstration of PCM switching operation. When the size of PCMDs scaled down, the thermoelectric effects cannot be omitted. To calculate the spatial electrical potential distribution, we not only iteratively solve the Laplace equation for each mesh element, but also consider additional generated current by Seebeck effects [13,16]. The current continuity equation is shown as

$$\nabla \cdot J = -\nabla \cdot [\ \sigma (\nabla V + S \nabla T)] = 0 \tag{1}$$

where J is the current density, σ is the electrical conductivity, V is the electric potential, S is Seebeck coefficient. In addition, we calculate the temperature distribution by solving the heating conduction equation, while we consider Joule heating induced by each mesh element, as well as Thomson heat within the GST and Peltier heat near the GST–TiN interface [12,17]. And the heat conduction equation is shown as

$$\mathrm{C}\,(dT / dt) - \nabla \cdot (\ \kappa \nabla T) = Q + Q_{\mathrm{th}} \tag{2}$$

where C is the volumetric heat capacity, T is temperature, t is time, κ is the thermal conductivity, Q is the Joule heat and Q_{th} is the contribution of thermoelectric effect. Then, according to the resulting temperature distribution, we model the phase-change process by the class theory of nucleation, and we adopt the Bruggeman effective medium approximation to discuss the percolation effect of a phase change material [16].

Table 1 shows the parameters used in our model at zero electric field and 300K room temperature, while experimental curves of detailed parameters utilized in our model is shown in Figure 1 [12-14,16].

 https://doi.org/10.1051/matecconf/201820106002

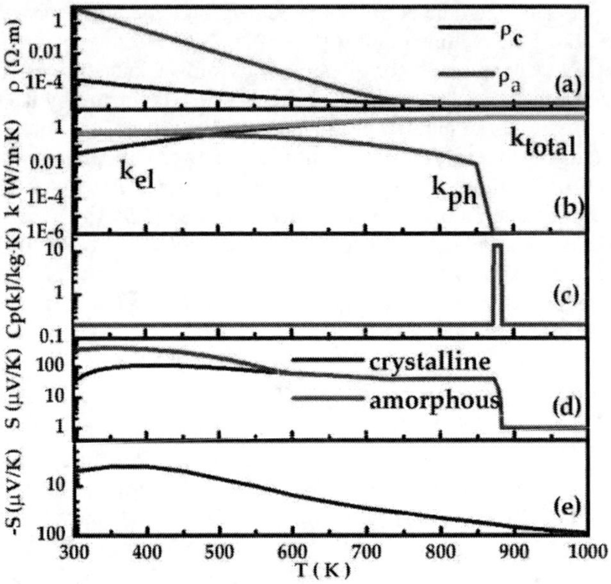

Fig. 1. (a) Electrical conductivity of crystalline and amorphous GST. (b) Constructed thermal conductivity of GST with phonon and electronic contributions shown. (c) Heat capacity for GST with a plateau at melting to include latent heat of fusion. (d) Seebeck coefficients for GST in amorphous and crystalline phases. (e) Negative Seebeck coefficient of TiN.

Table 1. parameters of materials. Taken from Refs. 12,13.

	ϱ_{elec}(Ω m)	κ(W/m K)	C(J/Kg K)
SiO_2	10^{14}	1.3	1050
TiN	10^{-6}	14	784
W	5.4×10^{-8}	175	132

3 Results

3.1 Scaling the cross section of pillar-type TiN

Figure 2 shows the effect of scaling pillar-type TiN, while the diameter of TiN changes in different values d_{TiN}= 50, 100, 150, 200 and 250 nm. In Figure 2a, with the diameter of TiN decreasing, to process a reset operation, the minimal programming current becomes lower, and the energy consumption decreasing either. In Figure 2c, it demonstrates that with the scaling of TiN, the dominated heating area generally concentrates and moves toward the GST/TiN interface. Figure 2b shows that with the cross section of TiN scaled down, the rate of current reduction caused by Peltier effect decreases while the rate of current reduction caused by Thomson effect increases. Overall, the total rate of current reduction decreases.

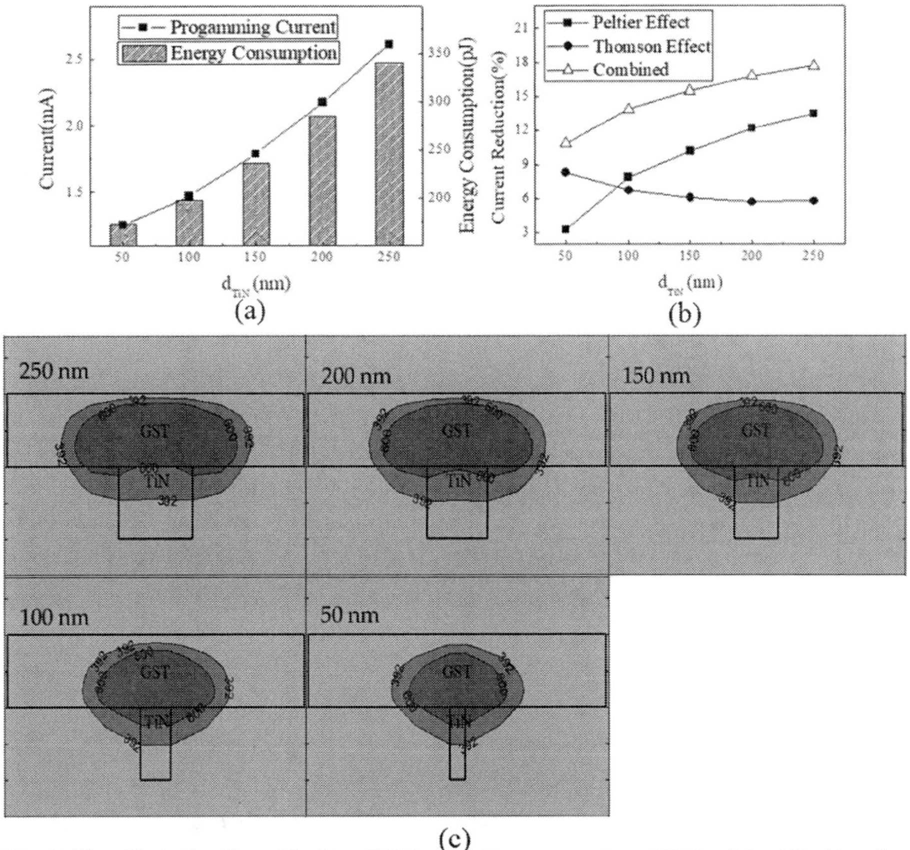

Fig. 2. The effect of scaling pillar-type TiN (scaling the cross section of TiN only), while d_{TiN} refers to the diameter of TiN: (a) programming current and energy consumption needed for a reset operation; (b) impact of thermoelectric effects on programming current; (c) at the end of a pulse, the temperature distribution of longitudinal section in a modeling device (isotherms in K are shown in each figure).

3.2 Scaling the thickness of GST layer

Figure 3 shows the effect of scaling the thickness of GST layer, while the thickness changes in different values h_{GST}= 50, 100, 150, 200, 250 and 300 nm. Figure 3a shows that both the programming current and the energy consumption increasing with the thickness decreasing, and the slope becomes larger when thickness is below 200 nm. In Figure 3c, it demonstrates that with the thickness scaling down the dominated heating area generally shrinks in the vertical direction. Figure 3b shows that considering different thermoelectric effects scaling the thickness of GST layer has different impact on the programming current in a reset operation. With the thickness of GST layer scaled down, the ratio of current reduction caused by Peltier effect decreases and the ratio of current reduction caused by Thomson effect slightly increases. Overall, the total rate of current reduction decreases.

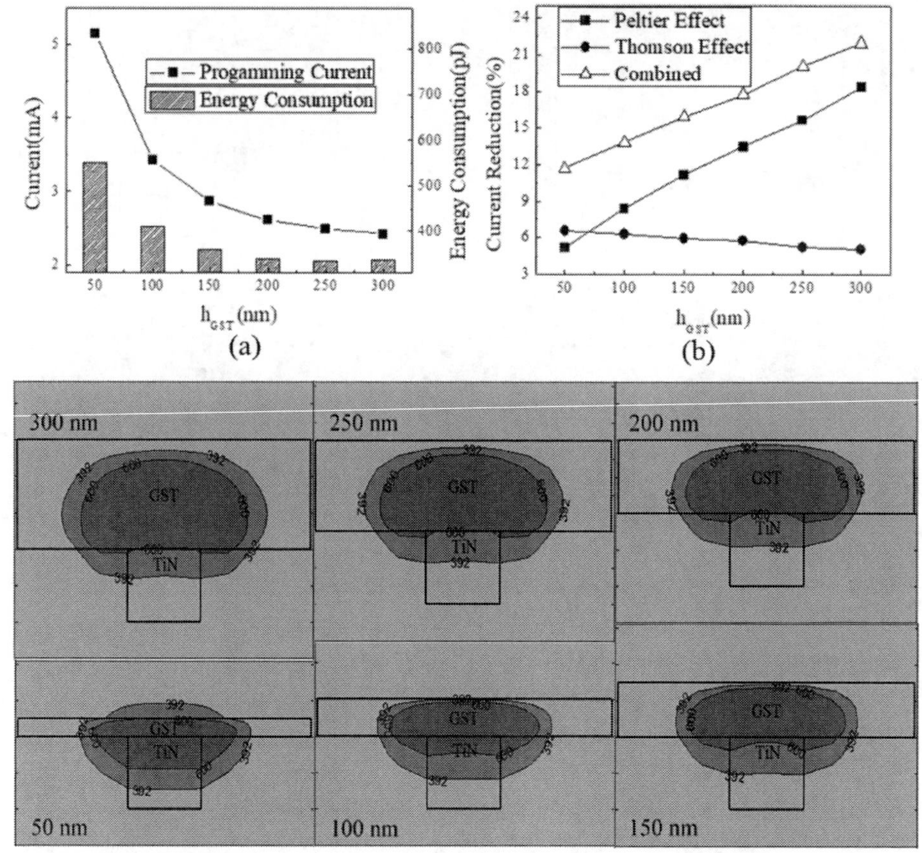

Fig. 3. The effect of scaling the thickness of GST layer, while h_{GST} refers to the thickness: (a) programming current and energy consumption needed for a reset operation; (b) impact of thermoelectric effects on programming current; (c) at the end of a pulse, the temperature distribution of longitudinal section in a modeling device (isotherms in K are shown in each figure).

3.3 Isotropic scaling the size of PCM device

Figure 4 shows the effect of isotropic scaling the size of PCM device, while the rate of scaling changes in different values 0.2, 0.4, 0.6, 0.8 and 1. Figure 4a shows the minimal programming current and corresponding energy consumption decrease at the end of a reset operation with the size of PCM device scaled down. Different thermoelectric effects have distinct impact on the programming current shown in Figure 4b. When the size of PCM device shrinks, the rate of current reduction caused by Peltier effect generally decreases, while the rate of current reduction induced by Thomson effect remains stable.

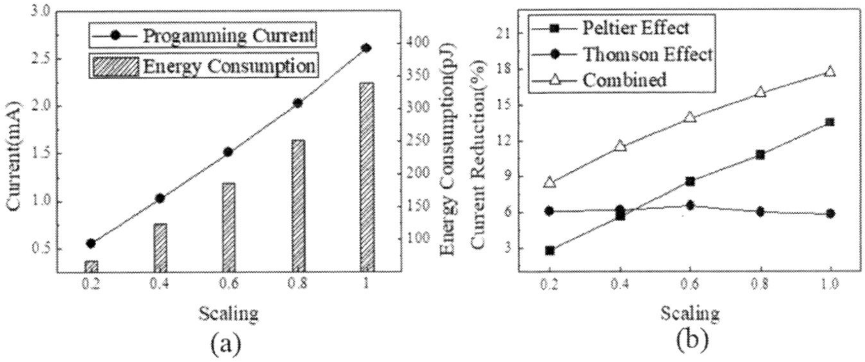

Fig. 4. The effect of isotropic scaling PCM device, while the horizontal axis represents the scale in both figures: (a) programming current and energy consumption needed for a reset operation; (b) impact of thermoelectric effects on programming current.

4 Discussion

With the cross section of TiN scaled down, both the increase of resistance of PCMS and the reduction of amorphous region for requirement of reset operation result in a smaller programming current. In this process, the prerequisite for a reset operation is the formation of an amorphous region which totally covers GST/TiN interface. Therefore, smaller the cross section of TiN, smaller the amorphous region covering heater, which means the area needed to be heated above the melting point in GST layer becomes smaller. In addition, the smaller cross section leads to a larger resistance of heater, which results Joule heating generated more efficiently via a fixed pulse current. On the other hand, with the cross section of TiN scaled down the weight of Peltier effect becomes lower owing to a significant decrease of the GST/TiN interface where the Peltier effect occurs, and the impact of Thomson effect on reset operation relatively increases due to an increasing temperature gradient caused by centralization of temperature distribution.

When scaling down the thickness of GST and keeping other conditions constant, although the volume needed to be heated above the melting point in the GST layer decreases due to the shorter thickness, the area that covers the interface and needs to be heated above the melting point remains constant, which means that relatively more region outside the GST layer is heated, leading to a notable heat diffusion. During a thickness reduction from 300 nm to 200nm, the dominated heating region is within the GST layer, while the heat diffusion is relatively weak, keeping the energy consumption basically constant. As the thickness is further reduced, to generate the same melting cover at the interface, heat diffusion becomes serious, while simultaneously the resistance of PCM device is lowered, making programming current and energy consumption increased. With the thickness of GST layer decreasing, the point of top temperature moves toward the GST/TiN interface, so the Peltier effect becomes less predominated for reset operation. On the other hand, it is harmful for reset operation that the Peltier effect leads to the heat diffusion occurring outside the GST layer, that explains the decreasing rate of current reduction by Peltier effect. In terms of Thomson effect, the temperature gradient in the vertical direction increasing dramatically with the thickness scaled down means the generation of heat by Thomson effect increasing as well. In addition, the point of top temperature moving toward interface leads to an increasing impact of Thomson effect on reset operation.

With the size of the PCM device scaled down isotropically, Because of the isotropic scaling, the temperature distribution ratios in different sizes remain the same, only the heating area decreases with the size scaled down, resulting in lower energy consumption. Nevertheless, inner temperature of GST layer increases more rapidly that leads to more serious heat diffusion toward outside. Due to the covered area at the interface decreasing, the Peltier effect weakens and the rate of programming current reduction declines. On the other hand, because of the equilibrium between a larger temperature gradient and a lower programming current, the Thomson effect has a basically constant impact on the heating efficiency, as well to maintain a stable effect on the programming current.

5 Conclusion

To put it in a nutshell, we have investigated thermal property and switching operation of PCM device based on a simulation of PCM device with different types of scaling. The simulation results show that the device scaling has an influence on temperature distribution, volume of the molten region, heat diffusion and switching operation of PCMD with the consideration of the thermoelectric effects. This simulation provides useful insights to understand the switching operation of the PCMDs under the impact of thermoelectric effects. The process is instrumental for a complete understanding of device operation and hence provides valuable feedback for fine-tuning the device design so as to enhance its efficiency.

This work was funded by National Key Research and Development Plan.

References

1. Geoffrey W. Burr, Matthew J. Breitwisch et al, Journal of Vacuum Science & Technology B, Nanotechnology and Microelectronics: Materials, Processing, Measurement, and Phenomena, 28, 223 (2010)
2. H. -S. Philip Wong, Simone Raoux et al, Proceedings of the IEEE. 98, 2201 (2010)
3. Y. N. Hwang, J. S. Hong et al, in VLSI Technology, Systems, and Applications, International Symposium, pp29–31(2013).
4. A. Pirovano, A. L. Lacaita et al, IEEE Transactions on Electron Devices, 51, 452 (2004).
5. Raoux S., Burr G. W. et al, IBM Journal of Research and Development, 52, 465 (2008).
6. Raoux S., Welnic W et al, Chemical Reviews, 110 (1), 240 (2010).
7. D. Ielmini, A. Lacaita et al, IEEE Electron Device Letters. 25(7), 507–509 (2004).
8. Y. N. Hwang, S. H. Lee et al, in IEDM Technical Digest, 2003, pp. 893–896.
9. U. Russo, D. Ielmini et al, IEEE Transactions on Electron Devices, 55, 2 (2008).
10. D. Ielmini, Physical Review B, 78, 035308(2008).
11. J. H. Park, S.-W. Kim et al, Journal of Applied Physics 117, 115703 (2015).
12. J. Lee, M. Asheghi et al., Nanotechnology, 23(20), 205201 (2012).
13. D.-S. Suh, C. Kim et al, Applied Physics Letters, 96, 123115 (2010).
14. U. Russo, D. Ielmini et al, IEEE Transactions on Electron Devices, 55, 2 (2008).
15. Y. Won, J. Lee et al, Applied physics letters, 100, 161905 (2012).

16. I. Cinar, O. B. Aslan et al, Journal of Applied Physics, 117, 214302 (2015);
17. L. W. da Silva, M. Kaviany, IEEE Transaction on electron devices, 47(10–11), 2417-2435 (2004)

AUTHOR INDEX

EDP Sciences – Web of Conferences
17, Avenue du Hoggar
Parc d'Activité de Courtabouf
BP 112
F-91944 Les Ulis Cedex A
France

ISBN 978-1-5108-7117-5

9 781510 871175

CURRAN ASSOCIATES INC.
proceedings.com

12th International Conference on Asia Agriculture and Animal (ICAAA 2025)

BIO Web of Conferences Volume 164 (2025)

Osaka, Japan
17-19 January 2025

edp sciences